ENCYCLOPEDIA
OF THE
CIVIL WAR

ENCYCLOPEDIA
OF THE
CIVIL WAR

GENERAL EDITOR
JOHN S. BOWMAN

JG
PRESS

Reprint 2001 by
World Publications Group, Inc.
455 Somerset Avenue
North Dighton, MA 02764

ISBN 1-57215-285-0

Printed in China

Page 1: Three Federal soldiers warm their
hands around an open fire.
Pages 2-3: The Battle of Stone's River
(December 31, 1862-January 3, 1863), as
depicted by Kurz & Allison
This page: Officers of the 55th New York
Infantry pose with a 32-pounder
Columbiad.

PREFATORY NOTE

Because America's interest in the Civil War seems never to wane, new books on the subject continue to appear every year. Many of these titles deal with particular subjects – with the life of an individual, for example, or with a specific battle or campaign – while others deal solely with aspects of the whole, such as naval operations or wartime party politics. Indeed, so much has now been written about the Civil War that only a few (usually multi-volume) general histories can still aspire to comprehensiveness.

Doubtless a good thing in itself, this explosion of information can nevertheless cause difficulties for the casual reader, who, increasingly, may be exposed to the problem of the unexplained allusion. A passage such as, for example, ''It was here, a year earlier, that Pleasanton's troopers made their attack on Fitz Lee's brigade,'' may seem all too opaque to a nonspecialist, who can be left wondering who Pleasanton and Fitz Lee were, which sides they were on, and in what context their action was fought. Similarly, unexplained references to Columbiads, the Baltimore Riot, the Wade-Davis Manifesto, the Lake Erie Conspiracy, panda, Laird rams and dozens of other topics can prove both baffling and annoying to the lay reader – and, often enough, to experts as well.

The *Encyclopedia* is intended, if not to banish such problems completely, at least to ease them. Its more-than-1000 entries and nearly 300 illustrations are, together, meant to form a kind of Civil War *vade mecum*, a reliable companion to all other Civil War reading. To that end it has been arranged in what the authors hope will be the most concise and accessible way possible.

The general scheme of organization is, in the formal sense of the term, discursive – that is, a heirarchy of interlocking entries. The longest entries deal with the broadest topics (the major campaigns, the greatest leaders, the most important issues and policies), and as entries decrease in length they tend to become more narrowly focused and summary. This implies that the reader will usually be rewarded by doing a little common-sense cross-referencing. For example, the *Encyclopedia* entry on Joshua Lawrence Chamberlain notes that he was awarded a Medal of Honor for 'his brilliant defense of Little Round Top at Gettysburg on July 2, 1863.' If the reader wishes to know more – where Little Round Top was located on the battlefield, why it was important, and how Chamberlain defended it – these and other details may be found in the longer entry on the Gettysburg Campaign and Battle. Only in cases where the reader might not necessarily assume that a cross-reference exists is the notation (*See*) employed – to have done otherwise would have produced a text so awash in (*See*)s as to the nearly unreadable. On other matters, such as the spellings of certain place names or whether a particular military engagement was important enough to be dignified by the title 'Battle of,' the authors have in all cases been content to follow the most common usage, though they freely acknowledge that variants exist.

That having been said, it remains only to add that the authors hope the reader may find this *Encyclopedia* not only useful and informative but also enjoyable simply for casual reading, for they intended that as well.

Abercrombie, John Joseph
(1802-1877) **Union general.**

Tennessee-born Abercrombie, an infantry veteran, was commissioned colonel in 1861. He commanded a brigade in the Peninsular Campaign, Abercrombie's Division in the defense of Washington, and the Fredericksburg depots before being mustered out in June 1864.

Ableman vs Booth

In March 1859 the US Supreme Court ruled that state courts may not free federal prisoners, overturning a Wisconsin ruling. The state had released a man named Booth who had been convicted of rescuing a fugitive slave. The ruling thus upheld the Fugitive Slave Act of 1850, and the federal government returned Booth to prison.

Citizens of Worcester, Massachusetts, in the 1830s gather on the town common to listen to an anti-slavery speech delivered by a local spokesman for the abolitionist movement.

Abolitionism

Abolitionists were those pre- and early-war antislavery radicals who favored immediate, uncompensated emancipation. The movement was divided in its aims and methods, encompassing such extremes as John Brown's violence and the moral suasion of Harriet Beecher Stowe's powerful novel *Uncle Tom's Cabin*. William Lloyd Garrison was a major influence on the rise of abolitionism in the 1830s, as were such periodicals as the *Liberator* and the *Emancipator* and the development of such national organizations as the American Anti-Slavery Society (founded 1833). Among many other orators, writers, and activists, Wendell Phillips, Frederick Douglass, Horace Greeley, and Harriet Tubman agitated for abolition through the 1830s and 1840s. In time, the Liberty Party (founded 1839), the Free-Soil Party (1848) and the Republican Party (1854) came to afford a broader-based political platform for the later phases of the antislavery struggle, and organized abolitionism was somewhat in decline in the years just before the outbreak of the Civil War.

Adams, Charles Francis
(1807-1886) **Diplomat.**

Son of John Quincy Adams, he was US minister to Great Britain from 1861 to 1868. In this crucial post his success in maintaining the neutrality of England (and thus Europe) was regarded as the diplomatic equivalent of winning a major military victory at home.

Adams, Daniel Weisiger
(1821-1872) **Confederate general.**

A Kentucky-born lawyer, he commanded the 1st Louisiana Regulars at Shiloh, then led a brigade at the battles of Perryville, Corinth, Murfreesboro, and Chickamauga, where he was wounded and captured. Eventually exchanged, he commanded the District of Central Alabama during the final months of the war.

Adams Revolver

Several thousand copies of this British service revolver were made under license in Massachusetts, though Union forces bought only an estimated 600. A potent sidearm, it did not need to be cocked; unlike the more widely used Colt, the Adams could be fired simply by pulling the trigger.

Ager Battery Gun

An early machine gun, the Ager used a crank-operated breech mechanism to deliver rapid fire from a single barrel. The designer claimed the gun could fire 100 rounds per minute. Union officials were unconvinced of its capabilities, however, and only about 50 were sold.

Alabama, CSS, and *Alabama* Claims

A Confederate raiding ship built at Laird's shipyard in England in 1862, the *Alabama* spent 22 months under Captain Raphael Semmes attacking Federal shipping in the Atlantic and Indian oceans. Powered by steam and sail and armed with eight guns (the largest of which was a 100-pounder rifled Blakely), she was by far the most successful of the Confederate commerce raiders, making a total of 66 captures, 53 of which she sank. She was sunk by the sloop-of-war USS *Kearsarge (See)* off Cherbourg, France, in June 1864. Partly because of the *Alabama*'s depredations, the US, during and after the war, initiated claims against England for the nearly $20 million in damage done to Union shipping by vessels built or outfitted in that supposedly neutral country. Britain finally paid the US $15.5 million in 1873.

Albemarle, CSS **Confederate ram.**

Operating on the Roanoke River, the *Albemarle*, James W. Cooke commanding, aided in the capture of Plymouth, NC, *(See)* in April 1864 and fought a seven-ship Federal blockading squadron to a standoff the following month. She was sunk in a daring midnight torpedo raid commanded by a Union Lieutenant named William B. Cushing *(See)* on October 27, 1864.

Aldie, *Virginia*

Federal cavalry under General Alfred Pleasonton attacked Fitz Lee's cavalry brigade, of James Longstreet's command, here on June 17, 1863. The bluecoats made a series of spirited attempts on enemy defensive positions, and the Confederates withdrew after dark. The Northern losses were 305, the Southern around 100.

Alexander, Edward Porter
(1835-1910) **Confederate general.**

A Georgian graduate of West Point, he fought at First Bull Run, in the Peninsular and Antietam campaigns, and commanded the artillery on Marye's Heights at Fredericksburg. He commanded James Longstreet's reserve artillery at Gettysburg. As Longstreet's chief gunner he also fought at

Spotsylvania, Cold Harbor, and Petersburg. He published his *Military Memoirs of a Confederate* in 1907.

Alexandria, *Louisiana*

As part of the Red River Campaign (*See*), Union General Nathaniel Banks had withdrawn his troops to Alexandria by May 1, 1864, covering his fleet's efforts to withdraw on the low river. There was a series of skirmishes around town through the 8th, as Richard Taylor's Confederates made probing attacks on land and on the water. Most notably, Southern cavalry captured or destroyed four enemy ships.

Alexandria Line

This was the name given Confederate defenses in Northern Virginia in the early weeks of the war. The Confederate government assigned 43-year-old General P. G. T. Beauregard to command the Alexandria Line on May 31, 1861.

Allatoona, *Georgia*

As part of Confederate General John Bell Hood's 1864 Franklin and Nashville Campaign, graycoats under Samuel G. French struck the Union supply depot at Allatoona on October 5. The battle, in which the Union garrison held out bravely against furious enemy assaults, became famous for W. T. Sherman's flag-signaled message as he marched to reinforce; this was roughly recounted as, 'Hold the fort. I am coming.' (Actually, French withdrew before Federal reinforcements arrived next day.)

Right: Charles Francis Adams, the singularly effective US minister to Great Britain from 1861 to 1868, played a key role in the Union effort to keep the British from extending diplomatic recognition to the Confederacy.
Below: The Southern raider *Alabama* attacks the *Hatteras* (foregound) in 1863. The Union complained bitterly about Britain's building such raiders for the Confederacy.

Allen, Henry Watkins *(1820-1866)*
Confederate general.

Allen was a Louisiana lawyer, planter, and legislator who fought at the battles of Shiloh, Vicksburg, and Baton Rouge, where he was badly wounded. Inaugurated governor of Louisiana in 1864, he restored the state's shattered economy by establishing trade routes through Mexico.

Amendments to Constitution

Since slavery was implicitly sanctioned by the Constitution, amendments were necessary to extend constitutional protection to blacks after the war. The 13th Amendment, enacted in December 1865, abolished slavery. The 14th Amendment, bolstering the Civil Rights Act of 1866, defined US citizenship to include blacks, forbade states to curtail federally mandated rights, and abrogated the 'three-fifths' clause of the Constitution. When Southern states objected, their readmission to the Union was made contingent on ratification. Ratification was announced in July 1868. The 15th Amendment guaranteed voting rights to every citizen regardless of race, color, or previous condition of servitude. Designed to end Reconstruction abuses, it went into effect in March 1870. (*See* also CONSTITUTION).

America

The Confederates used this famous yacht, which won the 'America's Cup' from the British in 1851, as a dispatch boat. Federal naval forces raised her sunken hull from a South Carolina River in 1862, and *America* again raced a successful cup defense in 1870.

The famous racing yacht *America*. In 1851 she beat a field of 18 other yachts to win what would afterwards be called the America's Cup.

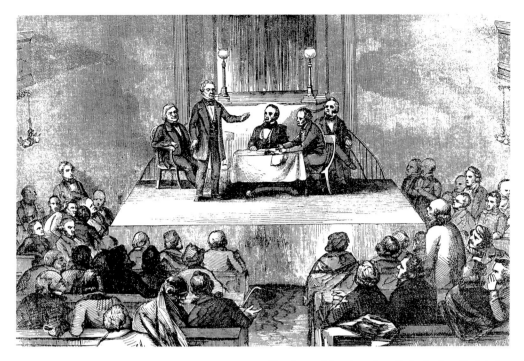

American Colonization Society

Antislavery activists established the society in 1816 to promote the return of blacks to Africa. Early returnees established the West African nation of Liberia, but by 1831 fewer than 1500 blacks had been resettled there.

American Flag Dispatch

Amid growing secessionist defiance in the South, US Treasury Secretary John A. Dix learned on January 29, 1861, that the captain of the revenue cutter *McClelland* had refused to surrender to federal authorities in New Orleans. Dix ordered the captain's arrest, adding, 'If anyone attempts to haul down the American flag, shoot him on the spot.'

Members of the American Colonization Society in Washington, DC, listen to an address by Massachusetts statesmen, educator and orator Edward Everett.

Ames, Adelbert *(1835-1933)*
Union general.

Wounded at First Bull Run ten weeks after his West Point graduation, Ames went on to participate in the Peninsular, Antietam, Fredericksburg, Chancellorsville, and Gettysburg campaigns; he led divisions in the Army of the Potomac in Virginia and North Carolina in 1864-65. He was a Reconstruction era governor of Mississippi.

Amistad Case

In August 1839, 53 Africans being transported between Cuban ports on the Spanish slave ship *Amistad* mutinied. They spared the lives of two crew members in order to reach North America, where a US warship escorted them into a Connecticut port. American courts rejected Spain's demand for the return of the slaves; in March 1841 the US Supreme Court upheld the lower court's decisions, and the Africans, freed, were returned to their homes in Africa.

Amnesty

On May 29, 1865, President Andrew Johnson proclaimed general amnesty to most participants on the Confederate side in the Civil War. Excepted were former-Rebels with property worth more than $20,000 and high ranking civil and military officers; these were required to apply individually to the president for a pardon. In the event, Johnson rarely refused such pardons, and with the pardons individuals' property rights (except for slaves) were restored.

Anaconda Plan

In order to avoid what he foresaw would be a bloody conflict, early in the war General Win-

field Scott proposed a Northern strategy of completely blockading the South. His plan called for both a coastal blockade and a line of 60,000 troops supported by gunboats along the entire length of the Mississippi to constrict the South like a 5000-mile-long snake. Derided as 'Scott's Anaconda,' the plan's value was proven by the general effectiveness of the coastal blockade adopted by Lincoln in 1861.

Anderson, 'Bloody' Bill (d.1864)
Confederate guerilla.

His band of near-criminals looted Centralia, Missouri, on September 27, 1864, murdering 24 unarmed Federals there. Two hours later, the gang ambushed a Union cavalry detachment, killing 124 troopers in what became known as the Centralia Massacre (*See*). Federals caught and killed Anderson near Richmond, Missouri, in late October.

Anderson, George Burgwyn
(1831-1862) **Confederate general.**

An 1852 West Point graduate from North Carolina, he led a brigade of home-state troops during the Seven Days' Battles of 1862 and was wounded at Malvern Hill. Wounded in the ankle while leading a brigade at Antietam in September, he died after an amputation on October 16, 1862.

Anderson, Richard Heron
(1821-1879) **Confederate general.**

In 1861 this South Carolinian career soldier joined the 1st South Carolina in time to support the bombardment of Fort Sumter; he won steady promotions, fighting in virtually every campaign of the Army of Northern Virginia – the Peninsular Campaign, Second Bull Run, Antietam, Fredericksburg, Chancellorsville, Gettysburg, the Wilderness, Spotsylvania, and the Shenandoah Valley Campaign of 1864. His greatest achievement was his role in the securing of Spotsylvania for Robert E. Lee in May 1864.

Anderson, Robert *(1805-1871)*
Union general.

This Kentucky-born career soldier taught artillery tactics at West Point and fought in the Seminole and Mexican Wars. After South Carolina seceded in December 1860, as commander of Charleston harbor he moved the garrison from Fort Moultrie to Fort Sumter, where he underwent the first bombardment of the war. Anderson commanded the Departments of Kentucky and the Cumberland before retiring as the result of physical disabilities in 1863.

Andersonville Prison

The most atrocious prison of the war was the Confederacy's Andersonville Prison, established at that Georgia town in February 1864 to house Union enlisted-men prisoners. In a stockade that eventually totalled 26 acres, over 30,000 prisoners were held at a time, most living in the open air with appalling sanitary conditions and inadequate diet. Disease, exposure, and general crowding killed over 13,000 prisoners before the end of the war. The Southern commander of the prison, Captain Henry Wirz, was hanged by the Union in November 1865, the only man to be tried and condemned for war crimes after the Civil War.

Then-Major Robert Anderson commanded Fort Sumter at the outbreak of the Civil War.

Andrews Raid

'The Great Locomotive Chase'

On April 12, 1862, Union spy James Andrews and a party of 21 Federal volunteers slipped into enemy territory to cut the important rail-

Ragged Union prisoners of war in 1864 await the distribution of rations at Andersonville, the South's most notorious prison camp.

road line between Chattanooga, Tennessee, and Marietta, Georgia. Near present Kenesaw, Georgia, the raiders seized the engine *General* and steamed toward Chattanooga. Southerners pursued in the engine *Texas*. Finally, near Graysville, the Federals ran out of wood for the boiler and bolted on foot. All were captured, Andrews and seven others to be hanged as spies and 14 others to be imprisoned. Of the latter, eight eventually escaped and the rest were paroled in 1863. The classic Buster Keaton film *The General* was loosely based on this incident.

Antietam, Campaign and Battle

(In Confederate chronicles called the Battle of Sharpsburg.)

Following the Confederate forces' successes in Virginia during the Seven Days battles and Second Bull Run, General Robert E. Lee decided that the time was propitious to take his Army of Northern Virginia into Maryland

in an invasion of the North. He notified CSA President Jefferson Davis of his intention on September 3, 1862, and Davis approved the plan. In the next days Lee's forces began crossing the Potomac River and concentrating in Frederick, Maryland. With this invasion Lee did not necessarily expect a quick victory, but he did expect to gain some important advantages: galvanizing anti-war sentiment in the North; perhaps arousing Maryland to join the Confederacy; tying up Federal troops that would be needed to protect Washington; moving the fighting out of Virginia; and, not least, impressing European governments, who might then be willing to recognize the Confederacy as a country rather than a rebellious territory, and therefore unlock the flow of weapons and supplies that the South desperately needed.

Marching into enemy territory, Lee took a bold gamble and divided his forces, sending Stonewall Jackson south with six divisions to capture the Federal garrison at Harper's Ferry, the gateway to Virginia's Shenandoah

Valley. Subduing that garrison would allow supplies to reach Lee's army from the rich farmland of the Shenandoah, and conversely would give him an avenue of retreat if needed. After the garrison was secured, Jackson was to rejoin Lee. This strategy, however, came close to disaster: General George B. McClellan, commander of the Federal Army of the Potomac, got hold of Lee's order detailing the disposition of the divided Confederate forces.

On September 13 a Northern soldier had found Lee's Special Order No. 191 lying in a field, inside an envelope and wrapped around two cigars. (Which of Lee's officers lost the order has never been discovered.) Perusing the captured order, General McClellan crowed, 'Here is a paper with which, if I cannot whip Bobby Lee, I will be willing to go home.' In characteristic fashion,

A Union army map shows the positions of the opposing armies at the end of September 17, 1862, the bloodiest day the US had ever seen.

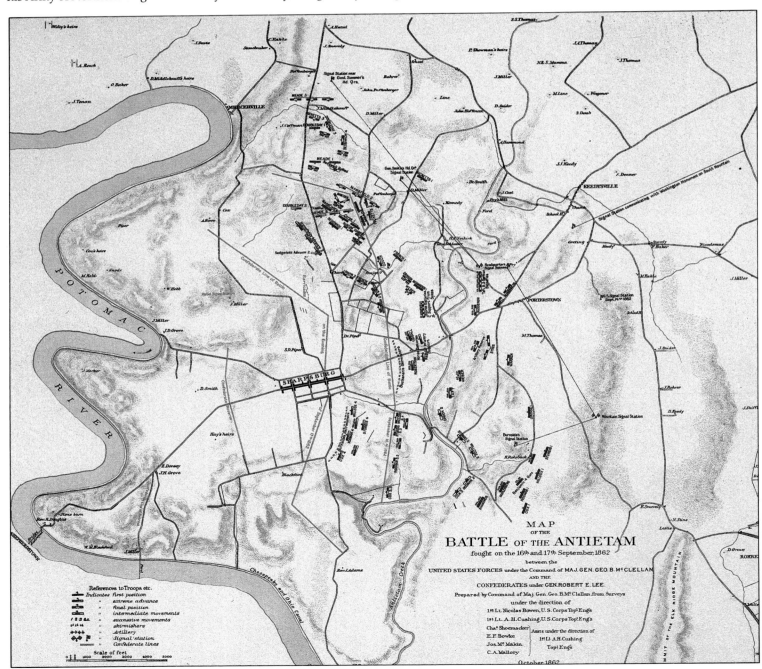

MAP
OF THE
BATTLE OF THE ANTIETAM
fought on the 16th and 17th September, 1862
between the
UNITED STATES FORCES under the Command of MAJ. GEN. GEO. B. McCLELLAN
AND THE
CONFEDERATES under GEN. ROBERT E. LEE.
Prepared by Command of Maj. Gen. Geo. B. McClellan from Surveys
under the direction of
1st Lt. Nicolas Bowen, U.S. Corps Topl Engs
1st Lt. A.H. Cushing, U.S. Corps Topl Engs
Chas Shoemacker
E.F. Bowke
Jos. Mc Makin.
C.A. Mallory
Assts under the direction of
1st Lt. A.H. Cushing
Topl Engs

October 1862

References to Troops etc.
Indicates first position
"   extreme advance
"   final position
"   intermediate movements
"   successive movements
"   skirmishers
"   Artillery
"   Signal station
"   Confederate lines

Scale of feet
0   1000   2000   3000   4000   5000

McClellan then proceeded to waste this golden opportunity by inching cautiously toward the enemy, thereby giving Lee time to discover that the order had been intercepted and to begin to march his troops toward Jackson's divisions.

On September 15 Jackson easily took Harper's Ferry, but that same day McClellan's army began to pull into position on the east bank of Antietam Creek, near Sharpsburg, Maryland. Across the creek stood 19,000 men of Lee's Army of Northern Virginia, their backs to the Potomac, while Jackson's 40,000 were still nearly a day's march away. Yet Lee, taking the measure of his opponent, elected to stand and fight. Thus the stage was set for the Battle of Antietam. The battle was not fought on the 16th, however, for McClellan spent the whole day positioning his forces rather than making an immediate attack.

No one is quite sure what McClellan's tactical plan was, and it seems to have been hazy to his officers at the time. In any event, the battle unfolded in three stages. The first began at dawn on the 17th when Union General Joseph Hooker led the three divisions of I Corps against Lee's left – one division south along the Hagerstown Turnpike, another moving into a cornfield, the third pushing through the East Wood. Their goal was to reach a little white church of the Dunker sect. All three divisions were soon fighting for their lives.

In the cornfield the opposing forces collided blindly in the dense head-high stalks, men grappling hand-to-hand, falling in waves from fire coming through the leaves. Fighting on the Federal right surged back and forth between the East Wood and West Wood, always centred on the cornfield. Finally, a jumbled collection of Federal troops

broke free and swarmed toward Dunker Church, but before they reached it a searing counterattack by John B. Hood's Texas Brigade sent the Northerners reeling back. By that time Hooker's corps had suffered nearly 2500 casualties, and Hooker himself was wounded, but Lee's losses were painfully heavy as well.

About 7:00 in the morning Union General Joseph Mansfield moved his XII Corps through the East Wood into the cornfield, supposedly in support of Hooker but too late to be of much help. Mansfield was fatally wounded as they reached the cornfield, and once again the fighting swept back and forth across the field to neither side's advantage. General George S. Greene's Federal division,

Union General Ambrose Burnside fights his way over the bridge that would later bear his name during the Battle of Antietam.

on Mansfield's right, made it past the Dunker Church and seriously threatened Lee's line, but Greene had to withdraw for lack of reinforcements from McClellan. That ended the first stage of the battle, leaving the Union I Corps devastated.

The next act began in the center, with Union General Edwin V. Sumner leading the II Corps at a right angle to Hooker's line of

An A. R. Waud sketch of a skirmish between the 14th Brooklyn and Confederate cavalry at the Battle of Antietam.

Skirmish between L. Brooklyn 14th and 300. Rebel Cavalry

An engraving made from an on-the-scene A. R. Waud sketch shows doctors attending to the wounded at Antietam. Combined casualties in the battle numbered well over 23,000.

attack, through the cornfield and the West Wood. They met little resistance at first; to shore up his middle, Lee was desperately stripping men from his right, where the Federals were also pressing, and throwing in troops that had begun to arrive from Harper's Ferry. As the men of Union General John Sedgwick's division emerged confidently from the West Wood into open fields and stopped to dress their lines, they were met by withering fire from left, front, and rear. In ten minutes 500 Federals fell without having fired a shot. The Northerners fled back through the woods and cornfield, suffering some 2500 casualties in about 15 minutes. By 9:30 in the morning nearly 12,000 men on both sides had fallen within a thousand-yard-square area. But the fighting in the middle was not yet finished.

South of Segwick's debacle, Federals under Greene mounted an assault on D. H. Hill's men, who were well-protected in a sunken road. The Union troops were thrown back in attack after attack, but with the help of reinforcements, and spearheaded by the Irish Brigade, they gained the sunken road, to find it choked with Southern dead. History remembers that little stretch of country road as 'Bloody Lane.'

McClellan and his Army of the Potomac were now on the verge of swamping Lee's army. The Southern line was ragged and shaky; Hood reported to Lee that his division was 'dead on the field.' James Longstreet's men, now out of bullets, turned back a Union charge with two cannons alone. But McClellan failed to grasp his advantage or to press it home in the center, where Southern lines were weakest. Instead, the Federal commander let the thrust of the battle shift to his right, where General Ambrose E. Burnside had spent the morning trying to get his forces

over a bridge every inch of which was covered by Southern gunfire.

Burnside is remembered in history as one of the most incompetent generals of all time, but he would end this day as a hero because, after suffering galling casualties, he at last got his men across the bridge at 1:00 in the afternoon. Unfortunately for Burnside's reputation, someone discovered later that Antietam Creek was so shallow that the Federals could have waded across at nearly any point and out of the way of enemy guns.

Nevertheless, his men pushed the Southerners back to the edge of Sharpsburg, and by 3:00 pm were advancing hard on Lee's vulnerable left. At that critical moment, however, Burnside's forces were blind-sided by Confederates under A. P. Hill, who had just arrived from Harper's Ferry after a 17-mile

forced march. The Federal advance faltered and collapsed, Burnside failing to commit two unused divisions. By evening both armies lay devastated and exhausted around the creek, neither having gained a clear advantage. The North had lost 2108 dead, 9549 wounded, and 753 missing of 75,316 effectives (McClellan had not committed another 24,000 troops); Southern losses were 2700 dead, 9024 wounded, 2000 missing. In all, nearly 25,000 men were dead or injured; the war would never see a worse day.

Lee stayed in position on September 18, daring McClellan to attack and actually planning a counterattack (Jackson and Longstreet had to talk their commander out of the idea). Later that day the Army of Northern Virginia began to withdraw across the Potomac, the invasion over and McClellan the nominal victor. Not worrying about the details, the North joyously celebrated its first major victory. But President Lincoln was not fooled by his general's performance. It would be McClellan's last battle, except for the one he fought, and almost won, as Lincoln's opponent in the election of 1864.

But Lincoln astutely took advantage of the victory at Antietam, however ambiguous, to release the Emancipation Proclamation, which transformed the war into the appearance of a crusade against slavery and therefore ended most of the South's hopes of gaining sympathy and support from Europe. Though the Proclamation actually freed no slaves at the time, it would in fact mark the beginning of the end of slavery in America.

Appomattox, Campaign and Surrender

Following the fall of Petersburg on April 2, 1865, General Robert E. Lee and the Confederate Army of Northern Virginia, by then reduced to 35,000 starving men, fled Peters-

In the house belonging to Wilmer McLean in Appomattox Court House, Va., General Robert E. Lee surrenders on April 9, 1865.

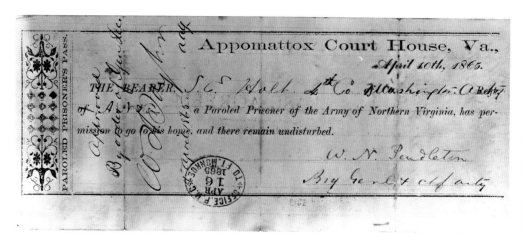

This pass, releasing a Union prisoner of the Army of Northern Virginia, was issued one day after Lee's surrender at Appomattox.

burg and Richmond and headed west. Lee was aiming for Amelia Court House, where he hoped to find a shipment of food and to put his army on the Danville Railroad for South Carolina. There he planned to join the army of Joseph E. Johnston and continue the fight for the Confederacy. In fact, both the army and the Confederacy were falling apart hour by hour. The collapse of Petersburg and departure of Lee had left the capital at Richmond defenseless, and the government there was fleeing as well. Meanwhile, Southern soldiers were deserting in hundreds.

Things were going as Union general-in-chief Ulysses S. Grant had hoped. He knew that William Tecumseh Sherman would arrive in the area with his army by the end of April, but he did not want to wait that long to run Lee to ground. 'I mean to end the business here,' he told his cavalry commander, Philip Sheridan. When the Rebel army bolted from Petersburg, Grant intended above all to keep Lee away from union with the forces of Joseph Johnston, so he sent Sheridan with cavalry and three infantry corps to shadow Lee's army. Sheridan cut the Danville Railroad on April 5, a day after President Lincoln had walked the streets of Richmond, accompanied by newly-freed slaves.

With his rail escape cut off and the food shipment having not arrived, Lee desperately struggled on toward the Shenandoah Valley, with Federals nipping at his heels. At Sayler's Creek on April 6 Union forces cut off and captured CSA General Richard Ewell's 6000 men, a quarter of Lee's remaining forces. On the next day Grant sent a surrender demand under flag of truce; Lee inquired after terms, but he was not ready to surrender yet. The army kept marching, dissolving as it went. Finally, on April 9, the spent Confederates arrived at the town of Appomattox Court House, there to find Sheridan's horsemen blocking the road. Lee would not give up without a fight. He ordered a cavalry charge that broke through for a moment; then lines of blue-clad infantry marched in to fill the gap, and two Federal infantry corps closed in on the Southern rear. The Army of Northern Virginia was now both surrounded and outnumbered.

At the last minute one of the Confederate staff suggested the desperate expedient of ordering the army to disperse and head for the hills, to fight on as guerrillas. Lee declined, saying that guerrillas 'would become mere bands of marauders,' and that rounding them up might devastate Virginia. Lee continued, 'There is nothing left for me to do but go and see General Grant, and I would rather die a thousand deaths.' A few moments later, now poised for a counterattack, the men of the North saw a Southern rider galloping toward them waving a white flag of surrender.

Lee and Grant had already exchanged several notes regarding surrender and terms, and now Lee, finally submitting to the inevitable, agreed to meet Grant at the brick home of Wilmer McLean in Appomattox. (McLean had earlier given up a house that had been shelled during First Bull Run and had come to Appomattox to escape the war, only to have the war now end in his parlor.)

Lee arrived first with his secretary, Charles Marshall, and an orderly. Grant arrived soon after with his staff; all were finally assembled in the parlor at about 1:30 in the afternoon. In history and legend, much would be made of the dress of the opposing commanders: Lee resplendent in dress uniform and jewelled sword (in fact, his field clothing had been destroyed in the retreat); Grant in his usual private's uniform, splattered with mud. In time the Confederate commander would come to represent the embodiment of the old chivalric tradition in war and of the old Virginia aristocracy. His opposite, a one-time failure and nobody who had raised himself to the highest responsibility by his own bootstraps, would represent the new age – rough, democratic, and ruthlessly efficient.

For a while the two men chatted about the weather and the past; Lee politely pretended to remember Grant from the Mexican War. Finally Lee asked for the surrender terms. They were discussed briefly, Lee seeing that the terms (which Lincoln had roughly outlined at the end of March in a meeting with Grant and Sherman) were generous: surrendered Southern soldiers would not be prosecuted as traitors and could go home, 'not to be disturbed by US authority so long as they observe their paroles and the laws in force where they may reside.'

Reading over the agreement, Lee dropped a hint that he wished all his cavalry and artillery might keep their horses, since most owned their own animals. Grant generously took the hint, and Lee responded, 'This will have the best possible effect upon the men . . . and will do much toward conciliating our people.'

While Grant's terms and Lee's letter of response were being copied out, Grant introduced Lee to his staff; Lee, visibly startled when he came to Colonel Ely Parker, a full-blooded Seneca Indian, finally said, 'I am glad to see one real American here.' 'We are all Americans here,' Ely replied.

Grant offered to send 25,000 provisions to the hungry Southern troops, and Lee said eagerly that 'it will be a great relief, I assure you.' After a few more minutes of conversation on matters both practical and aimless, Grant, Lee, and other officers signed the surrender agreement and Lee took his leave. As he mounted, Grant and the other Federal

In an unsigned sketch, probably by A. R. Waud, Union troops salute Lee as he rides away from the surrender site at Appomattox.

Union troops in 1864 pose before Robert E. Lee's confiscated home in Arlington, Va. Now called the Lee Mansion National Memorial, it is a part of Arlington National Cemetary.

officers saluted their great former enemy – saluted not militarily, but with a civilian tip of the hat. Lee responded in kind and rode back to his army.

At the formal surrender ceremony on April 12 the remaining men of the Army of Northern Virginia stacked their arms and banners before the ranks of a silent, and in many cases tearful, Federal Army of the Potomac. Though Johnston's and a few smaller Confederate armies had not yet given up, it was clear that the surrender of Lee had effectively ended the Civil War. The North was exploding in celebrations. President Lincoln, already making plans for the reconstruction of the South, had only a few days to live.

Arkansas Campaign of 1864

In support of Union General Nathaniel Banks's Red River Campaign, General Frederick Steele was given 12,000 infantry and cavalry troops and ordered to contain enemy forces in southwestern Arkansas, away from Banks. Steel's immediate goal was to tie up two Southern infantry divisions under Sterling Price, after which he planned to deal with three cavalry divisions in the area. In the end, the Confederate cavalry would rule much of the campaign.

W. T. Sherman had directed Steele to start at the beginning of March 1864, but the Federal column did not get out of Little Rock until nearly the end of the month. By that time, the Southern infantry divisions had marched to Louisiana to help CSA General Richard Taylor deflect Banks from his intended capture of Shreveport – exactly what Steele was in Arkansas to prevent. The Red River Campaign would never really recover from this initial setback.

As Steele's Federals marched south, they were continually harried by Southern cavalry; the end of March and the beginning of April saw a running series of skirmishes. On the night of April 9-10 Steele was reinforced near Elkin's Ford by troops under John M. Thayer; together they marched toward Spring Hill, hoping to draw Confederate cavalry after them. On April 15 Steele turned east and occupied Camden, Arkansas, where he learned that Banks had failed to take Shreveport. Meanwhile, Edmund Kirby Smith, commander of the Confederate Department of the Trans-Mississippi, was marching to attack Steele with several divisions of infantry. At Camden, on April 25, Kirby Smith sent a detachment to cut Steele's supply line; they captured a train of 211 wagons. Steele then retreated from Camden, suffering further losses in an attack at Jenkin's Ferry on April 29-30. After a thoroughly disastrous campaign, Steele arrived back in Little Rock on May 3. At that point the equally disastrous Red River Campaign was marooned by low water above Alexandria, Louisiana.

Arkansas Post (Fort Hindman)

Confederates used this Arkansas River fort as a base for gunboat forays on to the Mississippi River. Union Major General John A. McClernand captured it on January 11, 1863, after a brief campaign. Annoyed that McClernand should have been permitted by his political sponsors in Washington to undertake this campaign without reference to larger issues of strategy, Ulysses Grant had McClernand transferred and placed under Grant's command before Vicksburg.

Arlington, *Virginia*

The federal government confiscated Robert E. Lee's Arlington estate when he quit the Union army in 1861. The property, returned to the Lee family after the war, is the site of Arlington National Cemetery.

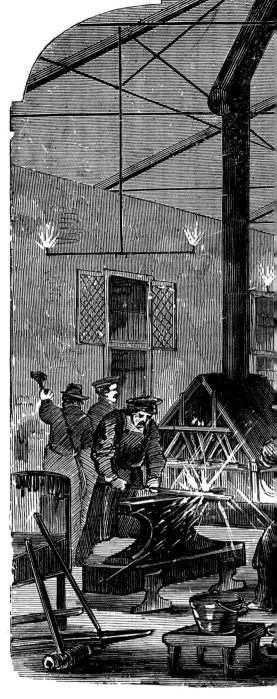

Armies

There was a certain looseness in what was defined as an 'army' during the Civil War; armies could range from relatively small ad hoc collections of troops to full-fledged, organized military units. Several Federal organizataions, such as the Armies of the Potomac and of the Mississippi, were named after rivers; others took their names from states, military departments, or regions (for example, the Armies of the Cumberland and of the Ohio). Southern armies tended to be named after regions, states, or departments: Army of Northern Virginia, Army of the Northwest, the Trans-Mississippi Department, etc. Similarities, such as the Army of the Tennessee (USA) and the Army of Tennessee (CSA), could, however, be confusing. During the course of the war there were about 16 in the North, 23 in the South.

Armistead, Lewis Addison

(1817-1863) **Confederate general.**

This scion of a distinguished North Carolina military family is chiefly remembered for the poignant symbolism surrounding his death at the Battle of Gettysburg. The brigade he commanded in George Pickett's division supposedly made the deepest penetration of the Federal line during the doomed 'Pickett's Charge' on the last day of the battle. Commanding the defending troops in this part of the line was Union General Winfield Scott Hancock, Armistead's best friend; Hancock would later have the sad duty of sending the fallen Armistead's spurs to his family. The inscription on the monument that today stands on the spot where Armistead fell refers to it as marking 'the high tide' of the Confederacy, though some other Rebel brigades may have penetrated equally far.

Armstrong Guns

One version of these technically-advanced English breech-loading rifled cannon could fire a projectile weighing as much as 600 pounds. Smaller field pieces fired a three-inch projectile, and models firing four-inch and 16-pounder shells were also used. Armstrongs were widely distributed in the Union forces; the Confederates acquired far fewer of these sophisticated weapons.

Arsenals (Armories)

These terms, loosely defined in popular usage, are generally used interchangeably to mean places of manufacture, repair, storage, and/or issue of ordnance and ordnance stores. Strictly speaking, however, an arsenal was a depository. It would have charge of an armory to manufacture arms; of a depot to

Ironwork for gun carriages being forged in the armory (*ie.*, the manufacturing sub-division) of the Union's Watervliet Arsenal in West Troy, New York.

collect, repair, and issue arms; and of a laboratory to make ammunition and develop standards and procedures. In practice, arsenals and depots often overlapped in their functions.

Artillery

The Civil War conclusively demonstrated the tactical effectiveness of long-range mounted guns. The dozens of types of artillery were classified by tactical use (primarily field, seacoast, and siege), by bore, by loading mechanism, by caliber, and by construction; the guns ranged from cannon (*See*) to howitzers (*See*) to mortars (*See*), and projectiles

Above: Though not a professional soldier, Turner Ashby was so good a leader of cavalry that by May 1862 the Confederacy had raised him to the rank of brigadier general.
Right: Field headquarters for correspondents of the *New York Herald*.

ranged from solid shot to shrapnel. Among important technological innovations were breech loading and the rifling of artillery for greater range and accuracy.

Artists, Writers, and the Civil War

Many of America's greatest writers lived through at least parts of the Civil War: Nathaniel Hawthorne (d. 1864), Herman Melville, Mark Twain, William Dean Howells, Henry James. Yet curiously none of them chose to deal with the war except in tangential ways. Indeed, it was left to a young man who was born after the war (1871) to write what is generally regarded as the finest novel inspired by the war – Stephen Crane's *The Red Badge of Courage* (1895).

Poets did not do much better: with the notable exception of Walt Whitman (*See*), few nineteenth-century poets were successful in conveying in words the great passions of the war. Twentieth-century American poets have occasionally turned to the Civil War for inspiration, but it is hard to think of a Civil War poem that many Americans know as well as, say, Longfellow's poems about the Colonial and Revolutionary periods.

Although many American graphic artists were active during the war and its aftermath, of the major painters only Winslow Homer (*See*) tried to make serious art out of the experience. Fortunately for history, some talented minor artist-journalists such as Alfred and William Waud, Edwin Forbes, Henri Lovie, and Arthur Lumley have left us compelling sketches and engravings of wartime scenes and personalities. As to sculpture, perhaps the only work of real distinction is Augustus Saint-Gauden's memorial to Robert Gould Shaw (*See*) and the black troops he led into battle.

The same general situation applies to music and drama. The war produced a rich legacy of popular music (*See* MUSIC OF THE CIVIL WAR) but little in the way of serious concert or operatic composition. And if there have been a few notable plays and films about the Civil War, they were, virtually without exception, presented long after the event.

Why artists should have drawn so little inspiration from what was probably the most traumatic, emotive, and important episode in American history is unclear. One possibility is that the war produced so many moving first-person memoirs, accounts, letters, and journals, so many graphic photographs, so many memorable songs, that artists may have felt they could not find ways adequately to transfigure a reality so overwhelming and – even today – so vividly alive.

Ashby, Turner *(1828-1862)*
Confederate general.

A Shenandoah Valley planter and politician, Ashby favored slavery but opposed secession. When Virginia seceded, however, he raised and led a mounted troop which, as part of the 7th Virginia Cavalry, defended the upper Potomac border, participating in First Bull Run. As Jackson's cavalry commander, he played an important role in the Shenandoah Valley Campaign of Jackson. He was killed in a rearguard action protecting Jackson's retreat from the Shenandoah Valley on June 6, 1862.

An artist-war correspondent at work. Since high-speed photography was not yet possible, artists still had a monopoly on all graphic images that involved action.

Our special Artist

Atlanta, Campaign and Battle

After losing the vital cities of Vicksburg and Chattanooga in 1863, the South had only two comparable centers left – the Confederate capital at Richmond, Virginia, and the manufacturing and rail center of Atlanta, Georgia. In the spring of 1864, when General Ulysses S. Grant began his great offensive against Richmond, his long-time partner, General William Tecumseh Sherman, was assigned to take Atlanta. Sherman's opponent, General Joseph E. Johnston, had returned the Confederate Army of Tennessee to fighting form, 62,000 strong, after their rout in the Battle of Chattanooga (*See*).

As usual in the war, the Federals fielded the larger army; Sherman commanded 100,000 men of the combined Armies of the Cumberland, the Ohio, and the Tennessee. Unlike many Federal generals, however, Sherman knew how to handle his superior forces. On May 7, 1864, the Federals moved against Johnston's left flank near Chattanooga, and the Southerners pulled back. That would set the pattern of the ensuing campaign: as in a formal dance, Sherman would move to one flank or another of his opponent, forcing the Confederates to withdraw to prepared positions farther south, each a step nearer Atlanta. Johnston knew that unless Sherman made an enormous blunder there was no way to resist this strategy, and Sherman was no blunderer. Still, Johnston also knew that his fighting withdrawal had a purpose that was highly promising: if Atlanta could hold out until the November presidential elections in the North there was a very good chance that Abraham Lincoln would be defeated, to be replaced by a Democrat who might make peace on something like the Conefederacy's terms.

While May wore into June the flanking-and-withdrawing dance continued slowly south through Georgia, with small encounters at Snake Creek Gap, Allatoona, and Dallas. Only once did Sherman make a serious mistake. At Kennesaw Mountain on June 27 an impatient Sherman mounted a frontal assault on well-prepared Southern positions. The result was a slaughter, the North losing 2000 men to the South's 442. A few days later Sherman resumed his flanking maneuvers, forcing Johnston back to the Chattahoochie River, the last Southern defensive position before the massive fortifications of Atlanta itself. At that point Confederate President Jefferson Davis stepped into the picture.

Rejecting the campaign of retreat, Davis abruptly removed Johnston from command and replaced him with General John B. Hood, a hard-fighting veteran of Lee's army. Hood was expected to take a more aggressive tack and did so – which was exactly what Sherman wanted.

On July 20 Hood mounted a surprise attack on an isolated Federal detachment at Peachtree Creek, nearly cutting off a sizable part of Sherman's army. But commanding there was dogged Union General George H. Thomas, the 'Rock of Chickamauga,' who in four hours of sharp fighting pulled his forces together and drove the Confederates back to Atlanta with heavy losses. Two days later, on July 22, the Battle of Atlanta opened when Hood's forces struck the left flank of Union General James B. McPherson's forces, who were trying to cut rail lines into the city. While his men were repulsing this attack, McPherson himself, riding out from Sherman's headquarters, ran afoul of some enemy scouts and was shot dead from his horse. When the body was brought to him, Sherman wept openly.

After his attack on the Union left faltered, Hood pitched into the enemy center, and for a time made progress before the Federals brought to bear a devastating artillery barrage. This was the turning point of the battle: torn by 17,000 rifles and several batteries belching grapeshot and canister, the center of the Southern line vanished and the rest withdrew. With losses of 8000 men compared to the Federals' 3722, Hood pulled back into the elaborate defenses of Atlanta, to which Sherman now lay siege.

As the election approached, with Lincoln's chances against his opponent General McClellan looking dark, Sherman methodically tightened his grip around the city. On August 31 Hood's last-ditch attack on Feder-

Federal soldiers destroy railroad tracks in Atlanta after the capture of the city by W. T. Sherman in September 1864.

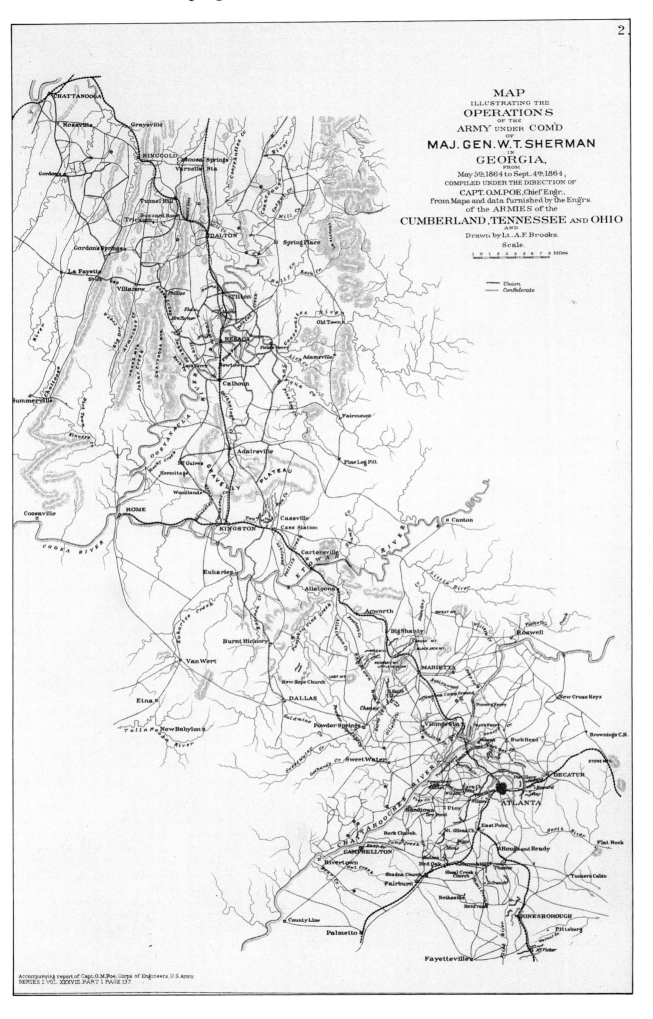

MAP
ILLUSTRATING THE
OPERATIONS
OF THE
ARMY UNDER COM'D
OF
MAJ. GEN. W.T. SHERMAN
IN
GEORGIA,
FROM
May 5th, 1864 to Sept. 4th, 1864,
COMPILED UNDER THE DIRECTION OF
CAPT. O.M. POE, Chief Engr.,
from Maps and data furnished by the Engrs.
of the ARMIES of the
CUMBERLAND, TENNESSEE AND OHIO
AND
Drawn by Lt. A.F. Brooks.
Scale.

Union
Confederate

Opposite: Sherman's route from Chattanooga to Atlanta is traced on this US Army map.
Above: The death of Union General James B. McPherson at the Battle of Atlanta, as shown on a Kurz & Allison color print.
Left: Federal troops man a battery emplaced in a redoubt on the northern side of what had formerly been the Confederate defenses of Atlanta. In the background, leaning on the parapet, is General Sherman.

als near Jonesboro failed; on the same day, Union forces cut the last rail line into Atlanta. That left Hood with no choices but surrender or precipitate flight.

On September 1 the remains of the Confederate army pulled out of Atlanta and marched south. Sherman telegraphed Lincoln, 'Atlanta is ours, and fairly won.' With that stunning Union victory the election turned around; Lincoln would win handily in November. Now Sherman would turn his ruthless attention to making sure Atlanta would never be of use to the Confederacy again, and from the ruins of the city he would set out on his famous March to the Sea in November.

Augur, Christopher Colombus (1821-98) **Union general.**

Augur, a New York-born career officer, fought on the Rappahannock and at the Battle of Cedar Mountain, was second in command under Nathaniel Banks in the 1862 New Orleans Campaign, commanded the District of Baton Rouge, and left field service in October 1863 to command the Department of Washington and XXII Corps.

Averell, William Woods (1832-1900) **Union general.**

New York State-born, a West Point graduate, and a pre-war Indian fighter, he proved to be one of the Army of the Potomac's more accomplished young cavalry leaders. He brought the Union cavalry its first taste of success in the engagement at Kelly's Ford (*See*) in March 1863, was one of George Stoneman's lieutenants at Chancellorsville, and served with distinction in the Shenandoah Valley Campaign of Sheridan in 1864. He ended the war a major general.

CORPS BADGES

Babcock, Orville *(1836-1884)*
Union army engineer.

An 1861 West Point graduate from Vermont, he worked on the Washington defense lines, fought in the Peninsular Campaign, and held senior engineering appointments in the army districts of Ohio and Kentucky. He served as Grant's aide-de-camp at the Wilderness, Spotsylvania, Cold Harbor, and Petersburg.

Badges

Devices used to identify members of Union corps, colored flannel badges were attached prominently to soldiers' caps. On Joseph Hooker's order, the Army of the Potomac adopted them in spring 1863; the West adopted them in 1864. Of the 25 Union corps, 23 wore badges in distinctive shapes such as stars, arrows, and lozenges. Eventually divisions were also designated by badges of red, white, blue, or green. Confederate corps did not wear badges.

Bagby, Arthur Pendleton *(1832-1921)* **Confederate officer.**

An Alabama-born West Pointer (1852) who quit the army to practice law in Texas, he led Texas troops at Galveston and in western Louisiana from 1861-63. He commanded a brigade in the Red River Campaign of March-May 1864 and saw action at Mansfield and Pleasant Hill.

Bailey, Theodorus *(1805-1877)*
Union naval officer.

A New Yorker, Bailey was a career officer who participated in the blockade of Pensacola and was second in command under Farragut at New Orleans. From November 1862 he led the East Gulf blockading squadron in intercepting 150 blockade runners; ill-health forced him ashore in 1864.

Baker, Edward Dickinson *(1811-1861)* **Union officer.**

An Englishman who became an Illinois lawyer and intimate and advisor of Lincoln, Baker declined a brigadier general's commission in 1861 to retain his Oregon Senate seat. As colonel of a Pennsylvania regiment, he was killed at Ball's Bluff (*See*) in October 1861.

Baker, La Fayette Curry *(1826-1868)* **US secret service chief.**

This New Yorker, a former San Francisco Vigilante, was a Union special agent throughout the war; his intelligence-gathering against Confederates, conspirators, and bounty-jumpers sometimes involved unconstitutional searches and arrests. Baker organized the pursuit and capture of John Wilkes Booth.

Baker, Laurence Simmons *(1830-1907)* **Confederate general.**

This West Point graduate left frontier Indian fighting for the North Carolina cavalry in

Various typical *shapes* of Union corps badges are shown above, but it should be noted that some corps symbols changed over time and that some corps used the same symbols.

May 1861. He fought in the Army of Northern Virginia in the Peninsular, Antietam, Fredericksburg, and Gettysburg campaigns. He assumed a North Carolina territorial command in 1864.

Balloons

In June 1861 President Lincoln observed an ascent by hot-air balloonist Thaddeus Lowe, who proposed the still-novel airships for scouting purposes. The Union experimented with balloons during the war, sending observers aloft during battle, but this had little impact either on the fighting or on the course of the war.

Ball's Bluff, *Virginia*

A raid across the Potomac here on October 21, 1861, blundered into a Confederate ambush that cost more than 900 Union casualties, including the Federal commander, President Lincoln's friend and advisor, Colonel Edward Baker, who was killed. Rebel casualties were fewer than 150.

Ball's Ferry, *Georgia*

In late November 1864, during W. T. Sherman's famous March to the Sea, a mixed force of Confederate cavalry and infantry briefly held up a the right wing of Sherman's Savannah-bound army at this Oconee River crossing. A Federal detachment crossed two miles upstream by flying bridge and turned the Rebels' flank, permitting the March to the Sea to resume.

Baltimore Crossroads

(also called Crump's Crossroads)

As the main opposing armies were fighting at Gettysburg on July 1-2, 1863, 6000 Federals under Erasmus Keyes (*See*) made a feint at Richmond. On the 2nd a Northern rearguard detachment was attacked at the crossroads.

Baltimore Riot

On April 19, 1861, as the first Northern regiment – the 6th Massachusetts – passed through the city en route to Washington, it was attacked by a pro-Confederate mob.

Their railroad cars surrounded, the militiamen were forced to march amid a hail of bricks and bullets; they returned fire indiscriminately. At least 13 people died, with dozens more wounded. Worried state officials forced a change in the military routes leading into Washington.

Banks, Nathaniel Prentiss (1816-1894) Union general.

Massachusetts-born Banks interrupted a long Congressional career to fight in the war. He commanded the Department of Annapolis, led V Corps during the Shenandoah Valley Campaign of Jackson in 1862, and II Corps at the Battle of Cedar Mountain in August of that year. Appointed to replace B. F. Butler in New Orleans late in 1862, he cooperated with Ulysses Grant in opening the Mississippi and was mainly responsible for the capture of Port Hudson, the last Rebel stronghold on the river, which fell in July 1863, soon after Grant's victory at Vicksburg. As commander of the Department of the Gulf, Banks led the Red River Campaigns of 1863-64. After the war Banks again served as a Representative from Massachusetts.

Barbee's Crossroads, *Virginia*

Union and Confederate cavalry tangled three times at this country road-crossing southeast of Manassas Gap. The most notable encounter took place on November 5, 1862, when Union General Alfred Pleasanton, with 1500 troopers, attacked 3000 Rebels under Wade Hampton with inconclusive results.

Above: The Union's Nathaniel Banks was a 'political general' who fought in numerous campaigns, seldom very successfully.
Below: Men of the 6th Massachusetts confront pro-Confederate rioters in Baltimore, Md., on April 19, 1861.

Small cavalry forces also skirmished here on July 25 and September 1, 1863.

Bardstown, *Kentucky*

Several skirmishes were fought here in October 1862 during CSA General Braxton Bragg's Kentucky Campaign (*See*). On July 5, 1863, Confederates under R. C. Morgan surrounded a detachment of the 4th US Cavalry at Bardstown and, after a 24-hour standoff, forced the Federals to surrender.

Barker, Mrs. Stephen
Sanitary Commission worker.

She accompanied her husband, chaplain to the 14th Massachusetts, to the war. A nurse attached to the 1st Heavy Artillery at Fort Albany for two years, she became the Sanitary Commission superintendent of several Washington hospitals in 1864.

Barksdale's Mississippi Brigade

Former US Congressman William Barksdale's hard-fighting Mississippians defended Marye's Heights against Union assaults at Fredericksburg in December 1862, holding the position with a loss of about 240 men. Federal attackers evicted the depleted brigade from Marye's Heights during the Chancellorsville Campaign in May 1863. Barksdale's losses in the latter action were nearly 600 killed, wounded, and missing.

Hospital worker and founder of the American Red Cross, Clara Barton did front-line duty not only in the Civil War but also in the Franco-Prussian and Spanish-American wars.

Union General Francis Barlow won distinction at Antietam, Gettysburg and the Wilderness.

Barlow, Francis Channing
(1834-1896) **Union general.**

He was a Harvard-educated New York lawyer. Despite several serious wounds requiring long recuperations, Barlow fought in most of the major campaigns of the Army of the Potomac from the siege of Yorktown to Sayler's Creek. He was a founder of the American Bar Association.

Barnard, John Gross *(1815-1882)*
Union general.

This Massachusetts-born army engineer specialized in coastal defenses, but as chief engineer successively of Washington, of the Army of the Potomac, and of the Armies of the Field, he also designed Washington's defenses and supervised Union engineering at First Bull Run, at the siege of Yorktown, and during William Tecumseh Sherman's Carolinas Campaign.

Barnett's Ford, *Virginia*

On February 6, 1864, Federal cavalry under Wesley Merritt drove enemy pickets back from the Robertson River to the Rapidan River, where Southern cavalry showed up to resist. The next morning saw an engagement as the reinforced Confederates prevented Merritt from crossing the river and inflicted 20 casualties.

Barry, John D. *(1839-1867)*
Confederate general.

A veteran of the Seven Days, Second Bull Run, and Antietam, he is believed to have given the order to fire that caused the mortal wounding of Stonewall Jackson at Chancellorsville. He led the 18th North Carolina in Pickett's Charge at Gettysburg. He briefly commanded a brigade in 1864-65.

Barton, Clara *(1821-1912)*
Humanitarian.

After the outbreak of war she left her clerkship in the Patent Office to provide nursing care and medical supplies to sick and wounded Federal troops, working behind the lines and earning the nickname 'the angel of the battlefields.' She supervised the hospitals of the Union Army of the James in 1864 and, at Lincoln's request, organized the postwar search for missing Union soldiers. Founder of the American Red Cross (1881), she worked extensively with the International Red Cross.

Baseball and the Civil War

American boys (and girls) and young men had already been playing games involving bats, balls, and bases for many decades when, in the 1840s, teams of young men in the Northeast began to try to introduce some rules that would make baseball a real game of skill and orderly contest. By the late 1850s, the so-called New York rules had generally prevailed, and representatives from 25 of the 60 to 100 teams – all in the Northeast or northern Middle West – that played by the New York rules formed the National Association of Base Ball Players. By 1860 these teams were even playing for an unofficial 'championship of the United States.'

With the advent of the Civil War organized civilian baseball, as might be expected, languished, though the game itself continued to be played informally in countless cities and towns. But at the same time, the game began to flourish within the military, for thousands of young men – often with plenty of time on their hands between the bloody battles – now

A baseball game in the Union army camp. One of the Civil War's better side-effects was to spread baseball's popularity nationwide.

took to playing baseball, and many US Army units formed their own teams and challenged those of other units. On Christmas Day in 1862 some 40,000 Union soldiers watched a game between an All-Star Union team and one from the 165th New York Volunteer Infantry: it is thought to have been the largest crowd at any sporting event in the nineteenth century.

It was largely via the prison camps, both Union and Confederate, that the South was introduced to the 'New York game,' for there Southern soldiers, as well as youths from the more remote communities of the still-youthful United States, could watch teams organized by Northeasterners play. (There is a famous contemporary lithograph of a Union team playing in a Confederate prison camp before a rapt crowd of their captors.) When the war ended, youths from all parts of the USA – and from all social classes and occupations – returned to their home towns and were soon introducing 'the New York game,' the new, more competitive version of the casual game they had formerly played. Thus, if the Civil War did not by itself make baseball into America's national sport, it certainly speeded the process amazingly.

Bate, William Brimage
(1826-1905) **Confederate general.**

Bate, a public servant and ardent secessionist in Tennessee, rose from private in the 2nd Tennessee to major general in four years. He was wounded three times in fighting at Shiloh, Stone's River, Missionary Ridge, and in both the Atlanta and Franklin and Nashville Campaigns.

Bates, Edward *(1793-1869)*
Union attorney general.

A Virginian by birth, Bates was a lawyer and moderate Republican political force in Missouri before the war. He lost his initial influence as Lincoln's attorney general by opposing Union military policies and what he considered the erosion of constitutional rights, and he resigned in November 1864.

Baton Rouge, *Louisiana*

On August 5, 1862, Confederate General Earl Van Dorn massed infantry, cavalry, artillery, and naval forces to attack Thomas Williams's 2500 Federals in Baton Rouge. Though the Federals were pushed back at first, the failure of Confederate naval support doomed the attack, and Van Dorn withdrew.

Battery Guns

These were primitive machine guns, usually multiple barrels mounted on a gun carriage and fired together. The Vandenberg, one such weapon, consisted of as many as 120 rifle barrels. Reloading so many barrels was slow work, and few Vandenbergs were manufactured. More successful types were the Ager Battery Gun (*See*) and the Billinghurst-Requa Volley Gun (*See*).

At the Battle of Baton Rouge, August 1861, one of the Rebel generals, John Breckenridge, was a former (1856-60) US vice president.

Battle Above the Clouds
(*See* Lookout Mountain)

Battle Hymn of the Republic

Probably the best-known song to survive from the Civil War is 'The Battle Hymn of the Republic,' with the words written by Julia Ward Howe (*See*) in 1861 after she had visited the Union Army camps around Washington, DC. Her words were published in the spring of 1862 in the *Atlantic Monthly*, and its editor actually assigned the poem its name. This much is widely recognized in standard reference books. But what of the stirring music? The composer was long ignored and then forgotten, but now he is generally conceded to have been William Steffe, an otherwise obscure early nineteenth-century composer who originally used the music for a hymn known as 'Fort Warren.' By the 1850s the music had been borrowed for a more widely sung spiritual known as 'Say, Brothers, Will You Meet Me?' Then in 1861, when the Massachusetts volunteers were marching through Baltimore on the way to the front, they are said to have been the first Union troops to introduce the new words, 'John Brown's body lies a-moldering in the grave . . . .' and soon this song was being printed and sung under the title, 'Glory Hallelujah.' And it was with this melody and those words in mind that Julia Ward Howe set out to write her own new verses – the ones that have endured (even in the face of endless parodies) over the decades. Some of Howe's other poems can be found in her 1878 collection *From Sunset Ridge: Poems Old and New*.

Union troops with fixed bayonets. Although bayonet charges were rare in the war, they could, as at Gettysburg, be devastating.

Battle Mountain, *Virginia*

Here Federal cavalry commander George Armstrong Custer's men struck the flank of James Longstreet's retreating forces on July 24, 1863, following the Confederate defeat at Gettysburg. The Southerners had to stop and fight a sharp rearguard action before pulling away to safety.

Baxter Springs, *Kansas*

On October 6, 1863, Confederate raiders under the ferocious guerrilla leader William Clarke Quantrill, all dressed in Federal uniforms, ambushed a small Union force here, killing 65, some atrociously.

Bayonet

Most Civil War soldiers carried this edged steel weapon, but it accounted for a very small proportion of casualties. Fewer than 1000 of 250,000 wounded men treated in Union hospitals were injured by bayonet or saber, according to Fox's *Regimental Losses*. Bayonet attacks were even rarer than bayonet wounds – only a few are recorded.

Bayou Teche, *Louisiana*

The war saw three minor actions in this town, all in support of the Union effort to bring the lower Mississippi River under Federal control. On November 3, 1862, there was indecisive fighting involving five Union gunboats and the 21st Indiana Volunteer Regiment. On January 14, 1863, four Union gunboats were engaged with the new Confederate XIX Corps. For the action of April 1863, *See* IRISH BEND AND FORT BISLAND.

Beale, Richard Lee Turberville
(1819-1893) **Confederate general.**

A Virginia legislator, Beale joined 'Lee's Light Horse' as a first lieutenant in 1861 and won early and rapid promotions, fighting in every campaign of the Army of Northern Virginia. In March 1864 his troops intercepted Ulric Dahlgren and discovered the Dahlgren Papers (*See*).

Bean's Station, *Tennessee*

Following his failed attack on the city in his 1863 Knoxville Campaign, Confederate General James Longstreet attempted on December 15 to capture three enemy cavalry brigades at Bean's Station. Due to the mistakes of some of Longstreet's subordinates – or so Longstreet maintained – the blue troopers escaped.

Beardslee Telegraph

This portable field telegraph enabled senior Union commanders to communicate when fog or battlesmoke obscured visual signals. A hand-cranked magneto powered the telegraph, which used an alphabet dial and pointed to send a message over a range of about ten miles. Unfortunately, the dials on the sending and receiving machines did not always synchronize, and gibberish could all too easily result.

Beauregard, Pierre Gustave Toutant *(1818-1893)*
Confederate general.

Beauregard, who officiated on the Confederate side at the beginning of the war, was born to a prosperous old Creole family in Loui-

siana. He was graduated from West Point and, after distinguished service in the Mexican War and years with the Corps of Engineers, became superintendent of West Point in January 1861. Within five days he was removed for saying that he would serve the South if it seceded. Soon he had his chance, being appointed the first brigadier general in the Confederate army (he would design the familiar Confederate flag).

As commander of the forces in Charleston, South Carolina, that opened hostilities and took Fort Sumter in April 1861, Beauregard reigned briefly as the South's first war hero. He went on to lead his forces to victory at the First Battle of Bull Run. Then his career foundered on two losses in 1862, the battles of Shiloh and Corinth. Relieved of command after the latter by President Jefferson Davis, he was sent to oversee the defenses of the coast from North Carolina to Georgia. At the end of the war Beauregard came to prominence again, defeating Union General Benjamin Butler at the Battle of Drewry's Bluff and turning back the first Union attempts on Petersburg in April 1864. After the surrender he worked in Louisiana in railroads and public works and wrote some important commentaries on the war.

Below: Union General W. W. Belknap, who would become Grant's war secretary.

Beaver Dam Station, *Virginia*

As part of Sheridan's 1864 Richmond Raid (*See*), on May 9-10 Federal cavalry under George A. Custer struck Lee's supply line at this place, destroying two locomotives, 10 miles of track, over 100 railroad cars, medical supplies, and hundreds of thousands of rations, in the process setting free 378 Union prisoners.

Bee, Barnard E. *(1824-1861)*
Confederate general.

A brigade commander at First Bull Run on July 22, 1861, he gave Thomas J. Jackson his nom de guerre during that battle. 'Look at Jackson's brigade – it stands like a stone wall!' Bee shouted, 'Rally behind the Virginians!' Mortally wounded shortly thereafter, he died the next day.

'Beecher's Bibles'

This was the ironic name for the Sharps carbines (*See*) smuggled into Kansas during the troubles over slavery there in the 1850s. The weapons allegedly were shipped in crates marked 'Bibles;' antislavery activist Lyman Ward Beecher believed slaveholders would have more respect for a single rifle than for a hundred bibles.

Above: Confederate General P. G. T. Beaugard. He won early fame as the commander of the Confederate forces at Fort Sumter and then as the victorious co-commander at First Bull Run.

Belknap, William Worth *(1829-1890)* **Union general.**

A pre-war lawyer and Democratic politician, he served with Iowa troops at Shiloh and fought at Corinth and Vicksburg. He led a brigade in W. T. Sherman's Atlanta Campaign. Belknap was accused of corruption as President Ulysses S. Grant's secretary of war from 1869-76, but the charges were eventually dropped.

Belle Isle

This Confederate prison on the James River in Richmond, Virginia, held 10,000 Union soldiers by the end of 1863. Union General Judson Kilpatrick led a cavalry raid on the prison in late February 1864; its failure cost the Federals 340 troopers, more than 500 horses, and hundreds of weapons. The Belle Isle prisoners were then moved to the notorious prison at Andersonville, Georgia.

Belmont *(Missouri)*, Battle of

In his first major operation of the war, General Ulysses S. Grant was ordered, in November 1861, to move his forces out of Cairo, Illinois, and down the Mississipi River in a diversion supporting a Union offensive in Missouri. On November 7 Grant landed one contigent of 3114 troops from river transports at Belmont, Missouri, to make a demonstration on the town. Hearing a report – erroneous, in fact – that enemy forces were heading for the area, Grant decided to turn his demonstration into an attack. His men

overran Confederate camps near town, then stopped because of enemy cannons threatening from nearby Columbus (the men also gave in to the temptation to loot and burn the camps). Soon Grant found Confederate General Leonidas Polk trying to get some 10,000 troops between the Federals and their transports, and the bluecoats had to make a dash back to the river with a few captured prisoners and supplies. In the better part of the day of fighting the North suffered around 600 casualties and the South about 650 of 4000 engaged. It was an inauspicious beginning for Grant, but he soon made up for it with his campaigns against Fort Henry and Fort Donelson (*See*).

Benjamin, Judah Philip
(1811-1884) **Confederate cabinet officer.**

Born in the British West Indies, he became a sugar planter, New Orleans lawyer, and, as a US Senator, an early secessionist. Appointed first Confederate attorney general, then secretary of war (September 17, 1861) and secretary of state (March 18, 1862), he was a pragmatist who, by 1864, was advising Jefferson Davis to arm and emancipate the slaves to win the war. After the war he emigrated to England, where he pursued a highly successful legal career.

Benning, Henry Lewis
(1814-1875) **Confederate general.**

Benning, a Georgia lawyer and legislator, was an early and extreme secessionist. In his military career he fought with distinction, if not brilliance, in nearly every campaign of the Army of Northern Virginia from Malvern Hill through Appomattox. Fort Benning, Georgia is named after him.

Shrewd and able, Judah P. Benjamin was easily the best of Confederate President Jefferson Davis's otherwise mediocre cabinet officers.

Benson, Eugene *(1839-1908)*
War correspondent and painter.

Benson trained at the National Academy of Design in the 1850s. In 1861, assigned by *Frank Leslie's Illustrated Newspaper* to sketch Charleston and its fortifications, he arrived just before the bombardment of Fort Sumter. After the war he painted and exhibited widely in Europe.

Bentonville *(North Carolina)*, Battle of

During W. T. Sherman's 1865 Carolinas Campaign, Confederate General Joseph Johnston massed 21,000 men at Bentonville to strike General Henry Slocum's isolated wing of Sherman's army. Slocum made contact on March 19 and held off fierce assaults. On the following day Sherman arrived with the rest of his force of around 100,000. Under attack and in danger of being cut off, Johnston pulled back on the 21st. This would be Johnston's last major attempt to contest Sherman's advance.

Bermuda Line

In mid-May 1864, after failing to take Drewry's Bluff (*See*) on the James River below Richmond, Virginia, Union General Benjamin Butler withdrew his Army of the James into defensive lines at Bermuda Hundred. Confederate forces followed up closely, effectively pinning the inept Butler's army in its own defenses and making it unable to assist Grant in his campaign against Richmond.

Berryville, *Virginia*

On the march to Gettysburg in mid-June 1863 a Confederate force of infantry and cavalry under Robert Rodes moved to trap an isolated Union cavalry brigade here. A Federal reconnaissance detected the move; the brigade commander, Colonel A. T. McReynolds, managed to withdraw most of his force, including the supply train.

Bickerdyke, Mary Ann Ball
(1817-1901)
Sanitary Commission worker.

A trained nurse, 'Mother Bickerdyke' ran field hospitals with Grant's army in Tennessee and Mississippi and then with Sherman's

Protected from Union attack by Britain's neutrality, Confederate blockade runners congregate in St. George harbor, Bermuda.

army in the Chattanooga and the Atlanta campaigns. Resourceful and efficient, she initiated army laundries and tirelessly nursed, foraged, and cooked through 19 battles.

Big Bethel *(Virginia)*, Battle of

This was the site of the first land battle of the war. On June 10, 1861, Union General B. F. Butler, whose division had recently arrived to reinforce the garrison at Fort Monroe, Virginia, ordered an assault on an enemy outpost at Big Bethel Church. The Rebels easily repulsed the clumsy attack. The Federals, with 4000 troops engaged, reported 76 casualties, the Confederates lost 11 of about 1400.

Billinghurst-Requa Volley Gun

This weapon, manufactured by a Rochester, NY, gunsmith named William Billinghurst, mounted 24 .60-caliber rifle barrels that took cartridges loaded from the breech. It fired an intimidating, if ragged, volley but never was produced in great quantities, though individual regiments made independent purchases of the weapon.

Birney, David Bell *(1825-1864)*
Union general.

Son of the abolitionist leader James G. Birney, this Philadelphia lawyer led a brigade in Philip Kearny's division in the Peninsular and Second Bull Run Campaigns, and then the division itself at Fredericksburg, Chancellorsville, and Gettysburg, where he also assumed Daniel Sickles's command after the latter was wounded. He died of malaria in October 1864.

Black Codes

Beginning with Mississippi on November 24, 1865, Reconstruction legislatures in Southern states passed a body of discriminatory laws regulating the conduct of newly freed blacks. These apprenticeship and vagrancy laws, penal codes, and guidelines for punishment restricted the opportunities of Southern blacks and codified their second-class status. Southern whites continued to apply many of these black codes until the Supreme Court ordered the integration of schools in 1954, forcing legal change.

Black Troops

The idea of using black soldiers on the Northern side met with great resistance at the beginning of the war, even though many freemen were eager to enlist. The pioneer units were organized in the fall of 1862, the first official one being the 1st Louisiana National Guard. Soon one state after another began calling for black volunteers. Lincoln was at first leery of this development, but after issuing the Emancipation Proclamation the president changed his mind and embraced the idea. In all black units during the war, officers were white. The first unit to see action was the 79th US Colored Infantry, in an engagement at Island Mounds, Missouri, in October 1862. After the gallant but doomed attack on Fort Wagner (July 1863 – *See*), in which the 54th Massachusetts Colored Infantry led the charge and lost 25 percent of its men, including commander Robert Gould Shaw, the *Atlantic Monthly* wrote, 'the manhood of the colored race shines before many eyes that would not see.' To those who still resisted black troops in the North and were indifferent to slavery Lincoln wrote, 'You say you will not fight to free negroes. Some of them seem willing to fight for you.' In the last months of the war a desperate Confederate government issued a call for the drafting of slaves, but the war ended before any saw action.

Blackburn's Ford, *Virginia*

On July 18, 1861, a Union reconnaissance in force bumped into two Confederate brigades guarding this Virginia ford on Bull Run. The Rebels repulsed the Federals, inflicting 78 casualties. Confederate losses were 68; they claimed this preliminary to the First Battle of Bull Run as an important victory.

English-born Elizabeth Blackwell, the first woman to receive a US medical degree.

A poster issued by the Union's Supervisory Committee for Recruiting Black Regiments. In all, about 186,000 black troops would serve in 140 Federal regiments.

Blackford's Ford, *Virginia*

As Lee retreated into Virginia from the 1862 Antietam battle, Federal units crossed the Potomac at this ford on September 19 and captured four guns of Lee's reserve artillery. Confederate General A. P. Hill counterattacked the next day, driving the bluecoats away. Federal losses were 92 killed, 131 wounded, 103 missing.

Blackwell, Elizabeth *(1821-1910)*
Physician.

The first-ever woman medical school graduate (1849), this Englishwoman helped found the New York Infirmary for Women and Children. Her initiative in organizing women's relief work in 1861 led to the establishment of the Sanitary Commission (*See*). She later became a prominent gynecologist and obstetrician in London and wrote numerous books and articles on health and education.

Blair, Francis Preston Jr. *(1821-1975)* **Union general.**

Kentucky-born Blair organized the Free-Soil and Republican Parties in Missouri and saved Missouri and Kentucky for the Union by seizing the St. Louis Arsenal in May 1861. He raised seven regiments and participated in the Yazoo expedition and the Chattanooga and Atlanta campaigns.

Blakely *(Alabama)*, Battle of

The last infantry battle of the war opened on April 1, 1865, when Federal cavalry, fighting dismounted, attacked Rebel outposts here. A Union force of 10,000 then besieged the town. Over the next few days new Union forces arrived, and on April 9 General Edward Canby attacked with 16,000 men, taking the town, more than 3400 Confederate prisoners, and some 40 guns.

Blakely Guns

Confederate forces bought small numbers of these rifled cannon of English design. The largest models – one Blakely fired a 12.75-inch shell from a barrel that weighed 27 tons – were used for coastal defense. Blakely field artillery pieces fired 3.1- and 8-inch solid and explosive projectiles.

'Bleeding Kansas'

Five years of intermittent warfare between pro- and antislavery factions followed the passage of the Kansas-Nebraska Act in 1854, which left the slavery question to the settlers' vote. Both factions sponsored immigration into the territory. John Brown and his followers killed several pro-slavery Kansans at Pottawatamie in 1856; pitched battles were fought at Franklin, Fort Saunders, and Hickory Point.

Blockade

The Union naval blockade of the Confederacy sometimes seemed ineffective in the short run, but during the course of the war it proved a potent means of choking off supplies to the South. President Lincoln first declared a blockade of Southern ports in April 1861. Though at first the Union fleet was ragtag and small, by the second year of the war the blockade was having a measurable effect. Eventually the 3550 miles of Southern coastline were patrolled by some 600 Union ships. Statistics tell the story: in 1861 only about one in ten Southern blockade-running ships was captured; in 1864 one in three such Confederate vessels was intercepted, out of a considerably reduced total.

'Bloody Angle'

Also known as 'the Salient,' this horseshoe-shaped bulge in the Confederate line at the Battle of Spotsylvania became one of the war's great killing grounds. At dawn on May 12, 1864, Union General Winfield Hancock's II Corps stormed the center of the position, taking 2000 prisoners and 20 guns. The Federals followed up with attacks on both flanks, but these lost heavily and failed to make ground. Hancock's troops held their gains against a ferocious Confederate counter-attack late in the day.

'Bloody Lane'

After hard fighting, Union troops took this stretch of sunken farm road in the center of the Confederate line at the Battle of Antietam on September 17, 1862. The Rebels fell back in disorder, but a shaken Union General George McClellan failed to follow up with his reserves. Lee reformed the line, then withdrew his army in good order the following night, September 18.

Blue Springs, *Tennessee*

In a preliminary to Confederate General James Longstreet's Knoxville Campaign 1700 Confederates under J. S. Williams occupied this eastern Tennessee town in late September 1863. Ambrose Burnside's Union forces attacked on October 10, forcing Williams to retreat into western Virginia with a loss of about 250 men.

'Bonnie Blue Flag'

This Confederate patriotic song, author unknown, was first sung in Richmond and New Orleans in 1861. The title refers to an early version of the Rebel flag, later replaced by the 'Stars and Bars.' (*See* also MUSIC OF THE CIVIL WAR).

After the Battle of Antietam Confederate dead lie in rows along the sunken road that is today remembered as 'Bloody Lane'.

John Wilkes Booth, Lincoln's assassin, was the brother of Edwin Booth, then America's foremost Shakespearean actor.

Booneville (*Mississippi*), Battle of

A large force of Confederate cavalry under J. R. Chalmers attacked Philip Sheridan's 2nd Cavalry Brigade at this halt on the Mobile & Ohio Railroad on July 1, 1862. Though heavily outnumbered, Sheridan counterattacked and routed Chalmers's troopers. His reward: a brigadier general's commission.

Booth, John Wilkes (*1838-1865*)

Born into an acting family and brother of famed Shakespearean Edwin Booth, John Wilkes Booth followed the family trade with some success before entering history as the assassin of Abraham Lincoln. Born in Maryland, he acted Shakespearean roles before seeing service with the Virginia militia that attacked John Brown at Harper's Ferry. During the war, while continuing his acting

The great photographer Mathew Brady (wearing the straw hat) watches a Union battery fire on Rebel positions at Petersburg in 1864.

career, he became a fanatical Southern patriot, toward the end of the war plotting without success to kidnap President Lincoln.

After the fall of Richmond and the imminent end of the war, an hysterical Booth gathered a group of conspirators to assassinate the president and other leaders, hoping this deed would inspire the South to fight on. Having enlisted accomplices also to kill Vice-President Andrew Johnson and Secretary of State William Seward (neither succeeded, though Seward was seriously injured), Booth slipped into Ford's Theater in Washington on the night of April 14, 1865, where Lincoln and his wife were watching a play, and mortally wounded the president (*See* LINCOLN ASSASSINATION).

Booth, fleeing with a broken leg, and co-conspirator David Herold were run to ground on April 26 in a barn near Bowling Green, Virginia. Herold surrendered, but Booth remained defiant. During the ensuing shoot-out the pursuers set the barn afire; when Booth emerged he was shot dead. Herold and three other accomplices were hanged in July 1865. For decades a rumor persisted that Booth had survived and lived in the South, but this was entirely fanciful.

Border States

After the 13 slave-holding states had seceded to form the Confederacy, four other slave-holding states remained, shakily loyal to the Union – Delaware, Kentucky, Maryland, and Missouri. These plus Virginia, which did secede, had been known as Border States because they divided free and slaveholding regions. Added to this group later in 1861 was West Virginia, an area sympathetic to the Union, that broke off after the rest of Virginia seceded. Especially in the early part of the war, the border states were considered potential allies by both sides and were thus vitally important. (Had four more states gone to the South, the Confederacy's chances of victory would have been vastly improved.) It

was therefore a great concern of President Lincoln to keep the remaining border states at least neutral. This was a primary reason for his early policy of fighting the war over secession rather than slavery: he could not afford to threaten the border-state slaveholders. By an adroit combination of coddling and periodic military action Lincoln managed to keep all these states from seceding, despite the Confederate sympathies of large minorities of their populations.

Bormann Fuse

Gunners used this Belgian-designed time fuse on explosive shells fired from field pieces and siege artillery but complained of its unreliability.

Bounties

Both armies, as well as state and local agencies, offered bounty payments as an inducement to volunteer. Congress voted a $100 bounty for three-year enlistees as early

as July 1861; by war's end, the federal government alone had paid out an estimated $300 million. The Confederate government generally offered a $50 bounty.

Bowie Knife

The name of Indian fighter James Bowie was given to almost any knife a Confederate soldier carried as a sidearm, but these various knives were all but useless in battle, and veterans learned quickly to toss them aside.

Boyd, Belle *(1844-1900)*
Confederate spy.

As a courier for P. G. T. Beauregard and Stonewall Jackson, this young Virginian was an intelligence agent and smuggler who proved especially useful to the Confederacy at the Battle of Front Royal. Three times arrested, she escaped to England in 1864, became an actress, and published a racy account of her espionage career.

Bradley, Amy Morris *(1823-1904)*
Sanitary Commission worker.

A regimental nurse at First Bull Run, Bradley later supervised hospital ships in the Peninsular Campaign. After December 1862 she transformed Camp Distribution, a squalid convalescent camp, into a clean, efficient operation and edited the *Soldiers' Journal*, a paper intended to disseminate practical information to Federal troops.

Brady, Mathew B. *(1823-1896)*
Photographer.

A highly acclaimed portrait photographer, he got Lincoln's authorization to photograph camp and battle scenes. Accompanying Federal troops with cumbersome wet-plate

Below left: A typical poster offering bounty payments to men willing to volunteer for service in the Union cavalry.
Below: The celebrated Rebel spy Belle Boyd helped Jackson during his Valley Campaign.

cameras, often a great personal risk, Brady and his assistants compiled a documentary record of 3500 photographs, preserving some of our most enuring and valuable images of the Civil War.

Bragg, Braxton *(1817-1876)*
Confederate general.

North Carolinian Bragg was graduated from West Point (1837), fighting in the Seminole and Mexican Wars and on the frontier before retiring to a Louisiana plantation in 1856. He commanded southern coastal defenses and, promoted to major general, served as Albert S. Johnston's chief of staff and commanded II Corps at Shiloh. A full general after April 1862, Bragg commanded the Tennessee Army through Bragg's Invasion of Kentucky, Perryville, Stone's River, the Tullahoma Campaign, Chickamauga, and Chattanooga. Replaced by Joseph E. Johnston after repeated misjudgments and failures to capitalize on battlefield gains, he became Jefferson Davis's military advisor and was captured with Davis in May 1865. Bragg was an intelligent military planner, but his war career was hampered by indecision, frequent illness, and personal unpopularity.

The high point of Rebel General Braxton Bragg's wartime career was probably his victory at Chickamauga in September 1863.

Bragg's Invasion of Kentucky

The slaveholding state of Kentucky had remained with the Union at the beginning of the war, despite its many Southern sympathizers. The Richmond government, wanting to make use of that sympathy to win the state for the Confederacy, acceded to General Braxton Bragg's plan for an invasion. Bragg, with 30,000 men, left from Chattanooga and arrived in Glasgow, Kentucky, on September

The Battle of Brandy Station in June 1863 was the war's first major cavalry action. Here, a charge by the 6th New York Cavalry.

13, 1861, then occupied Munfordville (*See*). (Meanwhile, CSA General Edmund Kirby Smith had left Knoxville and marched into Kentucky with his Confederate forces, planning on linking up with Bragg.) As Bragg moved north, however, the expected recruits and popular uprising failed to materialize, even after a Confederate governor was proclaimed at Frankfort on October 4. Finally, slow-moving Union General Don Carlos Buell assembled a large force and caught up with Bragg at Perryville. The ensuing battle on October 8 persuaded Bragg to give up the invasion.

Brandy Station *(Virginia)*, Battle of

Following the 1863 battle of Chancellorsville, as Robert E. Lee was gearing up for the Gettysburg Campaign, Federal Army of the Potomac commander Joseph Hooker sent cavalry under General Alfred Pleasonton to make a reconnaissance in force. The result, on June 9th, was the Battle of Brandy Station, the first true cavalry combat of the war and the largest. The Federals began with a surprise assault, and after a day of fierce fighting, much of it with sabers, the Union troopers had lost 936, Confederate General J. E. B. Stuart's cavalry 523. Though results of the fight were inconclusive, the action was perceived as something of a humiliation for Jeb Stuart and his Southern horsemen.

Breckinridge, John Cabell *(1821-1875)*
Confederate general and secretary of war.

A Kentucky politician, he was President James Buchanan's vice president and ran against Lincoln in 1860. Natural leadership outweighing his inexperience, Breckinridge fought at Shiloh, Stone's River, and Vicksburg, as well as with Braxton Bragg at Chickamauga and Missionary Ridge. Summoned by Robert E. Lee to the Shenandoah Valley, he won at New Market (*See*) in 1864. He served as the Confederate secretary of war after February 1865.

A Mathew Brady portrait of the Confederate general and statesman John C. Breckenridge.

Brentwood, *Tennessee*

On March 25, 1863, the Confederate cavalry commander Nathan B. Forrest surprised and surrounded a Union outpost held by the 22nd Wisconsin, then drove off reinforcements sent to rescue the captured Federals. Forrest reported taking more than 750 Union prisoners.

Brevet Rank

An honorary title awarded for gallant or meritorious action in war, a brevet rank carried none of the increases in authority, pay, or precedence of a real promotion. Brevet officers could occasionally claim the privileges of rank, but rules governing brevet rank were so vague that officers' titles and uniforms often failed to indicate their actual positions, and disputes were common. Abuses eventually caused the abandonment of the system.

Brice's Crossroads (*Mississippi*), Battle of

During his 1864 Atlanta Campaign, Federal General W. T. Sherman sent Samuel D. Sturgis and a mixed force of nearly 8000 to destroy Nathan Bedford Forrest's raiders, who had been wrecking Sherman's supply lines. With 4713 men, Forrest assaulted Sturgis's cavalry advance at the crossroad on June 10. As Union infantry arrived, exhausted from a forced march in severe heat, Forrest kept up the pressure; then, massing his forces, Forrest broke through the blue center and followed that with attacks on both flanks. Soon the Federals were fleeing in panic; the gray-

coats chased them all night and into the next day. With half the numbers of his opponent, Forrest had captured large quantities of supplies and arms and had inflicted over 2000 casualties (most in captured).

Brigades

These army formations consisted of two or more regiments; two or more brigades composed a division. Union brigades, designated by number (*i.e.*, 1st Brigade, 2nd Division) generally averaged about 2000 men. Confederate brigades, named for their commanding officers, were usually smaller. Two famous units were the Union 'Iron Brigade' of midwestern regiments and the Confederate Stonewall Brigade of Virginians.

Bristoe Campaign

This is the name given to a series of maneuvers and relatively small clashes between the Union Army of the Potomac and Robert E. Lee's Army of Northern Virginia in the autumn of 1863. After the Battle of Gettysburg the Confederate army had settled into Culpeper, Virginia, the Federals nearby across the Rappahannock River. By autumn both armies were somewhat weakened, having sent detachments to other theaters. Learning that his opponent, George Meade, had sent two corps to Chattanooga, Lee began the Bristoe Campaign to cut off the Federals; this produced a series of inconclusive engagements from mid-October through November: Bristoe Station, Catlett's Station, Buckland Mills, Rappahannock Bridge and Mine Run (*See* under each engagement). Meade, meanwhile, managed to pull his army back to a strong defensive position on the Bull Run, and by early December both armies had settled into winter quarters. The campaign is chiefly interesting as a demonstration of how Lee's losses at Gettysburg had deprived him of the ability to mount any further meaningful offensive operations.

Bristoe Station (*Virginia*), Battle of

As part of Robert E. Lee's attempts to cut off Union General George Meade in the Bristoe Campaign (*See*), Lee's lieutenant A. P. Hill sent a corps against the supposedly isolated Federal III Corps near Bristoe Station, Virginia. As the Confederates attacked, however, they were struck by the nearby Union II Corps; rather than retreat, they charged into the strong blue positions and were severely repulsed. In the day's fighting Lee suffered some 1900 casualties to the Union's 548.

Brooke Guns

This rifled artillery weapon, designed by the Confederate naval officer John Brooke, resembled the Parrott cannon widely used by both sides. The 3-inch field gun version fired a 10-pound projectile at a range of more than two miles.

Brooke, John Rutter (*1838-1926*)
Union general.

This Pennsylvanian led troops in virtually every campaign of the Army of the Potomac from the Peninsular to Cold Harbor, twice suffering serious wounds. He later commanded a division in the Army of the Shenandoah, and after the war joined the Regular Army.

Brooklyn, USS

Union commanders kept this wooden-hulled sloop-of-war, based at Norfolk, Virginia, on standby to reinforce Fort Sumter during the secession crisis of the winter of 1861, but for diplomatic reasons General Winfield Scott sent the unarmed *Star of the West* (*See*) in-

Just before the Battle of Bristoe Station (October 14, 1863) Union General George Meade hurries his men across Kettle Run. The battle would be a defeat for Robert E. Lee.

stead. The *Brooklyn* later served on blockade duty and took part in Admiral David Farragut's victories at both New Orleans and Mobile Bay.

Brooks, William Thomas Harbaugh *(1821-1870)* Union general.

An Ohio-born West Point graduate (1841), he fought in the Mexican War (under Robert E. Lee) and on the frontier. He led a division in the Peninsular Campaign and at Antietam in 1862, and at Drewry's Bluff, Bermuda Hundred, and Cold Harbor in 1864. He commanded X Corps during the Petersburg siege before resigning as the result of ill health in July 1864.

Brooks-Sumner Affair

On May 22, 1856, South Carolina Representative Preston Brooks delivered a savage caning to abolitionist Senator Charles Sumner, who had insulted Brooks's kinsman, a South Carolina Senator, in an antislavery speech two days before. Sumner suffered from the effects of the beating for three years, although he continued to represent Massachusetts in the Senate.

Brown, John *(1800-1859)*
Abolitionist.

Active in antislavery work throughout an itinerant early life, Brown was swept into radical activism in Kansas in 1855. He became leader of the Ossawatomie colony, gaining

South Carolina Congressman Preston Brooks attacks Massachusetts Senator Charles Sumner in the Senate Chamber in May 1856.

Fanatical abolitionist John Brown, author of the famous 1859 raid at Harpers Ferry.

national notoriety after massacring five proslavery men at Pottawatamie in May 1856. Claiming to be an instrument of God, and supported by leading Eastern abolitionists, Brown devised a plan to invade the South and free the slaves. He began by attacking Harper's Ferry (*See*) with 21 men in October 1859, occupying the town and its armory before being captured by Colonel Robert E. Lee. Convicted of treason, Brown was hanged in December and promptly became an abolitionist martyr. Passionate and eloquent, Brown was by some accounts insane; Emerson, however, praised him as 'a pure idealist of artless goodness.'

Brown, Joseph Emerson *(1821-1894)*
Confederate governor of Georgia.

Born in South Carolina and educated at Yale, Brown was a leglislator, judge, and, from 1857-65, governor of Georgia. A strong states' rights advocate, he opposed Jefferson Davis's centralization of the Confederate government. After the war Georgians deplored Brown's active support for Radical Reconstruction measures as opportunistic.

Brownell, Kady *(b.1842)*
Vivandiere.

Daughter of a British soldier, she accompanied her American husband to war and fought with his Rhode Island regiments at First Bull run, where she carried the colors, and at New Bern, where her husband was wounded. General Ambrose Burnside signed her discharge, and she received an army pension.

Brownlow, William Gannaway *(1805-1877)* Tennessee unionist.

A Virginia-born itinerant preacher, Brownlow edited influential Whig newspapers in Tennessee, notably the *Knoxville Whig*, and united the eastern Tennessee Unionists. Briefly imprisoned by the Confederates in 1861 for treason, he lectured in the North in 1862-63 and was elected Tennessee's governor in 1865.

Buchanan, James *(1791-1868)*
Fifteenth president of the United States.

Buchanan, a Democrat, became president in 1857. A states' rights advocate, he nevertheless opposed secession, yet his indecisiveness when Fort Sumter was threatened and Southern states seceded left Lincoln facing imminent war upon his inauguration. Historians judge Buchanan as politically unwise, but hardly as responsible for the war.

Buckner, Simon Bolivar *(1823-1914)* Confederate general.

An 1844 graduate of West Point, Buckner resigned from the army in 1855, settling into a business career in his native Kentucky. He organized and trained the state militia in 1860, meanwhile working to preserve Kentucky's neutrality. After the Federals invaded Kentucky, however, Buckner joined the Confederates. In February 1862 he surrendered Fort Donelson to Ulysses Grant. Exchanged in August and promoted to major general, he participated in Braxton Bragg's invasion of Kentucky, fortified Mobile, commanded East Tennessee during the summer of 1863, and led a corps at Chickamauga. Commanding the District of Louisiana after 1864, Buckner saw little further action, but after Appomattox he helped negotiate the surrender of the Trans-Mississippi armies.

Buell, Don Carlos *(1818-1898)*
Union general.

Buell, an Ohio native, was raised in Indiana, was graduated from West Point, and fought

A Mathew Brady portrait photograph of the last prewar president, James Buchanan.

in the Mexican War. He was commissioned brigadier general in 1861 and initially organized troops of the Army of the Potomac. Appointed commander of the Army of the Ohio in November, Buell moved to retake eastern Tennessee, occupying Bowling Green and Nashville and then forcing the Confederate retreat at Shiloh. After an unsuccessful expedition toward Chattanooga early in 1862 he led the Stone's River Campaign, in which his disappointing performance led to his replacement by William S. Rosecrans. After a seven-month investigation into his Tennessee and Kentucky Campaign, Buell resigned in June 1864. Though a solid general, Buell's early promise was unrealized. His reserved temperament neither inspired his troops nor allowed him to function effectively in the highly charged political climate of the Civil War.

Buford, Abraham (1820-1894)
Confederate general.

Born in Kentucky, he was graduated from West Point (1841), served in the Mexican War, and joined the Confederate Army in September 1862. He commanded a brigade at Stone's River, and fought with Nathan B. Forrest at the head of a cavalry brigade until he was wounded at Lindville in December 1864.

Buford, John (1826-1863)
Union general.

An 1848 West Point graduate from Kentucky, he commanded the Union cavalry screen that intercepted Confederate forces marching toward Gettysburg, Pennsylvania, on July 1, 1863. His decision to defend the town brought on the great battle there. Buford died of typhoid fever on December 16, 1863.

Built-up Guns

In this manufacturing method, the main components of cannon were produced separately, then joined by welding or other processes. Armstrong, Blakely, Brooke, Parrott, and Whitworth guns were made in this way. In the alternative method, cannon were cast in one piece.

Bull Run, First Battle of
(In Confederate chronicles called First Manassas)

In July 1861 General P. G. T. Beauregard commanded a Confederate army encamped at Manassas Junction, Virginia, some 25 miles southwest of Washington. President Lincoln ordered General Irvin McDowell to drive Beauregard away from that important rail junction. On the 16th McDowell advanced from Washington with 30,600 troops, primarily three-month volunteers and militia, many of them due to go home shortly (and thus less disposed to risk their lives). Having learned of the advance from spies in Washington, Beauregard called for reinforcements, and Confederate President Jefferson Davis ordered General Joseph E. Johnston to bring his 11,000 men by railroad from Virginia's Shenandoah Valley. (This was the first large movement of troops by rail in history.) Everyone expected a major battle; many expected it would decide the war.

The forces collided briefly on July 18th in a spirited skirmish at Blackburn's Ford on the Bull Run River, where General James Longstreet drove away a Federal reconaissance party. McDowell's green troops had marched slowly from Washington. The resulting delay in attacking allowed time for Johnston's reinforcements to arrive, giving Beauregard a force of well over 30,000 in his position west of the Bull Run. Both generals, who had been classmates at West Point, made identical plans for battle: feint with the left, attack on the right. If both had been successful, the two armies would have brushed past each other like a swinging door. In practice, however, the battle turned into a free-for-all.

At dawn on July 21 McDowell set his plan in motion with an artillery barrage. His strategy then fell apart, due largely to the slowness and inexperience of the Federal troops, who had insufficient drill and marching experience. McDowell made his feint on his left at a bridge on the Warrenton Turnpike, followed by a secondary attack on the enemy center. But to mount his flank attack on the right he had to march a detachment six miles through rough terrain. By the time these men had struggled to the enemy left Southern Colonel Nathan Evans had spotted the dust of the Union column on the march and had alerted Beauregard of the danger to his flank. By the time the bluecoats attacked two extra enemy brigades had been moved up to receive them.

Still, the badly outnumbered Southerners were slowly forced back in two hours of severe but confused fighting. At that point neither army was able to perform effective battlefield maneuvers. Finally the Confederates were pushed across the turnpike and up Henry House Hill, where hours of inconclusive fighting surged back and forth. As it began to appear that the exhausted Southerners were about to break and run, brigade commander Thomas J. Jackson moved up and formed his fresh troops into a defensive nucleus on the hilltop. It was then that Southern General Bernard E. Bee entered history in his last few moments of life, shouting to his men, 'Look at Jackson's Brigade – it stands like a stone wall! Rally behind the Virginians!' Soon the Confederate line had firmed up behind Jackson, who stopped the Union advance on the crest of the hill. From then on, the laconic, eccentric man who turned the tide of the battle would be called Stonewall Jackson, his troops the Stonewall Brigade.

Colonel (and soon-to-be General) Ambrose Burnside rallies his Rhode Island Brigade at the First Battle of Bull Run in this on-the-scene sketch by A. R. Waud.

Beauregard followed with a counterattack all along the line, using nearly every reserve he had (McDowell failed to commit two reserve brigades). As the Southerners drove into the Federals the eerie, frightening wail of the 'Rebel yell' was heard for the first time by most of the Northerners. Later a veteran would write of it, 'The peculiar corkscrew sensation that it sends down your backbone under these circumstances can never be told. You have to feel it.' The Northern men fell back in the face of the onslaught.

At dusk the Federals began an orderly retreat, with no pursuit from the exhausted and disorganized Confederates. Mixed in with the Federal troops were a number of civilians who had come to watch the battle, bringing picnic lunches. Suddenly a Southern battery fired some shells into the mass of Northern soldiers and civilians near a bridge over the Bull Run that constricted the column. A panic resulted, the retreat becoming a rout, everyone trying to get over the bridge at once.

The South had won its first major victory.

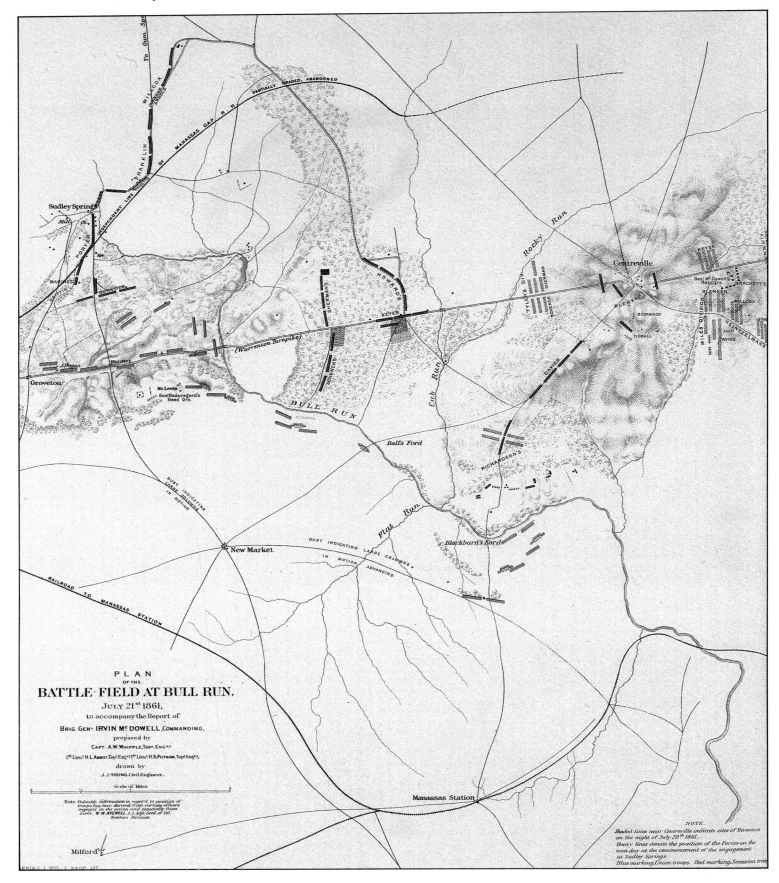

PLAN
OF THE
BATTLE-FIELD AT BULL RUN,
JULY 21st 1861,
to accompany the Report of
BRIG. GENl. IRVIN McDOWELL, COMMANDING,
prepared by
CAPT. A.W. WHIPPLE, TOPl. ENGrs.
1st Lieut. H.L. Abbot, Topl Engr & 1st Lieut. H.S. Putnam, Topl Engr,
drawn by
J.J. Young, Civil Engineer.

That night Washington learned of the disaster when the troops that had marched grandly off to battle returned to the city a dirty, demoralized rabble. The North was horrified, and none more so than President Lincoln. Newspaperman and Republican stalward Horace Greeley would write Lincoln that week, 'If it is best for the country and for mankind that we make peace with the rebels, and on their own terms, do not shrink even from that.' The South, naturally, erupted in celebration, though there were some bitter words about the army's 'failure' to march into Washington. Many in the South assumed the North would give up in short order, and nearly everyone gained an unrealistic sense of the Confederacy's fighting prowess. A Richmond newspaper wrote, 'The breakdown of the Yankee race, their unfitness for empire, forces dominion on the South. We are compelled to take the sceptre of power.' Against all resistance from both sides, Lincoln overrode his own despair and uncertainty and began to arrange for an extended war.

By the end of the First Battle of Bull Run about 18,000 troops had been engaged on each side. The North lost about 625 killed, 950 wounded, and over 1200 captured, the South some 400 killed and 1600 wounded. Among the other future luminaries of the war who fought in the battle were J. E. B. ('Jeb') Stuart and Wade Hampton for the South, and William Tecumseh Sherman, Oliver O. Howard, and Ambrose E. Burnside for the North. It would be eight months before the North tried anything major in Virginia again. An incidental outcome of the battle had to do with flags: noting that the original Confederate battle flag could be mistaken for the Union flag in the heat of action – there had been much confusion of sides in the fighting – General Beauregard designed the new flag of the Confederacy, white stars on a blue St. Andrew's cross on a field of red.

Bull Run, Second Battle of

(In Confederate chronicles called Second Manassas.)

After the successes of the Shenandoah Valley Campaign of Stonewall Jackson, in which three separate commands had failed to bring the rampaging Confederates to ground, Washington decided to combine those three armies into one – the short-lived Army of Virginia. Its commander, General John Pope, transferred from the Army of the Mississippi, starting off badly with a blustering address that began, 'Let us understand each other. I have come to you from the West, where we have always seen the backs of our enemies . . . I am sorry to find so much in vogue

Above: The Second Battle of Bull Run as it was imagined by Currier & Ives.
Opposite: Union army map of First Bull Run.
Below: A map showing what Union General Pope believed were the positions of Rebel forces two days before Second Bull Run.

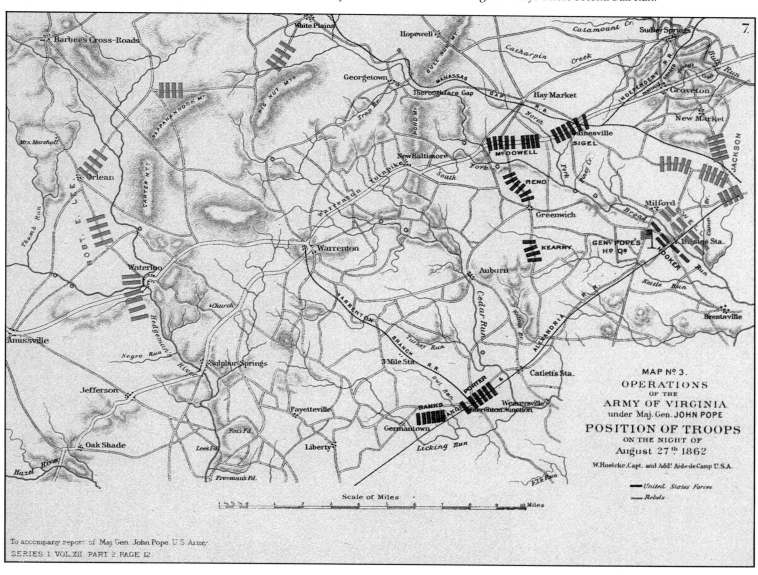

MAP No 3.
OPERATIONS
OF THE
ARMY OF VIRGINIA
under Maj. Gen. JOHN POPE
POSITION OF TROOPS
ON THE NIGHT OF
August 27th 1862
W. Hoelcke, Capt. and Add! Aide-de-Camp U.S.A.

Scale of Miles

United States Forces
Rebels

The armies had skirmished around Manassas long before Second Bull Run. These Rebel redoubts were photographed there in March.

amongst you . . . certain phrases [like] . . . 'lines of retreat' and 'bases of supplies' . . . Let us study the probable lines of retreat of our opponents, and leave our own to take care of themselves . . . Success and glory are in the advance, disaster and shame lurk in the rear.'

General Fitz-John Porter, on whom Pope would soon be shifting blame for his own mistakes, said of Pope's debut that he had 'written himself down, what the military world had long known, an Ass.' Pope's tendancy to sign his dispatches 'Headquarters in the saddle' prompted some to observe that his headquarters were where his hind-quarters belonged. Of the same opinion was General George B. McClellan, who at the end of July 1862 was ordered to join his forces to Pope's after the failure of the Peninsular Campaign. For his part, Pope considered McClellan incompetent and useless.

Confederate General Robert E. Lee, in Richmond following the Seven Days' Battles, was also outraged by Pope's ungentlemanly behavior in war. 'The miscreant Pope,' Lee proclaimed, must be 'suppressed.' More practically, he knew that the uniting of McClellan's 90,000-man Army of the Potomac and Pope's 50,000 troops must be prevented at all costs; even with two blundering and feuding generals in command, such a gigantic force would still be a serious threat to the Confederacy.

Lee had already grouped his still-new command into the organization that would lead the Army of Northern Virginia to victory time and again: Stonewall Jacakson, his strong right arm; his other division commanders James Longstreet, A. P. Hill, and D. H. Hill; and in command of cavalry the brilliant Jeb Stuart. In early August, Lee dispatched the commands of Jackson and A. P. Hill to deal with Pope before McClellan could reach him.

Jackson planned to strike the Federal advance units of the Union Army of Virginia and defeat them one corps at a time. But that plan was stymied when the opposing forces collided on August 9 at the Battle of Cedar Mountain, Virginia (*See*). There Federals under Nathaniel Banks drove back Jackson's men, and only a last-minute counterattack by A. P. Hill saved the day. A week later McClellan began to pull his Federal troops away from the Richmond area and ship them toward union with Pope. Now that Federal forces no longer threatened the Confederate capital Lee could move Longstreet's command from Richmond to back up Jackson and A. P. Hill.

For the first of several times Lee violated the old military maxim that forbids dividing forces in the face of equal or superior enemy numbers. Longstreet was ordered to spread his command along the Rappahannock River and hold the Federals in place while Jackson went on a wide envelopment. After marching over 50 miles in two days, on August 27 Jackson destroyed a Union supply dump at Manassas, Virginia, in Pope's rear, and then disappeared. The furious Northern commander put his army on the march in a futile attempt to find and destroy Jackson, whom he assumed to be fleeing. By the next day the Federals had reached nearby Groveton, where Jackson had concealed his men in a railroad cut. At that point the Southern commander faced a dilemma: he had only a third of Pope's strength, and Lee and Longstreet were still some distance away; yet if the Federals moved into strong defenses at Centreville, they could hold out until McClellan arrived. Taking a historic gamble, Jackson feinted at Pope on the evening of the 28th, deliberately revealing his position.

Pope gleefully gave orders to smash Jackson next day, meanwhile ignoring intelligence reports warning of Longstreet's approach. The Second Battle of Bull Run broke out in the morning of August 29 when 62,000 Federals made a series of uncoordinated frontal assaults on Jackson's 20,000 men. Well protected in the railroad cut, the Confederates turned back wave after wave throughout the morning. Though Jackson's lines nearly broke several times, the outcome became primarily a question of whether the Southerners would run out of ammunition before Longstreet arrived. Jackson rode back and forth behind his lines, entreating his men to hold out a little longer.

At 11:00 in the morning Longstreet's forces appeared and mounted a probing attack in the Federal center, relieving the pressure on Jackson. Pope persisted in ignoring Longstreet's presence and maintained that Jackson was about to retreat. On the next day the Federal commander learned better. After letting the Federals strike Jackson's left, Lee sent Longstreet on a crushing assault into the opposite Union flank, catching Pope in a pincers. The Northerners had no choice but to fall back. At Henry House Hill, scene of the hardest fighting in the First Battle of Bull Run, the battered Federals made a stand that stopped the Southern pursuit, but the next day Pope began a retreat toward Washington. On September 1 the Union rearguard turned back a Confederate attack at Chantilly, 20 miles from the Union capital; Washington broke into panic. In five days of fighting the Union had suffered 16,000 casualties of 65,000 engaged, to Lee's losses of 10,000 out of 55,000. Pope's army was merged into the Army of the Potomac, with McClellan still in command, and the hapless Pope was exiled to Minnesota to pacify fractious Indians.

When Lee had taken command of the Army of Northern Virginia in June, McClellan had been at the gates of Richmond. Since then, Lee had defeated two superior Federal armies and virtually cleared Virginia of enemy forces. Now the Confederate general was only 25 miles from Washington. He began to plan an invasion of the North, which would come to its conclusion at the Battle of Antietam.

Bulloch, James Dunwoody (1823-1901) Confederate naval officer.

This Georgian served in the US Navy from 1839 to 1854. As a wartime Confederate naval officer, he served in England and France, outfitting such ships as the *Alabama*, *Florida*, *Shenandoah*, and *Stonewall*. He later published a book about the Confederacy's secret foreign service.

Burnett, Henry Lawrence (1838-1916) Union officer.

This Ohio lawyer enlisted in 1861 and fought in Missouri and Kentucky. In 1863 Burnett became judge advocate for the Department of the Ohio. He prosecuted the Knights of the Golden Circle in Indiana, Chicago conspirators to free Confederate prisoners, and Lincoln's assassins.

Burns, John (1793-1872) 'The Old Hero of Gettysburg.'

The Union army repeatedly rejected Burns, a war veteran in his seventies who persistently tried to enlist. He walked onto the battlefield at Gettysburg; fighting all three days with various regiments, he was wounded three times. He later received a Congressionally mandated pension.

Union General Ambrose Burnside's legendary ineptitude is a part of military folklore.

Burnside, Ambrose Everett (1824-1881)

Union general.

West Pointer Burnside led troops in the first Battle of Bull Run and carried out the successful Expedition to North Carolina (*See* BURNSIDE'S EXPEDITION. . . .). He was then given a major command in the Army of the Potomac, whose left wing he led ineffectively at Antietam, and finally he was given command of the entire army, which he led into the disaster of Fredericksburg. Despite this colossal failure and his ensuing resignation, Burnside remained in important posts until his final and definitive debacle in the Petersburg Mine Assault. He would come out of the war still popular, and like many former soldiers would enter politics, going on to become governor of Rhode Island and a US Senator. History would remember Burnside, however, mainly for two things: that 'sideburns' were named for his facial whiskers; and for being one of the worst generals of all time. After the Petersburg failure, legend has Lincoln saying, 'Only Burnside could have managed such a coup: to wring one last spectacular defeat from the jaws of victory.'

Burnside Carbine

Union General Ambrose E. Burnside designed and patented an experimental carbine in 1856. During the war Union forces bought more than 55,000 of a successor design, a .54-caliber breechloader that weighed seven pounds. Burnside's company failed in 1860, and his patents assigned to creditors.

Burnside's Expedition to North Carolina

General Ambrose E. Burnside, who had been a Union brigade commander at the First Battle of Bull Run, received permission in October 1861 to create an amphibious division for coastal operations. While his troops were training at Annapolis, Maryland, he went to New York to assemble a flotilla for the operations; this turned out to be a motley collection of vessels ranging from gunboats to passenger ships to coal scows. Burnside's objective was to capture harbors in Virginia and North Carolina.

Setting out in January with 12,000 soldiers on board, the flotilla nearly came to grief before it saw action; on the 13th a gale off Cape Hatteras, North Carolina, scattered the ships and wrecked three. The expedition waited out two weeks of bad weather in Hatteras Inlet. Finally the weather calmed, and on February 7 Burnside reached Roanoke Island, his first target, with 65 vessels, 1666 men, and a 20-ship naval force under Admiral Louis M. Goldsborough. On the island, which controlled the passage between Pamlico and Albemarle Sounds, were 3000 Confederates and four artillery batteries under Henry A. Wise, who also had an inadequate 'mosquito fleet' of gunboats. Wise had pleaded for reinforcements from Richmond, but none had been sent; Confederate authorities seem to have no sense of the importance of keeping Southern ports open to frustrate the Union blockade.

Just before noon on the 6th Goldsborough's fleet began to shell the enemy forts and gunboats. That afternoon and evening Burnside landed 7500 troops on Roanoke Island. On the next day, having waded through swamps and over entrenchments, the Federals overwhelmed Wise's forces, capturing over 2500 prisoners with losses of only 264. Leaving occupying forces on the island, Burnside went on to take New Berne, North Carolina, on March 14 and Beaufort on April 11. From New Berne further Union operations were sent out along the coast. At very little cost Burnside's amphibious expedition had secured all but one North Carolina harbor, considerably tightening the Union blockade of the Confederacy and providing

Although too old for service in the Union army, septuagenarian John Burns insisted on fighting at Gettysburg anyway.

bases for further tightening. By April 1862 every major port on the Atlantic Coast except for Wilmington and Charleston would be closed to Southern blockade-running ships.

The feeble Southern effort to protect its ports caused a political firestorm in Richmond that led to the resignation of Confederate Secretary of War Judah Benjamin (his friend President Jefferson Davis immediately made Benjamin secretary of state). Meanwhile the North had a cheering victory and a new hero, Burnside, who would be promoted to major general. In July he would be sent with 7500 men to join McClellan's Peninsular Campaign in Virginia. Unfortunately for the Union, Burnside had not revealed his true capacities in the North Carolina expedition, which succeeded mainly due to the flimsiness of enemy resistance. The bewhiskered general's ensuing efforts – at Antietam, at Fredericksburg, and in the Petersburg Mine Assault – would add up to a career of legendary incompetance.

Bushwhacker

Sometimes spelled 'bushwacker'.

This word existed before the Civil War and refers to someone who beats down ('whacks') or clears away brush or vegetation to prepare a field for grazing; from this, it came to refer to someone who lives in or frequents the woods. During the war, it was applied specifically to Confederate supporters who engaged in guerrilla warfare, as did William Quantrill. It was also used to refer to deserters or draft dodgers who became outlaws – both during and after the war.

Union General Benjamin Butler (fifth from left, seated). Though an inept officer, he had a successful postwar political career.

Butler, Benjamin Franklin (1818-1893) Union general.

This New Hampshire native was a nationally influential Boston criminal lawyer and Democratic politician whose war career upheld his reputation for controversy. His 8th Massachusetts helped to garrison Washington after the Fall of Fort Sumter in 1861, then, commanding the District of Annapolis, he peacefully occupied Baltimore later that year. He was then disastrously engaged at Big Bethel before turning south, taking Forts Hatteras and Clark and, in May 1862, New Orleans. Butler proved an arbitrary and corrupt military governor there, issuing the notorious 'Woman Order' (*See*) and hanging a man for taking down a Union flag. Removed after international protests, Butler took over the Army of the James, and in October 1864 went to New York in anticipation of election riots. Incompetence at Petersburg and Fort Fisher finally cost him his command. Butler is considered typical of the politically-appointed generals who made such a generally dubious contribution to the Union war effort.

Butler Medal

In a private act, Union General Benjamin F. Butler ordered 200 medals from Tiffany's and awarded them to black troops of XXV Corps for valor at New Market Heights and Chafin's Farm, Virginia, in September 1864.

Butterfield, Daniel (1831-1901) Union general.

A New York merchant, Butterfield led the 12th New York, the first Union regiment to reach Virginia. He fought in West Virginia, in the Peninsular Campaign, and at Fredericks-

The brownish-gray 'butternut' hue of Rebel uniforms is well captured in this old print.

burg and was Chief of Staff to both Joseph Hooker and George Meade. He designed the corps badge system.

Butternuts

This nickname for Confederate troops derived from the color of their uniforms, a butternut brown. A dye made from walnut hulls produced the gray-brown hue.

Cabell, William Lewis *(1827-1911)*
Confederate general.

This Virginian West Point graduate organized the Confederate commissary and ordnance departments and was quartermaster to P. G. T. Beauregard and both Albert and Joseph Johnston. As brigadier general he fought in the Trans-Mississippi and, commanding northwest Arkansas, organized a first-rate cavalry brigade. Cabell was captured at Marais des Cygnes (*See*) in October 1864 and was imprisoned.

Cahaba Prison, *Alabama*

The Confederates used a decrepit, partially covered cotton shed here as a prison for Federal captives beginning in early 1864. By late in the year the shed, with 500 beds, and the stockade around it, held more than 2000 Yankees in a state of wretched squalor.

South Carolina statesman John Calhoun, the leading architect of secessionist theory.

Calhoun, John Caldwell *(1782-1850)* Southern statesman.

An immensely influential state's rights advocate from South Carolina, he served as vice president of the United States under both John Quincy Adams and Andrew Jackson. He resigned the latter vice presidency in 1832 to enter the Senate and argue his theory of nullification – in effect, the declaration of a state's right to void any federal law it deemed in violation of the voluntary agreement that formed the Union. As abolitionism waxed in the North, Calhoun also became increasingly outspoken in his defense of the institution of slavery. He thus articulated, more influentially than any man of his time, the legal, political, and moral assumptions that would ultimately lead the South to secession and plunge the nation into civil war.

Caliber

A measure of the diameter of the bore of a firearm or of the diameter of a projectile. For small arms, caliber measurements were in inches or millimeters (*e.g.* the Springfield musket had a caliber of .58 inches). Cannon often were designated both by the projectile's weight in pounds and by the caliber of the bore or projectile; thus the common 12-pounder Napoleon cannon measured 4.62 inches in caliber.

California Column

Commanded by Colonel J. H. Carleton (*See*), this Union column – 11 companies of infantry, two of cavalry, and two artillery batteries – was ordered to join General Edward Canby in New Mexico. It left California on April 13, 1862, reaching Santa Fe on September 20 after a march through hostile Indian territory. Confederate General Henry H. Sibley, already in retreat from his ill-fated invasion of New Mexico (*See*), ordered a further withdrawal to San Antonio on hearing of the Californians' arrival.

Cameron, Simon *(1799-1889)*
Union secretary of war.

As US Senator, Cameron organized the new Republican Party in Pennsylvania and became a lifelong political force there. As Lincoln's first secretary of war he presided over widespread fraud and corruption in military appointments and procurement; Lincoln transferred him to a diplomatic post in January 1862.

Camp Chase, *Ohio*

Initially a Federal training camp, this facility west of Columbus later held Confederate prisoners of war. By 1863 more than 8000 Rebels were imprisoned there.

Camp Douglas, *Illinois*

This camp south of Chicago, used at first to train Federal enlistees, became a prison after the fall of Fort Donelson, Kentucky, in February 1862. It eventually held about 30,000 Confederate prisoners of war.

Camp Ford, *Texas*

A Confederate prison near Tyler, it held Union officers and men from 1863 until the war's end. Captives built log dwellings, and though food, water, and sanitary arrangements were acceptable at first, later, as the camp became overcrowded with prisoners from the Red River campaign of 1864, conditions deteriorated badly.

Camp Groce, *Texas*

An open field with guard lines, this Confederate prison near Hempstead held Union officers and enlisted men from 1863 until the end of hostilities. Little else is known about the camp.

A photograph of Confederate prisoners of war confined in Camp Chase, Ohio.

Camp Jackson, *Missouri*

On May 10, 1861, Union troops under Nathaniel Lyon (*See*) captured a brigade of pro-Confederate militia encamped at Lindell Grove outside St. Louis. There were no casualties in the operation, but on the return march to the St. Louis arsenal Union troops fired into violent pro-Rebel crowds, killing 28 people. Among the observers that day were Ulysses S. Grant, an Illinois mustering officer, and William Tecumseh Sherman, who had not yet re-entered the army.

Camp Lawton, *Georgia*

The Confederates built this 42-acre stockade near Millen in the summer of 1864 to take the overflow from nearby Andersonville Prison (*See*). By the end of 1864 more than 10,000 Union prisoners were held here. They built their own huts from branches and other material left over from construction of the stockade and survived in great discomfort.

Camp Morton, *Indiana*

This former Indianapolis fairground became a Federal prisoner of war camp. The prison barracks, with no floors and rickety walls, were cold and drafty in the winter, and the Confederate inmates lived in dirty and uncomfortable conditions.

Campbell, John Archibald
(1811-1889) **Confederate statesman.**

Campbell, a Georgian, resigned from the US Supreme Court in 1861. From October 1862 until the war's end he was the Confederate assistant secretary of war and administrator of the conscription law. He was a commissioner at the Hampton Roads Peace Conference in 1865.

The war's classic field artillery pieces were the 12-pounder Napoleons, some of which are shown here on an ordnance wharf.

Campbell's Station, *Tennessee*

On November 16, 1863, Federal troops beat LaFayette McLaws's Confederate division to a crossroads here, enabling Union General Ambrose Burnside to move his supply trains safely into Knoxville (*See*). The covering action cost the Federals 318 casualties; the Rebels lost 174 men.

Canby, Edward *(1817-1873)*
Union general.

A career soldier (West Point, 1839), the Kentucky-born Canby held New Mexico (*See*) for the Union at the outbreak of the war. After serving in a staff appointment in Washington, DC, he commanded troops in New York

The largest siege cannon at the beginning of the war was the 24-pounder muzzle-loader. A smoothbore gun, it weighed 10,155 pounds.

City in the wake of the 1863 draft riots there. From May 1864 to May 1865 he commanded the Military District of Western Mississippi. Canby led the attack on Mobile and, at the war's end, accepted the surrender of Confederate forces in the district.

Cane Hill, *Arkansas*

When James Blunt's 1st Division of the Union Army of the Frontier surprised a force of 8000 Confederate cavalry under John Marmaduke here on November 28, 1862, the Rebels retreated into the Boston Mountains. Fearing

ambush, Blunt did not pursue. He reported 40 Federal casualties and a Confederate loss of 435 men.

Canister

A short-range defensive munition, this simple artillery projectile consisted of a tin can filled with iron or lead bullets, packed in sawdust. The can burst when it left the cannon's mouth, spraying its contents over a wide area. Canister could be used with effect up to a maximum range of 400 yards.

Cannon

The term describes all large firearms; the basic classifications, defined by their trajectories, are guns (flat), howitzers (angled), and mortars (arching). Iron, steel, and brass cannon were manufactured in a wide variety of sizes, with both smooth and rifled barrels, and for many specialized purposes. The most common field piece in both armies was the 12-pounder Napoleon gun-howitzer (*See*), a muzzle-loading smoothbore. There were at least 20 other standard types of field artillery, as well as many types of siege and coastal artillery. (*See* also ARMSTRONG GUNS, BLAKELY GUNS, BROOKE GUNS, COLUMBIAD, DAHLGREN GUNS, NAPOLEON GUN, PARROTT GUNS, RODMAN GUNS and WHITWORTH GUNS).

Cap-and-ball Firearms

These were percussion small arms that succeeded outmoded flintlock pistols, muskets, and rifles in the 1840s and 1850s, though in principle both methods of firing were similar. The newer weapons used a percussion cap, fitted onto the nipple of the chamber, to ignite the powder that propelled the ball or bullet out of the barrel.

Carcass

A hollow cast-iron artillery projectile filled with combustible material, this primitive incendiary device shot flame from four fuse holes to ignite fires where it landed.

Carleton, James Henry
(1814-1873) **Union general.**

A Maine native, Carleton was a career army officer whose frontier and western service continued through the war. In 1862 he raised the California Column (*See*) and led it to New Mexico. He commanded the Department of New Mexico from 1862 to 1865.

Carlisle, *Pennsylvania*

The Confederate cavalry commander J. E. B. Stuart shelled this town late in the afternoon of July 1, 1863, while in search of Richard Ewell's Confederate corps, then in action at Gettysburg. At Carlisle, Stuart finally learned of Lee's position and set off to rejoin the main army. He arrived too late to be of any use to the Confederates in the Battle of Gettysburg.

Carnifex Ferry, *West Virginia*

As part of the campaign to clear western Virginia of rebels, Union General William Rosecrans, with 7000 men, attacked 5800 Confederates under J. B. Floyd here on September 10, 1861. The Rebels were concealed in thick woods, and the attacks were inconclusive. Floyd withdrew during the night after a loss of 20 wounded. Federal casualties were 150 men.

Carolinas Campaign

Even though William Tecumseh Sherman's March to the Sea through Georgia would remain the operation most associated with him, the Carolinas Campaign that followed was actually more difficult and more significant in helping to end the war. After finishing his march to Savannah in December 1864, Sherman proposed to General-in-Chief Ulysses S. Grant that his army begin a similar and even more destructive campaign across the Carolinas, which had so far been largely untouched by the war. Grant agreed that Sherman should march north, laying waste as he went, and come up from the rear at Petersburg to help Grant 'wipe out Lee.' The latter part of the mission, it turned out, would be taken care of before Sherman reached Virginia.

The North had a particular sense of vendetta against South Carolina, which had led the Confederate states in seceeding. 'The whole army is burning with an insatiable desire to wreak vengeance on South Carolina,' Sherman wrote with his customary ferocity; 'I almost tremble at her fate, but feel that she deserves all that seems to be in store for her.' While the March to the Sea had largely spared Georgia's private dwellings, this Carolina march would leave smoking ruins and thousands of refugees in its path.

Sherman was to begin in mid-January 1865, but heavy rains (which would bedevil the whole campaign) delayed the start until February 1. Then the Federals pulled out of Savannah with 60,000 men. No major Confederate forces could be spared to oppose them, only scattered units amounting to some 22,500, including 6700 cavalry troops under Joseph Wheeler. Nearly half these forces were left for some time protecting Augusta and Charleston, South Carolina; rather than attacking, Sherman simply bypassed both cities. It would take the Southern forces in the area, eventually commanded by Joseph E. Johnston, until mid-March to organize any resistance to Sherman other than token skirmishing. By then it would be too little and too late. Meanwhile, Sherman sent detachments to occupy two coastal towns through which his supplies could come; Alfred Terry captured Fort Fisher on January 15, and Jacob Cox took New Bern on March 10.

As the Federals spread their trail of destruction through South Carolina they had to contend with numerous river, stream, and swamp crossings under the wettest conditions in two decades. Some roads had become streams themselves and had to be scouted by canoe. Confederate leaders were sure that Sherman could never get an army through the state. In fact, the Federals made a steady 10 or so miles a day, just as they had over much easier land in Georgia. Ahead of

Union and Rebel troops exchange fire in a South Carolina swamp during W. T. Sherman's brilliantly conducted Carolinas Campaign.

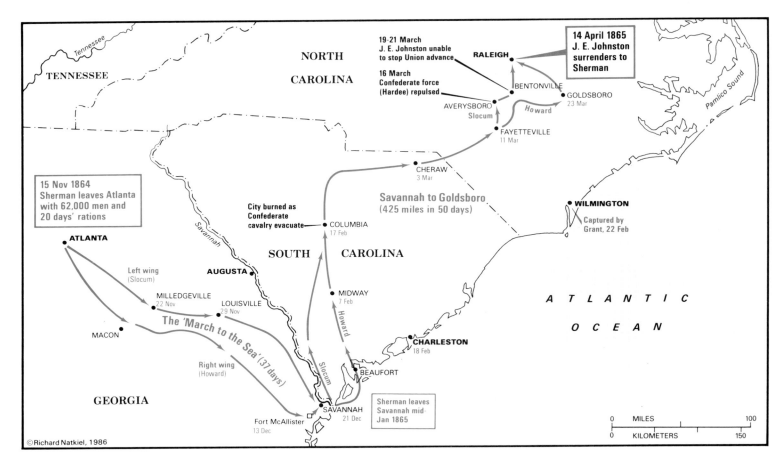

15 Nov 1864
Sherman leaves Atlanta with 62,000 men and 20 days' rations

City burned as Confederate cavalry evacuate — COLUMBIA 17 Feb

19–21 March
J. E. Johnston unable to stop Union advance

16 March
Confederate force (Hardee) repulsed

14 April 1865
J. E. Johnston surrenders to Sherman

Savannah to Goldsboro (425 miles in 50 days)

CHERAW 3 Mar

WILMINGTON
Captured by Grant, 22 Feb

MIDWAY 7 Feb

Left wing (Slocum)

Right wing (Howard)

The 'March to the Sea' (37 days)

MILLEDGEVILLE 22 Nov

LOUISVILLE 29 Nov

MACON

AUGUSTA

ATLANTA

GEORGIA

SOUTH   CAROLINA

NORTH
CAROLINA

TENNESSEE

RALEIGH

BENTONVILLE

GOLDSBORO 23 Mar

AVERYSBORO
Slocum

Howard

FAYETTEVILLE 11 Mar

CHARLESTON 18 Feb

BEAUFORT

Slocum

Howard

SAVANNAH 21 Dec

Fort McAllister 13 Dec

Sherman leaves Savannah mid-Jan 1865

ATLANTIC   OCEAN

Pamlico Sound

© Richard Natkiel, 1986

MILES   0 — 100
KILOMETERS   0 — 150

the army spread a wave of engineers and workmen, including many escaped slaves, who built bridges, felled trees to make corduroy roads, and erected causeways. At times Federal units waded out in water that was up to their armpits and full of snakes and alligators in order to drive away Wheeler's cavalry.

On February 17 Sherman's men arrived at Columbia, the capital of South Carolina, and Wade Hampton's Rebel cavalry pulled out just before the Yankees entered. That night fires consumed two-thirds of the city. It would never be certain just who was responsible for this, the worst episode of the Carolinas Campaign. Sherman blamed the fires on cotton bales set alight by Hampton's evacuating troops, but at least some other fires were probably the work of Federal soldiers who had located stores of liquor in the town and had made use of them. Nevertheless, it must be acknowledged that Sherman organized his forces to fight the fires throughout the night and that he personally took part in the effort, even though he did order the destruction of several installations of military importance the following day.

On February 19 units began to pull out of Columbia, heading for Goldsboro, North Carolina, where 30,000 more Northern soldiers were waiting. By March 16 Sherman was well into North Carolina, having fought a running series of skirmishes but without meeting any determined resistance. But Johnston had finally organized his Southern forces, and that day at Averasborough two Rebel divisions fought a delaying action against the Federals. But after suffering 865 casualties to the Union's 682 the Confederates fell back to Bentonville, where Johnston hoped to bring some 21,000 troops to bear against one of Sherman's two wings. That

effort, the largest battle of the campaign, flared up on March 19. The Federals drove Johnston's men back somewhat, but could not dislodge them until the other Northern wing appeared in support three days later. With Sherman's full force now threatening him, Johnston was forced to withdraw.

Above: By 1865 standards Sherman's advance over the difficult terrain of the Carolinas was remarkable. In slightly more than two months he effectively conquered two states.
Below: Sherman enters Columbia, the South Carolina capital, on February 17, 1865. That night a fire would destroy much of the city. How it started is still a matter of debate.

Rather than giving chase, Sherman continued his march toward Goldsboro. In three days of fighting at Bentonville, Johnston had lost 2606 men to Sherman's 1646. On April 9, the day Robert E. Lee surrendered at Appomattox, the bluecoats were marching on Raleigh with 80,000 men. The speed with which Sherman had moved through the Carolinas had been one of the major factors in forcing Lee to bolt from Petersburg and thus in setting him on the path to surrender.

Johnston held out until April 14, when he requested an armistice. Sherman was harshly criticized in the North for offering too-lenient surrender terms, which included a broad general amnesty for all Confederates and quick integration of existing Southern state governments into the Union. While these terms probably reflected Lincoln's ideas, expressed earlier to Sherman and Grant, Lincoln was now dead and the new administration in Washington rescinded Sherman's original surrender agreement. Johnston formally surrendered his 30,000 remaining men on April 26, on terms similar to those given Lee. Sherman would be bitter over the affair for the rest of his life; it was one of the main reasons he rejected all overtures to bring him into politics.

Carondelet, USS

A Union ironclad steamer carrying 13 guns, she fought at Forts Henry and Donelson in the winter of 1862. In April of that year *Carondelet* ran past Confederate batteries at Island No. 10 in the Mississippi River, forcing the Rebels to abandon the strongpoint.

A Democratic cartoon blames President Grant for the South's miseries under a carpetbag rule that is supported by federal troops.

Carpetbaggers

During the Radical Republican Reconstruction, some Northerners in search of financial opportunities streamed south. They collaborated with like-minded Southern politicians (*See* SCALAWAGS) to gain control of state and local governments in order to increase their personal fortunes; their self-serving behavior contributed greatly to the political chaos that afflicted the postwar South. Their nickname was inspired by the familiar sight of their luggage, or 'carpetbags.'

Carr, Eugene Asa *(1830-1910)*
Union general.

Carr was a New Yorker and West Point graduate whose long career as an Indian fighter was interrupted by the war. He fought at Wilson's Creek and Pea Ridge, commanded divisions in the Vicksburg and Mobile campaigns, and eventually commanded the District of Little Rock.

Carrick's Ford, *West Virginia*

In the Western Virginia Campaign of McClellan (*See*) this rear-guard action along the Cheat River during a Confederate retreat from Laurel Hill on July 13, 1861, cost the Rebels some 40 supply wagons and about 80 casualties. In another skirmish nearby, Union forces killed the Rebel commander, General Robert Garnett. He was the first Civil War general to die in battle.

Carrington, Henry Beebee *(1824-1912)* **Union general.**

In 1857 this Ohio lawyer and abolitionist reorganized the state militia, which was pre-

pared for duty in 1861 before any volunteers were ready. During the war he recruited 100,000 troops in Indiana.

Carroll, Anna Ella *(1815-1893)*
Union pamphleteer.

Encouraged by a war department official, she published pamphlets in 1861-62 justifying Lincoln's wartime assumption of executive prerogative. She spent the rest of her life unsuccessfully demanding payment for that service and for military strategy she claimed to have supplied the government.

Carson, Christopher *(1809-1868)*
Union officer and Indian fighter.

'Kit' Carson, a famous frontier fighter, trapper, and guide from Kentucky, guided John C. Frémont's expeditions of exploration in the 1830s and 1840s and fought in the Mexican War. In 1861 he organized a New Mexico regiment and spent the war fighting Indians in New Mexico and Texas. He was breveted a brigadier general in 1865.

Carter, Samuel Powhatan *(1819-1891)* **Union general.**

A Tennessee native, Carter interrupted his naval career for wartime army service, eventually holding a unique double rank: major general and rear admiral. He organized eastern Tennessee troops and held a series of field commands in the Ohio and Cumberland armies, finally commanding XXIII Corps. He is perhaps best remembered for a series of successful cavalry raids he con-

Propagandist Anna Carroll began her career as a publicist for the Know-Nothing Party.

ducted on Rebel supply lines in the upper Tennessee Valley in December 1862, a prelude to the Battle of Stone's River.

Case Shot

Grape, canister, and shrapnel were the three main types of case shot. All three types scattered small projectiles over wide areas at varying ranges. The term is sometimes used, imprecisely, as a synonym for canister and shrapnel.

Casey, Silas *(1807-1882)*
Union general.

A Rhode Island-born career soldier, his *Casey's Tactics* was a standard infantry manual. He was wounded in the Peninsular Campaign, then commanded a division defending Washington. He also examined prospective officers of black troops. His son Silas fought in the navy at Fort Sumter and in Charleston harbor.

Cass, Lewis *(1782-1866)* Statesman.

He rose to national prominence as governor of Michigan Territory (1813-31) and was afterwards a secretary of war and a US Senator. A strong unionist, Cass was President James Buchanan's secretary of state, eventually resigning over the president's failure to reinforce the Charleston forts.

Cast Metal Homogeneous

This method of gun construction, used to produce the Columbiad, Rodman, and Napoleon cannon, was obsolescent by the time of the Civil War. Modern technique in-

Lewis Cass was a state governor, a senator, a secretary of war and a secretary of state.

volved building the main parts separately, then joining them by welding, shrinking or screwing. The Armstrong and Parrott guns were produced by the newer 'built up' method.

Castle Pinckney, *South Carolina*

A Charleston harbor fort turned Confederate prison, it held mostly enlisted men, although some officers were also imprisoned there.

Castle Thunder, *Virginia*

Confederate prisons in Richmond and Petersburg, Virginia, both converted tobacco warehouses, carried this name. The Richmond prison held political prisoners and suspected spies, while the Petersburg prison held Union prisoners of war.

Casualties during the War

Casualties are defined as losses in manpower from all sources – not only killed in action, but also wounded, captured, deserted, died from disease, and so on. As to deaths in the Civil War, it should be borne in mind that over three times the number of soldiers died from disease than were killed in battle, that (roughly) 5.5 more men were wounded in battle for every one killed, and that of the wounded an estimated one out of seven eventually died (a far higher percentage than in modern wars). The total number of dead in the war has been estimated at 359,528 for the North, 258,000 for the South, some 618,000 in all, totalling about 33 percent and 40 percent of the active forces respectively. It was the costliest American war to date.

Civil War-related casualties were huge. The estimated 618,000 Americans killed exceeds by 33 percent those killed in World War II.

Catlett's Station, *Virginia*

This Virginia town was the site of two cavalry actions. First, on August 22, 1862, J. E. B. Stuart and 1500 troopers rode out to operate against Union General John Pope's supply lines. That night they raided a Federal camp near Catlett's Station, scattering the bluecoats and stealing supplies, including Pope's baggage and dress coat. Information gained from captured papers helped position Lee's forces for the Second Bull Run Battle. The second action at Catlett's Station occurred over a year later and also involved Stuart, who, on October 14, 1863, attacked several regiments of the Union II Corps in the area. The Federals withstood the assault, reporting 24 casualties and taking 28 prisoners.

Cedar Creek *(Virginia)*, Battle of

During his Shenandoah Valley Campaign of 1864 Federal General Philip Sheridan had routed Southern forces under Jubal Early at Fisher's Hill and Tom's Brook in the first weeks of October. Assuming that he had ended the threat from Early, Sheridan went to Washington on October 16 to confer with his superiors. On the way back two days later, he stopped for the night in Winchester, some 14 miles from where his army was encamped at Cedar Creek, near Middletown. On the next morning, October 19, Sheridan awoke to the sound of firing in the distance. An orderly told him it was probably skirmishing, so the general did not hurry. But as the

Of the many pictures of Sheridan's famous ride at Cedar Creek, this sketch by A. R. Waud may be the most authentic.

shooting continued, Sheridan mounted his charger, Rienzi, and took to the road in growing concern, stopping occasionally to listen. Close to Cedar Creek, he suddenly realized that the firing was approaching him faster than he was approaching it; that could only mean that his army was retreating under pursuit. Now thoroughly alarmed, he spurred his horse into a gallop.

Riding over the last ridge at about 10:30 in the morning, Sheridan saw his army coming toward him in full flight, the fields and roads covered by a tangle of men, horses, and wagons. Early had mounted a surprise attack on the left flank of the sleeping Federals at Cedar Hill, and four divisions had bolted out of camp and run for their lives. In a ride that would become legendary, Sheridan charged down the road waving his hat and shouting to cheering troops in his usual profane style: 'God damn you, don't cheer me! If you love your country, come up to the front. There's lots of fight in you men yet!' Word of his return spread out through the scattered army, electrifying the troops. Many of the veterans

had stopped to brew coffee along the road while they waited for orders, and the cavalry and VI Corps had not scattered. As Sheridan rode by, men began to kick over their coffee-pots, pick up their rifles, and head back to the front. It took several hours of painstaking work before the army was rounded up and formed into line of battle. Many of Early's men, meanwhile, had stopped at the captured Yankee camps to sample the abundant food and liquor. At about 4:00 pm Sheridan rode down the battle line waving a banner, and the Federals swept out to the attack; in short order the surprised and disorganized Confederates were running for their lives. In the battle Sheridan lost some 5665 of 30,829 engaged, Early 2910 of 18,410, plus most of his artillery and wagon train. It was effectively the end of Early's army and of major Confederate military presence in the vital Shenandoah Valley.

Cedar Mountain, Battle of

This is a name given to the opening engagement of the 1862 Second Bull Run Battle. On August 9 Stonewall Jackson and about 17,000 Confederates were moving toward Culpeper, Virginia, to strike John Pope's

advance units, when Jackson found himself under attack at Cedar Mountain by 8000 Federals under Nathaniel Banks. Jackson's men were retreating when A. P. Hill arrived with reinforcements and mounted a counterattack that drove the Northerners back and inflicted heavy losses on them.

Cemetery Ridge

The main line of the Union Army of the Potomac ran along this southeastern Pennsylvania ridge on July 2, 1863, the second day of the Battle of Gettysburg. In the shape of an inverted fish hook, it stretched, north to south, from Culp's Hill to Little Round Top. Both ends of the line were scenes of heavy fighting on the second day.

Centralia (Missouri) Massacre

On September 27, 1864, William ('Bloody Bill') Anderson (See) and his Confederate guerrillas captured a stagecoach in Centralia at 11:00 am. Half an hour later they hijacked and robbed a westbound train, murdering 24 unarmed Federal soldiers and two passengers on board. Major A. E. V. Johnson arrived in the afternoon with three companies of the 39th Missouri and led a dismounted attack; 124 of his 147 men were killed by Anderson's marauders.

Chain Shot

This missile, consisting of two balls linked by a chain, was used against the masts and rigging of ships. Its cousin, bar shot, consisted of two balls connected by a bar.

Chamberlain, Joshua Lawrence (1828-1914) Union general.

In August 1862 he left a professorship at Bowdoin College, Maine, to become lieutenant colonel of the newly raised 20th Maine. Chamberlain fought at Antietam and Fredericksburg, and conducted a brilliant defense of Little Round Top at Gettysburg on July 2, 1863; he received the Medal of Honor for this last action. He led a brigade at Spotsylvania

War artist Edwin Forbes made this sketch of the Battle of Cedar Mountain, the prelude to the Second Battle of Bull Run.

and Petersburg (where he was severely wounded) and during the Appomattox Campaign of April 1865. He returned to Bowdoin and eventually became its president (1871-83), after having served as governor of Maine (1867-71). His memoir of the war – especially his account of the surrender at Appomattox Court House – is widely quoted.

Chambersburg, *Pennsylvania*

Confederate General Jubal Early set fire to this town on July 30, 1864, after residents failed to pay a levy – demanded as reparation for Union damage to private property in Virginia – of $100,000 in gold or $500,000 in paper money. The 3000 inhabitants were evacuated late in the evening, and fire destroyed about two-thirds of the town.

Chambersburg Raid of Stuart

On his second ride around McClellan's Federal Army of the Potomac, October 9-12, 1862, J. E. B. Stuart and 1800 riders crossed the Potomac west of Williamsport, reaching Chambersburg, Pennsylvania, on the 9th. There they destroyed supplies and machinery useful to the North and left town next day with 500 captured horses. Stuart arrived in Leesburg, Virginia, on the 12th, having ridden 126 miles in four days, the last 80 miles of the journey nonstop.

Right: The South's two greatest commanders, Robert E. Lee and Stonewall Jackson, confer during the battle that will be remembered as their masterpiece, Chancellorsville.
Below: A Union army map of the Battle of Chancellorsville shows Jackson's undetected leftward shift to attack the Union XI Corps.

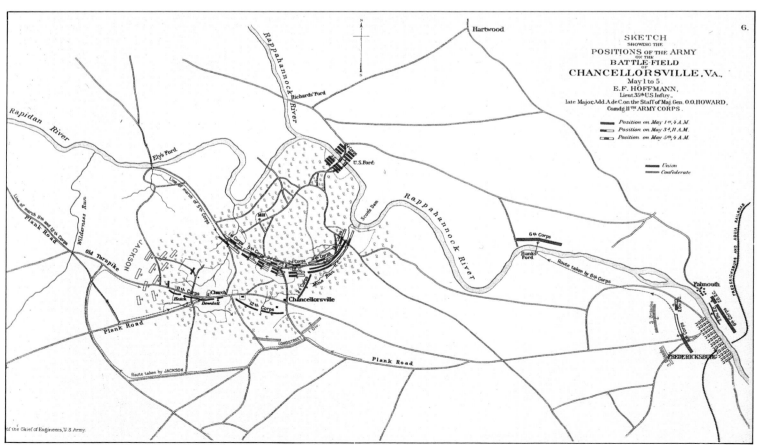

Champion's Hill, (Mississippi), Battle of

On May 16, 1863, 29,000 Union troops defeated 22,000 Confederates under John Pemberton here in a key battle in Ulysses S. Grant's Vicksburg Campaign. The hill, which dominated roads leading to the town from the east, changed hands several times before Federal forces under James McPherson prevailed. The Federals lost 2441 men; Confederate casualties exceeded 3800. This defeat obliged Pemberton to pull his forces back behind the Vicksburg defenses.

Chancellorsville, Campaign and Battle

At the end of January 1863 command of the Union Army of the Potomac passed from the hapless General Ambrose Burnside, who had just presided over the debacle at Fredericksburg, to General Joseph Hooker. After the army's latest defeats, 'Fighting Joe' was the only man who seemed to want the job of heading the Union's most important army and trying to bring down Robert E. Lee. Taking command, Hooker meticulously rebuilt the Army of the Potomac to fighting trim while evolving his plan of attack: he would leave a detachment to keep Lee's Army of Northern Virginia in their present position at Fredericksburg, meanwhile marching his major forces in a wide envelopment to come in behind the enemy from the west. It was a sound plan and might well have worked – if Lee had been willing to follow it.

Hooker had paid particular attention to building up his cavalry, which had never achieved the confidence and dash of Southern horsemen. In mid-April 12,000 cavalry under General George Stoneman were dispatched to tear up the Confederate supply lines. This raid, however, proved ineffectual, and Lee's cavalry head, J. E. B. Stuart, largely ignored it.

Hooker put his plan into motion on April 27, 1863, pulling 80,000 men of the Army of the Potomac out of their camps across the river from Fredericksburg and leaving 40,000 under John Sedgwick to hold the Army of Northern Virginia in their positions around the town. Lee had been waiting for some such move. Soon Jeb Stuart reported that the main body of Federals was gathering in the Southern rear, at a little road-crossing and clearing called Chancellorsville. Lee had sent two divisions out to forage and had on hand 60,000 men, about half Hooker's strength. As he had at Antietam, Lee took stock and decided to stake everything on his opponent's incompetence. Leaving a screening force of 10,000 at Fredericksburg, with orders to build many fires at night to fool the enemy, Lee marched the main body of his army toward Chancellorsville to meet Hooker.

Part of the Union general's strategy had been to push past the thick woods – called the Wilderness – that surrounded Chancellorsville and to engage Lee in open territory, where superior Union artillery could have clear lines of fire and the army room to maneuver. On May 1 the Union army was beginning to march out of the Wilderness as planned. Then, at mid-morning, skirmishers on the Federal advance unexpectedly ran into a line of Confederates blocking their way.

Hooker's generals pulled their units up into line of battle. After several hours of inexplicable silence, Hooker issued the astonishing order to pull back into the Wilderness and build defensive positions. His generals were outraged but did as ordered. As the Army of the Potomac entrenched in the Wilderness during the afternoon, Jeb Stuart's cavalry roamed around, looking for a weak spot in the Federal positions. Finally Stuart found it: the Union XI Corps, positioned on the Union right, was unprotected on the flank – 'in the air,' as it was called. Late that night Lee and Stonewall Jackson sat on cracker boxes, warming their hands over a fire and planning the next day's work.

That day, May 2, reached noon with no activity. General Hooker began to speculate that Lee was retreating. Reports came in about enemy movement across the Union front; some Federal troops even went out and captured some men from Jackson's division,

Jackson is fatally hit at Chancellorsville. He was not, as this Kurz & Allison print has it, killed in full battle but was hit by 'friendly fire' while riding in semi-darkness.

one of whom jeered, 'You wait until Jackson gets around on your right!' Hooker dismissed these clues, thereby failing to realize that Jackson was marching 30,000 men 12 miles on a small lane right in front of Union lines, out of sight in the dense woods, to assault the unprotected XI Corps on the Union right. If the Northern general had made any effort, he could have scattered Jackson's strung-out forces or swamped Lee's remaining 15,000; but as Lee had expected, the cowed Hooker did nothing.

About six o'clock in the afternoon of May 2, a wave of rabbits and deer suddenly poured into the positions of the XI Corps. They were followed by a screaming onslaught of Jackson's men, who swept up the confused Federal flank like a broom. Hooker learned of the disaster when a rabble of terrified survivors began pouring into the Chancellorsville clearing. The Union commander jumped on his horse and rode toward the right, organizing resistance as he went. Some Pennsylvania cavalrymen made a suicidal charge into the middle of the Southern advance that bought some critical moments; eventually dozens of cannon were pouring shot and shell into the Confederates. That barrage and the coming of darkness brought the Southern advance to a halt before it routed the entire Union army. Then, at nine o'clock that night, disaster struck Lee's army.

Stonewall Jackson had ridden out with some other officers to reconnoiter in the dark and had roused some Northerners, who opened fire as Jackson and the others galloped back toward their own lines. Hearing guns and approaching horsemen, Confederates on both sides of the road began firing into the dark; three bullets from his own men hit Jackson. He was taken away in an ambulance, and doctors subsequently amputated his left arm; within a few days a fatal case of pneumonia would set in. Also that night, hundreds of wounded men died in flames that the battle had started during the day.

The next morning, with Jeb Stuart now leading Jackson's command, the Confederates renewed the attack and began driving Federal units back toward the Rappahannock River. Hooker seemed confused and despondent as shells burst around his headquarters in a mansion at Chancellorsville. Meanwhile, to the east at Fredericksburg, Federals under Sedgwick stormed over weak Southern positions on the heights and headed west to reinforce Hooker. As Hooker waited on the porch for Sedgwick's arrival, a cannonball splintered a column and the concussion knocked him to the ground. Dazed, Hooker ordered a withdrawal to trenches already prepared between and the Rapidan and Rappahannock. With the Confederates swarming around them, the Army of the Potomac pulled back to the trenches.

Sedgwick would never make it. Lee, leaving 25,000 men to hold Hooker's retreating 75,000, sent 20,000 troops to meet the new Federal contingent. By the next morning Sedgwick found himself surrounded on three sides and fled back to the Rappahannock. With characteristic aggressiveness Lee planned to assault the Federal entrenchments on May 6, which might have proved disastrous for the South. But he never got the chance; Hooker withdrew his beaten and demoralized army across the Rappahannock on the night of May 5.

Hooker had gone into battle with twice the strength of his enemy and had let himself be outnumbered in every part of the engagement. Of 133,868 men, the Army of the Potomac had lost 17,278, to Lee's 12,821, out of 60,892 on the field. Chancellorsville was Lee's masterpiece and one of the most brilliant tactical achievements in military history. On the other hand, Lee had lost Jackson, his 'strong right arm.' On May 10 the wounded Stonewall Jackson cried out in delirium from his bed, 'Order A. P. Hill to prepare for action – pass the infantry to the front rapidly – tell Major Hawks . . .' Then, after a silence, came his last, oddly peaceful words: 'No, let us cross over the river and rest under the shade of the trees.'

Charleston, *South Carolina*

Charleston was at the forefront of Southern resistance before the war. The palmetto flag was raised there the day after Lincoln's election, and when South Carolina became the first state to secede six weeks later, the city's streets were wild with celebration. Part of Charleston's belligerence centered on its custody of Federal forts and arsenals; it is no accident that the war began here, at Fort Sumter.

Charleston (*South Carolina*), Naval Assault on

The advent of the ironclad ship raised hopes in the Union navy that large coastal forts might now be vulnerable to capture from the sea – a near impossibility for wooden-hulled warships. The theory was tested on April 7, 1863, when a Union squadron of nine ironclads attacked Fort Sumter and Fort Moultrie in Charleston Harbor. In the event, fire from the forts proved far too daunting for the assailants. Six of the ironclads were heavily damaged, one, USS *Keokuk*, so badly that it sank the next day. The squadron commander, Flag Officer Samuel DuPont, was forced to withdraw, having accomplished nothing save to demonstrate that the capture of big coastal forts was still, as in the past, properly a subject for combined operations.

Union Treasury Secretary Salmon P. Chase.

Chase, Salmon Portland
(1808-1873) **Union statesman and secretary of the treasury.**

Born in New Hampshire, he practiced law in Ohio, where he defended escaped slaves and led the Liberty Party, serving as US Senator and governor. As Lincoln's secretary of the treasury Chase had to finance the war; with the help of private financiers such as Jay Cooke, Chase managed the job fairly well, though in the process he was obliged to print 'greenback' paper currency that was inadequately backed by specie. An ambitious Radical Republican who was forever dissatisfied with what he considered Lincoln's undue moderation, Chase on several occasions came close to disloyalty to his president. Nevertheless, after Chase finally resigned from his cabinet post in mid-1864 Lincoln soon appointed him to fill the vacancy created by the death of Chief Justice of the Supreme Court Roger Taney, a post in which Chase served until his death.

Unable to take Charleston by naval assault in April 1863, the Union tried a combined operation in August. It also failed.

Chattahoochie River, *Georgia*

Confederate General Joseph Johnston, continuing his resistance to W. T. Sherman's 1864 Atlanta Campaign, pulled back on July 4 from Smyrna to a bridgehead north of the Chattahoochie River, northwest of Atlanta. Sherman ordered General George Thomas to hold Johnston in place while Sherman sent other forces to cross upstream. Threatened once again by envelopment, Johnston withdrew to the outskirts of Atlanta on the 9th.

Chattanooga Campaign

Following the devastating Union defeat at Chickamauga in September 1863 the Federal Army of the Cumberland had been besieged in Chattanooga by Braxton Bragg's Confederate Army of Tennessee. Even though the Union army thus held that vital rail center, it did them little good when they were trapped and starving. Meanwhile, their commanding general, William S. Rosecrans, seemed to be, in Lincoln's words, 'confused and stunned like a duck hit on the head' after his rout at Chickamauga. Lincoln and his advisors decided that someone else had to take over the job of lifting the siege.

On October 24, 1863, General Ulysses S. Grant arrived in Chattanooga with the command of the new Federal Division of the Mississippi, which included everything from that river to the Appalachian mountains. The route over which he had come to Chattanooga, a tortuous trail from Bridgeport, Alabama, was the only one left open to his army. Grant brought with him orders placing General George H. Thomas, the 'Rock of Chickamauga,' in immediate command, relieving Rosecrans. The new commanders faced a daunting challenge: Chattanooga lay in a bowl-shaped depression surrounded by hills and ridges on whose heights Braxton Bragg's men had dug in and had emplaced dozens of cannons.

Food, not fighting, was the first military objective. Grant put into motion a plan (actually originated by Rosecrans) for opening a supply route along the Tennessee River. The soldiers would call it the 'cracker line,' after the ubiquitous military biscuit. At the same time, Grant ordered 20,000 reinforcements under Joseph Hooker to march from Bridgeport, Alabama, where they had been stuck for two weeks after being moved there on trains from the Army of the Potomac (the fastest movement of a large body of troops ever seen before the twentieth century). Soon thereafter William Tecumseh Sherman would bring in 17,000 men of the Army of the Tennessee. As Hooker's men slipped into the city in the middle of the night, Union detachments drove Confederates from positions overlooking the river. Then, on the morning of October 30, the little ship *Chattanooga* steamed into town with 40,000 rations and tons of animal feed. The cracker line was open, and soon the Northerners would be in shape to fight.

A few days later Confederate President Jefferson Davis unwittingly helped Grant when he ordered Bragg to send 15,000 men under James Longstreet to join other Confederate forces in attacking Union-occupied Knoxville, Tennessee. Not only did this ill-advised

campaign fail, it deprived Bragg of a quarter of his forces. But the situation also created a problem for the Federals: to relieve the pressure on Knoxville, Grant had to attack Bragg soon. Despite the growing number of Federals accumulating in the city, Bragg still felt sanguine about his hilltop position, assuring an anxious citizen that 'There are not enough Yankees in Chattanooga to come up here. Those are all my prisoners.' It seemed a realistic assessment of the situation: as Robert E. Lee had found at Gettysburg, it is virtually impossible for an army to attack uphill into well-fortified positions.

Grant organized his forces and made his battle plans. On the morning of November 23 Union batteries opened up against the main enemy positions along Missionary Ridge; Southern cannons responded. From the city marched 20,000 Federal troops in dress uni-

On the outskirts of besieged Chattanooga Union pickets discover a Confederate patrol camouflaged as cedar bushes.

form, their ranks perfectly aligned. To the Confederates on the heights it looked like a parade until the ranks suddenly began charging up the slopes. The Battle of Chattanooga was underway, the Union army easily taking Orchard Knob, a hill between Missionary Ridge and the city, that would become Grant's command post.

During the night Sherman moved four divisions across the Tennessee River on a pontoon bridge, and the next day he attacked the northern end of Missionary Ridge. At the

A panoramic view, looking south, of the key Confederate rail center at Chattanooga. In the far background is Lookout Mountain.

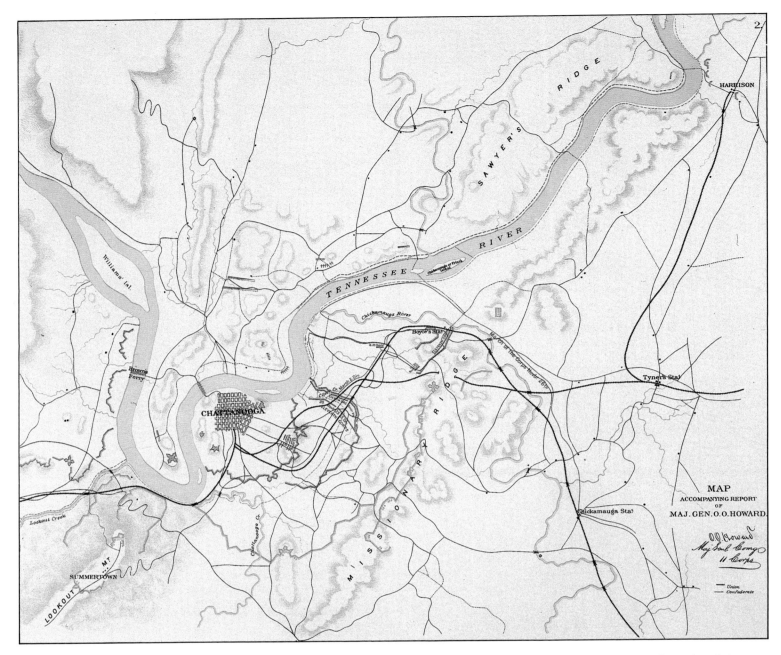

MAP
ACCOMPANYING REPORT
OF
MAJ. GEN. O.O. HOWARD.

Above: A union army map shows the relative locations of Chattanooga, Lookout Mountain, Missionary Ridge and the Tennessee River.
Left: The Missionary Ridge battlefield.

same time, Hooker was ordered to make a demonstration on the opposite flank at Lookout Mountain, part of a long ridge stretching south into Georgia. Due to the intermittent fog as Hooker's men scrambled up the slopes, the engagement would be dubbed the 'Battle Above the Clouds.' In fact, it was not much of a battle; the few Confederates in residence were easily driven away with fewer than 500 Federal casualties. On the left wing, Sherman seized enemy outposts on what his map told him was the northern end of Missionary Ridge, only to discover that he was stuck on an outlying hill with a ravine blocking the way to the ridge.

Dawn on November 25 revealed a huge Stars and Stripes flying from the summit of Lookout Mountain. Down in the city the Northerners cheered the sight amidst their preparations for battle. Grant had ordered Hooker and Sherman to press the main attack on the enemy flanks north and south of Missionary Ridge, but as the morning wore on neither general made much headway. After hours of indecisive fighting, in mid-afternoon Grant ordered Thomas's 23,000 men to advance on the center of the ridge, the heart of enemy strength, mainly as a demonstration to prevent Bragg from sending reinforcements to his flanks. To that end, and because a full-scale assault appeared suicidal, Grant ordered Thomas's forces to stop and regroup halfway up the ridge. What happened instead left everyone on both sides stunned with disbelief.

Thomas's men quickly overran the first line of Confederate rifle pits, partly because their occupants had received confusing orders from Bragg, and as the Southerners pulled out and ran, the Federals followed in pursuit, in the process overrunning the next line of defenses. An astonished Grant, watching from Orchard Knob with his staff, saw his troops continuing uphill in violation of orders. To Thomas he growled, 'Who ordered those men up the ridge?' The stolid Thomas replied that it wasn't he. 'Someone will suffer for it, if it turns out badly,' the lowering Grant warned.

By then Rebels all along the slopes had been swept up into flight, with Federals still hard on their heels. As they drove the enemy before them, the exultant Northern men began to chant the name of their recent humiliation: 'Chickamauga! Chickamauga!' By a combination of valor, luck, and the incompetence of their enemy, they were about to accomplish the impossible. Defenders at the top of the ridge found that they could not fire down the slopes without hitting their own men. For that reason, the Federals were quick to realize that their safest position was right behind the enemy. Moreover, Bragg's engineers had positioned their batteries on the very top of the ridge, whence they could not even be trained on to the slopes. Finally, the Southern troops had long lost faith in their commander, Bragg, and were more than ready to leave town. The Union assault rolled right over the fortifications at the top of the ridge and sent the Confederates running into Georgia. Rearguard forces stopped the Yankee advance, but the Rebels did not stop to regroup for 30 miles.

Casualties were relatively low for such a major battle; Union forces lost 5824 of 56,359 effectives, to the South's 6667 of 64,165. Besides taking one of the last remaining rail centers from the Confederacy, the Battle of Chattanooga dealt one more bitter blow to the sinking morale of the South and elevated U.S. Grant to the highest level of the Northern military command. His next opponent would be Robert E. Lee, in Virginia.

Cheat Mountain (West Virginia), Battle of

In his first campaign of the war, Confederate General Robert E. Lee was ordered to recapture parts of West Virginia that had been lost to the Confederacy in George B. McClellan's West Virginia Campaign (See). Lee's men first made contact with the Federals – under J. J. Reynolds – near Elkwater on September 10, 1861. Lee's complicated plans went astray over the next days due to wet weather,

the loss of surprise, and a Federal defensive position on Cheat Mountain that was made out to be much stronger than it actually was. Lee finally withdrew on the 15th; it was a dismal debut for the greatest of the war's field commanders.

Chesnuts, Mary and James

South Carolina-born James Chesnut Jr. (1815-1885) resigned his US Senate seat in November 1860, later sitting in the Confederate Congress. He was aide-de-camp to P. G. T. Beauregard at Fort Sumter and later to Jefferson Davis. Requesting field service in 1864, he commanded the South Carolina reserves. The Richmond journal of his wife Mary Boykin Miller Chesnut (1823-1886), one of the most sensitive chronicles of the wartime Confederacy, was published in 1905 under the title of Diary from Dixie.

Chickamauga, Campaign and Battle

The decisive year 1863 began in the middle of the Battle of Stone's River, near Murfreesboro in west Tennessee. This was a bloody but inconclusive three-day contest between the Federal Army of the Cumberland under William S. Rosecrans and Braxton Bragg's Confederate Army of Tennessee. At the beginning of summer, Washington ordered Rosecrans to start a new campaign to take the strategically vital rail center of Chattanooga and sweep Confederate forces out of Tennessee, a state that from the beginning had contained a strong contingent of Union sympathizers. To achieve his objective Rosecrans had to drive Bragg across the state, since Bragg would certainly fall back eastward to protect Chattanooga.

At the end of June, Rosecrans began his brief Tullahoma Campaign with a brilliant strategic coup, feinting at Bragg's left flank near Tullahoma. When the Southern general tried to respond, he discovered that two Union corps had gotten behind his right. Bragg had to pull back, and he decided to march all the way across the state to the strong defensive positions in Chattanooga, a nexus of rail lines running to the points of the compass. (During the Civil War, railroads became for the first time in history a vital element of strategy and logistics, moving troops and supplies at unprecedented speeds.)

The Confederate government at Richmond, worried about Bragg's position, took General James Longstreet and his men from Lee's army in Virginia and dispatched them by rail to Chattanooga. Before Longstreet arrived Rosecrans tried another strategic maneuver to get Bragg out of Chattanooga, diverting the Confederates with troops spread along the Tennessee River and then threatening the Southern rear again. In early September, Bragg pulled his forces from the city and headed south across the mountains and into Georgia. That same week, a hundred miles to the north, a Union army occupied Knoxville without firing a shot. Rosecrans now concluded that Bragg's forces were abandoning Tennessee and sent his men after them.

But the Federals were marching into a trap. Pursuing the supposedly fleeing enemy, Rosecrans divided his army to cross three mountain gaps some 50 miles apart. Meanwhile, Bragg was concentrating his forces in Lafayette, Georgia, whence they could strike

Nathan Bedford Forrest (right) was one of the two main leaders of Confederate cavalry at the Battle of Chickamauga.

This evocative sketch of the opposing lines of battle at Chickamauga was drawn by the ubiquitious war artist A. R. Waud.

each of the Northern contingents separately and overwhelm them one at a time. Bragg fumbled this opportunity, however, due mainly to the resistance of his subordinates, who disliked their choleric commander. Between September 10 and 13, Bragg's generals failed three times to attack as ordered. Meanwhile, Rosecrans finally realized why he kept running into parties of Confederates, all of whom seemed to be withdrawing toward Lafayette; sensing the danger he was in, the Federal commander ordered his three detachments to pull together on the west bank of Chickamauga Creek, near Lafayette. This was precisely the area where Bragg was awaiting the imminent arrival of Longstreet's forces, which would at last give him numerical superiority.

The Southern commander ordered a major attack on September 18, while the Union line was still highly vulnerable. Once again the attack failed to develop. By the evening of the 18th both commanders were ready to fight along Chickamauga Creek, whose Cherokee Indian name was said to mean 'River of Death.' Bragg intended to concentrate his next day's attack on the Union left and to cut off the Federals' only path of retreat, a road to Chattanooga. Rosecrans had anticipated this strategy and made sure his left flank was the strongest, the key position there being the steep horseshoe ridge of Snodgrass Hill where General George H. Thomas had been placed in command.

On the 19th the Battle of Chickamauga flared up by accident when a group of Federal cavalry scouts stumbled across some of Nathan Bedford Forrest's men north of the creek; the Confederates retreated under fire, and then Southern infantry pushed forward. Gradually the shooting spread down the line. There followed a bloody but disorganized day of fighting, during which a two-mile gap in the Union line remained undiscovered by Bragg. Thomas kept asking Rosecrans for re-

inforcements and gradually extended the Union left flank to protect the road to Chattanooga. For a time Confederates under John B. Hood (the first of Longstreet's forces to arrive) got on to the road, but then Thomas drove them away.

The costly but indecisive fighting ended in late afternoon with the Union line still in place. That evening Longstreet arrived with two more divisions, experienced veterans of Robert E. Lee's army, and now Bragg had the numerical upper hand. He ordered Leonidas Polk to begin at dawn with a strong assault on Thomas at Snodgrass Hill; after Polk's move on the Union left, the rest of the Southern forces were to join in successively down the line. Meanwhile, across the way, Union troops spent the night building log breastworks. Rosecrans met with his generals, cautioning them above all to keep closed up to the left. That was the beginning of a chain of coincidences adding up to disaster for the Federal Army of the Cumberland.

At dawn, with fog blanketing the thick woods, Bragg waited for Polk's attack. After an hour of silence a messenger was dis-

patched; he found Polk having a leisurely breakfast in a farmhouse. After vociferous prodding from Bragg, Polk finally assailed Thomas and slowly began to push the Union left flank back toward the critical road to Chattanooga.

Responding to urgent requests from Thomas for more reinforcements, Rosecrans ordered in J. S. Negley's reserve unit. But now confusion began to creep into Union deployments, for it was discovered that Negley was actually in line of battle and T. J. Wood was in reserve, where Negley was thought to be. As Negley's men were pulled out and sent to shore up Thomas on the left, and Wood was moved into line of battle on the right, the confusion snowballed. Negley and his men got lost, wandering over to Rossville; meanwhile, Rosecrans assumed that Negley had joined Thomas.

These confusions in deployment came to a head when an excited scout arrived to tell Rosecrans that there was a quarter-mile gap in the Federal line between the divisions of Wood and J. J. Reynolds. To seal that dangerous gap Rosecrans sent an order to Wood to 'close up on and support' Reynolds. This baffled Wood, since the scout had been mistaken: the line of battle in that area was Wood/Brannan/Reynolds, just as it was supposed to be; the woods and fog were so thick that the scout had not seen J. M. Brannan's division and had *assumed* there was a gap. Puzzling over the order, Wood decided that Rosecrans must mean for him to pull out of line and march behind Brannan to join Reynolds. Thus, as he pulled his troops out of line, Wood really did create gap.

At that moment, in Southern lines opposite the gap, apparently by sheer coincidence Longstreet moved to the attack. A column of Confederates charged straight into the gap, wheeled to the north, and in short order the whole Union right wing was fleeing up the road toward Chattanooga. During the rout the North lost thousands in dead, wounded, and captured. Among those retreating was Rosecrans, who ran into Negley and drew

Parts of the Rebel line in the Chickamauga Woods. This battle, which cost the South nearly 18,000 in dead or wounded, was to be the Confederacy's last major victory.

the mistaken conclusion that Negley had been with Thomas and thus that the left wing had broken as well. Thinking his whole army was on the run, the despairing Rosecrans continued on to Chattanooga.

But the Union army had not been entirely routed. General Thomas was still holding on as Longstreet's forces swarmed around the steep slopes of Snodgrass Hill. When ammunition ran low in late afternoon, however, it looked like the end, and Thomas ordered his men to fix bayonets. Then, at the last possible minute, a column of troops appeared in the Union rear. For a few moments Thomas was unsure if they were friend or foe; they turned out to be reserves under General Gordon Granger, who had violated Rosecrans's order to stay put and had marched to reinforce Thomas. With Granger's help Thomas was able to fight until nightfall and then make an orderly withdrawal to Chattanooga. The Confederates had won the field, but Thomas was the hero of the battle; forever after he would be the 'Rock of Chickamauga.'

Losses in the two days of battle were among the worst of the war: of 58,222 Federals engaged there were 1657 dead and 9756 wounded; of 66,326 Confederates, 3212 were dead and 14,674 wounded. Bragg failed to follow up his victory and pursue the enemy. By the time the Southern commander finally dispatched troops to Chattanooga on September 21 he found the enemy in strong defensive positions. Bragg dug his forces onto the heights around the city and settled down to starve the Yankees out. There things stayed until the arrival of U. S. Grant in October. (See CHATTANOOGA CAMPAIGN.

Chickasaw Bluffs (*Mississippi*), Battle of

As part of his early (and unsuccessful) attempt to take Vicksburg, Mississippi, during late 1862 Ulysses S. Grant ordered two corps under the command of W. T. Sherman to attack Chickasaw Bluffs, a Confederate strongpoint north of the city overlooking Chickasaw Bayou and the Yazoo River. Meanwhile, Grant was to take another

General George Thomas directs the heroic defense of the Union left at Chickamauga.

detachment overland along a railroad line to operate against the city. Due to enemy raids on his Holly Springs supply depot, however, Grant had to call off his overland advance, which gave John Pemberton in Vicksburg the chance to shift forces to meet Sherman's threat. Because Union telegraph lines had also been destroyed, Grant was not able to get a word to Sherman to call off his attack.

Sherman landed his troops from the Yazoo, spent two days working some 20,000 men across the tangle of waterways and swamps of the bayou, and ordered the assault on Chickasaw Bluffs for December 29 at noon. The attack never had a chance, being repulsed by fierce enemy artillery fire from the heights. Sherman called off the attack after suffering some 1800 casualties (to the enemy's 207). It would be next spring before more promising approaches to the city presented themselves.

Churchill, Thomas James *(1824-1905)* Confederate general.

This Kentucky native was an Arkansas planter who raised a regiment and fought at Wilson's Creek, surrendered to Union General John McClernand at Arkansas Post, then fought again in the Red River Campaign of 1864 and at Jenkins's Ferry. He finally surrendered reluctantly in Texas in 1865.

Civil Rights Acts of 1866 and 1875

The Civil Rights Act of 1866 superseded the Dred Scott decision(*See*) by granting American-born blacks citizenship and guaranteeing their civil rights (while excluding Indians and upholding state segregation laws). Concern over its constitutionality led to passage of the 14th Amendment (*See*). The Civil Rights Act of 1875 guaranteed equal rights to whites and blacks in public places and forbade blacks' exclusion from jury duty. In 1883 the Supreme Court ruled this act invalid since it protected social rather than political rights, ruling further that the 14th Amendment protected civil rights from infringement by states, but not by individuals. Racial discrimination by individuals was legal until the Civil Rights Act of 1964.

Clark, William Thomas *(1831-1905)* Union general.

A Connecticut-born Iowa lawyer, he raised the 13th Iowa and fought at Shiloh, Corinth, Port Gibson, Champion's Hill and Vicksburg. From February 1863 to April 1865 he was James McPherson's adjutant general. After the war Clark was a 'carpetbagger' Representative from Texas.

Clay, Cassius Marcellus *(1810-1903)* Union general.

Clay was a staunchly abolitionist editor, lawyer, and politician in Kentucky. On his way to a ministerial posting in Russia in 1861 he paused to organize troops to defend Washington. In 1862-63 he briefly suspended his diplomatic appointment to accept a commission, but he refused to fight until slavery was abolished.

Clay, Henry *(1777-1852)* Statesman.

Representing Kentucky in Congress, Clay was an eloquent voice for moderation, from the Missouri Compromise of 1820, of which he was the chief sponsor, through his own compromise resolutions of 1850 (*See* COMPROMISES OF 1820 AND 1850). He was also the author of the compromise Tariff of 1833, which de-fused the dangerous Nullification Crisis of the preceding year (*See* NULLIFICATION DOCTRINE). Facing increasing sectionalism in the 1850s, he urged gradual emancipation and warned against the dangers of secession.

Cleburne, Patrick Ronayne *(1828-1864)* Confederate general.

Irish born, this Arkansas druggist and lawyer seized the Little Rock arsenal with a militia in 1861. The 'Stonewall Jackson of the West' performed impressively at Shiloh, Richmond (Kentucky) and Perryville, Stone's River, Chickamauga, Chattanooga, and in the Atlanta Campaign, but he hurt his chances of promotion by advocating arming the slaves.

Kentucky-born Henry Clay was 'The Great Compromiser' of the prewar years.

Cobb, Howell (1815-1868)
Confederate general.

He was a Georgia-born lawyer, US Representative, governor of Georgia (1851-54), and Buchanan's secretary of the treasury (1857). A Unionist, he became a secessionist after Lincoln's election and chaired the Montgomery Convention (See). He organized the 16th Georgia and, despite his lack of military training, achieved a distinguished war career, fighting at Shiloh and Antietam and commanding Georgia's reserve forces and then the District of Georgia. His brother, lawyer and author Thomas Reade Rootes Cobb (1823-1862), was killed at Fredericksburg.

Coehorn Mortar

Union forces employed this light, portable weapon, named for its seventeenth-century Dutch inventor, in siege operations. A 24-pounder version weighed only 164 pounds, used powder sparingly, was easy to site, aim, and fire, and was accurate at ranges of up to 1200 yards.

Cold Harbor, Battle of

After the inconclusive Wilderness Battle (See) of early May, 1864, that began his campaign against Robert E. Lee and the Confederate Army of Northern Virginia, General Ulysses S. Grant had written defiantly to Washington, 'I propose to fight it out on this line if it takes all summer.' Since failing to overwhelm Lee for a second time at Spotsylvania, Grant had repeated the same maneuver for the third time, slipping around Lee's right flank in an effort to reach Richmond. As before, Lee had anticipated the move and had put his army in the way at the North Anna River.

The Southern lines there lay in a wedge-shaped formation; on May 23 Grant's Army of the Potomac made probing attacks and split in half along the wedge. Lee then had a rare opportunity to strike at the halves of his enemy's army in succession, but at that point

Previous pages: The Battle of Chickamauga, as depicted by Kurz & Allison.
Below: A battery of the Union's VI Corps in action at Cold Harbor in June 1864.

he was bedridden with fever and could not direct his forces. After two more days of indecisive fighting along the North Anna, Grant again 'sidled' the army of the Potomac to the left, flanking Lee, while the Confederates shadowed the move.

On May 31 Philip Sheridan's Federal cavalry found enemy cavalry at the crossroads of Cold Harbor, and a spirited fight broke out, leaving the Northerners in control of the road junction. The next day saw some fruitless Southern infantry attacks on the position. On the night of June 1 both armies entrenched on a line seven miles long between the Topopotomy and Chickahominy rivers. By that time the Federals had 109,000 men available, Lee 59,000. Grant ordered assaults for the next day, but slow troop movements and rain forced a postponement. The Union commander apparently was frustrated; three battles in a month had failed to crack his opponent's lines. Yet he now believed the Southerners to be exhausted and demoralized. So Grant decided to send his army in full strength against the Cold Harbor breastworks and try to overwhelm them in one blow. This would prove the most disastrous decision he ever made. The impossibility of the assignment was plain to the soldiers; the night before the battle many were seen sewing name tags on their clothes so their bodies could be identified.

The Battle of Cold Harbor on June 3 was in essence a series of charges on Confederate positions that were all but invulnerable, a maze of zig-zagging 'works within works and works without works.' The first assault struck the right and center of the Southern line at 4:30am. As the Federals approached, an observer recalled, 'there rang out suddenly on the summer air such a crash of artillery and musketry as is seldom heard in war.' Union men fell in waves. For a few minutes this first charge reached the outer trenches, but a countercharge drove the Federals back. Within the first half hour of fighting thousands of bluecoats dropped before the gray line. Yet after that devastating repulse Grant ordered a second general assault. It was carried out raggedly, with many troops holding back, and failed. A third order to attack produced no more than a token attempt.

By the time Grant ended the attacks at

noon Union casualties totalled some 7000, added to 5000 from the previous two days. Lee meanwhile had lost less than 1500. And the horror continued. Apparently neither general was willing to imply that he was beaten by asking for the usual truce to collect the wounded. As a result, no stretcher parties went out for four days, and hundreds of men died, in full view of both lines, of wounds, exposure, and thirst.

Grant would admit at the end of June 3, 'I regret this assault more than any one I have ever ordered.' A later commentator would more bluntly call the day, 'a horrible failure of Federal generalship.' General George Meade, still nominally in command of the Army of the Potomac, wrote to his wife, 'I think Grant has had his eyes opened, and is willing to admit now that Virginia and Lee's army is not Tennessee and Bragg's army.' (See CHATTANOOGA CAMPAIGN.) The army, for its part, was not likely to countenance further orders to attack breastworks.

Yet the Union cause had nonetheless been furthered in the last four inconclusive battles. In a month of ceaseless marching and fighting the Federal Army of the Potomac had suffered 50,000 casualties, 41 percent of its original strength, and numbers of men had experienced physical and mental breakdowns from the stress. Yet while the losses of Lee's Army of Northern Virginia had been numerically less, 32,000, that represented 46 percent of Confederate strength. Though Grant had been forced into a game of attrition only by Lee's continuing resistance, the Federal general well knew that as long as he stayed in the field the war could be decided by the simple and brutal matter of numbers. Union losses could be replaced, and Confedrate losses could not; the South was reaching its last reserves of manpower. Having failed four times to hammer Lee into submission in open battle, however, now Grant would change his strategy of inching toward the Confederate capital and fighting Lee in the trenches and barricades as he went. Now he would turn for Petersburg, the back door to Richmond.

Cold Spring Foundry

Under the supervision of Robert P. Parrott (See), this plant across the Hudson from the US Military Academy produced some 1700 guns and 3 million projectiles during the war. It was also called the West Point Foundry.

Colquitt, Alfred Holt (1824-1894)
Confederate general.

Colquitt was a Georgia lawyer, planter and extreme states' rights politician who fought in the Peninsular Campaign and led Colquitt's Brigade at Antietam, Fredericksburg, Chancellorsville, the Wilderness, Spotsylvania, and Petersburg.

Colt Revolvers and Rifles

From 1848 on, Samuel Colt produced several successful cap-and-ball (See) revolver models for US forces, the most famous Civil War types being the .36-caliber Model 1851 and 1861 'Navy' weapons and the .44-caliber Model 1860 'Army' weapon; the war depart-

Capt Stevens battery on the 6th Corps skirmish line. A R Waud

ment bought more than 100,000 examples of the Model 1860, which became the official US Army pistol.

Columbia (*South Carolina*), Burning of

(*See* CAROLINAS CAMPAIGN)

Columbiad

This large cannon, first fired in the War of 1812, was produced in calibers of 8, 10, and 15 inches and was used for coastal defense. The 15-inch version, weighing nearly 50,000 pounds, fired a 320-pound shell.

Compromises of 1820 and 1850

For over a generation before the Civil War, indeed from the time of the Revolution, the rising tensions between the slave-holding and free regions of the United States had been heavily focused on the problem of what the status of states newly admitted to the Union should be, since this directly affected the voting power of the two regions in Congress. The first major test of the question came in 1820. At that time the free and slave regions were exactly balanced, each being composed of 11 states; but now it was proposed that Maine, a free territory, be admitted as a 23rd state. Southern objections to this upsetting of the balance were so extreme that in the end a compromise was adopted whereby Missouri would be admitted as a slave

state in 1821. Another provision of this compromise, alternatively known as the Compromise of 1820 or the Missouri Compromise, barred the extension of slavery elsewhere in the territory of the Louisiana Purchase above 30° 30′ N.

But the problems surrounding the admission of new states became steadily more complex and envenomed in the years that followed, and particularly after the annexation of Texas and the large acquisition of new territory following the Mexican War. Matters came to a boil again in 1849 with the proposed admission of California as a free state. In

The Union attack at Cold Harbor was bloodily repulsed. Grant later said he regretted the assault more than any he ever ordered.

1850, largely thanks to the efforts of Senators Henry Clay and Stephen A. Douglas, a new series·of compromise measures (known collectively as the Compromise of 1850) was passed to allay the crisis: California would

A selection of revolvers typical of the kind being produced by Samuel Colt's factory in Hartford, Connecticut, in the 1850s. Colt received his first patent for a 'revolving gun' in 1836.

enter as a free state, the territories of Utah and New Mexico would decide their status by local vote, slavery would be abolished in the District of Columbia, and the provisions and enforcement of the Fugitive Slave Acts would be strengthened. Although these measures placated majorities in both regions temporarily, no one was really satisfied, and the work of this last great federal effort at compromise would soon be undone by the effects of the Kansas-Nebraska Act, the Dred Scott Decision, and other divisive occurences that multiplied in the 1850s.

Confederate Army

There never was an official standing Confederate army; the collection of volunteers called the Provisional Army was established by President Jefferson Davis in February and March of 1861. Estimates of men fighting for the South during the war are highly speculative; one estimate has been 1,082,119. Only 174,223 were left to surrender at the end of the war, most of the depreciation being due to desertion.

Confederate Flags

The original 'Stars and Bars,' the first of four Confederate flags, had two horizontal red stripes with a white one in between, seven white stars in a circle, and a blue field. After First Bull Run, General P. G. T. Beauregard introduced the more familiar blue St. Andrew's cross on a red field, with 13 stars superimposed on the blue. A 'National Flag,' adopted in May 1863, was white with Beauregard's battle flag in the upper corner. In March 1865 a vertical bar was added to the edge of the National Flag.

Confederate Money

Beginning with a $1 million authorization in March 1861, the Confederate government issued paper notes payable six months after the ratification of a peace treaty. More than $1.5 billion was eventually issued. The money depreciated steadily. In December 1861 a Confederate dollar was worth 80 cents in gold; by the surrender at Appomattox it took up to $1000 in Confederate notes to buy $1 in gold or Union paper.

Representative of Confederate army units was Charleston's Palmetto Battery.

Confederate Navy

The Confederate navy was nonexistent in 1861, with no ships, no navy yards or manufacturing to build a fleet, and few officers or merchant seamen. Confederate Navy Secretary Stephen R. Mallory devised a resourceful strategy of coastal and river defense using ironclads, mines, and submarines, and he provided for blockade-running and commercial raiding by using converted small craft and British-built cruisers. The Southerners succeeded in disrupting Northern commerce and, at least to some extent, in puncturing the Union blockade.

Confederate States of America

The Confederate States of America was the name adopted by the 11 states that seceded from the US between December 1860, and June 1861. There were also separate Confederate 'governments' in sympathetic regions of two slaveholding but unseceded states, Kentucky and Missouri. The Confederacy, in short, proposed to be a separate country that differed from the US primarily in protecting the institution of slavery.

Previous pages: The Battle of Cold Harbor. *Above*: By early 1865 Confederate paper money was worth less than are these facsimiles now.

The theoretical basis for the idea of secession was the concept of States' Rights, which held that individual states had the right to nullify Federal laws – especially antislavery laws – to which they objected, and in extreme cases to withdraw from the Union. Southern states held the election of Abraham Lincoln to the presidency to be such an extreme case: Lincoln had long been an eloquent voice of the antislavery movement, and the newly-formed Republican Party he represented was part of that movement.

The first state to secede was South Carolina, on December 20, 1860, two weeks after Lincoln's election. The ordinance of secession concluded: 'the union now subsisting between South Carolina and other States, under the name of "The United States of America,"is hereby dissolved.' By the time Lincoln took office on March 4, 1861, six other states had followed suit: in order, Mississippi, Florida, Alabama, Georgia, Louisiana, and Texas. After the fall of Fort Sumter in mid-April, four other states from the upper

This design was intended to be the great seal of the Confederate States of America.

South would secede – Virginia, Arkansas, North Carolina, and Tennessee.

Delegates from six of the original seven states (the Texas delegation arrived late) met in provisional congress on February 4 at Montgomery, Alabama. On the 8th a provisional constitution was adopted, closely resembling the US Constitution in the organization of government, but with strong provisions protecting slavery and the rights of individual states. The following day Jefferson Davis was elected provisional president and Alexander Stevens vice-president. The provisional congress also declared that any US laws not directly contradicting stated Confederate laws were still to be in force. Davis, who learned of his election after the fact, was sworn in on February 18 and on the next day announced a cabinet.

On the 28th the congress directed Davis to call for 12-month military volunteers; he would ask for 100,000. By the fall of Fort Sumter in mid-April the Confederate army con-

Confederate President Jefferson Davis (at left end of table, seated) and his cabinet get a battle report from Robert E. Lee.

sisted of some 35,000 men. The Confederate capital would be moved to Richmond, Virginia, on May 20, 1861, where it would remain until the end of the war.

The Confederate government proved to be fractious and inefficient, both because of the nature of the government and the character of its members. Davis, a former US Senator and secretary of war, was an able man dedicated to his cause, but he was personally cold, humorless, and unskilled in the persuasions and manipulations of politics. Chronic and painful illnesses exacerbated these problems. He also overrated his military abilities, directing the Confederate war effort himself rather than appointing a general-in-chief. Especially in the South, he thereby hobbled his armies by his tendency to favor weaker generals (such as Braxton Bragg) and hold down outstanding ones (notably Nathan B. Forrest).

The very states-rights basis of the Confederacy made concerted action by the government difficult and often impossible, since representatives of each state tended to insist on their own interests and independence. Representatives were also taken from a population given to fights and duels to settle matters, and this made for tumultuous debates. In the later stages of the war the government proved unable to stem shortages of food and other civilian supplies or to combat massive inflation of Confederate currency. Moreover, Davis had a great deal of trouble every time he stepped on the prerogatives of delegates and/or states; thus there were bitter wrangles over such vital issues as drafting soldiers, taxes, and emergency suspension of civil laws. Davis was also beset by the resistance of his vice-president to many of his policies; after a while Stevens virtually cut off communication and worked steadily against the president.

One of the few things the Confederate government turned out to be good at was supplying its armies with military equipment. By a combination of manufacturing and foreign purchases, the government managed to keep ample arms and ammunition

flowing to its forces for the duration of the war. Notable in the cabinet was Secretary of the Navy Stephen R. Mallory, who virtually created a Confederate navy out of thin air, organized a brilliantly effective blockade-running fleet, and led the way in the historic development of ironclad ships. At the same time, the government was shockingly lax in other important elements of military logistics, notably in providing clothing and food; Rebel soldiers often marched and fought ragged, barefoot, and hungry, even when supplies were available in the South. On the whole, it is probably safe to say that Confederate military fortunes prospered as long as they did in the war less because of the government than despite it.

Confiscation Acts

A set of three Congressional measures approved in 1861-62, they declared freedom for slaves used in the transportation of military goods or the construction of military facilities. The acts also proclaimed that all slaves who lived in areas occupied by Union forces would be freed.

Congressional Medal of Honor

The highest award for valor given to US forces, Congress authorized it for Navy enlistees in December 1861 and for soldier enlistees in July 1862. In March 1863 Army officers were made eligible. (Navy and Marine officers did not become eligible until 1915.) More than 1200 such medals were given during the Civil War; award standards for later wars were much more strict.

Conner, James *(1829-1883)*
Confederate general.

A South Carolina lawyer and secessionist, he joined Wade Hampton's Legion in May 1861. He fought at First Bull Run, on the Peninsula, and at Chancellorsville and Gettysburg. After court martial duty, he commanded brigades during the Petersburg Campaign and the Shenandoah Valley Campaign of Sheridan, ending field service after losing a leg at the Battle of Fisher's Hill in September 1864.

Constitution

The US Constitution, drafted in 1787, appeared to sanction slavery by counting each slave equal to three-fifths of a white person in calculating Congressional representation; by permitting the slave trade to operate until 1808; and by providing for the return of fugitive slaves to their owners. The Bill of Rights (1791) guaranteed the rights of white Americans only. Three Amendments to the Constitution (*See*) passed after the Civil War extended Constitutional protection to black Americans.

'Contrabands'

General B. F. Butler coined the term in May 1861 when he denied a Virginia slaveholder's request for the return of three runaway slaves who had sought refuge in Fortress Monroe. The word eventually became slang usage for any slave or freedman.

Cook, Philip *(1817-1894)*
Confederate general.

A Georgia lawyer, Cook fought with the 4th Georgia in the Seven Days' Battles, at Antietam, at Fredericksburg, and at Chancellorsville. He sat in the state legislature briefly in 1863-64, returning to fight with Jubal Early in the Shenandoah Valley in 1864. He was wounded and captured by Union forces at Petersburg in April 1865.

Cooke, John Esten *(1830-1886)*
Confederate general.

This Virginian, a nationally known writer, served throughout the war. He was J. E. B. Stuart's ordnance officer and Robert E. Lee's inspector general of the Horse Artillery. He surrendered with Lee at Appomattox. Cooke published biographies of Stonewall Jackson and Lee, among other books about the war.

Cooke, John Rogers *(1833-1891)*
Confederate general.

A Missouri-born, Harvard-educated engineer, he resigned from US Army frontier duty in 1861 to raise a Confederate artillery company. Cooke fought at First Bull Run, Seven Pines, Fredericksburg, Bristoe Station, and the Wilderness, suffering several wounds. His father, Philip St. George Cooke, was a Union officer.

Cooper, Joseph Alexander *(1823-1910)* Union general.

This Mexican War veteran, a Tennessee farmer, recruited and trained Union troops in Tennessee. He fought at Stone's River, Chickamauga, and Chattanooga. Rapidly promoted, he led a brigade at Atlanta and participated in eastern Tennessee operations until the end of the war.

Peace Democrats in the form of copperhead snakes assail Columbia, spirit of the Union, with (presumably poisonous) peace proposals in this Northern cartoon.

A lightly-constructed corduroy road runs up the main thoroughfare of these 1862 Union army winter quarters (a former Confederate camp) in Centreville, Virginia.

Cooper, Samuel *(1798-1876)*
Confederate general.

Cooper, a New Jersey-born career officer and West Point graduate, was married to a Virginian and offered his valuable administrative experience to the Confederates in 1861. A full general, he was their highest ranking officer serving as adjutant- and inspector-general.

Copperheads

(Also known as Peace Democrats)

These Northern Democrats opposed the war, advocating a negotiated peace and restoration of the Union largely on Southern terms. They influenced the adoption of a peace plank in the Democratic platform for the 1864 presidential election. Particularly strong in Ohio, Illinois, and Indiana, their leaders included Alexander Long, Fernando Wood, and Clement L. Vallandigham (*See*). Their name derived from their identifying badges: the head of Liberty cut from copper pennies.

Corcoran Legion

Michael Corcoran, an Irish-born Union officer, raised this brigade, composed of the 155th, 164th, 170th, and 182nd New York, in November 1862. After serving for nearly a year in the Washington, DC, area, the legion joined the II Corps of the Army of the Potomac in May 1864.

Corduroy Road

A road with large branches or tree trunks laid side-by-side on top, it permitted passage for troops and vehicles over soft ground.

Corinth *(Mississippi)*, Battles of

The first major military operations around Corinth followed the battle of Shiloh, from the end of April to mid-June 1862. General Henry Halleck, commanding the Federal Department of the Mississippi, effectively relieved Ulysses S. Grant from command of the Army of the Tennessee, despite Grant's victory at Shiloh; the ostensible reason was Grant's falling victim to the surprise attack that opened, and nearly ended, that battle. Naming Grant to the functionless position of second in command, Halleck personally took charge of the three Union armies in the area – of the Tennessee, Ohio, and Mississippi – and marched on Corinth, Mississippi, where the army of P. G. T. Beauregard, the loser at Shiloh, was located.

So obsessed with detail and so cautious was Halleck, however, that his march from the Shiloh battlefield area to Corinth proceded at the snail's pace of 20 miles per day, from April 29 to May 25. On the way there had been minor skirmishing, but nothing to

seriously impede the Federals. Arriving on the outskirts of town, Halleck prepared to lay siege. Beauregard saw that even with the 70,000 men he had collected (many wounded or sick) he could do little to resist a Federal army of 110,000; so he pulled his forces out of town during the night of May 29-30 and marched for Tupelo, Mississippi. Halleck decided not to mount a major pursuit but rather decided that he would consolidate his position in Tennessee.

Because of this victory by way of maneuver and his earlier writings on military strategy, Lincoln and his advisers decided that Halleck was the man to run the war. In July the general was called to Washington to become general-in-chief – not a very effective one, in the end. Beauregard's career would never recover from his loss at Shiloh and his withdrawal from Corinth.

By October of 1862 Federal forces were dispersed in four contingents around the area, with 23,000 men holding Corinth under the command of General William Rosecrans. Confederate forces in the area, having escaped Grant's attempt to swamp them at the Battle of Iuka (*See*), were organized by General Earl Van Dorn for a strike at Rosecrans. Van Dorn, commander of the Confederate District of Mississippi, got off to an inauspicious start by underestimating Federal strength in the city; in fact, the Federals outnumbered his forces by 1000. Scouts informed Grant of Van Dorn's approach, but the Union general could not discover which of his four contingents the enemy was planning to strike.

The Battle of Corinth broke out in the morning of October 3, when Van Dorn mounted an attack that drove the Federals back two miles into their inner line of breastworks. Through a day of desperate enemy onslaughts the Union lines held. Grant, learning of the attack in the morning, dispatched reinforcements. On the 4th Van Dorn mounted another assault, but in heavy fighting made no headway. The battle was over by afternoon, when Federal reinforcements began to arrive.

Grant hoped to catch Van Dorn in a pincers between the reinforcements and Rosecrans's men moving out of town. But because of the slowness of Rosecrans (or so Grant believed), Van Dorn got away with most of his forces, though he lost 300 men captured when he was caught crossing the Hatchie River. The Federals broke off pursuit at Ripley, and Van Dorn continued by Holly Springs. By the end of the battle and ensuing retreat the Union had lost 2520 men, the South 2470 dead or wounded and 1763 missing and captured. Though Grant was disappointed that Van Dorn got away, and was thereafter cool to Rosecrans, the battle was a considerable strategic victory. From then on Grant would hold most of the cards in the Mississippi theater, and his campaign against the strategically crucial city of Vicksburg could go forward.

Corps

An organizational unit consisting of two or more army divisions. Unofficial Union corps early in the war relied on the use of numerals I through VI, identifying themselves further by the army to which they belonged. Union corps were officially authorized on July 17, 1862. Commanded by major generals, their numbers reached to XXV Corps. Confederate corps, commanded by lieutenant generals, were authorized on September 18, 1862; before then divisions were for the most part simply grouped under a commander's name – *e.g.*, 'Longstreet's Wing.'

Corse, Montgomery Dent (1816-1895) **Confederate general.**

This Virginia banker fought at First Bull Run, on the Peninsula, at Second Bull Run, and at Antietam; his own regiment reduced to seven men, he took over Pickett's brigade and participated at Fredericksburg, Gettysburg, Chickamauga, the Wilderness, and in the Appomattox Campaign. He was captured with Richard Ewell at Sayler's Creek.

A Kurz & Allison version of the Battle of Corinth, fought on October 3 and 4, 1862. A strategic, rather than tactical, victory for the Union, it seriously weakened Rebel strength in what would soon become the war's pivotal theater, the Mississippi.

Rebels burn cotton to prevent its falling into the hands of approaching Federals. By the war's end cotton was relatively scarce.

Cotton

The importance of the institution of slavery to the South lay largely in its provision of unpaid labor to grow cotton, the region's principal crop, so that it could be exported at competitive prices. Through the 1850s demand and production of cotton skyrocketed, until some Southerners proclaimed that 'King Cotton' made them 'the controlling power of the world.' By 1860 the South was producing some 5 million bales of cotton annually. But this specialization was to exact a price in self-sufficiency during the war, since the expansion of cotton farming had been at the expense of raising edible crops. Confederate authorities at first confidently predicted that Europe would be forced both to trade with the South and to recognize secession in order to maintain its supply of cotton, but this was not the case. After running through its considerable surplus stocks of raw cotton, Europe simply turned to alternative suppliers such as Egypt and India.

Cox, Jacob Dolson *(1828-1900)*
Union general.

An Ohio lawyer, legislator and radical anti-slavery activist before the war, Cox fought in the Kanawha Valley Campaign (*See*) and at South Mountain and Antietam. He commanded the Department of West Virginia and District of Ohio, and led divisions in the Atlanta and Franklin and Nashville Campaigns.

'Cracker Line'

(*See* CHATTANOOGA CAMPAIGN)

Crater, Battle of the

(*See* PETERSBURG SIEGE)

Crawford, Samuel Wylie *(1829-1892)* **Union general.**

A Pennsylvanian, this army surgeon led a battery at Fort Sumter and, as a brigadier general, fought at Winchester, Cedar Mountain, Antietam, and Gettysburg. He participated in all the Potomac Army operations of 1864-65 and was present at the Appomattox surrender.

Crittenden, John Jordan *(1787-1863)* **Statesman.**

Kentucky-born governor of Kentucky, US attorney general and US Senator, Crittenden was an anti-secessionist who supported Lincoln and worked to keep Kentucky in the Union. On December 18, 1861, he offered the Senate the Crittenden Compromise, proposing the extension of the Missouri Compromise line to the Pacific, but this peacekeeping measure was rejected by both sides.

Crook, George *(1829-1890)* **Union general.**

Crook was a West Point graduate from Ohio who suspended his outstanding career as an Indian fighter long enough to compile a successful Civil War record. He fought at South Mountain, Antietam, and Chickamauga and in the Shenandoah Valley Campaign of Sheridan and the Appomattox Campaign.

Cross Keys (or Union Church) and Port Republic *(Virginia)*, Battles of

These were the climactic battles of the 1862 Shenandoah Valley Campaign of Jackson. On June 7 Thomas J. Jackson found himself between two pursuing Federal forces under John Frémont and James Shields. On the 8th Frémont advanced from Cross Keys, but Jackson's lieutenant, Richard Ewell, stopped the 10,500 bluecoats with only 6500 Rebel troops. On the next day, keeping Frémont at

bay with a burned bridge and a screening force, Jackson massed most of his troops and after several hours of bloody fighting drove Shields from Port Republic.

Cullum, George Washington *(1809-1892)* **Union general.**

A New Yorker, this army engineer published numerous works on engineering and military history. He held staff positions under Winfield Scott and Henry Halleck and was chief engineer of the Departments of Missouri and Mississippi. At the end of the war he was superintendent of West Point.

Culp's Hill

The northeastern anchor of the Union position at the Battle of Gettysburg, it was the scene of especially heavy action on the second and third days of the battle.

Cumberland Gap

This strategic mountain pass on the Tennessee-Virginia line changed hands several times during the war. Federal forces under Ambrose Burnside took it for good on September 10, 1863, capturing a Confederate garrison of 2500 men and 36 guns and severing direct Confederate rail communications between Chattanooga and the east.

Cumming, Alfred *(1829-1910)* **Confederate general.**

A Georgia-born West Point graduate, Cumming resigned from frontier duty in 1861 and commanded Confederate troops in the Peninsula. He led brigades at Antietam, Mobile, and the siege of Vicksburg; captured and exchanged, he fought at Chattanooga and in the Atlanta Campaign. He was wounded at Jonesboro and discharged.

Curtis, Newton Martin *(1835-1910)* **Union general.**

Curtis was a New York farmer and lawyer who fought as a captain in the 16th New York at First Bull Run. Steadily promoted, he fought at Cold Harbor, Petersburg, and Fort Fisher, where he was badly wounded and earned a Medal of Honor.

Union general George Crook won postwar fame as an able (and enlightened) Indian fighter.

The Union so valued spy Pauline Cushman's work that she was made an honorary major.

Curtis, Samuel Ryan (1805-1866)
Union general.

This West Point graduate and civil engineer resigned his Iowa Congressional seat in 1861. As commander of the Army of the Southwest, he won at Pea Ridge and occupied

Still a lieutenant when this photograph was taken, cavalry leader George Custer would be promoted faster than any Union officer, rising to the rank of major general by 1865 and becoming a national celebrity.

Helena, then commanded successively the Departments of Missouri, Kansas, and the Northwest.

Cushing, William Barker (1842-1874) Union naval officer.

He resigned from Annapolis in 1861 and joined the North Atlantic blockading squadron. Cushing performed brilliantly in Florida and the Carolinas, destroyed the Confederate ram *Albemarle* in a daring night torpedo attack made in a small boat in October 1864 and led an assault of sailors at Fort Fisher.

Cushman, Pauline (1835-1893)
Union spy.

Born in Louisiana and raised in Michigan, this actress turned spy and was sent south in 1863 to gather military intelligence. Arrested near Tullahoma, Tennessee, and sentenced to death by the Confederates, she was spared by their sudden retreat and so was able to pass on valuable information to Union General William Rosecrans during his Tullahoma Campaign in mid-1863.

Custer, George Armstrong (1839-1876) Union general.

Young, flamboyant, and controversial, Custer compiled an outstanding war career, fighting in virtually every battle of Army of the Potomac from First Bull Run until the surrender at Appomattox. His greatest triumph was his relentless pursuit of Lee's retreating army in April 1865: Custer accepted the Confederate truce flag. His postwar campaigns on the plains ended in the fatal 1876 ambush at the Little Big Horn. (*See* also BATTLE MOUNTAIN, BEAVER DAM STATION, NAMOZINE CHURCH, and WAYNESBORO).

Dabney's Mills

(Also called Hatcher's Run and Boydton Road

During the siege phase of his Petersburg Campaign, Ulysses S. Grant ordered D. M. Gregg's Federal cavalry to strike enemy supply wagons on the Boydton Plank Road; Gregg had no success. From February 5-7, 1865, there was fighting in the area, particularly on the 6th, when Confederates attacked Gouveneur Warren's division near Dabney's Mills and inflicted 2300 casualties. By the 7th the Federal siege lines extended to Hatcher's Run at the Vaughan Road.

Dahlgren Guns

Admiral John Dahlgren designed this weapon, dubbed the 'soda water bottle' on account of its shape. Primarily a naval gun, Dahlgrens were manufactured in 9-, 11-, 15- and 20-inch calibers. All the Dahlgren guns were smoothbores but were designed to fire either solid or explosive ammunition.

Dahlgren, John Adolphus Bernard (1809-1870) Union admiral.

Son of the Swedish consul in Philadelphia, he became a US naval ordnance officer. He invented the Dahlgren Gun (*See*). Dahlgren was appointed commander of the Washington Naval Yard in 1861 and in 1862 was named chief of the Ordnance Bureau. After July 1863 he commanded the South Atlantic Blockading Squadron, sealing Charleston and helping capture Savannah before finally entering Charleston in February 1865. Ulric Dahlgren (*See*) was his son.

Dahlgren, Ulric (1842-1864)
Union army officer.

The son of the admiral who invented a widely used naval gun, he served as a staff officer with Ambrose Burnside, Joseph Hooker, and George Meade successively. Wounded after Gettysburg, he had a leg amputated. He was killed during the notorious Kilpatrick-Dahlgren raid (*See*), of which he was the co-leader, in March 1864.

Dahlgren Papers

These documents, which detailed a plan to assassinate Jefferson Davis and his cabinet, were allegedly found on the body of Colonel Ulric Dahlgren (*See*), killed in the Kilpatrick-Dahlgren Raid of late February-early March 1864 (*See*). There were claims the papers had been forged, but recent research suggests they were authentic.

Dallas (*Georgia*), Battle of

Confederate General Joseph Johnston, continuing his resistance to W. T. Sherman's 1864 Atlanta Campaign, threw his forces in the path of Federals attempting to envelop him through Dallas. In heavy fighting on June 25 the Federals failed to break through. On the 27th another several hours of battle were inconclusive but costly, including some 1400 Federal casualties. Frustrated in his envelopment, Sherman then tried a disastrous direct assault the same day on Johnston's position at Kenesaw Mountain (*See*).

Dalton (*Georgia*) Federal Demonstration on

On February 22, 1864, Union General George Thomas's Federals in Chattanooga began a reconnaisance of Joseph Johnston's Confederate army at Dalton, Georgia, to see if Johnston was still at full strength. After driving Confederates from Varnell's Station and Tunnel Hill, the Federals failed to break through Buzzard Roost Gap on the 25th. Finding that the Confederates were still strong, the bluecoats withdrew on the 26th. W. T. Sherman's Atlanta Campaign followed soon after this action.

'Damn the Torpedoes'

Admiral David Farragut is said to have made the comment as his fleet ran past Fort Gaines and Fort Morgan during the Battle of Mobile Bay on August 5, 1864.

In October 1864, outside Petersburg on the Darbytown Road, Union troops repel a Rebel attempt to turn the Federal flank.

Dana, Napoleon Tecumseh Jackson (*1822-1905*) **Union general.**

This West Point graduate and Mexican War veteran became a Minnesota banker. He fought at Ball's Bluff, on the Peninsula, and at Antietam. He commanded Philadelphia's defenses during the Gettysburg Campaign. He also led a successful expedition against the Texas coast in 1863.

Darbytown and New Market Roads, *Virginia*

During the 1864 Federal siege in the Petersburg Campaign, Robert E. Lee's Confederates made an unsuccessful attempt on October 7 to recapture Union-held positions on these roads.

Davidson, John Wynn (*1823-1881*) **Union general.**

A Virginian, West Point graduate and career cavalryman, Davidson declined a Confederate commission in 1861. He fought with the Federals on the Peninsula and commanded Missouri districts and departments, a cavalry division in the Arkansas expedition, and the Division of the West Mississippi.

Davis & Davis Escape from Harper's Ferry

During the Antietam Campaign, Dixon S. Miles's Union forces were surrounded at Harper's Ferry. On September 14, 1862, Colonel B. F. Davis of the 8th New York Cavalry and Lieutenant Colonel Hasbrouck Davis of the 12th Illinois Cavalry led a column of 1300 Federal cavalry in a spectacular escape; they reached Greencastle, Pennsylvania, without losing a man, incidentally capturing a Confederate ammunition train with a 600-strong escort along the way.

Davis, Charles Henry (*1807-1877*) **Union admiral.**

This Massachusetts-born naval officer helped plan Union naval war strategy. He held commands in the Port Royal Expedition and in

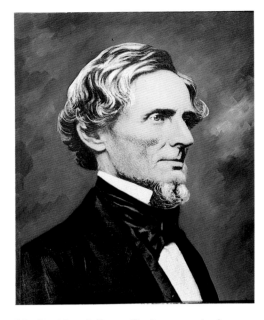

CSA President Jefferson Davis was a mixed blessing to the Confederacy, dedicated and brave but also quarrelsome and inflexible

the upper Mississippi gunboat flotilla, fighting at Memphis and Vicksburg and on the Yazoo River. Davis was chief of the Bureau of Navigation from July 1862 throughout the remainder of the war.

Davis, Edmund Jackson (*1827-1883*) **Union general.**

A Texas lawyer stung by losing an election for the secessionist convention, Davis organized a Unionist regiment in Mexico which spent most of the war in Louisiana, unsuccessfully attacking Laredo in 1864. Elected governor of Texas in 1869, Davis presided over a notoriously corrupt carpetbag administration.

Davis, George (*1820-1896*) **Confederate attorney general.**

He was a North Carolina lawyer who participated in the Peace Conference in Washington in February 1861 but afterward denounced its recommendations. A Confederate Senator and advisor to Jefferson Davis, he became the CSA's attorney general in January 1864.

Davis, Jefferson (*1808-1889*) **Confederate president.**

One-time United States secretary of war, Congressman, and Senator, Jefferson Davis ended his political career as the president of the Confederacy. In his public and private life he seemed to embody many of the elements that both made and unmade the Southern cause. Born in Kentucky, he was taken as a child to Mississippi, where his father was a farmer. In 1824 he gained an appointment to the US Military Academy.

After graduation in 1828 Davis served as an officer in remote posts in Wisconsin and Illinois, seeing a little action in the Black Hawk Indian War of 1832. The former commandant at one of his early posts was future President Zachary Taylor, whose daughter Davis married against her father's wishes;

she died within three months. For the next decade Davis remained in isolation, running a plantation in Mississippi. During this period he came to identify with the Southern plantation mentality – the social system (including slavery), pride in one's State, and a feeling that the South must be allowed to choose its own ways. Encouraged by an older brother, Joseph, a man of some wealth and influence, Davis ran successfully for the House of Representatives in 1845. In the same year he married Varina Howell, daughter of one of the local planter aristocrats.

Davis was in Washington only a few months before he resigned his seat to fight in the Mexican War; he saved the day at the Battle of Buena Vista, gaining national attention and confirming his vision of himself as an outstanding military man. In 1847 he returned to Washington as a Senator; he became a staunch defender of slaveholding and advocated extending slavery into new territories. President Franklin Pierce appointed Davis secretary of war in 1853, and during an active and successful tenure Davis took an expansionist approach to foreign affairs, one that he saw as consonant with the Southern desire to extend slavery. He then returned to the Senate.

For all his defense of slavery and the Southern way of life, Davis was opposed to seces-

President and Mrs. Jefferson Davis, as they appeared soon after the war's end. He was at this time still under arrest.

sion and continued through the Democratic conventions of 1860 to urge some type of compromise. With the election of Lincoln, however, and upon the new president's declaration that he was opposed to adding more slaveholding territories, Davis saw no alternative to going along with secession and formally withdrew from the Senate on January 21, 1861.

His ambition was to command the Southern armies, but he was soon asked to become the Confederacy's provisional president – mainly because the delegates could not agree on any other candidate – and was inaugurated on February 18, 1861, becoming regular president the next year. He faced immense challenges. The Southern states were unprepared for war, lacked weapons and resources for large military enterprises, and were subject to a Union blockade that gradually choked off supplies from abroad. Moreover, the states-rights basis of the Confederacy made the position of the central government weak and ambiguous when it attempted to take such necessary actions as drafting troops and levying taxes.

Davis faced other problems, among them his own inflexible nature, hot temper, and ill health. His wife called him 'a mere mass of throbbing nerves.' Nearly everything that transpired during his presidency exacerbated these difficulties. He quarreled constantly with other leaders civilian and military, and with his friends – such as cabinet secretary Judah Benjamin – and tended to be unpopu-

lar with Southerners. He often elevated mediocre generals (such as Braxton Bragg) and held down outstanding ones (such as Nathan B. Forrest), and, overrating his own military prowess, insisted on telling his generals how to run the war, the notable exception to this being Robert E. Lee, whom Davis trusted thoroughly. Toward the end of the war, with the Confederacy on the brink of collapse, Davis caused widespread outrage with a proposal to draft 40,000 slaves and free them after the war – in other words, to emancipate these slaves.

Davis put up a brave and hopeful front to the end, even declaring, as the Confederate government fled Richmond, that victory was assured. Davis was soon captured by Federal forces, on May 10 near Irwinville, Georgia, and clapped in irons at Fort Monroe, Virginia. Before long, however, he was given comfortable quarters that he shared with his wife. Despite many demands for it, he was never prosecuted for treason but simply released on bond in May 1867. His home, health, and fortune lost, he spent some time traveling in Europe and eventually regained some equilibrium. He settled with his family at an estate on the Gulf of Mexico, where he wrote an account and defense of the Confederacy. Mississippi wanted to return him to the Senate, but could not because he refused to request an official pardon from the Federal government – a position typical of his inflexible sense of honor. He died in New Orleans on December 6, 1889.

Davis, Varina Howell *(1826-1906)*

Wife of Jefferson Davis.

Born in Mississippi, she married Davis in 1845 and forged an intellectual and political partnership with him. As first lady of the Confederacy she was controversial because of her Northern ancestry and considerable political influence.

The inauguration of Jefferson Davis at the statehouse in Montgomery, Alabama, in 1861.

Dayton, *Virginia*

In October 1864, in retribution for the murder of one of his staff officers, Union General Philip Sheridan ordered the burning of all houses within fives miles of this Shenandoah Valley village. He calmed down and changed his mind, however, and ordered instead the taking of all able-bodied men in the area as prisoners of war.

Decorations

The Civil War saw the creation of the first individual military decorations to award gallantry or merit, including the Medal of Honor. Other Federal decorations included the Fort Sumter and Fort Pickens Medals, the Kearny Medal and Kearny Cross, and the Butler Medal, awarded to black troops. The Confederate government was unable to supply medals and emblems for the decorations it planned and instead simply published a Roll of Honor after each battle.

Deep Bottom Run *(Virginia)*, Battles of

The first battle of Deep Bottom Run, Virginia, was a Union operation to draw off Southern troops prior to the Petersburg Mine Assault and/or to fight into Richmond, if feasible. Federal units attacked along Deep Bottom Run on July 27, 1864, but stiff Southern resistance frustrated the advance. On the 28th Philip Sheridan's cavalrymen made some gains, enough to draw Rebel strength from Petersburg as planned, but made no headway toward Richmond. The second operation, also part of the Petersburg siege, came the next month. It involved another Federal attack in force on supposedly weak defenses at Deep Bottom. In a series of encounters beginning on August 13 Confederate defenses once again proved unexpectedly strong, and the Union offensive gained nothing significant. By the 20th the North had suffered 2899 casualties, the South probably less than half that.

Democratic Party

The modern Democratic Party grew out of the political organization that Andrew Jackson assembled when he gained the presidency in 1828; during the next three decades Democrats tended to control both the presidency and Congress. Although the party was fairly well united in its belief in states' rights and limited central government, its varied supporters did not agree on much else. Particularly divisive was the issue of slavery, and despite the efforts of leading Democrats to work out compromises, the party was clearly splitting into Northern and Southern wings. In 1860 the Northerners nominated Stephen A. Douglas, but the Southern Democrats went off and nominated John C. Breckinridge. This allowed the candidate of the recently formed Republican Party, Abraham Lincoln, to gain the presidency. During the war, 'Peace Democrats' opposed Lincoln and the war, while 'War Democrats' supported both. With the end of the war and the institution of Reconstruction policies by Republicans, the South in general adopted the Democratic Party as its own, giving rise to a 'Solid (*i.e.*, solidly Democratic) South' that would survive until the 1970s.

Denver, James William *(1817-1892)* **Union general.**

By 1861 he had been a lawyer, newspaper editor, California legislator, and Kansas Territory Representative and governor. He held commands in Kansas and the Army of the Tennessee and fought at Shiloh and Corinth, resigning in March 1863. Denver, Colorado was named after him.

Departments

Both Union and Confederate armies organized territory into departments, generally naming their field armies after the departments they operated in. A department could consist of all or part of a single state (Department of Maryland); a group of states (Department of New England); a broad geographical area (Department of the West); or a key city or region (Department of Norfolk, Department of the Potomac). Departments were grouped into larger territorial units called divisions.

Desertions

Wartime desertions were numerous on both sides as a result of inadequate food and clothing, the impoverishment of soldiers' families, the Union bounty system (*See* BOUNTY JUMPERS), and, among the Confederates, the inevitability of defeat. Neither conscription nor amnesties on both sides were able to solve the manpower problem: Union desertions totalled 268,000 men, while Confederate absenteeism rose steadily, an estimated two-thirds of Southern soldiers having abandoned their ranks by 1864.

Devall's Bluff, *Arkansas*

Several minor actions were fought at this place on the White River. On July 6, 1862, 2000 Federal troops broke up a body of 400 Confederate cavalry, inflicting more than 80 casualties. In early January 1863 about 10,000 Federals advanced westward up the White River while Union cavalry approached from the opposite direction, a pincer operation that yielded both supplies and prisoners.

Devens, Charles *(1820-1891)* **Union general.**

A Harvard-educated lawyer and Massachusetts public official, Devens was a commander in the Army of the Potomac. He was wounded at Ball's Bluff, Fair Oaks and Chancellorsville, fought at Fredericksburg and Cold Harbor, and led the advance on Richmond. Camp Devens, Massachusetts, is named for him.

Dewey, George *(1837-1917)* **Union naval officer.**

This Vermont-born Annapolis graduate held junior commands on the old side-wheeler *Mississippi* at New Orleans and Port Hudson, on Farragut's lower Mississippi flagship *Monongahela*, and on the *Colorado* at Fort Fisher. He later achieved international fame by his great victory at Manila Bay in 1898.

'Dictator'

The Union army used this 13-inch seacoast mortar in the siege of Petersburg in 1864. The Dictator could sent a 200-pound projectile a maximum 4325 yards. From July 9 to 31, 1864, it sent 45 rounds into the Petersburg lines from its flatcar mount on the Petersburg & City Point Railroad.

Divers, Bridget **Union Army nurse.**

This vigorous Irishwoman accompanied her husband to war with the 1st Michigan Cavalry. A vivandière, nurse, and Sanitary Commission agent, 'Michigan Bridget' fre

A captured Union deserter is hanged outside Petersburg in June 1864. Despite the threat of such punishment the rate of desertion in both armies mounted steadily.

The Dictator, the big flatcar-mounted Union mortar used in the siege of Petersburg.

quently fought with her regiment and at Cedar Creek rode through enemy lines.

Dix, Dorothea Lynde (1802-1887)
Social reformer.

She reformed the treatment of the insane, establishing many state hospitals for their care. Superintendent of Women Nurses throughout the war, she hired and closely supervised female nurses. Her authoritarian style, lack of administrative experience, and broad interpretation of her duties made her a controversial figure.

Dorothea Dix began her crusade to reform treatment of the insane in the 1840s when she wrote an influential memorial about the subject to the Massachusetts legislature.

Dix, John Adams (1798-1879)
Union secretary of the treasury and general.

Dix was a powerful lawyer and Democratic force in New York. As Lincoln's secretary of the treasury (January-March 1861) he laid a sound basis for financing the war and issued the American Flag Dispatch (See). Commissioned a major general, he later commanded VII Corps and the Departments of Virginia and of the East.

'Dixie'

The origins of this common name for the South are obscure. The song of this title was composed by Daniel Emmett, a minstrel and son of an Ohio abolitionist, who first performed it in New York in 1859. The Confederacy appropriated 'Dixie' as a war song, first playing it officially at Jefferson Davis's inauguration in February 1861. The song was also popular in the North. Indeed, it was reported to have been one of President Abraham Lincoln's favorite melodies.

Dodge, Grenville Mellen (1831-1916) Union general.

A Massachusetts native, he was an Iowa engineer and merchant whose important contributions to the Federal army included construction of numerous bridges and railroads. Dodge held a series of commands in the Armies of Southwest Missouri and the Tennessee. He was wounded at both Pea Ridge and Atlanta.

Donelson, Daniel Smith (1801-1863) Confederate general.

A West Point graduate, Donelson was a Tennessee planter and secessionist legislator who built Fort Donelson (See) while in the provisional army. As a brigadier general he led brigades in West Virginia and at Perryville, Stone's River, and Shelbyville before commanding the Department of East Tennessee. Sources disagree on the place and circumstances of his death.

Double Shotting

In a crisis the charge of canister, grape, or even solid shot fired from an artillery piece could be doubled. 'Double shot those guns and give 'em hell,' General Zachary Taylor was said to have ordered Captain Braxton Bragg at the Mexican War Battle of Buena Vista in 1847.

Doubleday, Abner (1819-1893)
Union general.

This Mexican and Seminole Wars veteran aimed the Federals' first shot from Fort Sumter. He won successive promotions through the Shenandoah Valley Campaign of Jackson, Second Bull Run, South Mountain, Antietam, and Fredericksburg. At Gettysburg he led John Reynolds's corps after the latter was killed, but, failing to get the permanent command, he served out the war in administration. Historians agree that Doubleday had nothing of any significance to do with baseball, although he is popularly credited with 'inventing' the game in 1839.

Douglas, Stephen Arnold (1813-1861) Statesman.

Born in Vermont, he was a Democratic Senator from Illinois whose brilliant oratory made him the nation's foremost advocate of compromise in the prewar years. He was, along with Henry Clay, instrumental in confecting the Compromise of 1850, and his chairmanship of the Committee on Territories put him at the heart of the national debate on slavery; he articulated the doctrine of popular sovereignty (See) during the Kansas-

Stephen A. Douglas, one of the few truly great US statesmen of the prewar era.

Born a slave, Frederick Douglass ended his exemplary career as US minister to Haiti.

Nebraska Act debates (1854). Although he won a Senate race against Lincoln in 1858, their debates propelled his unknown opponent to national prominence. After losing the 1860 presidential race Douglas made public shows of support for Lincoln, finally abandoning his compromise stance after the attack on Fort Sumter and endorsing the president's call for volunteers. He died of typhoid fever on a northwestern tour to rally support for the war.

Douglass, Frederick (c. 1817-1895)
Abolitionist.

Douglass was born into slavery as Frederick Augustus Washington Bailey. Having been taught to read by his master's wife, he escaped in 1838, becoming a Massachusetts Anti-Slavery Society lecturer. He published an autobiography in 1845, then, famous and fearful of arrest as a fugitive slave, went to England, returning in 1847 to buy his freedom and found the abolitionist paper *North Star*. Douglass persuaded Lincoln to allow blacks to fight in the Civil War and personally recruited black troops. The most famous black man of his age, Douglass remained a powerful champion of civil rights until his death in 1895.

Draft Riots

In August 1862 President Lincoln authorized states to fill their enlistment quotas with draftees if there were not enough volunteers. This led to some unrest in the North, but nothing like what happened after the Enrollment Act of March 3, 1863, which mandated the three-year enlistment of all able-bodied men between 20 and 45. The bill also provided that those who had the money could buy their way out of service. It was largely this provision that touched off the ensuing wave of riots.

In New York City, soon after the first draft drawing, resentment boiled over into a four-day riot that began on July 12, 1863. A mob of over 50,000 people, most of them Irish working men, swarmed into the city draft office, setting it afire and nearly killing its super-

intendent. Over the next days the rioters burned an evacuated black orphanage and the offices of Horace Greeley's pro-war *Tribune*. Increasingly, the violence was directed toward blacks, who were attacked and killed at random, but the rioters also burned and looted businesses, beat to death a Union colonel, and assaulted the home of the mayor. At length Federal troops quelled the mob, leaving over 1000 dead and wounded in the darkest homefront episode of the war and the worst race riot in American history. Less serious riots broke out in Boston and other towns in the East and in Ohio.

Dragoon

The term denotes a cavalryman who dismounts to fight. With some exceptions, American cavalry fought dragoon-style – that is to say, essentially as mounted infantry – during the Civil War.

The Supreme Court's decision in the 1857 Dred Scott case outraged many Northerners.

Drayton, Thomas Fenwick (1808-1891) **Confederate general.**

A South Carolina planter and legislator with substantial previous army experience, Drayton proved an ineffectual field commander. He directed the defense of Port Royal, led brigades at Second Bull Run, South Mountain, and Antietam, and, after brief court martial duty, assumed various commands in both Arkansas and Texas.

Dred Scott Decision

Scott was a slave whose Missouri master took him (from 1834 to 1838) both to Illinois, a free

Federal troops open fire on the mob during the 1862 New York City draft riot.

state, and to the Wisconsin Territory, where the Missouri Compromise prohibited slavery. Back in Missouri in 1846, Scott sued for his freedom, arguing that residence in free territory had annulled his enslavement. In *Scott v. Sandford* (1857) the Supreme Court ruled against Scott. Its major holdings, articulated in Chief Justice Roger B. Taney's majority opinion, were that slaves were not citizens and were not entitled to sue in US courts, and that Congress could not prohibit slavery in territories – which in effect meant that the Missouri Compromise of 1820 was unconstitutional. The Court's inflammatory endorsement of slavery in this decision hastened the coming of the Civil War.

Drewry's Bluff (*Virginia*), Battle of

As part of Ulysses S. Grant's overall plan to win the war in the summer of 1864, Federal General Benjamin Butler was ordered to take his Army of the James up the Virginia peninsula between the James and Appomattox rivers toward Richmond. Butler began landing his army from the James on May 5. At that point Richmond was highly vulnerable to attack, but Butler moved cautiously and ponderously as P. G. T. Beauregard organized Southern resistance. Arriving at the defenses of Drewry's Bluff, Butler spent the 15th arranging his own defenses – notably, for the first time in war, wire entanglements made out of scavenged telegraph wire. In a full-scale battle on the 16th the entanglements worked quite well, but Butler nevertheless ordered a retreat well before it was clear that he was actually beaten. The result was that Beauregard was able to keep Butler's army bottled up on the peninsula for the rest of the campaign.

Dumfries Raid of Stuart

This was the last and most elaborate of several raids by Confederate cavalry leader J. E. B. Stuart against supply lines of the Army

of the Potomac under Ambrose Burnside. Stuart left Fredericksburg, Virginia, with 1800 men and four guns on December 26, 1862, and headed east. His columns attacked a Union garrison at Dumfries and overran enemy camps at Occoquan, meanwhile skirmishing and stealing horses and supplies. Capturing a Union telegraph at Burke's Station, Stuart sent a cable to Washington complaining about the quality of captured mules. He rejoined Robert E. Lee on the 31st, not long after the Battle of Fredericksburg, with some 200 captured prisoners, many horses, and other equipment.

Dupont, Samuel Francis (1803-1865) **Union admiral.**

Born in New Jersey, DuPont was a career naval officer. The first commander of the South Atlantic Blockading Squadron, he enforced the blockade in 13 of 14 stations, capturing Port Royal (*See*) in November 1861, seizing ships, forts, and islands, occupying the Georgia sounds, and taking Jacksonville and St. Augustine. DuPont retired after suffering the worst Union naval setback of the war in his assault on the Charleston harbor forts in April 1863.

Dutch Gap Canal

In the summer of 1864, as part of Ulysses Grant's advance on Richmond, General B. F. Butler ordered a canal to be cut at Dutch Gap, Virginia, to enable Union gunboats to bypass Confederate water batteries on the James River. Black troops were assigned most of the work. They completed the canal only in April 1865, too late to be used militarily and one more of Butler's dubious achievements.

Dyer Projectile

Made of cast iron, this 3-inch explosive projectile carried a corrugated cap at the tip that channeled flame from the propellant charge to ignite the fuse.

Early, Jubal Anderson (1816-1894) **Confederate general.**

Early was a Virginia-born West Point graduate, lawyer, and state legislator. Nicknamed 'Old Jube' or 'Jubilee,' he held commands in all the 1861-64 campaigns of the Army of Northern Virginia, after June 1864 leading an independent corps in Early's Washington Raid (*See*) and raids in the Shenandoah Valley. Defeated by Philip Sheridan and routed by George Custer at Waynesboro in March 1865, he lost his command.

Early's Washington Raid

In the summer of 1864 Robert E. Lee, besieged in Petersburg, ordered Jubal Early and 17,000 Confederates to embark on a raid toward Washington that was intended to draw Union forces from the siege. Early crossed the Potomac on July 5 and headed

The massive (and, as it turned out, useless) Dutch Gap Canal under excavation.

north through Maryland. Washington broke into panic, and an unwilling Ulysses Grant was in fact obliged to detach a few units from Petersburg. On July 11 Early reached Silver Springs, Maryland, on the outskirts of Washington. (During skirmishes around Fort Stevens, President Lincoln twice stood on the parapets and watched as the bullets flew.) Finding the defenses of the city too strong, Early withdrew on the 12th and headed back to Virginia. That in the end the raid accomplished so little was largely due to Grant's steadfast refusal to be impressed by it, but Grant did nevertheless dispatch Philip Sheridan on his Shenandoah Valley Campaign the following month in part to ensure that no such future raids would occur.

Eaton, John Jr. *(1829-?)*
Union officer.

He entered the service as chaplain of the 27th Ohio in August 1861. Ulysses Grant chose him in November 1862 to direct aid programs for contrabands (*See*) in the departments Tennessee and Arkansas. He later became Freedman's Bureau commissioner for Washington, DC, Maryland, and parts of Virginia.

Echols, John *(1823-1896)*
Confederate general.

Echols was a Harvard-educated Virginia lawyer. He fought at First Bull Run, in the Shenandoah Valley Campaign of Jackson, at New Market, and at Cold Harbor and commanded the District of Southwest Virginia and the West Virginia Department.

Edged Weapons

This classification includes bayonets, sabers, swords, cutlasses, knives, pikes, and lances. Even bayonets (*See*) and cavalry sabers, the

Below: Elmer E. Ellsworth.
Below right: A commemorative version of the Emancipation Proclamation.

most widely used edged weapons, inflicted few casualties during the Civil War. In practical terms, a sword's chief purpose was to symbolize an officer's authority.

Edmonds, Sarah Emma Evelyn *(1841-1898)* **Union soldier.**

As a runaway adolescent Edmonds sold Bibles disguised as 'Frank Thompson,' the same name she used to join the 2nd Michigan in 1861. She fought in the 1861-62 Potomac Army campaigns, deserting in 1863; later pensioned by the army, she joined the Grand Army of the Republic.

Ellsworth, Elmer Ephraim *(1837-1861)* **Union officer.**

As a young Chicago lawyer Ellsworth organized and toured nationally with a Zouave troop before the war. In May 1861 his New York Zouave regiment helped to take Alexandria, where he was killed in a dispute. A friend and election aide of Lincoln, Ellsworth was the first prominent Union casualty of the Civil War.

Elmira (*New York*) Prison

Opened in a former Union barracks in May 1864 after the prisoner exchange system broke down, it could house only half its 10,000 Confederate captives indoors. The rest lived in tents, even in the severe upstate New York winter. The death rate at Elmira averaged about 5 percent a month.

Emancipation Proclamation

Lincoln's great proclamation pronounced all slaves in areas still in rebellion 'forever free.' Applying only to areas where Lincoln's government lacked jurisdiction, the Proclamation actually emancipated no one. It did, however, turn the war from a campaign to preserve the Union into a crusade to free the slaves. It also marked Lincoln's abandon-

Marine engineer John Ericsson in 1865. His *Monitor*, a steam-driven ironclad vessel with a revolving gunturret, revolutionized international warship design.

ment of his own hope for gradual emancipation. The Proclamation was issued five days after the Battle of Antietam in September 1862, and took effect on January 1, 1863. Southerners and Northern conservatives were predictably outraged, but support for the Union surged in the North and abroad. The 13th Amendment, passed in December 1865, legalized national emancipation.

Enchantress Affair

The Confederate privateer *Enchantress*, carrying prize master Walter W. Smith and a crew from CSS *Jeff Davis*, was captured by Union authorities on July 22, 1861, and her crew was convicted of piracy. The Confederate secretary of war retaliated by ordering 14 Federal prisoners designated as hostages for Smith and the crew of another captured Confederate privateer. The convictions were overturned, however, the courts ruling that the Confederate crews were not pirates, but prisoners of war.

Enfield Rifle

The Union imported more than 500,000 examples of this muzzle-loading British Army rifle, and Confederate arms agents bought tens of thousands more for the Southern service. The Enfield, the British Army's standard rifle from 1855 to 1867, fired a .577-caliber bullet with remarkable accuracy at ranges of up to 1000 yards. With bayonet, it weighed 9 pounds, 3 ounces.

Enrollment Act

The US Congress approved this draft measure on March 3, 1863. It provided for the conscription, for a term of three years, of all able-bodied male citizens of ages 20 to 45. In fact, because of exemption loopholes, it supplied only 175,000 new soldiers in 1863-64. In February 1864 Lincoln called for the conscription of an additional 500,000 men.

Famed orator Edward Everett was an eminent educator, diplomat, and public servant.

Ericsson, John *(1803-1889)*
Marine engineer.

Swedish born, he moved in 1840 to America. His numerous military and naval inventions included the screw propeller and a recoil mechanism for gun carriages. Ericsson designed the *Princeton* (1840), the first warship with underwater propelling machinery, and in 1861 designed and built the *Monitor*, an ironclad ship with a revolving gun turret. After the *Monitor*'s victory over the *Merrimac*, Ericsson designed other ironclads.

Etheridge, Anna Blair *(b. 1844)*
Union army nurse.

Born in Detroit, 'Gentle Annie' enlisted with the 2nd Michigan and tended Michigan regiments throughout the war, often working under fire and once being wounded. She earned the Kearney Cross for bravery.

Everett, Edward *(1794-1865)*
Statesman.

In his distinguished public service career, Everett was noted for brilliant oratory. His many wartime lectures throughout the North rallied support for the government and were

The final surrender of Confederate General Richard Ewell's corps after the Battle of Sayler's Creek, April 6, 1865.

judged by some to be Everett's primary achievement; the most famous was his two-hour speech preceding Lincoln's brief Gettysburg address.

Ewell, Richard Stoddert *(1817-1872)* **Confederate general.**

Born in Washington, DC, this West Point-trained career officer, one of the South's 'fighting-est' commanders, fought at First Bull Run. As a major general he won victories at Winchester and Cross Keys in the Shenandoah Valley Campaign of Jackson and participated in the Peninsular Campaign and the Battles of Cedar Mountain and Second Bull Run. Despite losing a leg at Groveton, he led II Corps at Gettysburg, the Wilderness, and Spotsylvania. He was captured by Philip Sheridan at Sayler's Creek in April 1865.

Ewing, Thomas Jr. *(1829-1896)*
Union general.

He was a Kansas lawyer, antislavery activist, and delegate to the 1861 Peace Convention in Washington. Ewing recruited the 11th Kansas, fought in Arkansas, and as a brigadier general commanded the Border District (where he issued Order No. 11, which depopulated western Missouri) and St. Louis.

Exchange of Prisoners

Early in the war prisoners were released on parole (*See*). An agreement on the formal exchange of prisoners was concluded on July 22, 1862. Internal policy disagreements and differing policies of successive commanders-in-chief had largely halted exchanges by the time Ulysses Grant assumed command and suspended them altogether, but the South, overwhelmed by the number of Federal prisoners, began releasing them in 1864.

Ezra Chapel *(Georgia)*, Battle of

In this action of the Atlanta Campaign the Confederate commander John Bell Hood attempted to parry W. T. Sherman's bid to cut his lines of communication to the south. Heavy fighting broke out at 2:00 pm on July 28, 1864, and continued until after dark, when Hood withdrew into the Atlanta defense lines, having lost nearly 5000 men. The battle is also known as the Battle of Ezra Church and as Hood's Third Sortie.

Fair Oaks and Seven Pines *(Virginia)*, Battles of

As Union General George B. McClellan's Peninsular Campaign closed in on the Confederate capital of Richmond, Virginia, from the east in May 1862, Erasmas D. Keyes's IV Corps became isolated south of the rain-swollen Chickahominy River. Southern General Joseph E. Johnston decided to attack that isolated corps. The main thrust of the attack was given to James Longstreet, who was to envelop Keyes's right flank, cutting him off from the Federals north of the river.

The plan, however, snarled around dawn on March 31 when Longstreet took the wrong road, entangling his troops with two other units. The Southern attack finally got underway just after noon. Though disjointed, it made some headway, driving the enemy left flank back through the village of Seven Pines (which is the Confederate name for the battle). Then the Federals, with the help of reinforcements sent by McClellan (Edwin V. Sumner's II Corps), stopped the Confederates at Fair Oaks. Johnston was severely wounded in the fighting. On the next day further Confederate attacks were ordered, but in confused fighting these made no headway. By the end, of close to 42,000 engaged on both sides in the battle, the North had suffered 5031 casualties and the South 6134. At midday on June 1 a new Southern general arrived to break off the fighting and take over from the wounded Johnston. This was Robert E. Lee, who would command the Army of Northern Virginia thereafter.

Fairfax Court House, *Virginia*

While Robert E. Lee's main army was invading Pennsylvania, J. E. B. Stuart's Confederate cavalry attacked and broke up two companies of the 11th New York Cavalry here on June 27, 1863; only 18 Federals escaped death or capture. This was the largest of several small encounters that took place at Fairfax Court House during the war.

Falling Waters, *West Virginia*

Two Union cavalry divisions attacked a Confederate rearguard here on July 14, 1863, during Lee's retreat from Gettysburg. Henry Heth, the Rebel commander, managed to withdraw in fair order, even though he lost two guns and some 500 stragglers.

Farmville and High Bridge, *Virginia*

As the Confederate General James Longstreet retreated toward Farmville on the night of April 6, 1865, remnants of Richard Ewell's and Richard Anderson's beaten corps crossed the Appomattox River at nearby High Bridge (actually two bridges, one for the railroad and the other for wagons). William Mahone, commanding the covering division, waited too long to order the burning of the bridges, and Union troops rushed across, speeding the pursuit that ended on April 9 with Lee's surrender at Appomattox.

Farnsworth, Elon John *(1837-1863)* **Union general.**

This Michigan native joined the 8th Illinois Cavalry in September 1861, fighting in every operation of his regiment until his death, serving as acting chief quartermaster of IV Corps and later as Alfred Pleasanton's aide-de-camp. Farnsworth was killed leading a disastrous cavalry charge on the third day at Gettysburg.

Farragut, David Glasgow *(1801-1870)* **Union admiral.**

This Tennessee-born career naval officer moved north in 1861 and, despite his inexperience in war, assumed command of the vital New Orleans Expedition (*See*). In a brilliant attack in April 1862 he succeeded in opening up the Mississippi to Vicksburg, becoming an instant celebrity. He won another famous victory in Mobile Bay (*See*) in

A veteran of the War of 1812, Union Admiral David Farragut was a commander bred in the tradition of England's great Horatio Nelson.

August 1864; the ranks of vice admiral and then admiral were created to reward him for his stellar accomplishments. Farragut was by far the greatest naval commander of the war and one of the greatest in US history.

Feint

In battle tactics a feint is a pretended attack with the deceptive purpose of drawing the enemy's attention while the real blow is delivered elsewhere.

Ferrero, Edward *(1831-1899)* **Union general.**

This Spanish immigrant, a New York dancing instructor and militiaman, fought under Ambrose Burnside in North Carolina, led Potomac Army troops from Second Bull Run through Fredericksburg, and joined Ulysses S. Grant's army at Vicksburg and Knoxville. He won notoriety at the Petersburg mine assault by abandoning the black division after ordering them to charge.

Fessenden, James Deering *(1833-1882)* **Union general.**

A Maine lawyer, he trained troops in Virginia in 1861, became General David Hunter's aide-de-camp in the Carolinas in March 1862, and fought at Charleston and in the Chattanooga and Atlanta Campaigns. While on Hunter's staff Fessenden organized the first black Union regiment, which the authorities, however, disbanded.

'Fire-eaters'

These were pre-war radical Southern secessionist politicians. They included Edmund Ruffin, W. L. Yancey, and R. B. Brett; none held high office in the Confederate government or military.

Fisher's Hill *(Virginia)*, Battle of

A battle in the 1864 Shenandoah Campaign of Sheridan. On September 22, after pursuing Jubal Early's fleeing Confederates for two days following the Battle of Winchester, Philip Sheridan struck strong enemy positions at Fisher's Hill with a flank attack, then moved his whole line forward. Early's men were routed once again, but would be back to fight at Cedar Creek. Federal losses were 528, Southern losses over twice that.

Confederate flag and jack flying, the Rebel commerce raider *Florida* lies at anchor in the neutral French port of Brest.

Five Forks *(Virginia)*, Battle of

As part of the Appomattox Campaign, in spring 1865 Ulysses Grant ordered Philip Sheridan to outflank the right wing of Robert E. Lee's defenses at Petersburg. On March 30 Rebel cavalry under Fitzhugh Lee repulsed a Federal advance on Five Forks. In the next two days Sheridan was reinforced, and as Confederate forces under George Pickett withdrew toward Five Forks on April 1 the Union general mounted an overpowering assault that captured over half of Pickett's force of some 10,000. This was the turning point of the Siege of Petersburg; on the next day Grant would break through Lee's weakened lines defending the city.

Fixed Ammunition

In this type of ammunition the projectile, propelling charge, igniter, and primer are a single unit – as, indeed, they are in all modern small-arms ammunition.

Flanking Position

As a defensive posture, a flanking position is one that forces an advancing enemy to expose his flanks or line of communications if he continues his forward movement. To assume such a position a defender needs good defensive ground, protection for his own communications, and the ability to strike the enemy on his vulnerable flanks if he continues the advance.

Flintlocks

These muskets used a flint in the hammer to strike a metal plate and produce the spark that ignited the powder. Although percussion firing had made them obsolete, flintlocks were used extensively during the early part of the Civil War.

Florida, CSS

Built for the Confederacy in a British shipyard in 1862, she raided in the Atlantic from New York to Brazil. The USS *Wachusett* captured her off Bahia, Brazil, in October 1864. The Federal vessel towed the *Florida* back to Hampton Roads, where she was scuttled.

Floyd, John Buchanan
(1806-1863) Confederate general.

A pre-war governor of Arkansas and war secretary in President James Buchanan's cabinet from 1857 to 1860, he led a brigade in western Virginia in the early months of the war. He was in command at Fort Donelson, Kentucky, when Ulysses S. Grant approached in early 1862. Floyd turned the fort over to his next in command and had gone by the time Union forces captured the fort on February 15, 1862.

Fogg, Isabella
Sanitary Commission worker.

She joined a Maine regiment as a nurse when her son enlisted in 1861. Fogg served the Army of the Potomac in field hospitals and behind the lines from the Seven Days' Battles through the Wilderness. In January 1865 she was permanently disabled by a fall sustained on a hospital ship.

Food Shortages

Confederate troops and civilians alike were underfed during the war, a problem exacerbated by the Union forces' destruction of crops, livestock, farm implements, and mills in their Southern campaigns. A bread riot in Richmond, Virginia, on April 2, 1863, was dispersed only under threat of militia fire; on September 4 that year hungry women looted Mobile, Alabama. The Confederate government's confiscation of food supplies in Virginia for Robert E. Lee's troops in January 1864 added to civilians' misery.

Foote, Andrew Hull (1806-1863)
Union admiral.

This Connecticut-born naval officer publicly opposed the slave trade in the 1850s. He commanded upper Mississippi naval operations in 1861, fighting at Forts Henry and Donelson, and, invalided, directed the Bureau of Equipment and Recruiting in 1862. Foote died in June 1863 en route to assume command of Samuel DuPont's squadron off Charleston, South Carolina.

Forbes, Edwin (1839-1895)
War correspondent and artist.

Sent by *Frank Leslie's Illustrated Newspaper* to illustrate the operations of the Army of the Potomac, Forbes stayed in the field from 1861 to 1864, sending back a series of sketches which he later etched as *Life Studies of the Great Army* (1876).

Force Bills

These were Congressional authorizations for executive use of force. In 1833 President Andrew Jackson asked Congress for authority to enforce the tariff, an early sectional issue dividing North and South. Congress approved a force bill in 1870 as a means of blocking Ku Klux Klan efforts to deny blacks the right to vote.

Forrest, Nathan Bedford
(1821-1877) Confederate general.

A self-made Memphis businessman with little education and no military training, Forrest enlisted as a private in 1861 and emerged from the war a lieutenant general. His modest explanation of his military success ('I just . . . got there first with the most men') belied real military genius. Forrest raised and equipped a cavalry regiment and escaped with his men through enemy lines at Fort Donelson. He was seriously wounded at Shiloh before beginning a series of raids in Tennessee which made him famous. He fought at Chickamauga and figured in the infamous Fort Pillow Massacre of April 1864 (*See*). He conducted brilliant operations during the Atlanta Campaign and then swung back to participate in the Franklin and Nashville Campaign. After this spectacular string of victories he was defeated at Selma, Alabama, in April 1865 and surrendered in May. Violently pro-slavery, Forrest was Grand Wizard of the newly founded Ku Klux Klan from 1867 until 1869. (*See* also FORREST'S RAIDS and BRICE'S CROSSROADS).

Union General Philip Sheridan's victory at Five Forks on April 1, 1865, ended the siege of Petersburg and thus doomed the South.

Forrest's Raids

In Murfreesboro, Tennessee, in the summer of 1862, after having served under other commanders, Rebel cavalry leader Nathan Bedford Forrest was given his own command and ordered to raid Union supply lines, which would be his prime task for most of the war. On July 13 Forrest and 1000 cavalrymen surprised a Federal garrison under Thomas Crittenden at Murfreesboro. He captured the entire garrison of 1000 men, as well as supplies worth a million dollars, and wrecked the railroad that was the main Union supply line. Federals under Don Carlos Buell chased Forrest into the Cumberland Mountains and repaired the railroad, but soon the raiders reappeared to cut the line again. By the end of July, Federal operations in Tennessee, especially Buell's intended Chatanooga campaign, were seriously threatened, and Forrest had been made a brigadier general. His raiding in Tennessee would continue through the year.

In west Tennessee in 1862-3, raiding Grant's supply lines during the Federal operations on Vicksburg, Forrest's 2000 riders tore up Grant's rail supply line during the summer, defeated Federal cavalry at Lexington on December 18, and uprooted rails and telegraph lines for miles into Kentucky, meanwhile outfighting or outwitting several enemy garrisons and cavalry detachments. In the process he captured immense stores of equipment and accounted for 2000 Federal casualties. At the end of the year, at Parker's Crossroads, two blue detachments managed to catch Forrest between them. Legend says that when his officers asked him what to do, Forrest replied, 'Charge them both ways!' In any case, that is what happened, his men slowing both enemy wings long enough for the Confederates to escape. The raiding continued into the next year.

At the end of April 1863 Federal General William Rosecrans, harrassed by Forrest during Union operations in Tennessee, sent a mounted column of some 1500 men under Colonel Abel Streight to hunt Forrest down. Instead, Streight found himself under pursuit, chased out of Tennessee and into Alabama. For two weeks the Federals retreated in growing exhaustion. The Confederates were near exhaustion themselves when they found a shortcut that allowed Forrest to get in front of Streight, who then asked for a truce. As the two commanders conferred, Forrest kept his two cannons and his troops circling around; eventually Streight caved in to apparently overwhelming odds. Streight then discovered that he had surrendered his 1466 Federals to Forrest's 500 troopers.

In 1864, after serving unhappily under Braxton Bragg at Chickamauga, Forrest was again given an independent command and began a highly successful series of raids against W. T. Sherman's supply lines as the Federals in Chattanooga prepared for the Atlanta Campaign. Finally Sherman sent some 7000 cavalry under W. Sooy Smith to neutralize Forrest. On February 21 Smith's men were scattered by Forrest near West Point, Mississippi. On the following day, at Okolona, Smith's retreating troopers were overtaken by Forrest and attempted to make a stand. But the 7th Indiana, under withering assault, broke and ran. A series of delaying actions over a nine-mile line covered the Union retreat until 5:00 pm, when the Federals stood up to a Confederate cavalry charge. But this was only a delaying action, the Federals continuing to withdraw in great disorder to Memphis. (For Sherman's next effort to rid himself of Forrest's depredations *see* BRICE'S CROSSROADS).

Fort Darling, *Virginia*

This Confederate battery at Drewry's Bluff on the James River, seven miles south of Richmond, halted the advance of the Federal ironclads *Monitor* and *Galena* in May 1862. Union General Benjamin Butler failed to take the battery in his Drewry's Bluff (*See*) attack two years later in May 1864.

Fort Donelson *(Tennessee)*, Capture of

Union forces under Ulysses S. Grant marched overland from Fort Henry (*See*) to invest this Cumberland River strongpoint, arriving on February 12, 1862. The defenders repulsed a gunboat attack on February 14, then tried a breakout attack the following day. When Union troops contained the attack, the Confederate Commander, General Simon B. Buckner, asked for surrender terms. Grant's return note insisted, famously, on unconditional surrender. (*See* also HENRY AND DONELSON CAMPAIGN).

Fort Fisher *(North Carolina)*, Capture of

In December 1864 a Union expedition under General Benjamin Butler failed to take this strongpoint and shut down Wilmington, the most important remaining Confederate port. Ulysses Grant then assigned General A. H. Terry to mount a second expedition. On January 13, 1865, 8000 Union troops landed near the fort. The attack opened with a naval bombardment on the 15th, and at 2:00 pm Terry's infantry began to advance. Rebel resistance collapsed after several hours' hard fighting. Union troops claimed 2000 prisoners; Federal losses were about 1300, including naval forces.

Fort Henry *(Kentucky)*, Capture of

Grant's 1862 invasion of the South began with the capture of this Tennessee River strongpoint on February 6, 1862. The fort, nearly awash in floodwaters, surrendered after a short bombardment by gunboats under the command of Flag Officer Andrew Foote. On February 11 Grant began his move eastward to Fort Donelson (*See*) on the Cumberland River. (*See* also HENRY AND DONELSON CAMPAIGN).

Fort Hindman (*See* ARKANSAS POST)

Fort Macon *(North Carolina)*, Capture of

Federal forces under Ambrose Burnside captured this outwork on April 25, 1862, after a month-long siege. Along with the fort, the Federals took 400 Confederate prisoners.

Fort McAllister *(Georgia)*, Capture of

Union General W. B. Hazen's division took this strongpoint on December 13, 1864, during W. T. Sherman's brief siege of Savannah. The action enabled Sherman's forces to reach the Atlantic coast, where they could be supplied by the Navy. The Confederates lost about 300 men, including 250 prisoners; Union casualties were 134.

Fort Pickens, *Florida*

This strongpoint on the tip of 40-mile-long Santa Rose Island guarded Pensacola Bay, the best natural harbor on the Gulf of Mexico.

A view of the interior of Fort Fisher after the devastating Union naval bombardment that was delivered on January 15, 1865.

Union forces refused to surrender the fort after Florida seceded; in May 1862 the Confederates abandoned their positions on the mainland, leaving the harbor and navy yard to the Federals.

Fort Pillow Massacre

Confederate cavalry under Nathan Bedford Forrest attacked this Tennessee outpost on April 12, 1864. The 1500 Rebels took the fort with comparative ease. Union forces lost 231 killed and 100 seriously wounded out of a garrison of about 550 men, including 262 blacks.

The Federals charged that the Confederates - shouting 'No quarter! Kill the damned niggers!' – shot many soldiers – mostly black – after they had surrendered.

Fort Pulaski (Georgia), Capture of

In the first action in which rifled guns were used against a masonry fort, Federal forces attacked this fort on April 10, 1862. The Confederates surrendered the next afternoon after a continuous bombardment lasting 30 hours. The rifled guns so damaged the fort that it became indefensible.

A Northern artist's version of the massacre that occurred at Fort Pillow in April 1864. It was one of the war's worst atrocities.

Fort Sanders (Tennessee), Assault on

Confederate General James Longstreet sent three brigades, totalling about 3000 men, against this well-sited bastion at Knoxville on November 29, 1863. The attack failed to carry the position, and the Rebels lost more than 800 men, to about 100 for the defenders. Longstreet did not try again to penetrate Ambrose Burnside's Knoxville defenses.

Fort Stedman (Virginia), Battle of

The action at this Federal bastion was Robert E. Lee's last offensive foray from Petersburg. On March 25, 1865, Confederates under John B. Gordon took the fort and some positions beyond. A Federal counterattack led by John F. Hartranft drove Gordon's troops back into Fort Stedman, where about 1900 surrendered rather than retreat through a heavy Federal crossfire. Total Rebel losses were 3500.

Fort Stevens, District of Columbia

Confederate General Jubal Early probed here during his raid (See EARLY'S RAID) of July 1864, but decided not to order a full-scale attack. Lincoln, inspecting the defenses here, twice exposed himself to fire from Early's nearby raiders.

Rifled artillery of Union forces under the command of General Q. A. Gillmore bombard Fort Pulaski, Cockspur Is., Georgia, in 1862.

Fort Sumter (South Carolina), Capture of

Fort Sumter, where the Civil War began, entered history as an unfinished brick stronghold three miles out in the harbor of Charleston, in South Carolina, the first Southern state to secede. In April 1861 it contained 48 guns, nine officers, 68 noncommissioned officers and privates, eight musicians, and 43 noncombatants, all under the command of Major Robert Anderson. Its significance was less military than symbolic: if the Union evacuated the garrison as the newly-formed Confederate government demanded, it would be a concession to Southern claims on Federal property within its borders – and an implicit

recognition of the existence of the Confederacy. There seemed little hope, meanwhile, that the fort could hold out if attacked; at this point it was encircled by a ring of Confederate batteries and was in addition low on food and ammunition.

Beset on all sides by conflicting opinions, President Lincoln, in a masterstroke of policy, decided neither to surrender the fort nor to initiate hostilities, but rather to ship provisions to the garrison, thereby leaving the critical decision to the other side: either the Confederacy would back down or it would initiate hostilities; in either case, the Union would win a moral and political victory even if it lost the fort. He notified the governor of South Carolina of his intention

and waited to see what the South would do. The answer came as the provision ships were en route on April 11: General P. G. T. Beauregard, Confederate commander in Charleston, sent Major Anderson a demand for surrender. Playing for time, Anderson replied that he would evacuate on the 15th unless further orders came from Washington. At 3:30 the next morning, April 12, a note arrived

Below: A US Army map showing Confederate positions in and around Fort Donelson.
Opposite top: Ulysses Grant's capture of Fort Donelson on February 16, 1862.
Opposite bottom: Confederate General James Longstreet's 1863 attack on Knoxville's Fort Sanders failed, sparing the city.

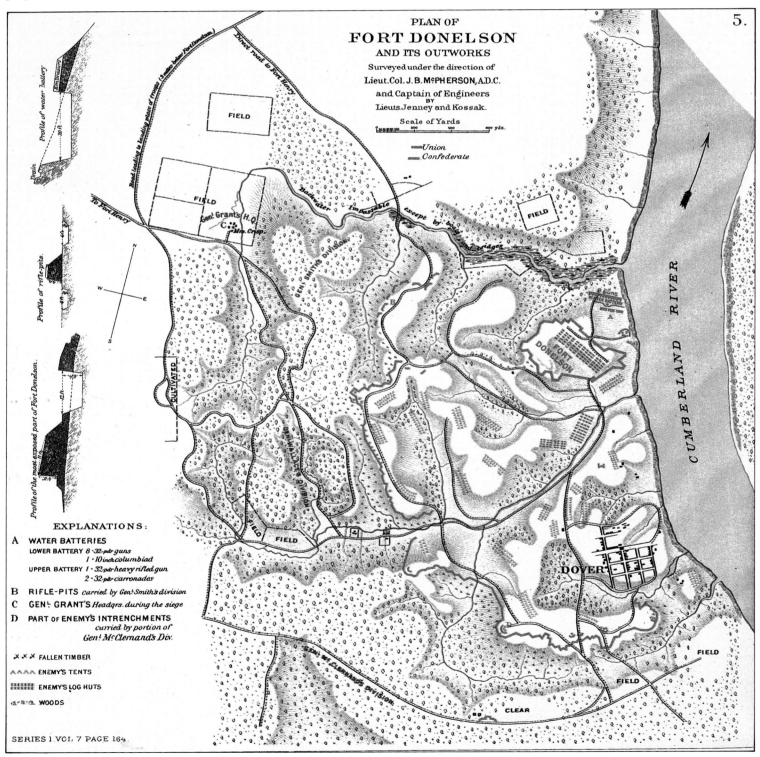

PLAN OF
FORT DONELSON
AND ITS OUTWORKS
Surveyed under the direction of
Lieut. Col. J. B. McPHERSON, A.D.C.
and Captain of Engineers
BY
Lieuts. Jenney and Kossak.

Scale of Yards

Union
Confederate

5.

EXPLANATIONS:

A   WATER BATTERIES
    LOWER BATTERY 8 · 32-pdr guns
                  1 · 10 inch columbiad
    UPPER BATTERY 1 · 32-pdr heavy rifled gun
                  2 · 32-pdr carronades

B   RIFLE-PITS carried by Gen.ˡ Smith's division

C   GEN.ˡ GRANT'S Headqrs. during the siege

D   PART OF ENEMY'S INTRENCHMENTS
             carried by portion of
             Gen.ˡ McClernand's Div.

××× FALLEN TIMBER
^^^^ ENEMY'S TENTS
|||||| ENEMY'S LOG HUTS
~~~~ WOODS

at the fort: 'We have the honor to notify you that [Beauregard] will open the fire . . . in one hour from this time' At 4:30 am on April 12, Confederate Captain George S. James pulled the lanyard of a ten-inch mortar, and the first shot of the Civil War arched into the sky.

The shell burst a hundred feet over the parade ground in the center of the fort. Immediately dozens of Confederate cannons and mortars opened up. Major Anderson did not return fire until daylight, but even then it was only token – he was outgunned and his shells could have little effect on the well-protected enemy batteries. At midmorning the Federal provision ships appeared in the harbor, saw the bombardment, and turned back. During that day's action Beauregard tried the experiment of using hot shot, cannonballs heated red-hot before firing; these set off some small fires in the fort. On the following day Beauregard used more hot shot, this time setting the Union barracks ablaze. The Federals, busy fighting the flames and trying to keep them for the magazine, could fire off only one return shot every five minutes. Clearly there was no point in continuing. Shortly after noon on the 13th Anderson ordered a white flag run up on the stump of a flagpole.

A Confederate delegation arrived at the fort; after some confused negotiations it was decided that the Federals could depart the next day after saluting their flag with cannons. At that point there had been no casualties on either side, but as Anderson's men fired their salute on April 14 sparks from the smoldering fire in the fort touched off a paper cannon cartridge as it was being loaded. The explosion claimed the first life of the war, Private Daniel Hough, and wounded five others, one of whom later died. Then, with the band playing 'Yankee Doodle' and Southerners cheering from the shore, the Northern men boarded a boat for New York, and Confederate soldiers marched into Fort Sumter.

Confederate guns in Fort Moultrie fire on Union-garrisoned Fort Sumter in Charleston harbor, thus beginning the Civil War.

On the next day Lincoln mobilized 75,000 militiamen for 90 days to put down the 'insurrection.' On both sides tens of thousands rallied to the colors and four more states – the last ones – seceded: Virginia, Arkansas, North Carolina, and Tennessee. Despite sustained Union efforts to recapture the fort, the flag of the Confederacy would not come down until the end of the war: the fort was destined to remain a powerful symbol of Southern resistance.

Fort Wagner, *South Carolina*

Federal troops unsuccessfully assaulted this strongpoint guarding Charleston Harbor on July 10 and 18, 1863. In the first try, the Federal brigade engaged lost 339 men. In the second, the black 54th Massachusetts penetrated the fort but was evicted before reinforcements could arrive. Union casualties totaled more than 1500; the 54th lost 25 percent of its strength.

Fortress Monroe, *Virginia*

Union forces retained control of this fort after secession and kept it throughout the war. Early in the war, runaway slaves sought refuge here; by July 1861 a harried General B. F. Butler reported he had more than 900 slaves in his custody.

Forts Gaines, Morgan, and Powell, *Alabama*

These forts protected the strategic Confederate port city of Mobile. On August 5, 1864, a Union fleet under Admiral David Farragut ran past the forts, opening the Battle of Mobile Bay. Forts Gaines and Powell fell quickly; Fort Morgan held out until the end of August.

'Forty Acres and a Mule'

By 1865 blacks were farming much Confederate land seized under the Federal Confiscation Acts of 1861-62, giving rise to the widespread misconception that the Federal government would redistribute land to them permanently. The Proclamation of Amnesty restored all Southern property, except slaves, to its former owners.

Fougass

A form of land mine, it used a strong charge of gunpowder to spray an advancing enemy with stones or metal pellets. Fougass mines were often used as part of the outer defenses of fortifications.

Fowle, Elida Barker Rumsey *(1842-1919)* **Philanthropist.**

Too young to enlist as an army nurse, she developed a private relief effort, visiting camps and hospitals and raising money. She and her fiance founded the Soldiers' Free Library in Washington, DC, and became such famous field nurses that they were married before a joint session of Congress.

Fox, Gustavus Vasa *(1821-1883)* **Union naval officer.**

Born in Massachusetts and graduated from Annapolis, Fox headed an expedition in April 1861 to reinforce Fort Sumter, arriving in time to evacuate the Federals after their surrender. As first assistant secretary of the navy throughout the war, Fox proved an able planner of naval operations.

Franklin and Nashville Campaign

After being forced out of Atlanta in September, 1864, Confederate General John B. Hood did not give up hope of regaining the initiative with his Army of Tennessee. He decided to march north, around his opponent, W. T. Sherman, and invade Tennessee. If he could conquer Nashville, now occupied by Federals under George H. Thomas, Hood reasoned that he might force Sherman to withdraw from Georgia to protect Tennessee. In this strategy Hood showed both his usual aggressive style and his usual lack of judgment: he had 40,000 men left, Thomas had 60,000; and the latter had earned his nickname 'Rock of Chickamauga' for being an exceptionally able and tenacious fighter.

Hood learned that Thomas had divided his forces, some 30,000 Federals under John M. Schofield being at Pulaski, Tennessee, 75 miles south of Thomas in Nashville. In the last week of November 1864 Hood attempted to get his forces between those of Schofield and Thomas. Hood's immediate goal was Columbia, but Schofield anticipated that and pulled back to protect the town; there followed several days of inconclusive skirmishing along the Duck River near Columbia. On the 28th Hood sent Nathan B. Forrest's cavalry on a wide flanking maneuver, but Schofield again anticipated the move and fought off the gray horsemen at Spring Hill.

Opposite top: Black troops of the Union's 54th Massachusetts make an heroic attempt to take Fort Wagner on July 18, 1863.
Opposite bottom: The Battle of Franklin in November 1864 cost CSA General John Bell Hood's Army of Tennessee 7000 casualties.

The Federal commander then pulled farther back to Franklin, Tennessee, 15 miles from Nashville, and ordered his men to entrench.

On November 30 Hood struck in typical determined but ill-considered style: in a repeat of Robert E. Lee's doomed charge on the third day of Gettysburg, but with even less chance of success, Hood had his Confederates march out in a broad front, without artillery preparation, over two miles of open ground toward carefully built enemy barricades. Although they were torn apart on the approach by artillery and rifle fire, a few segments of the advance reached and briefly held sections of the Union line, struggling hand-to-hand with the defenders before being overwhelmed. Otherwise, it was an unrelieved slaughter for six hours. When fighting ended, the Confederates had suffered some 7000 casualties, including six generals killed and 54 regimental commanders killed or wounded; Union losses were 2326.

Schofield pulled out of Franklin that night and marched to join Thomas in Nashville. Hood followed, digging in his army south of the extensive defenses of the Tennessee capital. As Thomas carefully organized his plans and forces, Ulysses Grant wired increasingly imperative orders to attack. When Thomas was finally ready, an ice storm stalled his plans. Grant, exasperated with the inactivity, sent General John A. Logan toward Nashville to replace Thomas in command; but before Logan arrived the ice had melted, and Thomas had unleashed his full force of 50,000 on Hood's 25,000.

On December 15 the Battle of Nashville began, the Federals following Thomas's plan to hold the enemy in place on the Union left while mounting a series of crushing attacks on the right. After enduring these attacks all day the Confederates pulled back to tighter lines that night, on the Brentwood Hills outside the city. On the next day Thomas followed the previous day's tactic, holding with one flank, pounding away with the other,

The camp of the 125th Illinois in Nashville, one of the Union regiments in the Franklin and Nashville Campaign of 1864.

Union General Ambrose Burnside supervises artillery bombarding Fredericksburg, soon to be the site of a major Union disaster.

and finally he worked his cavalry around behind the enemy left. The Confederate line began to collapse from left to right, until thousands were surrendering and the rest were fleeing as a leaderless mob. Thomas's cavalry chased the enemy for two weeks, from Tennessee to Alabama to Mississippi.

By the time the Army of Tennessee came to rest in Tupelo, Mississippi, in January 1865, it had lost half the 40,000 men it started with. Hood, having finally battered his army to pieces against the Union juggernaut, resigned his command. Some of his men wandered off to join other armies, many returned to their homes and farms. This disaster, combined with the humiliation of Sherman's March to the Sea, was a dire blow to the South's sinking morale.

Franklin's Crossing, *Virginia*

Union General Joseph Hooker ordered a reconnaissance in force here on June 5, 1863, to determine whether the Confederates were pulling out of Fredericksburg. Units from John Sedgwick's VI Corps crossed the Rappa-

hannock and attacked Confederate positions at Deep Run, taking 35 prisoners at a cost of 41 killed and wounded. It was a preliminary skirmish in the Gettysburg Campaign.

Fraternization

Informal truces between front-line troops were common. Opposing pickets often exchanged notes and traded in tobacco, coffee, and newspapers. Even front-line troops, as at Petersburg during the 1864 siege, sometimes negotiated informal truces, agreeing not to fire unless fired upon.

Fredericksburg, Campaign and Battle

After Robert E. Lee had retreated from Maryland following the Battle of Antietam in September 1862 President Lincoln had publicly gone along with the Northern celebrations of victory and the congratulations to General George B. McClellan, commander of the Federal Army of the Potomac. Privately, Lincoln knew better: McClellan had blundered through the battle and let Lee escape with his Army of Northern Virginia. Then, in October, Lee's cavalry under Jeb Stuart had gone on a second embarrassing ride completely around the Union army. McClellan had eventually set out after Lee at his usual slow pace, but Lincoln had seen enough; he relieved McClellan and replaced him as head of the Army of the Potomac with General Ambrose E. Burnside.

This bewhiskered officer (*sideburns* were named after him) was well-liked and was so far successful, having won a string of victories in North Carolina. Even his bungling attacks at the Antietam bridge had been interpreted as a success. Burnside himself, however, doubted his own ability to lead a major army in a major campaign, and events would more than confirm those doubts. He would end the war still popular and with a fine career in politics ahead of him, but history

would remember him as one of the most incompetent generals of all time.

Burnside's strategy for the Army of the Potomac was simply to make straight for the Confederate capital of Richmond, en route occupying Fredericksburg, Virginia, on the Rappahannock River. It was there that Lee decided to contest the Union advance. On November 17, 1862, Federal units began to pull into Falmouth, across the river from Fredericksburg, a day before James Longstreet's command in Lee's army arrived in the town. At that point, Burnside could easily have sent his men across the river and taken Fredericksburg. Instead, he collected his forces and waited over a week for the delivery of pontoon bridges. (They had not come sooner because Washington had misunderstood Burnside's orders, which were typically vague.) During that week's delay Lee arrived with the full Army of Northern Virginia and erected virtually impregnable defenses, along Marye's Heights behind the town, and stretching southeast along the river. Although he had 78,500 men to Burnside's 122,000, Lee awaited the coming Federal attack with visible confidence.

Burnside compounded his initial delay with an incredible decision: noting that Lee was expecting Union forces to cross above or below the town, out of range of Confederate guns, Burnside ordered a crossing right in front of Lee, saying 'the enemy will be more surprised' by this move. Lee's response was less surprise than incredulity: he had the approach covered so thoroughly that, as a Confederate officer noted, 'a chicken could not live on that field when we open on it.' In fact, however, Lee was perfectly prepared to

let the Federals cross, since they apparently planned to make a frontal assault that could well cost them virtually their whole army.

On December 11 Federal troops began constructing pontoon bridges across the Rappahannock. Lee had decided to offer token resistance, posting sharpshooters in the town who claimed dozens of Union casualties

Above: Union troops cross the Rappahanock to begin their assault on Fredericksburg in December 1862. Robert E. Lee's Confederates wait for them in the hills behind the town.
Below: An Arthur Lumley sketch of Federals looting Fredericksburg just before the main battle began. The sketch was not published because Lumley's editor felt that it showed Union soldiers in a bad light.

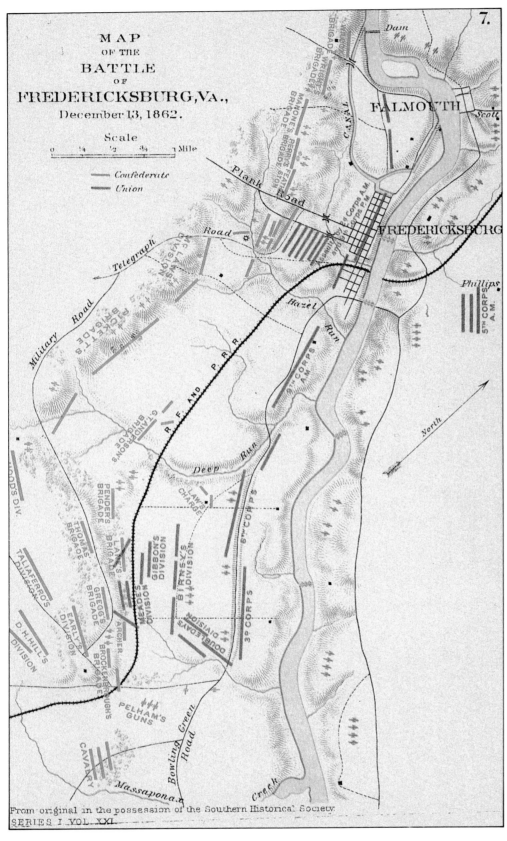

MAP
OF THE
BATTLE
OF
FREDERICKSBURG, VA.,
December 13, 1862.

Scale

0   ¼   ½   ¾   1 Mile

—— Confederate
—— Union

From original in the possession of the Southern Historical Society
SERIES I VOL XXI

A Confederate map shows the disposition of the opposing armies at Fredericksburg.

during the preparations. When the bridges were finished, the Army of the Potomac poured across the river and spent the night of the 12th ransacking the town.

On the morning of December 13 the area was blanketed by thick fog. Suddenly, at 10:00 am, it swept away and revealed to the Southerners rank upon rank of bluecoats pre-paring to attack. On the right, William Franklin's division advanced on Stonewall Jackson's position; Jackson's artillery opened up, tearing wide holes in the Union lines. Then George Meade's division found a chink in Jackson's lines and got behind the enemy, threatening to roll up the Confederate flank; but Franklin failed to press his advantage and a Southern countercharge drove the Federals away. Watching with satisfaction from his command post, Lee uttered his famous lines:

'It is well that war is so terrible – we should grow too fond of it.'

There would be no further chances for the Union that day. Wave after wave of Federals threw themselves at the enemy positions along Marye's Heights, where four ranks of defenders behind a stone wall were firing virtually at a machine-gun rate. No Federals made it closer than 50 yards from the wall. Some units lost 50 percent and more in casualties. Southern General Longstreet later wrote: 'At each attack the slaughter was so great that by the time the third attack was re-pulsed, the ground was so thickly strewn with dead that the bodies seriously impeded the approach of the Federals.'

By the end of the fighting the North had lost 12,700 killed and wounded of 106,000 engaged; the South lost less than half that – 5300 casualties of 72,500 engaged. Burnside had to be talked out of personally leading a suicidal charge the next day. In January he made one more attempt to dislodge Lee, ordering the Army of the Potomac to march upstream and attack from behind. Coming as it did in the middle of a thaw, the operation ground to a halt in a sea of mud. With that Mud March, as it was named, Burnside had crowned a deba-cle with a fiasco. He was relieved at his own request at the end of January 1863.

Hearing the reports of the defeat, Lincoln said, 'If there is a worse place than Hell, I am in it.' Across the North the disaster created widespread gloom. Washington was filled with rumors that Lincoln was going to resign or be deposed; some hoped that General George McClellan would step in and lead a military government, and the ambitious McClellan did not discourage the idea. None-theless, Lincoln pulled himself together to turn back challenges to his authority by Re-publican Senators and some of his own cabi-net. The war would continue with Lincoln still holding the reins, but he and the entire North were deeply shaken.

Freedman

This term described all slaves liberated after the adoption of the 13th amendment, which abolished slavery. Some 4 million blacks were freed.

Free-Soil Party

A political party founded in the 1840s with the slogan, 'free soil, free speech, free labor, and free men.' It supported free homesteads and called for any new territories, chiefly those acquired from Mexico, to outlaw slavery. The Free-Soilers held the balance of power in the 1848 presidential election, but, their influence eroded by the expansion of the southern Democratic Party, their num-bers dwindled, and they merged with the antislavery Republican Party after 1854.

Frémont, John Charles (1813-1890) Union general.

A Georgian, Frémont earned national fame as a young western frontier explorer and soldier. In 1856 he ran unsuccessfully for the US presidency on the Republican ticket. From July 1861 he commanded the Depart-ment of the West, a difficult job made worse

by the flamboyance, recklessness, and corruption of his administration and by the excessive harshness of his policies toward slave-holders (which ultimately caused his removal). Sent abruptly to the Mountain Department in March 1862, Frémont failed to stop T. J. Jackson in the Shenandoah Valley Campaign of Jackson and was relieved of his

In Union service John C. Frémont dissipated most of his heroic prewar reputation

command in June when he refused to serve under his old adversary, John Pope. He was the favored candidate of the Radical Republicans to run against Lincoln in 1864, but he withdrew from the race in September. After the war both his fortunes and his reputation declined steadily.

French, William Henry
(1815-1881) Union general.

A Maryland-born West Point graduate and career artilleryman, he held commands in the Gulf and Washington's defenses in 1861-62 and fought on the Peninsula, at Antietam, at Fredericksburg, at Chancellorsville, and at Gettysburg. He lost his command of III Corps as the result of criticism of his performance in the Battle of the Wilderness in 1864 and saw no further field service in the war.

Frigate

A type of wooden-hulled full-riged naval ship (*i.e.*, one with three square-rigged masts and a bowsprit) that carried its main battery on a single covered deck. By the 1860s many frigates had auxiliary steam power. Although more powerful than sloops-of-war (*See*), frigates were not ranked as battleships, a class defined as having a minimum of two covered battery decks.

Fritchie, Barbara Hauer
(1766-1862) Patriot.

Eponymous heroine of John Greenleaf Whittier's 1863 poem. According to popular legend, as T. J. Jackson's troops marched out of Frederick, Maryland, in September 1862, the 90-year-old patriot Barbara Fritchie defiantly waved Union flags. No historical evidence exists for this encounter.

Front Royal (*Virginia*), Battle of

A battle in the 1862 Shenandoah Valley Campaign of Stonewall Jackson. Feinting at the 7000 Federals of Nathaniel Banks's Union army in Strasburg with cavalry, T. J. Jackson took his infantry across Massanutten

A village of freedmen (*ie.*, former slaves liberated after December 1865 by the 13th Amendment) in Arlington, Virginia.

Mountain and joined with Richard Ewell's forces, which raised the strength of Jackson's army to 16,000 men. With these he struck Colonel J. R. Kenly's 1000 Federals at the Front Royal on May 23, capturing most of the bluecoats. This victory put Jackson dangerously on Banks's flanks, forcing the Union general to retreat northward and eventually to leave the Valley.

Fry, Birkett Davenport
(1822-1891) Confederate general.

This Virginian, a Mexican War veteran and Alabama businessman, joined an Alabama infantry regiment in 1861. Fry was wounded at Seven Pines and fought at Antietam, Chancellorsville, and Gettysburg, where he was captured in Pickett's Charge. Exchanged, he fought at Cold Harbor and commanded the District of Augusta.

Fugitive Slave Act

Amending a 1793 act, the 1850 Fugitive Slave Act provided for the return of escaped slaves to their masters. The Act troubled Northerners with its strictness (inspiring *Uncle Tom's Cabin*, published in 1851) and angered Southerners, who viewed it as interference. Its constitutionality was upheld by the Supreme Court in 1859, though free states' 'personal liberty' laws (*See*) and the growing success of the underground railroad steadily eroded its effectiveness.

Fuses

Explosive artillery projectiles were fitted with three types of fuses. The shock of firing or impact set off a concussion fuse. In a percussion fuse, fulminate set off by impact exploded the charge. A time fuse, ordinarily a wooden or paper tube cut to a specific length, was lit by firing; when it burned down, it set off the charge. Civil War time fuses were, for the most part, unreliable.

Gag Rule

In May 1836 Southern representatives in Congress engineered passage of a rule aimed at blocking discussion of the slavery issue. The House approved such a rule at the start of every session through 1844, but it failed to lay the slavery debate to rest.

Gaines's Mill (*Virginia*), Battle of

Third of the 1862 Seven Days' Battles. On June 27 Robert E. Lee tried an assault on Union General Fitz-John Porter's new defensive position near Gaines's Mill. In heavy fighting Porter was at first driven back, but then his line firmed up and the fighting ended inconclusively. That night Porter got most of his men back across the river, where CSA General John Magruder's bluffing had held the main Union army of George McClellan at bay. The North lost some 4000 killed and wounded and 2800 captured at Gaines's Mill, but Lee lost 9000, one of his costliest days in the war. McClellan, having inflicted heavy losses on the enemy in two days of fighting, nonetheless decided to pull back to

Union batteries of 12-pounder Napoleon guns fire cannister at advancing Rebel infantry in the 1862 Battle of Gaines's Mill.

a base on the James River, giving up his attempts on Richmond. The Savage's Station battle followed (*See*).

Gallatin, *Tennessee*

Confederate cavalry under John Hunt Morgan captured the Federal garrison here during Kirby Smith's invasion of Kentucky in August 1862. Morgan's troopers took 200 prisoners and partially burned a key bridge on the Louisville & Nashville Railroad. Federal infantry chased the Rebels from the town the next day.

'Galvanized Yankees'

These were Federal prisoners of war who had taken an oath of alliegance to the Confederacy and enlisted in the Confederate service. There were such Confederates, too; Rebel prisoners filled six newly formed US infantry regiments in 1864 and saw service on the western frontier.

Galveston, *Texas*

Federal warships shelled this Confederate port in August 1861 but did not occupy it until October 5, 1862. On January 1, 1863, Confederates under John Magruder recaptured the town after a four-hour battle. The Federal fleet resumed the offshore blockade, and the port remained in Rebel hands until after the Confederate surrender in 1865.

Gamble, Hamilton Rowan
(*1798-1864*) Union governor of Missouri.

A Virginian by birth, he was a Missouri lawyer, legislator, and judge who left retirement in 1861, becoming provisional governor when secessionist officials fled the state. Gamble opposed the government's right to draft soldiers as unconstitutional but led the militia against Southern guerrillas, keeping Missouri free and in the Union.

Garfield, James Abram
(*1831-1881*) Union general and 20th president of the United States.

Leaving the Ohio legislature for the 42nd Ohio in 1861, Garfield earned rapid promo-

A photograph of future-President James A. Garfield when he was a Union general.

tions, leading brigades at Middle Creek, Pound Gap, and Shiloh. He was William Rosecrans's chief of staff in the Chickamauga Campaign before resigning in December 1863 to join the US Congress. He was elected president on the Republican ticket in 1880.

Garnett, Richard Brooke
(*1819-1863*) Confederate general.

A West Point graduate and career officer, this Virginian led the Stonewall Brigade under T. J. Jackson in the Shenandoah Valley Campaign of Jackson, Pickett's brigade in the Maryland Campaign, and his own brigade at Fredericksburg and Gettysburg. He was killed in Pickett's Charge at Gettysburg.

Garnett's and Golding's Farms, *Virginia*

This minor engagement in the Seven Days' Battles consisted of holding attacks south of the Chickahominy while the main event un-

William Lloyd Garrison, influential editor of the abolitionist journal *The Liberator*.

The lethality of the Gatling machine gun was never fully grasped in the Civil War.

folded at Gaines's Mill (*See*). In two days of fighting, June 27-28, 1862, the Confederates lost 461 men; Union casualties were 368.

Garrison, William Lloyd
(1805-1879) **Abolitionist.**

This Massachusetts printer-turned-editor sounded some of the earliest calls for an immediate end to slavery, which he called 'not only a crime but the sum of all criminality.' An uncompromising abolitionist, Garrison made innumerable speeches, published the influential journal *The Liberator* (1831-65) and helped found the American Anti-Slavery society in 1832. His reform agenda encompassed women's and Indians' rights, capital punishment, and prohibition.

Gatling Gun

This rapid-fire weapon, powered first by a hand crank and later by an electric motor, saw limited service in the Virginia theater during the war; the army did not formally adopt the Gatling until 1866. It fired .57-caliber and, later, .45-caliber bullets out of multiple (usually six) barrels.

General War Orders

In this extraordinary series of four presidential orders, issued from January to March 1862, Lincoln sought in vain to force General George McClellan into military action. Number One named February 22 as the date for Federal forces to move against the Confederates. Numbers Two and Three reorganized the Army of the Potomac and assigned Union troops to defend the capital. Number Four removed McClellan as general-in-chief.

'Get there first with the most'

See NATHAN BEDFORD FORREST.

Getty, George Washington
(1819-1901) **Union general.**

Born in Washington, DC, this West Point graduate and war veteran commanded artillery in the Peninsular Campaign, at South Mountain, Antietam, and Fredericksburg, constructed entrenched lines at Norfolk and Portsmouth, and fought in the Wilderness, the Shenandoah Valley Campaign of Sheridan, Petersburg, and the final pursuit of Robert E. Lee.

Gettysburg Address

At the beginning of November 1863 President Lincoln was invited to present a few words at the dedication of a new cemetery at Gettysburg, Pennsylvania, for the dead of the battle there. The main address was to be given by the celebrated orator Edward Everett (*See*). Contrary to later legend, Lincoln's speech was not jotted on an envelope on the way to Gettysburg but rather begun two days earlier. At the ceremony on November 19 Everett spoke for two hours. Afterward, Lincoln rose to deliver what was intended as a sort of ceremonial benediction. Neither Lincoln nor anyone else realized at the time that it would become the most famous speech in American history:

'Four score and seven years ago our fathers brought forth, upon this continent, a new nation, conceived in Liberty, and dedicated to the proposition that all men are created equal.

'Now we are engaged in a great civil war, testing whether that nation, or any nation, so conceived, and so dedicated, can long endure. We are met here on a great battlefield of that war. We have come to dedicate a portion of it as a final resting place for those who here gave their lives that that nation might live. It is altogether fitting and proper that we should do this.

'But in a larger sense we cannot dedicate – we cannot consecrate – we cannot hallow – this ground. The brave men, living and dead, who struggled here, have consecrated it far above our poor power to add or detract. The world will little note, nor long remember, what we say here, but it can never forget what they did here. It is for us, the living, rather to be dedicated here to the unfinished work which they have, thus far, so nobly carried on. It is rather for us to be here dedicated to the great task remaining before us – that from these honored dead we take increased devotion to that cause for which they here

A facsimile of the manuscript of Lincoln's Gettysburg Address. The eloquent speech was not at first recognized as a masterpiece, and Lincoln supposed it to be a failure.

gave the last full measure of devotion – that we here highly resolve that these dead shall not have died in vain; that this nation shall have a new birth of freedom; and that this government of the people, by the people, for the people, shall not perish from the earth.'

Gettysburg, Campaign and Battle

Soon after his defeat of the Federal Army of the Potomac at Chancellorsville in May 1863 General Robert E. Lee decided for the second

time to invade the North with his Confederate Army of Northern Virginia. There were a number of reasons for this decision. Even though Lee had just won a brilliant victory, things were bad in the Confederacy and getting worse: Ulysses S. Grant was about to secure Vicksburg for the Union, inflation was running wild in the South, badly needed European recognition had not come, the Confederate government was torn by partisan squabbles, the Union blockade along the Southern coast was growing steadily more effective, and antiwar sentiment was fading

in the North. A major Confederate victory on enemy soil might ameliorate all those problems. Moreover, after their string of victories Lee and his men had begun to believe – fatally, as it turned out – that they were virtually invincible.

General James Longstreet, Lee's second in command since the death of Stonewall Jackson, objected to the invasion from the beginning. Longstreet entreated his commander to

A Confederate map of the armies' positions on the second day at Gettysburg.

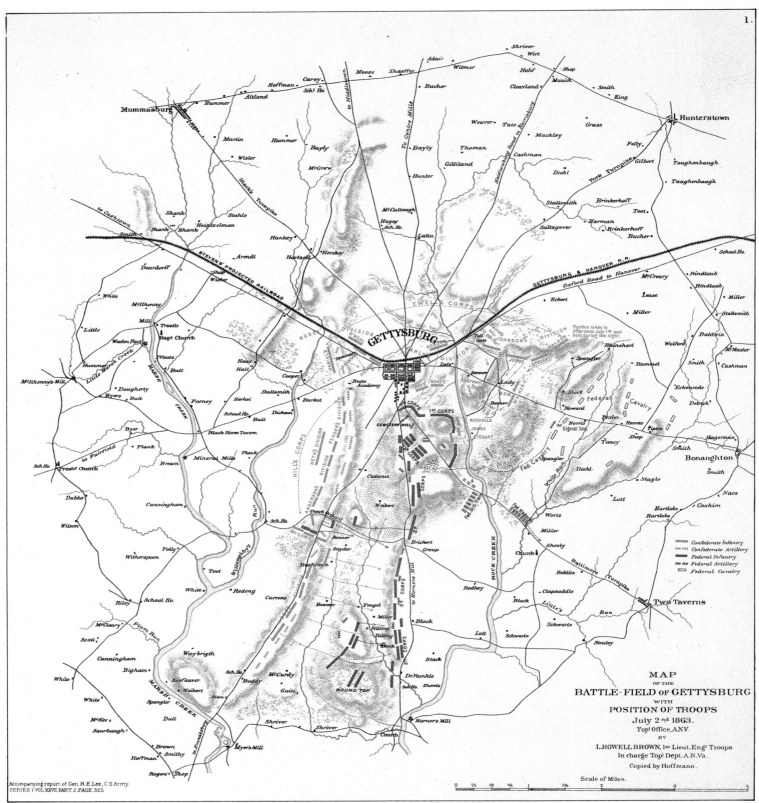

1.

MAP
OF THE
BATTLE-FIELD OF GETTYSBURG
WITH
POSITION OF TROOPS
July 2nd 1863.
Top! Office, A.N.V.
BY
L. HOWELL BROWN, 1st Lieut. Eng! Troops
In charge Top! Dept. A.N.Va.
Copied by Hoffmann.

Scale of Miles.

Accompanying report. of Gen. R.E.Lee, C.S.Army.
SERIES I VOL XXVII PART 2 PAGE 325

Opening engagement.

Retiring with prolonge.

Shelled out.

Position on the 3rd and 4th July.

Leaving the field. July 5th.

pursue a defensive strategy in Virginia and to send troops to reinforce Braxton Bragg in Tennessee; this might compel General Grant to send some of his forces to reinforce William Rosecrans's Union army in Tennessee, thus relieving the pressure on Vicksburg. Longstreet's ideas were sound, but Lee insisted on his invasion plan; his instincts invariably told him to take the offensive.

Thus, in early June 1863, the Army of Northern Virginia pulled away from Fredericksburg and headed for Pennsylvania with 89,000 men. At that point its adversary, the Federal Army of the Potomac, was still under the command of General Joseph Hooker; but after Hooker's humiliating defeat at Chancellorsville, Washington was trying to ease him out of command. Learning of the Confederate move, Hooker put his 90,000 men on the march, shadowing Lee. The two armies marched to the northwest on parallel routes, neither quite sure where the other was, the opposing cavalries fighting a running series of skirmishes that kept Rebel cavalry leader Jeb Stuart's scouts at a distance.

That disturbed Lee, who had always been able to depend on Stuart's detailed reports. Finally Lee ordered Stuart to take his cavalry on an independent ride to assess the enemy strength and position. Intepreting the ambiguously-worded order as an opportunity to ride around the Army of the Potomac as he had twice in the past, Stuart began a wide circle around the Federals, constantly detour-

ing to avoid scattered enemy forces. In the end, Stuart would be gone for ten days, not returning until a battle was in progress. With Stuart gone, Lee was marching blind in enemy territory and would stumble into a fight at a time and place not of his choosing.

On June 28 Washington countermanded an order of Hooker's, hoping the general would resign in protest; Hooker did as hoped. The new commander – appointed over his own protest – was General George

Random scenes of the Battle of Gettysburg, from the initial engagement of July 1 to the beginning of the Union pursuit on the 5th.

Gordon Meade, who had been a corps commander under Hooker. This general was as experienced as any, but he was also irascible and much troubled by a wound from the pre-

A somewhat fanciful rendering of the third day of the Battle of Gettysburg.

The little town of Gettysburg, as the Union XI Corps would have seen it from Cemetery Hill. The road is the Baltimore Turnpike.

vious year. Nonetheless, he would prove to be the first successful commander of the Army of the Potomac. His appointment came almost on the eve of battle; by coincidence, both commanders decided to concentrate their forces at the same small Pennsylvania town with convenient road crossings: a place called Gettysburg.

There, on July 1, Federal cavalry commander John Buford was scouting with 2500 men. From the west Buford saw a column of enemy troops marching in his direction. They were a division of A. P. Hill's corps looking for a supply of shoes rumored to be in town (many Confederate troops marched barefoot). Buford's cavalrymen spread out in a thin line and began firing with their new Spencer repeating carbines (*See*), and the enemy returned fire. The greatest battle ever fought on American soil had begun.

By mid-morning Southern troops were pouring into line. Union General John Reynolds arrived and hurried his I Corps forward to take over from Buford's cavalry; shortly after giving his orders, Reynolds, whom many believed the best general in the Union army, was shot dead from his horse. The fighting escalated steadily, commanders on both sides desperately pulling troops into position. As it had been at Chancellorsville, the Union XI Corps was hit by a flank attack; its men fled into the town, where hundreds were killed or captured in the streets. By evening the Federals had been driven from their original line in the west to a position south of town, on Cemetery Ridge. Just before dusk Lee asked General Richard Ewell to attack Cemetery Ridge 'if practicable.' In a fateful decision, Ewell decided that it was not practicable. In fact, Union lines were still very weak at that point; during the night, however, Meade shored them up into a formidable defensive position along the ridge.

Still, the Army of Northern Virginia had clearly won the first day's battle. Lee decided on the next day that he would attack with everything he had. Over the objections of Longstreet, who saw the strength of the Union defensive positions, Lee ordered Longstreet to make a dawn assault on the Federal left flank at Little Round Top, a hill at

the southern end of Cemetery Ridge, with Ewell supporting with a diversion at Culp's Hill, at the northeast end of the Ridge. On July 2, however, nothing went as planned: Longstreet's attack did not take shape until the afternoon, and Ewell made only mild probes at Culp's Hill. Nonetheless, Federal General Daniel Sickles handed the enemy a golden opportunity when he moved his III Corps out of position on the Federal left to slightly higher ground in front of the Ridge at the Peach Orchard. There Sickles found himself amidst a devastating barrage from Southern cannons, and his men had to fight their way back to where they began. Meanwhile, Confederate forces began closing in on Little Round Top, the linchpin of the Union left. A successful attack on that point could have spelled disaster for the entire Northern line.

Federal General Gouverneur K. Warren arrived on the rocky hillock of Little Round Top to find the enemy approaching and dangerously few defenders at the position. At the last minute, a few cannon arrived to slow the Southern advance. Then came 350 men of the 20th Maine under young Colonel Joshua Chamberlain to man the extreme left position. After the Maine men had expended all their ammunition, incredibly, they mounted a bayonet charge that sent the

startled Confederates back down the hill. (Bayonet charges were rare in the war, and much feared.) The men of Maine had saved the Army of the Potomac. A day of bloody, inconclusive fighting ended with engagements on the middle and right of the Federal line.

That night General Meade assembled his generals and took the unusual step of asking for a vote on whether the Army of the Potomac should retreat, attack, or wait to receive Lee's attack. The vote strongly advised the last; the Federals would wait.

The third day, July 3, began with a brief but intense assault by Ewell on Culp's Hill, the curving top of the hook-shaped Union line. This attack was easily repulsed, and then for some hours the battlefield was quiet. As the Union men watched, Confederate cannons began to appear opposite them to the west, on Seminary Ridge, finally amounting to 150 guns on a line two miles long. Though some Northern generals thought the guns were covering a retreat, the real answer was the opposite. Lee had decided to risk everything

An A. R. Waud sketch shows Union Lt. Col. G. H. Stevens's 5th Maine Battery in action on Culp's Hill. The large gate on Cemetery Hill is clearly visible in the distance.

Some of the Gettysburg dead. Of the more than 51,000 combined casualties, over 7000 were killed. Lee lost a third of his army.

on a grand charge into the center of the Union line on Cemetery Ridge.

Though history would remember this as 'Pickett's Charge,' named for division commander George E. Pickett, Longstreet was actually in command. And once again Longstreet strongly opposed the offensive tactics of his commander. Their discussion ended with Lee angrily pointing with his fist and proclaiming, 'The enemy is there, and I am going to strike him!' Visibly anguished, Longstreet made arrangements for the assault; with tears in his eyes he would ask Pickett to give the final order to move out.

But before the charge began the Southern cannons all opened up together at noon, in the next hour and a half producing what may have been the heaviest barrage in history to that time. Yet this effort to soften up the Union line failed; Confederate gunners were firing slightly too high, sending most of their shots to the Union rear.

Then the guns fell silent, and the Northern soldiers in the center rose to their feet to see 15,000 men of the Army of Northern Virginia marching toward them, rifles gleaming, flags flying, bands playing, officers galloping back and forth, on a front a mile wide and three ranks deep. This picture-book spectacle ended when the Confederates came into range of Northern guns. Ragged holes soon appeared in the line as a storm of bullets and shot and shells tore into it. The Confederate right flank began to drift, and the left flank gave way. Finally a Southern spearhead of two or three hundred men crossed the low stone wall that marked the Union front. Leading was General Lewis Armistead, holding his hat aloft on his sword to show the way. That moment was the high tide of the Confederacy, its deepest penetration into enemy territory, and one of the legendary images of American history.

It did not last long. Federal reinforcements arrived and swarmed around the Southern spearhead to attack with pointblank firing, bayonets, gunstocks, and fists. Soon General Armistead was on the ground, mortally wounded, and the spearhead had turned into a rabble of frightened men, some throwing down their arms and surrendering,

others pouring back down the hill. Lee's great gamble had failed; the Battle of Gettysburg was over. On the next day, Lee began his retreat in a driving rain.

It had been by far the most terrible battle of the war. Of 88,289 Federals engaged, 3155 were killed, 14,529 wounded, and 5365 were missing, a total of 23,049 casualties. Of 75,000 engaged for the South, 3903 were killed, 18,735 wounded, and 5425 were missing, for a total of 28,063 casualties. Lee had lost over a third of his army.

Gettysburg was a monumental battle, but it was less decisive than what was simultaneously happening in the West; it was Grant's taking of Vicksburg, Mississippi, that same week that really doomed the Confederacy. Both armies would meet in battle many times more. But Gettysburg was a terrible blow to Southern morale and to Lee's reputation for invincibility. It would live in history as the greatest battle of the war and as a defining event in the consciousness of Americans, much as the battle for Troy has haunted the Greek imagination through the centuries.

Gillmore Medals

Union General Quincy Gillmore (*See*) awarded these bronze medals, carrying the inscription 'For Gallant and Meritorious Conduct,' during operations in the Charleston, South Carolina, area from July to September 1863. Some 400 medals, which were given only to enlisted soldiers, were struck.

Gilson, Helen Louise (*1835-1868*)
Sanitary Commission worker.

A Massachusetts native, she joined the Sanitary Commission in 1862, working in the campaigns of the Army of the Potomac from the Peninsula through Gettysburg, Cold Harbor and Petersburg, and organizing contraband and freed blacks to provide kitchen and other services to Union troops.

Globe Tavern (*Virginia*), Battle of

Ulysses S. Grant's effort to extend his siege lines westward and cut off communications to Petersburg from the south led to sharp fighting here from August 18-21, 1864. Confederate forces attacked Gouverneur Warren's V Corps when it reached the Weldon

Railroad near this place on the 18th, and followed up with fresh attacks the next day and on the 21st. Union troops held their ground, with the loss of about 4400 men, including more than 3100 missing, of the 20,000 engaged. Confederate casualties were 1600 out of 14,700 involved.

Goldsborough, Louis Malesherbes (*1805-1877*)
Union naval officer.

A 45-year veteran when war broke out, he commanded Union naval forces in the highly successful joint operations with Ambrose Burnside along the North Carolina coast in August 1861. Heavily criticized in 1862 when the James River flotilla he commanded failed to reach Richmond, Virginia, he asked to be relieved of his command. He held administrative jobs for most of the rest of the war.

Gordon, John Brown (*1832-1904*)
Confederate general.

Gordon, a lawyer and mine official, worked in Alabama and his native Georgia before the war. An untrained but gifted officer, he fought at Seven Pines, Malvern Hill, Antietam, Chancellorsville, Gettysburg, and Spotsylvania, and led the assault on Fort Stedman at Petersburg. His wife, Fanny Haralson Gordon, accompanied him in the field throughout the war.

Grand Army of the Republic

Established in November 1866 in Indianapolis, Indiana, the GAR became the most influential of the Civil War veterans' organizations. The GAR often allied itself closely with Republican policies and lobbied for legislation that aided Union veterans.

Grand Review

More than 150,000 Union soldiers, members of the armies of the Potomac, the Tennessee, and Georgia, marched in review past President Andrew Johnson and other high officials in Washington, DC, on May 23-24, 1865. Afterward, the volunteers were swiftly mustered out of service.

Grant, Ulysses Simpson (*1822-1885*) **Union general and 18th president of the United States.**

U. S. Grant became a great commander of Federal armies and went on to be an unsatisfactory but still popular president of the United States. Grant was born in Point Pleasant, Ohio, on April 27, 1822. His father was a tanner and farmer, and the boy worked at these trades until he gained an appointment to West Point. On admission he was incorrectly listed as Ulysses S. Grant (his real first name was Hiram); rather than try to fight army bureaucracy, he accepted the new name and used it for the rest of his life. He was graduated in 1843, having distinguished himself in little but horsemanship. Two years later he led troops in the Mexican War, where he earned citations for bravery. Then his military career apparently coasted to a halt; during six years of languishing in remote posts away from his wife, Grant began to drink heavily and in 1854 resigned, apparently to avoid being cashiered.

For the next six years Grant lived in St. Louis, fruitlessly pursuing farming and other endeavors. Finally, in 1860, he moved to Galena, Illinois, to be a clerk in his brothers' leather-goods store. On the beginning of the Civil War he was quick to look for military command; in June 1861 he became colonel of a regiment of Illinois volunteers. By September he had been made a brigadier general and was assigned to command a district with headquarters in Cairo, Illinois. He first saw action in an assault on Confederate camp at Belmont, Kentucky, that ended with his troops retreating before a counterattack. Soon after came his first successes and the beginning of his enduring fame.

In February 1862 Grant led brilliant campaigns on Forts Henry and Donelson in western Tennessee. It was during his assault on

Scenes from the military career of Ulysses S. Grant. Though not a brilliant tactician, he was probably the war's best strategist.

the latter that Grant issued his famous ultimatum to the enemy commander: 'No terms except an unconditional and immediate surrender can be accepted.' The result was the capture of nearly an entire Confederate army, the Union's first important victory, and a nickname everyone in the country knew – 'Unconditional Surrender' Grant. He was made a major general and given command of the Federal Army of the Mississippi.

The implacable drive to victory that his nickname implied would be characteristic. He was a quiet and rather shy man, awkward in gait and shabby in dress, whose face showed the effects of long struggle against failure and the bottle. He began the war with absolutely nothing to lose and an undiscovered genius. During its course, and despite some blunders, Grant would prove himself one of the great military minds of all time, able to organize vast strategic combinations to outmaneuver his opponents. In battle more the bulldog than the fox, Grant was several times outfought, ordered several disastrous assaults (notably at Cold Harbor), and was accused by his own side of being a

A careworn General Grant at Cold Harbor in June 1864. The errors he made in this battle haunted him the rest of his life.

butcher; but he never lost a campaign, and he captured three enemy armies whole (ending with Robert E. Lee's). The existence of the United States as it is today owes as much to him as to anyone in its history.

Fort Donelson made Grant a hero, but his next major engagement nearly ended his career. At the Battle of Shiloh in April 1862 Grant allowed his forces to be surprised and nearly overwhelmed, though on the second day he struck back to sweep the field. To demands for Grant's removal after the battle, Lincoln replied astutely, 'I can't spare this man. He fights.' Grant redeemed himself with his masterpiece, the campaign to conquer the Mississippi River city of Vicksburg. Its fall in June 1863 was arguably the single most important event of the war. Following that, late in the year, Grant took over an apparently hopelessly besieged Union army in Tennessee and by the end of the Chattanooga Campaign had put the enemy to flight.

Having risen to preeminence among Union generals, in March 1864 Grant received the rank of lieutenant general and was named general-in-chief of Union armies. In that post he planned the broad strategy that would end the war, even though several minor elements of that strategy failed: his own success and that of his friend Sherman would prove sufficient.

Rather than manning a desk, Grant took to the field with George Meade's Army of the Potomac, whose task was to run to ground Lee and his army. Grant would pursure that supremely difficult assignment for a long and bloody year, in the Wilderness, at Spotsylvania and Cold Harbor, at the siege of Petersburg, and finally at Appomattox. In that yearlong campaign of attrition he would lose over half his army before he had hammered the fight out of his opponents. At the surrender of Lee on April 9, 1865, Grant offered generous terms that began, at least, the postwar era on a note of goodwill.

Rose O'Neal Greenhow, head of a Confederate spy ring in Washington, DC, is shown here with her daughter in a Union prison.

His career would ascend from that point in title but not in success. In 1866 Grant became the only man besides George Washington to hold the rank of full general. As head of the army he was obliged to pursue Southern reconstruction measures more punitive than he liked. Becoming the Republican presidential nominee in 1868, Grant was assured of election against the inept Andrew Johnson. But as president, the general was out of his element – aimless, bewildered with politics, innocently loyal to untrustworthy friends. As a result, his eight years in office were marked by the worst corruption and scandal Washington would see until the 1970s and 80s. Though scandals such as the Crédit Mobilier affair and the Whiskey Ring never touched Grant personally, many held him responsible for allowing his administration to

New York *Tribune* editor Horace Greeley's political views were confusingly erratic.

get out of control. To much of the nation, however, he remained America's most popular war hero throughout his term.

After leaving office and mounting a triumphant world tour that he hoped might bring him back into politics, Grant was ruined by a corrupt bank. To regain his fortune and provide for his family, he began writing about his experiences in the war. He finished his *Memoirs*, some of the finest of their kind in military literature, a few days before his death from cancer on July 23, 1885.

Grape Shot

A form of case shot (*See*), grape usually consisted of nine iron balls in an assembly of top and bottom iron plates, rings, and a connecting pin. Alternatively, the balls were lashed together with cord and encased in a canvas bag. Used at short ranges, grape gradually was replaced by the more effective canister (*See*) after 1861.

Gratiot Street Prison

A Federal prison in St. Louis, Missouri, it held Union army deserters, bounty jumpers, captured guerrillas, and Confederate prisoners of war. The building had a capacity of about 500 prisoners, but it usually held twice as many. On at least two occasions inmates set fire to the place.

Greeley, Horace (1811-1872)
Editor and politician.

Greeley founded the influential New York *Tribune* in 1841 and edited it until 1872. The newspaper was a forum for those promoting anticompromise and antislavery views and urging immediate emancipation. At first a powerful moral spokesman for the North, Greeley eroded his popular support by withholding support from Lincoln and opposing conciliatory peace policies throughout most of the war, and then, toward its end, urging Lincoln to negotiate a peace treaty favorable to the South. He ran as a Democrat in the 1872

presidential election, was soundly defeated by Ulysses Grant, and died, apparently insane, two months later.

Greene, George Sears (1801-1899)
Union general.

Rhode Island-born, this West Point graduate engineered and built railroads. He fought under Nathaniel Banks in the Shenandoah Valley Campaign of Jackson and fought at Cedar Mountain, Antietam, Chancellorsville, and Gettysburg. Seriously wounded in the Wauhatchie Night Attack in October 1863, he returned to field duty for the North Carolina Campaign.

Greenhow, Rose O'Neal (c. 1815-1864) **Confederate spy.**

A proslavery activist and well-connected Washington political hostess, she relayed the Federals' plans for First Bull Run to P. G. T. Beauregard and continued to transmit information after her subsequent arrest. After her release she traveled to England as a Confederate agent. She was drowned when she was returning home.

Gregg, David McMurtrie (1833-1916) **Union general.**

This Pennsylvanian was a West Point-trained cavalryman and Indian fighter. Commanding various Potomac Army cavalry units, he compiled a distinguished war career, seeing almost constant action from the Peninsula until his resignation in February 1865. He published an account of the activities of the 2nd Cavalry Division at the Battle of Gettysburg, during which Gregg had won special praise for foiling J. E. B. Stuart's attempt to get behind the Union lines on the third day.

Grierson, Benjamin H. (1826-1911) **Union general.**

A one-time Illinois music teacher who did not like horses, he won fame in perhaps the most daring Federal cavalry raid of the war. As a diversion in support of Ulysses Grant's Vicksburg Campaign, Grierson was ordered to raid south through Mississippi in mid-April 1863; he reached Baton Rouge, Louisiana, within two weeks, having inflicted 100 casualties on the enemy, taken 500 prisoners, destroyed 50 miles of railroad, and captured 1000 horses and mules, all at the cost of only 24 Union casualties. Later, he played a prominent role in W. T. Sherman's 1864 Meridian Campaign (*See*). Grierson remained in the army after the war, commanding the 10th Cavalry in Indian campaigns on the frontier.

Griffin, Charles (1825-1867)
Union general.

Ohio-born, Griffin was a West Point graduate and veteran artilleryman who fought, among many other campaigns and engagements, at First Bull Run, the Peninsula, Antietam, Fredericksburg, Chancellorsville, Gettysburg, and in the Petersburg and Appomattox Campaigns. As commander of V Corps he served as one of the surrender commissioners at Appomattox.

H

Habeas Corpus, Suspension of

Both Union and Confederate governments suspended this basic right, which protects citizens from being jailed without charge. Lincoln, who believed the threat to public safety outweighed the civil liberties issue, ordered the first of several suspensions on April 27, 1861, after rioting in Baltimore. On February 27, 1862, the Confederate Congress gave Jefferson Davis authority to suspend the writ of *habeas corpus*.

Hagood, Johnson (1829-1898)
Confederate general.

A South Carolina lawyer and planter, Hagood fought at Fort Sumter and First Bull Run, participated in the defense of Charleston and returned to the field for the Wilderness and Weldon Railroad battles and the Petersburg Campaign. He was later governor of South Carolina.

Union General Henry Halleck was better at administration than field command.

Haines's Bluff

W. T. Sherman's forces shelled Confederate positions here on April 30 and May 1, 1863, and threatened an infantry assault as a diversion from the landing of Ulysses Grant's main force at Port Gibson, Mississippi, during the Vicksburg Campaign. With Grant's army safely across the Mississippi, Sherman withdrew.

Halleck, Henry Wager (1815-1872) **Union general.**

Halleck, a New Yorker, was graduated third in his class at West Point in 1839; his army nickname was 'Old Brains.' He retired after Mexican War service in California's military government to establish a business career there. Appointed major general in 1861, Halleck restored honesty and order to the Missouri Department after John C. Frémont's maladministration and, thanks largely to successes won by Ulysses Grant, John Pope, and other of Halleck's field commanders, he was briefly appointed commander of the Department of the Mississippi, winning his only field victory at Corinth in April 1862. He was Lincoln's military advisor and general in chief (a position he called 'political hell') from July 1862 until March 1864, when Grant demoted him to the administrative position of army chief of staff. Austere and aloof, and inept as a strategist, Halleck nevertheless contributed substantially to the Union's wartime army administration.

Hamlin, Hannibal (1809-1891)
Vice president of the United States.

This Maine lawyer was an antislavery Democratic state legislator and US congressman who turned Republican in 1856 and was vice president during Lincoln's first term. Hamlin enjoyed good relations with Lincoln while promoting the Radical Republican agenda. His sons Cyrus and Charles were Union officers in the war. In 1869 Hamlin was elected by Maine voters to the US Senate and served in that capacity until 1881. From 1881 to 1882 he was the US minister to Spain.

Hampton Roads Peace Conference

On February 3, 1865, Lincoln and Secretary of State William Seward met Confederate peace commissioners aboard the *River Queen* in the Hampton Roads for peace talks. Their four-hour conference failed, largely because Lincoln, having nearly won the war, was disinclined to negotiate. He insisted on union and the abolition of slavery, while the Confederates wanted a truce to precede any substantive agreements.

Hampton-Rosser Cattle Raid

During the Petersburg siege Confederate cavalry under Wade Hampton raided a Union camp at Coggin's Point, Virginia, on September 16, 1864, and returned with 2486 cattle to feed Robert E. Lee's hungry army. Union forces suffered 400 casualties defending the corral; the Confederate losses were about 50 men.

Confederate General Wade Hampton was one of the South's best cavalry leaders.

Hampton, Wade (1818-1902)
Confederate general.

Born in South Carolina to wealthy planters, he held minor offices and came to doubt the economic benefits of slavery and the wisdom of Southern secession. Nevertheless, he raised the Hampton Legion, which he led at First Bull Run and in the Peninsular Campaign. He went on to fight at Antietam and Gettysburg, and succeeded J. E. B. Stuart in commanding the cavalry corps of the Army of Northern Virginia. He made his famous cattle raid on Ulysses Grant's commissariat in September 1864 (*See* HAMPTON-ROSSER CATTLE RAID), and in February 1865 he was given command of the cavalry of the Army of Tennessee, while simultaneously commanding a division of the Army of Northern Virginia. After the war he was governor of, then Senator from, South Carolina.

Hancock, Winfield Scott (1824-1886) **Union general.**

Pennsylvania-born, he served on the frontier and in the Mexican War after graduation from West Point in 1840. He commanded a brigade in several battles of the Peninsular Campaign, and led the 1st Division of the II Corps at Antietam and Fredericksburg. Hancock commanded the II Corps at Gettysburg and was badly wounded; though the wound troubled him long afterward, he led the corps at the Wilderness, Spotsylvania, Cold Harbor, and Petersburg. He was the unsuccessful Democratic candidate for the United States presidency in 1880.

Hanover, *Pennsylvania*

J. E. B. Stuart's cavalry attacked a body of Federal cavalry here on June 30, 1863, during the Gettysburg Campaign. After losing some prisoners and wagons, the Federals counterattacked and scattered the Rebels, nearly taking Stuart prisoner.

Hardee, William Joseph (1815-1873) **Confederate general.**

This Georgian, the author of a definitive infantry manual used by both sides in the

General Winfield Scott Hancock played a key role in the Union victory at Gettysburg.

war, resigned his commission when Georgia seceded and joined the Confederates. He organized 'Hardee's Brigade' in Arkansas and led a Kentucky corps at Shiloh, Perryville, and Stone's River. Hardee played a leading role in the Confederate fight against W. T. Sherman during the latter's Atlanta Campaign, March to the Sea, and Carolinas Campaign. Hardee eventually retreated to North Carolina, where he was captured near the end of the war.

Harpers Ferry Arsenal and Brown's Raid

After his murder of five pro-slavery men in a Kansas raid of 1856, fanatical abolitionist John Brown began to plan a raid in the South, hoping to unleash a massive black insurrection that would end slavery and take revenge on white Southerners in one blow. Brown believed he was directed to this task by God, who would insure its success. In fact, it was a hopeless scheme from its concept to its tragic conclusion.

Brown's first step was to capture the US Arsenal at Harpers Ferry, Virginia, a large complex containing thousands of muskets and machine shops for making weapons. With arms seized from the arsenal he would march south, gathering slaves in his column, and bring the white South to its knees. The liberated slaves would then form their own nation. He gained approval and funds from several important Eastern abolitionists (black leader Frederick Douglass refused help, saying accurately, 'you will never get out alive'); but in the end he could find only 21 men to join him. In October 1859 Brown set out for Harpers Ferry with this group, not notifying any potential recruits, without rations or escape plans, and with no strategy beyond seizing the arsenal. It is possible, in other words, that he had already decided to make himself a martyr to the abolitionist cause.

On the night of October 16 Brown arrived at the armory complex with 18 men, five of them black, and found it guarded by one watchman, who was overpowered. Brown then sent out some men to seize white hostages and recruit slaves; they returned with

hostages but no black volunteers. By the next day the alarm had gone out and local militia appeared to seal off the armory. In the shooting, eight of Brown's men were killed, including two of his sons; seven other raiders escaped and three townspeople died.

That night, the 17th, a US Marine detachment arrived under the command of Colonel Robert E. Lee and Lieutenant J. E. B. Stuart. Brown had holed up in a small fire-engine house with his remaining men and hostages. The Marines attacked and broke into the engine house, killing two raiders and capturing Brown. Thus ended the insurrection, less than two days after it started. Attempting to stem reaction in and out of the South, Virginia authorities acted fast to try Brown; within six weeks he had been convicted of treason, murder, and formenting insurrection and was hanged on December 2. Six other raiders followed him to the gallows.

If he had in fact desired to shake things up and achieve martyrdom, Brown achieved his goal, not least with his eloquent and dignified behaviour during his trial and execution. He ably played the part of saint and martyr, saying at one point, 'I am worth inconceivably more to hang than for any other purpose.' The aftershocks rolled around the country. Southerners saw in his raid the spectre of their deepest fear, a slave revolt; in the ensuing revelations concerning his abolitionist supporters and admirers, the enraged South saw Northerners endorsing violence against slave-holders. To abolitionists,

At Harpers Ferry, US Marines storm the engine house where John Brown, his raiders and his remaining hostages have been surrounded.

Harrison's Landing (and McClellan's Letter)

After his failure in the Peninsular Campaign, Union General George McClellan positioned his army at Harrison's Landing on the James River, where Lincoln visited him on July 8, 1862. McClellan handed the president a presumptuous letter offering advice on prosecuting the war, articulating a conservative Northern Democratic position and specifically cautioning that adherence to radical abolitionist views would cost the Union the war. The letter probably hastened McClellan's downfall.

Hartford, USS

A steam-propelled sloop-of-war built in 1858, *Hartford* was Union Admiral David Farragut's flagship at the Battles of New Orleans in

Left: A view of Harpers Ferry in 1864. The town occupied a key position at the northern end of the vital Shenandoah Valley.
Below: Future President Benjamin Harrison saw distinguished service as a general in the Union army during the Civil War.

Brown became an idol, though a troubling and ambiguous one. Quite possibly he touched off the simmering tensions that led directly to the war, whose blueclad soldiers would march to the song 'John Brown's Body.' Thoreau called Brown 'a crucified hero.' Herman Melville called him, more appropriately, 'the meteor of the war.'

Harris, Eliza
Sanitation Commission volunteer.

In addition to bringing aid and comfort to Union wounded, Harris wrote vivid newspaper accounts of life at the front which inspired financial donations to support the commission's work. She nursed wounded from First Bull Run to Gettysburg and worked in hospitals in Chattanooga and Nashville in 1863-4.

Harris, Nathaniel Harrison
(1834-1900) **Confederate general.**

In 1861 Harris organized an infantry company in Vicksburg, where he was practicing law. Joining the 19th Mississippi, he fought in the upper Shenandoah, at Williamsburg, in the Maryland Campaign, at Chancellorsville and Gettysburg, and in every main engagement from Spotsylvania through Petersburg, later participating in the defense of Richmond and in the ensuing confrontations that led to Appomattox.

Harrison, Benjamin *(1833-1901)*
Union officer and 23rd president of the United States.

An Indiana lawyer and politician, he helped raise the 70th Indiana, and, despite his inexperience, held a series of commands in the Army of the Cumberland, eventually joining W. T. Sherman for the Atlanta Campaign, March to the Sea, and Carolinas Campaign. A Republican, he was elected president of the United States in 1888.

A view of some of the 22 9-inch Dahlgrens that made up the main battery of the famous Union sloop-of-war USS *Hartford*.

April 1862 and Mobile Bay in August 1864. Wooden-hulled and equipped with a full suit of sails, she could, under both sail and steam, make 11 knots. Her main battery consisted of 22 9-inch smoothbore guns.

Hatteras Inlet, *North Carolina*

A combined Federal force under Admiral Silas Stringham captured two coastal forts here with light casualties on August 28-29, 1861. Union forces took some 670 prisoners and 35 cannon.

Hawley, Joseph Roswell (1826-1905) Union general.

A North Carolinian by birth, he was a newspaperman and Republican organizer in Connecticut. He fought at First Bull Run, along the Confederacy's east coast, and in Virginia, led a peacekeeping force in New York during the 1864 election, and at the war's end was General Alfred Terry's chief of staff.

Hay, John Milton (1838-1905) Author and statesman.

Hay was an Illinois lawyer whose Springfield connections led to his appointment as Lincoln's private secretary in 1860, a job he performed with great ability for five years. With John Nicolay, Hay later wrote the important 10-volume study, *Abraham Lincoln: A History,* published in 1890.

Hayes, Rutherford Birchard (1822-1893) Union general and 19th president of the United States.

An Ohio lawyer and local politician, Hayes was commissioned a major in 1861 and had a varied, if undistinguished, war career, fighting in western Virginia, under John Frémont in the Shenandoah Valley Campaign of Jackson in 1862 and then in the Shenandoah Valley Campaign of Sheridan in 1864. After winning the disputed presidential election of 1876, Republican Hayes kept his promise to Southerners by withdrawing the last Union troops from the South on April 20, 1877, thus ending Reconstruction.

Henry and Donelson Campaign

In February 1862 Federal forces under Ulysses S. Grant prepared for an attack on Confederate Fort Henry (*See*) on the Tennessee River. The Federals arrived outside the fort on February 6 to find that the enemy commander had sent most of his forces to reinforce the more important Fort Donelson (*See*) on the Cumberland River in northwestern Tennessee. The 100 artillerymen left in Fort Henry, faced with Grant's 15,000 men and seven gunboats, surrendered after brief but costly resistance. Grant then marched for Fort Donelson.

The Federals besieged that 21,000-man garrison on February 13; on the next day the gunboats arrived to shell the fort, but the Donelson batteries drove them off. On the 15th, with Grant away downriver, the Confederates emerged from the fort to open up a potential escape route toward the east. At that point, however, Southern General John Floyd called in his forces and, as the Federals closed in again, fled with some 2000 men. It was assumed that General Simon B. Buckner, remaining in command inside the fort, would get favorable surrender terms from his old army acquaintance Grant.

When Buckner requested terms, however, he received the answer that would make Grant famous: 'No terms except unconditional and immediate surrender can be accepted.' With no other choice, Buckner surrendered with perhaps over 10,000 men (records are unclear) on the 16th. It was the first decisive Federal victory of the war, claiming much of Tennessee for the Union and virtually ending Confederate hopes of conquering Kentucky. The campaign also took Grant from obscurity to fame, with the nickname 'Unconditional Surrender Grant'.

Henry Repeating Rifle

This 16-round lever-action carbine used a .44-caliber rimfire cartridge. Union arms buyers favored the Spencer carbine, but state militia forces bought the Henry in quantity.

Henson, Josiah (1789-1883) Black leader.

Born into slavery in Maryland, Henson escaped from a brutal master in 1830 and became an Ontario preacher and internationally renowned emancipation advocate. Having published his autobiography in 1849 and told his story to Harriet Beecher Stowe, Henson was widely regarded as the inspiration for the character Uncle Tom in *Uncle Tom's Cabin*.

Hickok, James Butler (1837-1876) Union scout and spy.

'Wild Bill' Hickok, born in Illinois, was a Kansas stagecoach driver who served the Federals as a Missouri-based scout and spy in a war career characterized by dramatic adventures, arrests, and escapes. He later became an American legend as a fast-drawing Kansas marshal.

High Bridge, *Virginia*

Ulysses S. Grant ordered this bridge on Robert E. Lee's line of retreat toward Farmville (*See*) burned on April 6, 1865. Confederate defenders routed their attackers, however, capturing 780 Federals. A Confederate rear guard failed to destroy High Bridge the next day, permitting the Federals to continue their fast pursuit of Lee toward Appomattox.

Hill, Ambrose Powell (1825-1865) Confederate general.

This Virginian was a hero of the Peninsular Campaign, leading 'Hill's Light Division,' so called for its fast marches, in the Seven Days' Battles. He fought at Cedar Mountain, Second Bull Run, Harpers Ferry, Antietam, and Fredericksburg. Assuming the wounded Stonewall Jackson's command at Chancellorsville, Hill led III Corps through the Gettysburg and Wilderness Campaigns. He was killed in the final assault on Petersburg.

Hill, Daniel Harvey (1821-1889) Confederate general.

A West Point graduate from South Carolina, Hill was superintendent of the North Carolina Military Institute in 1861. After organizing a North Carolina instruction camp, he led the 1st North Carolina at Big Bethel and in the Peninsular and Antietam Campaigns. Prominent in the Battle of Chickamauga, he subsequently recommended Braxton Bragg's removal, earning himself demotion to a minor command in North Carolina, where he surrendered with Joseph Johnston.

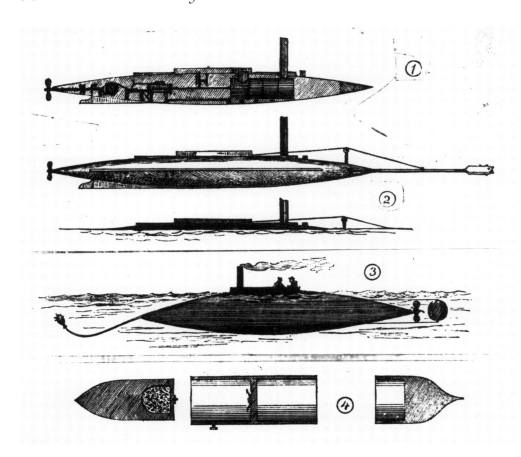

prolific than such fellow war artists as Edwin Forbes (*See*) and Alfred Waud (*See*), but, unlike them, Homer subsequently worked up a number of his sketches into full-fledged paintings, some of them (*e.g.*, *The Briarwood Pipe*, 1864, and *Prisoners from the Front*, 1866) among his most famous works.

Hood, John Bell (1831-1879)
Confederate general.

Kentucky-born Hood was graduated near the bottom of his West Point class in 1853 and fought on the frontier before resigning to join the Confederates. He commanded John Magruder's cavalry at Yorktown and the 'Texas Brigade' at Gaines's Mill, Second Bull Run, and Antietam. As a major general he led a division at Fredericksburg and Gettysburg (where his left arm was crippled) and James Longstreet's corps at Chickamauga (where Hood lost his right leg). Riding strapped to his horse, Hood commanded the Army of the Tennessee in the disastrous Atlanta and Franklin and Nashville Campaigns. He was relieved at his own request and fought with

Left: Sketches of the submarine CSS *Hunley*, the first such craft to sink an enemy ship.
Below: A Winslow Homer sketch was the basis for this engraving showing a sewing circle making clothes for soldiers. Lithography plainly did not enhance the artist's work.

H. L. Hunley, CSS

This Confederate submarine became the first such vessel to destroy a warship when it sank the USS *Housatonic* with a spar torpedo off Charleston, South Carolina, on Febraury 17, 1864. Unfortunately, the blast also swamped the *Hunley*, and the submarine followed the *Housatonic* to the bottom.

Holabird, Samuel Beckley (1826-1907) **Union officer.**

Born in Connecticut, Holabird was a West Point-trained career officer. He served during the war as quartermaster to Robert Paterson, Nathaniel Banks, Joseph Mansfield, and A. S. Williams and, after December 1862, was chief quartermaster of the Department of the Gulf. He continued on active service in the army until 1890.

Hollins, George Nichols (1799-1878) **Confederate commodore.**

A Maryland native, Hollins resigned from the US Navy in 1861 to join the Confederate navy. He commanded the James River defenses, the New Orleans naval station, and the upper Mississippi naval forces. After New Orleans fell in April 1862 he sat on various naval boards.

Homer, Winslow (1836-1910)
Painter and war correspondent.

This great Boston-born artist began his career as a war correspondent for *Harper's Weekly*, starting in 1861. His frontline sketches, reproduced (usually to the artist's disadvantage) as lithographs in *Harper's*, won the young Homer a national reputation. He was less

'Home, Sweet Home' was the title Winslow Homer gave this pensive painting of Union army soldiers in their camp.

P. G. T. Beauregard in Tennessee, surrendering at Natchez, Mississippi, in May 1865. 'The Gallant Hood,' though too headstrong and no match for tacticians of the stripe of W. T. Sherman, was an unparallelled brigade and division commander: 'Hood's Brigade' set a standard to which other troops aspired.

Hooker, Joseph *(1814-1879)*
Union general.

Born in Massachusetts and graduated from West Point (1837), Hooker resigned after the Seminole and Mexican Wars to farm in California. He participated in Washington's defenses and fought with distinction in the Peninsular and Second Bull Run Campaigns and at Chantilly. Promoted to major general, he led a corps at South Mountain and Antietam (where he was badly wounded) and commanded the Centre Grand Division at Fredericksburg. In January 1863 Hooker assumed command of the Army of the Potomac, receiving a famous letter from Lincoln frankly deploring his public criticisms of both the man he replaced, Ambrose Burnside, and the administration, and urging him to 'give us victories.' Hooker lost the Battle of Chancellorsville, however, and, after vainly seeking reinforcements, resigned his command five days before the Battle of Gettysburg. He left the field after the Chattanooga and Atlanta Campaigns. Hooker received the Thanks of Congress for defending Washington and Baltimore against Robert E. Lee. 'Fighting Joe,' a nickname he regretted, arose from typesetters' misinterpretation of a dispatch heading: 'Fighting – Joe Hooker.'

Hornet's Nest

A nickname given by Confederate troops to a position in a wooded area on the left center of the Union line on the first day (April 6, 1862) of the Battle of Shiloh.

Hot Shot

Confederate gunners used heated solid shot in the bombardment of Fort Sumter, and it could be effective in setting fire to buildings and ships. A 24-pound ball could be brought to a red heat in less than half an hour.

Hotchkiss Projectile and Gun

The projectile, designed by Union arsenal superintendent Benjamin Hotchkiss, consisted of three parts: a body, an expanding lead ring, and an iron cup. Upon firing, the iron cup drove the lead into the rifling of the gun. The projectile sometimes gave its name to the gun that fired it.

Hough, Daniel *(d. 1861)*
Union soldier.

On April 14, 1861, Hough, a private in Battery E, 1st US Artillery, was accidentally killed as a salute was fired before the Federal evacuation of Fort Sumter, making him the first fatality of the war. He was buried in the grounds of the fort.

Howard, Joseph Jr. *(1833-1908)*
War correspondent.

He sent *New York Times* dispatches from First Bull Run, but is best remembered for a journalistic hoax: in May 1864 he helped forge a presidential proclamation announcing the failure of Ulysses Grant's advance on Richmond and calling for 500,000 new Federal recruits. Two newspapers printed the story; Howard was briefly imprisoned.

Howard, Oliver Otis *(1830-1909)*
Union general.

Howard, a Maine native, was trained and taught at West Point. Joining the 3rd Maine, he fought at First Bull Run and in the Peninsular Campaign (where he lost an arm at Fair Oaks). After Antietam he led a division of II Corps and then led XI Corps at Chancellorsville, where his troops were routed in T. J. Jackson's famous flank attack. He served with distinction at Gettysburg, Lookout Mountain, and Missionary Ridge, then accompanied W. T. Sherman on his Atlanta Campaign, March to the Sea, and Carolinas Campaign, in the process becoming commander of the Army of the Tennessee. After the war he won more fame as an Indian fighter. A founder of Howard University (named for him), he was its president from 1869 to 1873.

Howe, Julia Ward *(1819-1910)*
Author and social reformer.

Born in New York City, she married Dr. Samuel Gridley Howe (1801-1876), a prominent Boston philanthropist, and with him edited the abolitionist newspaper *Commonwealth*. Although a prolific writer of both prose and verse and the first woman elected to the American Academy of Arts and Letters, she will always be best remembered as the composer of the lyrics for 'The Battle Hymn of the Republic' (*See*).

One of the 'fighting-est' Union generals of the Civil War, Oliver O. Howard was also a founder of Howard University.

Howitzers

Designed to fire at high angles, dropping low-velocity explosive shells behind the enemy's cover, howitzers exemplified the traditional artillery that predominated during the Civil War. Wartime howitzers were smoothbores, usually bronze, and most dated from 1840s. A 12-pounder howitzer, 5 feet long, was 3.67-inch caliber and could fire 6-pound balls to 1500 yards. A battery typically consisted of four guns and two howitzers mounted on wooden carriages.

Huff, John A. (c. 1816-1864)
Union soldier.

A prizewinning veteran sharpshooter, Huff was a private in the 5th Michigan Cavalry when he fatally wounded Jeb Stuart at Yellow Tavern on May 11, 1864. Huff himself died of wounds received at Haw's Shop, Virginia, 17 days later.

Hunt, Henry Jackson (1819-1889)
Union general.

In the 1850s Hunt, a West Point graduate, helped develop the artillery tactics used throughout the war. He commanded artillery units in the Army of the Potomac from the Peninsula through Gettysburg (where he was chief of artillery) and the Wilderness, and he directed the siege at Petersburg.

Hunter, David (1802-1886)
Union general.

Born in Washington, DC, this West Point graduate fought at First Bull Run, commanded various departments and sat on courts martial. Hunter authorized the first black regiment (the 1st South Carolina). Lincoln annulled Hunter's unauthorized proclamation of May 1862 freeing all the slaves in the Southern Department.

Massive 8-inch gun-howitzers are mounted in Fort Corcoran, one of the fixed defenses surrounding Washington, DC.

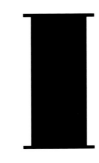

Income Tax

The war was financed in the North largely through loans and the issue of paper money. Adding to government revenues in the war years, however, were various taxes, including an income tax. An August 1861 income tax of 3 percent on annual incomes above $800, though authorized, was never levied. However, a revised bill passed in July 1862 imposed a 3 percent charge on incomes of $600-$10,000 and 5 percent on higher incomes. By 1865 income taxes generated 20 percent of the Federal government's receipts. The Federal income tax expired in 1872, not finally to be reinstituted until 1913. The Confederate government – acknowledging its financial deterioration but angering Southerners opposed to its centralization of power – reluctantly introduced a graduated income tax in April 1863.

Indian Territory

The term defined the area that is now the state of Oklahoma, less its panhandle. Confederate forces occupied the territory through the war, and raised some Indian troops, most notably those who fought in the battle of Pea Ridge (*See*) in March 1862.

Indian Troubles

Skirmishes with Indians in the West drained Federal resources throughout the war. In August 1862 Henry Sibley's Union troops attacked the Sioux after the massacre of 450 white settlers in Minnesota. A year later Colonel 'Kit' Carson's volunteer cavalry moved against the Navaho in Arizona Territory in an operation culminating in the infamous 'Long Walk' – a 300-mile forced march to Fort Sumner, New Mexico.

Inflation

By February 1863 inflation had so weakened the Confederate dollar that its buying power had dropped to about 20 cents. In some places, bread sold for as much as $25 a loaf. The Northern war economy was also somewhat inflationary, but its tremendous agricultural and industrial production capacity meant that supply and buying power never fell critically out of balance.

Irish Bend and Fort Bisland, *Louisiana*

Union General Nathaniel Banks advanced toward Alexandria, Louisiana, with 15,000 men during his Red River Campaign of 1863. On April 13 he opened an attack on about 2700 Confederates under Richard Taylor at Fort Bisland; when the attack resumed next morning the defenders had vanished. Taylor reappeared to launch a flank attack at Irish Bend later that morning, then completed his escape. Federal pursuit was – as were all Union actions in this campaign – sluggish.

Irish Brigade

This brigade of the 1st Division, II Corps, Army of the Potomac, originally consisted of the 63rd, 69th, and 88th New York. Massachusetts and Pennsylvania regiments were added later. The brigade's best-known action came against Marye's Heights at the Battle of Fredericksburg in December 1862.

Iron Brigade of the West

Four midwestern regiments, the 19th Indiana and the 2nd, 6th, and 7th Wisconsin, formed this brigade, one of the most famous fighting units of the war. Also known as the Black Hats, the brigade lost 33 percent of its strength at Second Bull Run. With the addition of the 24th Michigan, it recovered in time to earn its nickname at Antietam. The Iron Brigade was nearly destroyed at Gettysburg, where it lost two-thirds of the 1800 engaged.

Ironclad Oath

A July 1862 act of Congress required every Federal military or civilian officeholder to declare allegiance to the Constitution and to swear that he had never fought against the Union or aided the rebellion in any other way. After the war, the oath was used to keep former Confederates out of authority.

A Northern cartoon implies that Confederates were implicated in the bloody 1862 Indian uprising in Minnesota.

Ironclads

This was the generic term for vessels sheathed in protective iron armor. Both sides used armored gunboats and ocean-going warships, though the Union had a tremendous advantage in technical resources and production capacity. Probably the best-known American ironclad was USS *Monitor*, which fought a famous duel with the Confederate *Merrimac* in March 1862. Ironclads were not an American invention, the first armored ship being the French frigate *Gloire*, launched in 1858, but the Americans were the first to test the type in battle. Because ironclads proved nearly impervious to most naval (though not shore-based) gunfire, they for a time upset the traditional balance between offense and defense in naval warfare. That balance was restored only after the war with the development of high-velocity armor-piercing munitions. By then, the age of the 'wooden walls' had vanished forever.

Island No. 10

See NEW MADRID AND ISLAND NO. 10.

Iuka (*Mississippi*), Battle of

In mid-September 1862 Confederates under Sterling Price had occupied Iuka. U. S. Grant, Federal commander in the area, ordered converging forces under Edward Ord and William Rosecrans to catch Price in a pincers. The day before the intended Federal attack, however, Price moved out and struck Rosecrans; Ord, who was within supporting distance, did not hear the battle because of an 'acoustic shadow.' But Price was nevertheless outnumbered and withdrew from the town, ending plans for a contemplated Confederate invasion of Tennessee.

Iverson, Alfred (*1829-1911*)
Confederate general.

This Georgia veteran, lawyer, and businessman fought in the Seven Days' Battles, at South Mountain, and at Antietam and led a brigade at Fredericksburg, Chancellorsville, Gettysburg, and in the Atlanta Campaign, where he captured Federal General George Stoneman at Hillsboro in July 1864.

Aground on the shoals of a Louisiana river, the Union ironclad *Barritaria* is harassed by gleeful Confederate marksmen.

Jackson, *Mississippi*

Situated, as it was, due east of Vicksburg, and a base for Rebel forces, Jackson played a key role in Ulysses S. Grant's Vicksburg Campaign. After the fall of Vicksburg, Union forces under W. T. Sherman besieged the town from July 9 to 16, 1863. Rebels under J. E. Johnston withdrew without giving battle. Smaller actions were fought in or near the Mississippi capital in February and July 1864.

Jackson, *Tennessee*

Confederate cavalry under Nathan B. Forrest threatened this outpost in December 1862. With infantry reinforcements, Union troops attacked on December 19 and drove Forrest away. The Federals estimated Rebel losses at 73 and reported six casualties, including one killed, of their own. This action, also known as Salem Church, is part of Forrest's Second Raid (December-January 1862-63).

Jackson, Thomas Jonathan ('Stonewall') *(1824-1863)*
Confederate general.

Gaining his nickname from an heroic stand he and his troops made at the First Bull Run Battle, Stonewall Jackson went on to become the brilliant architect of the 1862 Shenandoah Valley Campaign that bears his name and the right-hand man of General Robert E. Lee. Born in Virginia, Jackson was graduated from West Point in 1846, fought in the Mexican War, and taught for a decade at Virginia Military Institute. Throwing his lot with the Confederacy at the beginning of the Civil War, he commanded a brigade at First Bull Run.

In 1862, now a major general, he led his fast-moving troops in the Shenandoah Valley Campaign of Jackson, a diversionary operation that would take him into military history. Afterward, joining his forces to Lee's in the Peninsular Campaign, Jackson became a corps commander in the Army of Northern Virginia. Though, because of his exhaustion, he impeded Confederate operations in the Seven Days Battles, he hit his stride again at the Second Bull Run Battle of August 1862, where he outwitted and outfought more numerous Federal forces. Further distinc-

tions followed in the great battles fought at Antietam in September and Fredericksburg in December, though Jackson did not play a central role in either.

His most remarkable and final achievement with Lee's army was at Chancellorsville in early May 1863, when Jackson marched his army secretly across the front of the Army of the Potomac and struck a devastating blow on the Union right wing. On the night of May 2, however, Jackson was wounded by his own men as he rode back from a reconnaissance. After losing an arm, Jackson steadily declined and died of pneumonia on May 10. Eccentric, obsessively pious, and ambitious, Jackson would be remembered as one of the handful of great generals in the war, a man who was always able to live up to his own primary maxim of strategy: 'Always mystify, mislead, and surprise the enemy.'

Jacksonville, *Florida*

Union forces, including black troops under Theodore Higginson (*See*), occupied this port town in late March 1863. The Federals raided upriver, taking a handful of prisoners and some horses and cotton, then burned part of the town before withdrawing on March 31.

James, Union Army of the

Organized in April 1864, it was formed by Ulysses S. Grant to threaten Richmond from south of the James River while the Army of the Potomac moved against Robert E. Lee in the north. He chose General B. F. Butler to command its two corps and single cavalry division, a total of about 20,000 troops. General E. O. C. Ord succeeded Butler, who had failed to make effective use of his forces, in January 1865.

The South's second-greatest commander: the brilliant and eccentric Stonewall Jackson. His death was a heavy blow to the CSA.

James Brothers

Frank (1844-1915) and Jesse (1847-1882) James served their criminal apprenticeship in Quantrill's (*See*) guerrilla force in Missouri. Quantrill did not survive the war; the James Brothers went on to become among the most notorious outlaws of the western frontier.

James River Bridge

This Union pontoon bridge, said to be the largest continuous bridge of its type ever used in warfare, carried the Army of the Potomac across Virginia's James River toward Petersburg after the Battle of Cold Harbor in 1864. Some 450 engineers bridged the 2100-foot-wide river in the course of an eight-hour workday on June 15, 1864, using 101 pontoons and three schooners.

Johnson, Andrew *(1808-1875)*
Lincoln's vice president and 17th president of the United States.

An uneducated tailor's apprentice, Johnson settled in Tennessee and entered public service in 1830. A moderate Democrat, he was the only Southern Senator who retained his seat after secession. Lincoln rewarded him with the military governorship of Tennessee in 1862 and the vice presidential nomination in 1864. His presidency was besieged by hostile Radical Republicans, and Johnson narrowly survived impeachment in 1868 for dismissing Secretary of War Edwin M. Stanton in violation of the Tenure of Office Act. Johnson was not thereafter able to act effectively in moderating the growing harshness of Washington's Reconstruction policies. He was passed over by both parties in the 1868 presidential election, but in 1875, shortly before he died, he succeded in winning an election as Senator from Tennessee.

Johnson, Richard W. *(1827-1897)*
Union general.

An 1849 West Point graduate, he was a veteran of Indian campaigns on the prewar frontier. From 1861 on, he served in the Western Theater. As a brigade commander, he took part in the siege of Corinth. He commanded a division at Stone's River, Chickamauga, and Missionary Ridge, and during W. T. Sherman's Atlanta Campaign.

Johnson's Island, *Ohio*

A Federal prison camp in Sandusky Bay in Lake Erie, the island held about 3000 Confederate officers by the war's end.

Johnsonville, *Tennessee*

Confederate forces under Nathan B. Forrest opened fire on this Federal supply depot on the Tennessee River on November 4, 1864. The attack set off a panic among the defenders. Fires set by the shelling, by the destruction of Federal vessels and supplies to keep them from falling into Forrest's hands, and by individual looters caused an estimated $2.2 million in damage. For all the chaos and destruction they caused, Forrest's troops never actually entered the town.

Lincoln's successor, Andrew Johnson, was a man of modest capacities who had the bad luck to come into office at the time when the nation was still riven by war-bred hatreds.

Johnston, Albert Sidney
(1803-1862) Confederate general.

Born in Kentucky and graduated from West Point in 1826, Johnston resigned in 1835 only to rejoin the army after fighting in the Mexican War; after leading the Utah expedition (1858-60) he commanded the Pacific Department. A powerful and commanding personality, Johnston was regarded in 1861 by Jefferson Davis, among others, as 'the greatest soldier . . . then living,' an assessment not shared by later historians. He refused the Federals' offer to be Winfield Scott's second in command, instead taking charge of the Confederate Western Department as a full general. Johnston captured Bowling Green, but after losses at Logan's Cross Roads and Forts Henry and Donelson, he withdrew to Nashville, then to Corinth. He died of a leg wound at Shiloh.

Johnston, Joseph Eggleston
(1807-1891) Confederate general.

Though J. E. Johnston began and ended the war with considerable respect, he was largely fated to oversee losing campaigns. Virginia-born and West Point-educated, he was wounded fighting the Indians and in the Mexican War. Named quartermaster general of the US Army in 1860, he resigned next year to take a commission in the Confederacy, and was in overall command at the victorious First Bull Run Battle (though Beauregard spent more time on the scene).

Appointed to command the Department of the Potomac, Johnston was wounded at the

Confederate General Joseph E. Johnston was a fine commander fated to win few battles.

battle of Seven Pines in May 1862 and was replaced in command by Robert E. Lee. On recovery he took over the Department of the West, where his subordinates managed to lose the Vicksburg and Chattanooga Campaigns. Johnston then took over from the disastrous Braxton Bagg as head of the Army of Tennessee, but in that position he could only withdraw – which he did skillfully – before W. T. Sherman's oncoming forces in the Atlanta Campaign of 1864. Relieved in command by the unfortunate John Bell Hood, Johnston ended the war hopelessly trying to resist Sherman in the Carolinas. He surrendered to Sherman on April 26, 1865, the last significant general to do so. After years of working in railroads and insurance, and after a term in Congress, Johnston died of pneumonia contracted at Sherman's funeral (out of respect for Sherman he had stood bareheaded in an icy rain).

Joint Committee of Fifteen

This group, formally titled the Joint Congressional Committee on Reconstruction, was formed in December 1865 to develop measures for the Reconstruction of the defeated Confederate states. Radical Republicans, who favored harsh policies, dominated the committee.

Joint Committee on the Conduct of the War

This Congressional committee was established in December 1861 after a series of early Union defeats, notably Ball's Bluff, to investigate the conduct of the war. The Joint Committee interrogated officers about specific battles and campaigns and became both controversial and politicized, sometimes shaping its findings to serve political ends; but the record of its proceedings is an important resource for Civil War historians.

Jonesboro (Georgia), Battle of

This was the climactic battle of W. T. Sherman's 1864 Atlanta Campaign. After O. O. Howard's Federals repulsed John Bell Hood's forces in an August 31 attack at Jonesboro, Union General John Schofield's men cut the last Confederate railroad line at the town of Rough and Ready, and Hood began evacuating Atlanta. On September 1 Hood's forces completed their evacuation, blowing up munitions and stores behind them. Fighting also continued at Jonesboro, with Sherman's men trying unsuccessfully to prevent the escape of General William Hardee's Confederates.

Jones's and Imboden's West Virginia Raid

In April 1863 Confederates William E. Jones and John Imboden set out at the same time by different routes to attack the Baltimore & Ohio Railroad, a main Federal east-west supply route. Jones, with a brigade of cavalry, carried out his part of the operation, destroying several bridges along the line and at one point threatening Wheeling and Pittsburgh. Imboden, who led a mixed force of infantry and cavalry, failed to reach the B&O.

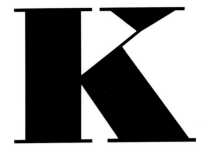

Kanawha Valley *(West Virginia)* Campaign

In September 1862 Confederate General William Wing Loring captured several West Virginia towns, including Charleston, while Union forces were being withdrawn to check Robert E. Lee's invasion of Maryland. After the Battle of Antietam, the Federals returned and drove Loring's small Confederate force out of the state.

Kansas-Nebraska Act

Passed in May 1854, the Act divided Kansas and Nebraska into separate territories and empowered them to settle the slavery question by popular sovereignty, the erroneous assumption being that pro- and anti-slavery settlers would each choose a territory. Undoing the Compromise of 1820, the Act produced five years of political chaos and violence in Kansas (*See* BLEEDING KANSAS) and led militant antislavery groups to form the Republican Party.

Kearny, Philip *(1814-1862)*
Union general.

Kearny opposed the wishes of his socially prominent New York family to fulfill a romantic dream of being a cavalry officer. A dashing leader whose dragoons rode matched dapple-gray horses and whose troops wore distinctive scarlet, diamond-shaped 'Kearny patches,' he compiled an outstanding war record at Williamsburg, Seven Pines and Second Bull Run. He was killed while reconnoitering in September 1862. General Winfield Scott called him 'a perfect soldier.'

Kearsarge, USS

This 7-gun Union sloop-of-war sank the 8-gun Confederate raider *Alabama* off Cherbourg, France, after a sea fight on June 19, 1864. Having been cornered by *Kearsarge* in Cherbourg harbor, *Alabama*'s Captain Raphael Semmes informed *Kearsarge*'s Captain John Winslow of his intention to sortie into the open sea and fight. Winslow gladly accepted the challenge, and this second-

most-famous of Civil War single-ship duels took place, beginning at 10:57 am, on a quiet Sunday morning. The opponents were fairly evenly matched in size, speed, and armament, but the better discipline of the Union gun-crews eventually prevailed. *Alabama* slid beneath the waves at 12:24 pm. Semmes escaped capture, having been picked up and carried to England in the British yacht *Deerhound*. Union naval officers considered that Semmes's failure to surrender personally was a breach of naval etiquette.

Kelly's Ford *(Virginia)*, Battle of

On March 17, 1862, newly organized Federal Army of the Potomac cavalry were sent out

Hulled by the Union sloop *Kearsarge*, the Confederate raider *Alabama* sinks in the English Channel off Cherbourg, France.

under W. W. Averell to attack enemy cavalry around Culpeper, Virginia. With 2100 men, Averell advanced on 800 enemy under Fitzhugh Lee at Kelly's Ford on the Rappahannock. In a full day's fighting Averell's Federal forces gained about two miles, suffering 78 casualties and inflicting 133 (including mortally wounding famed Southern artillerist

Armed Southerners pour into Kansas in the 1850s to ensure that it will be pro-slavery when it attains statehood – an unintended result of the 1854 Kansas-Nebraska Act.

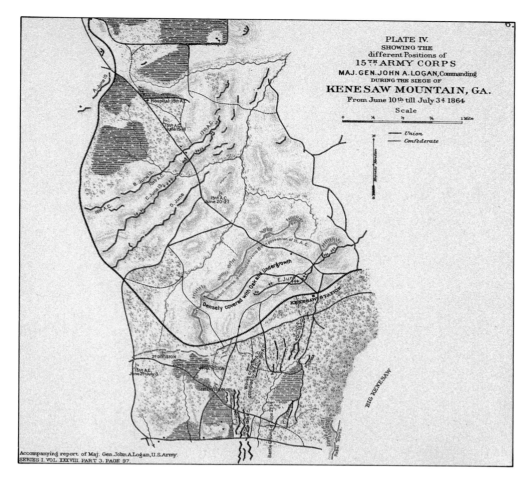

A Union army map shows the disposition of opposing forces in the June 1864 Battle of Kennesaw Mountain, fought during Union General W. T. Sherman's advance on Atlanta.

John Pelham), and then withdrew. It marked the first time Northern cavalry had stood up well to Southern horsemen.

Kennesaw Mountain (Georgia), Battle of

During his 1864 Atlanta Campaign, General W. T. Sherman, losing patience with his slow but effective campaign of maneuver against Joseph Johnston's Confederates, decided to try a decisive blow with a frontal assault on enemy positions at Kennesaw Mountain, Georgia. On the morning of June 27, however, three Federal assaults failed to capture any of the enemy breastworks, and casualties were staggering: nearly 2000 Federals were killed or wounded of 16,225 engaged, while Southern casualties were 442 killed or wounded of 17,733 engaged. A chastened Sherman once again resumed his campaign of deliberate maneuver.

Kentucky, Invasion of

See SMITH'S INVASION OF KENTUCKY.

Kentucky, Union Department of

Both sides treated this border state as neutral ground at the start of the war. The Federals established the military department under General Robert Anderson in May 1861 but did not officially occupy the state until September fo that year.

Kernstown (Virginia), First and Second Battles of

There were two engagements during the war in this Virginia town, usually called 'First' and 'Second Kernstown.' The first came on March 23, 1862, at the beginning of the Shenandoah Valley Campaign of Stonewall Jackson. Ordered to keep Federal forces in the valley occupied, Jackson attacked what he thought was a small detachment of Federals under James Shields at Kernstown. In fact, the bluecoats outnumbered Jackson considerably and routed the attack. Nonethe-

less, this loss was as good as a victory for the South: it gave government leaders in Washington a fright and led them to withhold forces from reinforcing George McClellan's Peninsular Campaign, which is exactly what Jackson had hoped to accomplish. 'Second Kernstown' came on July 23-24, 1864, as part of Confederate General Jubal Early's Washington Raid. During his retreat from Washington, Early drove George Crook's Federals from the town with heavy losses.

Ketch, Bomb

These small vessels were designed to fire mortars. They were used on western rivers to bombard fixed positions, notably during Union Admiral David G. Farragut's advance up the Mississippi toward the Confederate port of New Orleans in April 1862.

Keyes, Erasmus Darwin
(1810-1895) Union general.

Keyes, a Massachusetts-born West Point graduate and career officer, was Winfield Scott's military secretary in 1861. Commanding a brigade at First Bull Run, he led IV Corps throughout the Peninsular Campaign, notably at Seven Pines (*See* FAIR OAKS AND SEVEN PINES). During the Battle of Gettysburg he conducted a feint toward Richmond: it had little effect on the battle. He sat on an army board before retiring in May 1864.

Kilpatrick, Hugh Judson
(1836-1881) Union general.

Known as 'Kill Cavalry,' this flamboyant officer at first served in the Virginia theater, where he led the unsuccessful Kilpatrick-Dahlgren Raid on Richmond (*See*). In April 1864 he went west at W. T. Sherman's request and commanded Sherman's cavalry during the Atlanta Campaign, the March to the Sea, and the Carolinas Campaign.

A Kurz & Allison version of the Battle of Kennesaw Mountain: this frontal assault was Sherman's only major error in the campaign.

Kilpatrick-Dahlgren Raid

As Union fortunes soared at the beginning of 1864 an impetuous Federal cavalry general named Hugh Judson Kilpatrick (See) convinced President Lincoln and other superiors to back his plan for a raid into Richmond, in which his cavalry would try to create panic, release Union prisoners, and perhaps even seize the Confederate government. Kilpatrick left the Army of the Potomac on February 28, 1864, his 3584 cavalrymen heading toward Richmond in two wings. Commanding 500 men in the other wing was young Colonel Ulric Dahlgren (See), son of Navy Admiral John Dahlgren.

With little trouble Kilpatrick's wing reached the defenses north of Richmond on March 1; but after having a look he turned back and left the other wing to its fate. Dahlgren's now-divided column, meanwhile, was under heavy enemy pursuit. Within three miles of the city they were attacked and reduced to 100 riders (most of the rest escaped). On the following day, March 2, Dahlgren was ambushed and shot dead, and his remaining men were captured.

Papers found on Dahlgren's body stated, among other things, that 'The city must be destroyed and Jeff Davis and his Cabinet killed.' The South erupted in rage at this planned atrocity, and Robert E. Lee

An 1864 Republican election poster condemns the activities of the Knights of the Golden Circle as being traitorous.

demanded an explanation from Washington. None was forthcoming, and history has never discovered if the papers were authentic or who, if anyone, authorized the assassinations of Confederate officials.

King, Rufus *(1814-1876)*
Union general.

A West Point alumnus and Milwaukee newspaper editor, he organized Wisconsin's 'Iron Brigade.' King participated in Washington's defenses and led a divison at Second Bull Run, where his retreat from Gainesville on August 28 was erroneously blamed for the Federal loss. He retired in ill-health in October 1863.

Knights of the Golden Circle

Established in the South in the 1850s to promote the extension of slavery, this organization evolved into a secret Northern order of Confederate sympathizers, particularly Peace Democrats (See). Clement Vallandigham was prominent in this movement, which in 1863 became known as the Order of American Knights and then, in 1864, as the Sons of Liberty.

Knoxville Campaign

On November 4, 1863, as Ulysses S. Grant was organizing his forces in Chattanooga for the Chattanooga Campaign, Confederate General Braxton Bragg, who had been holding the Federals under siege, sent a detachment under James Longstreet to attack Union-held Knoxville, Tennessee. This campaign, planned by CSA President Jefferson Davis, was ill-advised in the extreme, given that Union forces in Chattanooga were clearly planning a breakout. It was done in part, apparently, because of friction between Bragg and Longstreet, and in part because Union General Ambrose Burnside, then in Knoxville, was preparing a march into Kentucky, an operation that Richmond was interested in stopping.

Longstreet, who at that point had 10,000 infantry and artillerymen and 5000 cavalry under youthful Joseph Wheeler, put his forces on the rails and reached Louden, Tennessee, on the 12th. On the next day Wheeler's troopers drove some blue cavalry out of Maryville, and Confederate forces began to move toward the city. Burnside responded by ordering in his outposts. At Cambell's Station on the 16th Longstreet tried and failed to cut off the enemy withdrawal. Now Burnside had all his men inside the elaborate fortifications of Knoxville.

His forces too limited to undertake a full-scale siege, Longstreet decided to concentrate on attack on a salient to the northwest that the Federals called Fort Sanders. After over a week of preparation and delays, mainly to await reinforcements, the Confed-

The Ku Klux Klan, 'an invisible empire' of Southern white-supremacist terrorists, was founded within a year of the war's end.

In the 1863 battle for Knoxville, Tennessee, Union troops repel a Rebel assault on Fort Sanders, a key to the city's defenses.

erate assault began on November 29. Rather than beginning with an artillery bombardment, which might have opened a breach in the steep parapet of Fort Sanders, Longstreet sent in his infantry. The advance, made in bitter cold, was slowed by Federal wire entanglements and then became bogged down in a ditch, the attackers lacking scaling ladders adequate to reach the parapet. Unable to advance, Longstreet called off the assault; the Federals captured 200 Southerners in the ditch. This mishandled effort ended the South's last chance to capture Knoxville; four days earlier, Grant's army had chased Bragg off the heights around Chattanooga.

Learning that W. T. Sherman was approaching from Chattanooga with two Federal corps to relieve Burnside, Longstreet withdrew to Greenville, Tennessee, for the winter. Showing his usual ineffectiveness, Burnside subsequently failed to drive Longstreet out of Tennessee and thus forced Grant to deploy considerable forces until next summer to keep Longstreet at bay. Having already received much criticism for failing to help William Rosecrans after the rout at Chickamauga, Burnside was now relieved at his own request, as he had been after his debacle at Fredericksburg. The bewhiskered Federal general would play one more major role in the war, as the architect of the Petersburg Mine Disaster (See PETERSBURG SIEGE). Longstreet brought charges against some of his officers for alleged failures in the Knoxville Campaign.

Ku Klux Klan

The Ku Klux Klan was one of several white supremacist vigilante groups organized in the South after the war. Six Confederate veterans founded the Klan in Tennessee in 1866 and adopted a constitution calling for the formation of an 'invisible empire' opposing blacks and carpetbaggers. Nathan Bedford Forrest became its first Grand Wizard. At first supported by the Democratic Party, the Klan quickly became a front for racial violence and was formally disbanded in 1869. Its clandestine activities continued, however. In two Ku Klux Klan Acts (1870, 1871) Congress outlawed the Klan's vigilante activities and attacks on blacks' voting rights. A flourishing revival in the 1920s subsided after lurid public revelations about murders and torture by Klan members.

Laird Rams

After strong Union protests, the British government on September 5, 1863, seized two ram warships being built for the Confederates at Laird's shipyard in Liverpool. Laird's also built the Confederacy's most successful commerce raider, the *Alabama*, which by late 1863 had captured or destroyed more than 60 vessels.

Lake Erie Conspiracy

A scheme by two Confederate agents to release Confederate prisoners held on Johnson's Island in Lake Erie and organize them into an army to operate in the area. The plan called for the capture of the Federal gunboat *Michigan*. Captain John Yates Beall successfully commandeered two boats on September 19, 1864, but his partner, Charles H. Cole, was discovered aboard the *Michigan* and was arrested. Beall escaped.

Lamar, Lucius Quintus Cincinnatus *(1825-1893)*
Confederate statesman.

A Mississippi lawyer and states' rights politician, he drafted his state's secession ordi-

nance. Lamar raised and led the 19th Mississippi until his health failed in 1862, later representing the Confederacy in Europe (1862-63) and serving as a judge advocate in the Army of Northern Virginia (1864-65).

Land Mines

Also called booby traps, these new weapons, usually artillery shells buried a few inches underground, exploded when stepped on. A Confederate officer appears to have been the first to introduce them, at Yorktown in May 1862, but Federal forces soon were setting booby traps of their own.

Lane, James Henry *(1833-1907)*
Confederate general.

This Virginian, a teacher educated at Virginia Military Institute, fought throughout the war with the Army of Northern Virginia, scouting before Big Bethel and surrendering at Appomattox. Three times wounded, he was a brigadier general at twenty-nine; his troops called him 'The Little General.'

Lawrence, *Kansas*

In what amounted to a terrorist attack, Confederate guerrilla William Quantrill (*See*) raided this town at dawn on August 21, 1863, killing 150 civilians and wounding about 30. Quantrill's 450 raiders then set the town afire before vanishing.

Lawrence Priming System

This disk primer magazine, patented in 1857, replaced an older priming system on Sharps rifles and carbines. The Lawrence primers were fed mechanically by the cocking of the weapon's hammer.

Lawton, Alexander Robert *(1818-1896)* **Confederate general.**

Lawton was a West Point graduate, Georgia lawyer, and secessionist legislator. He commanded the Georgia coast, took part in the

British ship-of-the-line *Majestic* guards Laird rams earmarked for the Confederacy.

Shenandoah Valley Campaign of Jackson, and fought from the Seven Days' Battles through Antietam. Wounded and reassigned, he was a reluctant but effective quartermaster general until the war's end.

Lee, Fitzhugh *(1835-1905)*
Confederate general.

Robert E. Lee's nephew, he served on the frontier in the prewar army. He served as a staff officer during the Peninsular Campaign, then led a cavalry brigade under Stuart in the Antietam, Chancellorsville and Gettysburg Campaigns. Seriously wounded at Winchester in the Shenandoah Valley Campaign of Sheridan in September 1864, he returned to command the Army of Northern Virginia's cavalry during the Appomattox Campaign. Fitzhugh Lee returned to active service in 1898, commanding the US VII Corps in Cuba during the Spanish-American War.

Lee, George Washington Custis *(1832-1913)*
Confederate general.

Robert E. Lee's eldest son, Custis Lee served for most of the war as President Jefferson Davis's aide-de-camp. He commanded Richmond's defenses during the Kilpatrick-Dahlgren Raid (*See*). In 1871 he succeeded his father as president of the institution that was then named Washington & Lee University.

Lee, Mary
Sanitation Commission Worker.

An English-born Sanitation Commission worker from Philadelphia, she served almost continuously in Union field hospitals in the Virginia theater from the Peninsular Campaign to the Confederate surrender.

The principal Confederate generals surround their great leader, Robert E. Lee.

Robert E. Lee confers with his 'strong right arm', Stonewall Jackson, before the 1863 Battle of Chancellorsville.

Lee, Robert Edward *(1807-1870)*
Confederate general.

Brilliant commander of the Confederacy's most important army, Robert E. Lee emerged from the war with remarkable respect from both sides, due not only to his military genius but to his magisterial personality. Lee was born on the family estate in Westmoreland County, Virginia, on January 19, 1807, son of an old aristocratic and military Virginia family and of Revolutionary War hero 'Lighthorse Harry' Lee. Robert attended West Point and compiled a fine record, being graduated second in his class in 1829 with not one demerit on his record. He spent the next 17 years in the Engineers Corps, a prestigious post for young officers.

With many other future Civil War leaders Lee saw his first service in the Mexican War of 1846, where he distinguished himself in a series of battles and ended the war a colonel. For three years he served as superintendent of West Point, but left that post for cavalry service. In that capacity he led the detachment that captured abolitionist raider John Brown at Harpers Ferry (*See*).

As the Southern states began to secede at the beginning of 1861, Lee, considered by many the best man in the US army, was offered command of the Union army in the field. Despite personal objections to both slavery and secession, Lee declined; and when his home state of Virginia seceded he felt obliged to resign his commission, saying he could not raise his hand against his own people. Soon he accepted a general's commission in the new Confederate army, serving as personal military adviser to Confederate President Jefferson Davis. For a year he directed campaigns from behind the scenes, always having to defer to Davis, who largely

ran the Southern war effort. In his first field command Lee failed to prevent the loss of West Virginia. When General J. E. Johnston was wounded in the Battle of Fair Oaks in May 1862, Lee, at 55, took command of that army, renamed it the Army of Northern Virginia, and wrote it into military history with a brilliant series of victories over the Federal Army of the Potomac.

Though his first major engagements during the Seven Days Battles were disorganized and hardly victorious, they did serve to drive superior Federal forces out of Virginia. Lee would have the upper hand over his enemy for most of the remaining war. His string of successes began at Second Bull Run in August 1862, aided there, as later, by his extraordinary team of Stonewall Jackson and cavalryman Jeb Stuart. Lee faltered on the battlefield only when he moved into enemy territory, as he first did in September 1863, when he fought to a draw with vastly superior Union forces at the Battle of Antietam but was nevertheless obliged to pull back from his invasion of Maryland with heavy losses.

Lee was incomparable as a battlefield tactician, fiercely aggressive for all his courtly manners, able to respond to the changing conditions of battle to gain local superiority over superior enemy forces, and able to inspire his men to remarkable feats. A gambler and iconoclast, Lee in several battles (notably Chancellorsville) violated the old military maxim against dividing forces in the face of superior enemy forces. His great enemy later in the war, Ulysses S. Grant, was the better strategist, a genius at large maneuvers; but not Grant or any other Federal general was able to bring Lee to bay on the battlefield, even with twice the men. (Lee's one major defeat, at Gettysburg – another ill-advised invasion – was lost mainly by his own inexplicable decision to gamble all on Pickett's Charge (*See*).) Lee's primary weakness was exactly in large-scale strategy, particularly logistics – his army fought hungry, ragged, and often shoeless, even when these supplies were available. Nonetheless, such was the power of Lee's personality and leadership that time and time again his men outfought a better-fed, better-equipped, and outnumbering enemy.

Lee's masterpiece was the Battle of Chancellorsville in May 1863, but that battle also marks the summit of his success. There he lost Stonewall Jackson, his right-hand partner, and followed up that loss by another over-ambitious invasion which came to grief at Gettysburg in July 1863. (Typically, Lee took full responsibility for the defeat and offered to resign. Equally typically, the resignation was refused and his men lost none of their faith in him.)

From then on, Lee was forced into fighting a defensive war, which did not suit his aggressive style; but he did it with the same brilliance as before, fighting Grant and the Army of the Potomac to a standstill in the battles of the Wilderness, Spotsylvania, and Cold Harbor. But as Lee settled into Petersburg to withstand Grant's siege in summer 1864, he knew as well as anyone that only a miracle could save the Confederacy; the South had reached the bottom of the barrel in supplies of food, matériel, and fighting men.

When Lee was finally named general in chief of Confederate armies for the first time in February 1865, it was virtually an empty title.

Forced out of Petersburg in early April 1865, Lee doggedly attempted to escape to the Carolinas with his army, but Grant finally ran him to ground at Appomattox. On April 9 the two generals signed the surrender of the Army of Northern Virginia, which both knew was effectively the end of the war. Lee was paroled home and officially indicted for treason, but he was never brought to trial. When he applied for a pardon in June 1865, he urged his troops and all Southerners to accept the outcome and get on with rebuilding. In the campaign of 1868 some Northerners even backed Lee for president. Instead, he became president of small, destitute Washington College in Virginia (later renamed Washington and Lee). Still in that post, Lee died in Lexington, Virginia, on October 12, 1870. A Southern tradition holds that his last words were, 'Strike the tents.'

Later, many would note that Lee, the courtly Virginia aristocrat, represented perhaps the last vestige of the old chivalric tradition in war. Certainly his own time was not inclined to ask the question of how such a breathtaking gambler and such an extraordinarily aggressive killer on the battlefield could be reconciled with so mild and dignified a personality. As to the question of who was really the greatest general of the war, that will forever be debated among partisans of Lee, Grant, Jackson, Sherman, Forrest, and others; but, at least in the popular imagination, no other Civil War commander has even attained quite the same near-mythic stature as Robert E. Lee.

The text of Lee's farewell address to his beloved Army of Northern Virginia.

After four years of arduous service, marked by unsurpassed courage and fortitude, the Army of Northern Virginia has been compelled to yield to overwhelming numbers and resources. I need not tell the brave survivors of so many hard-fought battles, who have remained steadfast to the last, that I have consented to this result from no distrust of them; but feeling that valor and devotion could accomplish nothing that would compensate for the loss that must have attended a continuance of the contest, I determined to avoid the useless sacrifice of those whose past services have endeared them to their countrymen. By the terms of agreement officers and men can return to their homes and remain until exchanged. You will take with you the satisfaction that proceeds from the consciousness of duty faithfully performed, and I earnestly pray that a merciful God will extend to you His blessing and protection. With an increasing admiration of your constancy and devotion to your country and a grateful remembrance of your kind and generous consideration of myself, I bid you all an affectionate farewell.
APRIL 10th, 1865.

Lee, William Henry Fitzhugh
(1837-1891) **Confederate general.**

Robert E. Lee's second son, 'Rooney' Lee led W. W. Loring's cavalry during West Virginia operations of 1861. He fought with Jeb Stuart at Antietam, Fredericksburg, Chancellorsville, and Gettysburg. Taken captive while he was recovering from a wound received at Brandy Station in June 1863, he was exchanged in 1864. Rooney Lee commanded Rebel cavalry in the retreat from Petersburgh to Appomattox in the spring of 1865.

Legal Tender Acts

Congress issued treasury notes in 1862, 1863 and 1864 to help finance the war. Some $450 million-worth of these notes, called greenbacks, were printed; they circulated at fluctuating values.

Leggett, Mortimer Dormer
(1821-1896) **Union general.**

This Ohio school superintendent volunteered as George McClellan's unpaid aide-de-camp in 1861 and went on to raise the 78th Ohio, fighting at Fort Donelson, Shiloh, Corinth, and Vicksburg and participating in the Atlanta Campaign and the March to the Sea. The hill he captured and held at Atlanta was renamed Leggett's Hill.

Legion

This term describes a military formation composed of infantry, artillery, and cavalry. The Union's Corcoran (*See*) and the Confederacy's Hampton (*See*) were two notable Civil War legions.

Le Mat Revolver

A New Orleans-born physician named J. A. F. Le Mat invented this nine-shot, double-barreled pistol. He could not get the machinery to produce his weapon in the Confederacy, so he sailed to Europe on the British packet ship *Trent* (*See*) and manufactured about 3000 pistols and carbines there.

Former Confederate POW camp, Libby Prison, in 1865. A year earlier it was the scene of the war's most spectacular jailbreak.

Letters of Marque

Generally issued by a recognized government, they distinguish commerce-raiding privateers from common pirates. On April 17, 1861, President Jefferson Davis announced that the Confederate government would accept applications for letters of marque. At about the same time, Lincoln announced that Union naval forces would blockade Southern maritime ports.

Lexington, *Tennessee*

In a preliminary to the Stone's River battle, Nathan B. Forrest's Confederate cavalry attacked and routed the 11th Illinois Cavalry here on December 18, 1862. The 11th retreated toward Jackson with a loss of 124 troopers. The action was part of Forrest's Second Raid of December-January 1862-63.

Libby Prison Escape

More than 100 Union officers escaped from notorious Libby Prison on the James River in Richmond on February 9, 1864, fleeing down a tunnel they had dug. Of the 109 who escaped in this largest prison break of the war, 48 were recaptured, two drowned, and 59 reached the Federal lines.

Lincoln, Abraham *(1809-1865)*
Sixteenth president of the United States.

Every people needs its success stories, its great leaders, its saints, its martyrs. The importance and the mythical presence of Abraham Lincoln in American history results from his being all those things. Rising from obscurity to lead the nation through its greatest trial, he brought to the presidency a nobility of character and moral courage combined with a genius for politics, for statesmanship, and for soul-stirring language.

Lincoln was born in a log cabin near Hodgenville, Kentucky, on February 12, 1809, son of a barely educated frontier farmer. The family moved to Indiana when he was seven. From his youth he aspired to a life beyond small farming. Though he attended school less than a year, he studied on his own, sometimes walking miles to borrow books. His self-education led him to the study of law after he had moved to New Salem, Illinois, in

Abraham Lincoln, as he looked on November 8, 1864, 11 days before the Gettysburg Address.

1831. Reading law while he worked at various jobs, he was admitted to the bar in 1836 and moved to the state capital of Springfield to begin his practice.

His political career had already begun. Elected to the Illinois house of representatives as a Whig in 1834, he spent seven years there as a lackluster legislator. By the time he left, his law practice was prospering and he had wed Mary Todd, high-spirited if sometimes unstable daughter of a prominent family. As a circuit-riding lawyer, Lincoln gradually made himself known in political circles statewide. In 1846 he ran successfully for the US House of Representatives but after two eventless years was back in Springfield, disillusioned with politics.

It was his opposition to slavery that brought him back to politics. In 1856 he joined the new antislavery Republican Party and two years later was its candidate for the Senate against Stephen A. Douglas, who had accommodated pro-slavery forces with the Kansas-Nebraska Bill (*See*). The two began a series of debates which were to make Lincoln a national figure, even though he lost the election. His reputation bore fruit in 1860 when Lincoln gained the Republican presidential nomination and rode a split in the Democratic party to win in Electoral votes (he lacked a popular majority). As had been feared, however, some Southern states responded to his election by seceding from the Union. When Lincoln took office in February 1861, he already faced a rival slaveholding country of seven states, with its own constitution, president, and military. After the fall of Fort Sumter, six more states seceded, but three other slaveholding states nevertheless remained in the Union.

He came to Washington an unknown, with only two years of experience in national politics and those unsuccessful. His position on slavery was moderate and politically expedient: he had written, 'If slavery is not

wrong, then nothing is wrong,' and, 'A house divided against itself cannot stand'; but, nonetheless, for the moment he was willing to tolerate slavery in the South to preserve the Union, but he firmly objected to its spread into new territories.

Lincoln's gift with words had made him famous, but in manner and appearance he was less inspiring. His voice was high and flat, his frame gaunt and awkward, his clothes ill-fitting, and his face rough-hewn (though there was about it an unmistakable quiet dignity and nobility). He had a disconcerting habit of cracking jokes at inappropriate moments (though the jokes were often memorable, as when he took to bed with a mild case of smallpox saying, 'At last I have something I can give everybody.') A member of his cabinet dismissed Lincoln as 'the original gorilla.' He seemed an unlikely man to save the Union.

Yet in test after test, decision after decision, political maneuver after maneuver, Lincoln would prove equal to the most daunting tasks a president ever faced. As tensions grew over Southern demands for the Union to evacuate of Fort Sumter, he made sure that if the crisis came to conflict, it would be the South that began the hostilities, thereby giving the Confederacy responsibility for starting the war. When Sumter fell Lincoln raised a Union army by decree before Congress could get a word in. He successfully placated the slaveholding Union states (and the racism of the time) by steadily maintaining that the war was entirely over secession, not slavery; then, at the politically opportune

Lincoln meets with General George McClellan in the field on October 1, 1862, two weeks after the savage Battle of Antietam.

time, January 1863, he released the Emancipation Proclamation (*See*) that indeed made the conflict a war over slavery, in the process making it morally impossible for Europe to support the Confederacy. He deliberately appointed to his cabinet strong-minded men of varying political pursuasions, several of whom aspired to replace him as president, and managed to fight off their challenges to his power while exploiting their considerable abilities. With a stubborn and often near-mutinous Congress he did likewise. In the end, this strange, homely, depressive, and elusive figure was able to secure the loyalty of most of the North and many of his former enemies, not to mention his soldiers, who voted for him overwhelmingly in the election of 1864. His immortal Gettysburg Address of November 1863 remains the most succinct and eloquent statement of American ideals.

On April 14, 1865, less than a week after Lee's surrender at Appomattox, Lincoln was assassinated by actor John Wilkes Booth at Ford's Theater in Washington (*See* LINCOLN'S ASSASSINATION). Had he lived, he would have faced a task as difficult as the war, the task of trying to secure his conciliatory vision of Southern reconstruction against the Radical Republicans who demanded revenge and supression. His second inaugural address had ended, 'With malice toward none, with charity for all, with firmness in the right as God gives us to see the right, let us strive on to . . . bind up the nation's wounds, to care for him who shall have borne the battle and for his widow and his orphan – to do all which may achieve and cherish a just and lasting peace among ourselves and with all nations.' The final tragedy of his death was that it left these great tasks to be performed by lesser men.

This Mathew Brady photograph of the much-criticized Mary Todd Lincoln was apparently made sometime in 1861.

Lincoln, Mary Todd *(1818-1882)*
Wife of Abraham Lincoln.

Born into a genteel Kentucky family, she settled in Illinois in 1839 and married Lincoln in 1842. Her close Southern family ties, political interference, and unpredictable temperament attracted criticism during Lincoln's presidency, but his affection for her was apparently unwavering.

Lincoln's Assassination

While living in Washington, actor and fanatical Southern patriot John Wilkes Booth (*See*) assembled a group of conspirators in 1864 and with them planned to abduct President Lincoln and make him a hostage in the South. None of these plots came to fruition. After Lee's surrender at Appomattox on April 9, 1865, Booth turned to the idea of assassinating the president, perhaps in hopes this would inspire the Confederacy to fight on.

Learning that Lincoln planned to attend Ford's Theatre in Washington on the night of April 14, to see a comedy called *Our American Cousin*, Booth quickly collected his current conspirators and handed out assignments: he would shoot the president, George Atzerodt would kill the vice-president, Lewis Paine (a.k.a. Powell) would kill Secretary of State William Seward, and David Herold would help Booth escape. (The slow-witted Atzerodt would lose his nerve, but Paine would seriously wound Seward in his bed.)

Arriving at the presidential box in the theater, Booth found it unguarded, slipped in, and shot Lincoln behind the ear as he sat next to his wife and amidst a party of several people. Booth then leapt from the box to the stage (in the process breaking his leg), where he apparently shouted the phrase *Sic semper tyrannus!* ('Thus be it ever for tyrants'). Lincoln died next morning in a rooming house

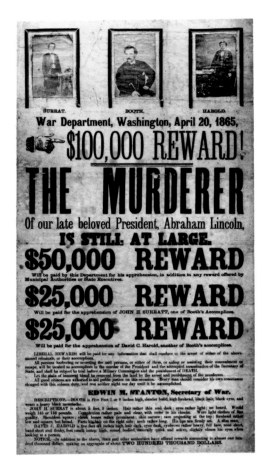

Signed by Secretary of War Stanton, this poster offers rewards for the capture of the conspirators in Lincoln's assassination.

across the street, the first president to fall victim to assassination.

With Herold, Booth fled to Virginia, where they were run to ground and Booth was killed. Later, Herold, Paine, and Atzerodt were hanged, along with Mary Surratt, Booth's landlady (who may well have been innocent). Four other supposed conspirators were sentenced to life imprisonment but received pardons in 1869.

Little Rock, *Arkansas*

Confederates captured the US arsenal here on February 8, 1861. Federal forces returned to the Arkansas capital in September 1863.

Little Round Top

A small hill lying between Cemetery Ridge and the Round Top at the southern end of the Union line at the Battle of Gettysburg, it was the pivot of battle on the second day.

Livermore, Mary Ashton Rice *(1820-1905)*
Sanitary Commission organizer.

A Chicago writer and editor when war broke out, she helped set up the Sanitary Commission's Northwestern Branch. After becoming a national director of the Sanitary Commission, she inspected battlefields and lectured widely, work that led her later into feminist activism. Her memoir, *My Story of the War*, contains much valuable information on the work of the Sanitary Commission.

Logan, John Alexander *(1826-1886)* **Union general.**

This Illinois Congressman left Washington to fight at First Bull Run. He participated at the capture of Fort Donelson, the Vicksburg and Atlanta Campaigns, the March to the Sea, and the Carolinas Campaign, commanding XV Corps and, briefly, the Army of the Tennessee. Logan later founded the Grand Army of the Republic and established Decoration (Memorial) Day.

Logan's Cross Roads *(Kentucky)*, Battle of

About 4000 Confederates under George B. Crittenden attacked a 4000-strong Union force under George H. Thomas here as part of the defense of the Cumberland Gap (*See*) on January 19, 1862. After a hard fight Crittenden's line broke, forcing the Rebels to retreat across a rain-swollen stream and leave their heavy equipment behind. Thomas's Federals took 12 guns, a quantity of small arms, and about 1000 horses and mules. The action is also called the Battle of Mill Springs.

'Long Tom'

The Confederates dubbed a 30-pounder Parrott captured at First Bull Run a Long Tom, and eventually it became the name for all guns of that type. US troops in World War II used the name for a 155-millimeter cannon.

Longstreet, James *(1821-1904)*
Confederate general.

South Carolina born and West Point trained, Longstreet led a Confederate brigade at First Bull Run and became Robert E. Lee's primary infantry commander in 1862; after Antietam he was promoted to lieutenant general. His record with Lee was outstanding at times, at other times less so. A man of strong convictions, he opposed Lee's plan to invade Pennsylvania and bitterly objected to 'Pickett's Charge' at Gettysburg, though he was ordered to organize that charge and did so. He was later sent south and fought with distinction in the Chickamauga Battle and with less distinction in the Knoxville Campaign before returning to Lee's army for the Wilderness Battle in 1864 (where he was seriously wounded) and for the ensuing battles and campaigns of the Army of North-

Confederate General James Longstreet.

ern Virginia up to Appomattox. His postwar years were shadowed by the South's blaming him – unfairly – for the failure of Pickett's Charge; he ended up a Republican and supporter of the presidency of his one-time enemy, Ulysses S. Grant.

Lookout Mountain *(Tennessee)*, Battle of

On Ulysses Grant's orders, Joseph Hooker assaulted this natural strongpoint, which rises 1100 feet above the Tennessee River, as part of the Chattanooga Campaign. Hooker sent two divisions up the mountain on the foggy morning of November 24, 1863. After some sharp fighting around Craven's Farm, the Rebels pulled back a few hundred yards to new positions. Attackers and defenders then settled down for the night. After midnight, the Confederate forces were withdrawn. Because of the fog, this engagement has also been called 'The Battle Above the Clouds.'

Loring-Jackson Incident

When Confederate War Secretary Judah P. Benjamin granted General William Wing Loring's appeal and overrode an order from Stonewall Jackson in western Virginia in January 1862, Jackson threatened to resign

The murder of Abraham Lincoln by John Wilkes Booth in Ford's Theatre, Washington, DC.

The Battle of Lookout Mountain in November 1863 was one of two actions by which Grant broke the Rebel siege of Chattanooga.

from the army. Benjamin reversed himself and backed Jackson. A few weeks later General Loring was transferred away from Jackson's command.

Loudon Rangers

The Federals recruited this force from among the German settlers around Leesburg, Virginia, in the spring of 1862. The Rangers were assigned to track the Confederate John S. Mosby's (See) Partisan Rangers, but were no better suited to the task than the regular Union units that constantly tried and failed to catch Mosby's men.

Lovejoy's Station, *Georgia*

John Bell Hood's Confederate army concentrated here after the evacuation of Atlanta (See ATLANTA CAMPAIGN) in September 1864, and here W. T. Sherman's IV and XXIII Corps attacked CSA General William Hardee's forces, which had begun to prepare defensive positions, on the morning of September 2. Skirmishing continued for another three days. Hood's main forces were in place by September 4, and on the 5th the Federals withdrew into Atlanta.

Lovell Court of Inquiry

A West Point graduate (1842), Mansfield Lovell resigned as deputy street commissioner for New York City to enter Confederate service. He commanded at New Orleans (See) when Union forces captured the city in April 1862. A Confederate court of inquiry concluded in 1863 that Lovell had defended New Orleans with energy and competence, given the resources at his disposal.

Union General Nathaniel Lyon (left) with Colonel (soon-to-be-General) Franz Sigel.

Lowe, Thaddeus Sobieski Coulincourt *(1832-1913)*
Aeronaut and inventor.

As a scientist investigating air currents from a hot-air balloon, Lowe was briefly arrested as a Union spy on a flight over the Carolinas in 1861. He pioneered air-to-ground telegraphy and aerial photography and became supervisor of the Union army aeronautics corps, a balloon fleet that observed the battles of the Army of the Potomac from First Bull run through Gettysburg.

Loyalties of Military Men

In 1861 only 26 of the 15,000 enlisted men in the Regular Army left to join the Confederate forces. Of the 620 officers from the North, 16 men, all married into Southern families, joined the Confederate Army. Among the Southern officers, about half of the 330 West Point graduates but only one of the 130 civilian appointees – Winfield Scott – fought on the Federal side.

Lynchburg, *Virginia*

Federal forces under David Hunter attacked and were repulsed here on June 18, 1864. Some of the Confederate defenders were newly arrived from Jubal Early's corps. When Early began his advance up the Shenandoah Valley, a preliminary to his Washington Raid (See), the dismayed General Hunter retreated northward in haste.

Lyon, Nathaniel *(1818-1861)*
Union general.

Born in Connecticut, this West Point-trained career soldier became a Republican polemicist while stationed in 'Bleeding Kansas.' Commanding the arsenal and then the Federal troops in St. Louis, his decisive operations against the Confederates probably saved Missouri for the Union. He was killed at Wilson's Creek in August 1861.

adoption. Designs included the battery gun, the Vandenberg, the mechanically loaded Ager Battery Gun and Williams Gun, and the Gatling Gun, patented in 1862. Union General Benjamin Butler bought a dozen Gatlings with his own money and used them at Petersburg, but they were not officially procured until after the war.

Mackenzie, Ranald Slidell (1840-1889) **Union general.**

First in his class at West Point (1862), this New Yorker compiled a distinguished war record as an engineer officer with the Potomac Army from Kelly's Ford through Petersburg and served as a commander in the Shenandoah Valley Campaign of Sheridan and the Appomattox Campaign. Ulysses S. Grant called Mackenzie 'the most promising young officer in the army.'

Maffitt, John Newland (1819-1886) **Confederate naval commander.**

Born at sea, Maffitt was a career naval officer. Commanding the Confederate ships *Savannah, Florida*, and *Albemarle*, he was engaged in combat and blockade-running; he ran the Federal blockade of Mobile against nearly unsuperable odds and captured dozens of Union ships.

Magruder, John Bankhead (1810-1871) **Confederate general.**

Virginia-born Magruder was a West Point graduate and Mexican and Seminole Wars veteran whose courtliness earned him the nickname 'Prince John.' He failed to sustain the decisiveness he had initially shown at Big Bethel, Yorktown, Mechanicsville, and Gaines's Mill, and after he had made some critical errors late in the Peninsular Campaign he was transferred to the District of Texas, where he captured Galveston. He lectured about the war in later years.

MacArthur, Arthur (1845-1912) **Union officer.**

Massachusetts born, he joined the 24th Wisconsin Volunteers in August 1862 and fought at Perryville, Stone's River, and Missionary Ridge (where his conspicuous bravery won him a Medal of Honor) and in numerous battles of the Atlanta campaign, becoming one of the youngest regimental commanders of the war. He would later serve in the Spanish American War and would be the military governor of the Philippines in 1900-1901. He retired a lieutenant general. Douglas MacArthur was his son.

Machine Guns

The Civil War saw the first combat use of machine guns, but the indifference of military experts forestalled their widespread

One of the best of the war's proto-machine guns was the .58 caliber Ager 'Coffee Mill' but the Union bought only 63 examples of it.

Stephen Mallory did excellent work as the Confederacy's secretary of the navy.

Mahan, Dennis Hart (1802-1871) **Military educator.**

A New Yorker trained in engineering at West Point, he taught civil and military engineering there for 40 years. Among his numerous publications, the treatises *Field Fortification* (1836) and *Advance-Guard, Out-Post . . .* (1847) were standard military texts for officers on both sides throughout the Civil War. His son, Alfred Thayer Mahan (1840-1914), who served as a Union naval officer during the war, eventually became one of the world's greatest naval historians.

Mahone, William (1826-1895) **Confederate general.**

A Virginia railroad president in 1861, 'Little Billy' commanded the Norfolk District and fought in the Army of Northern Virginia virtually continuously from the Peninsula through Spotsylvania. Promoted to major general for heroism at the Petersburg crater, he led 'Mahone's Brigade,' famous for its *esprit de corps*, through Appomattox.

Mallory, Stephen Russell (1813-1873) **Secretary of the Confederate navy.**

Raised in Florida, Mallory was a customs inspector, judge, and, by 1861, a US Senator of ten years' standing who opposed secession and the war. Nevertheless, he resigned and served as secretary of the Confederate navy throughout the war with creditable resourcefulness against great odds (*See* CONFEDERATE NAVY). Arrested with Jefferson Davis in May 1865, Mallory practiced law in Florida after his release.

Malvern Hill (Virginia), Battle of

In the last of the Seven Days' Battles, on July 1, 1862, Robert E. Lee's Confederates attacked George McClellan's Army of the Potomac north of Richmond. The utterly disorganized attack was met by a withering Federal artil-

Although the Union won the 1862 Battle of Malvern Hill, General McClellan persisted in his retreat down the Virginia peninsula. Here, Union gunboats cover the retreat.

lery barrage from Malvern Hill. By the end of the day Lee had suffered 5355 casualties to the Federals' 3214; both armies had over 80,000 engaged. Though McClellan had inflicted a devastating repulse, he continued his retreat to Harrison's Landing.

Manassas, First and Second

Southern names for the two great battles that are called in Northern histories First and Second Bull Run.

Marais des Cygnes (*Kansas*), Battle of

On October 25, 1864 Confederate General Sterling Price's forces, retreating after their month-long raid in Missouri (*See* PRICE'S RAID), paused to fight a rearguard action against Federal cavalry; the fighting cost the Confederates 1000 prisoners, including Generals John Marmaduke and William Cabell and four colonels.

March to the Sea

In October 1864 Southern general John B. Hood moved his army into Tennessee to attack Federal supply lines, trying to make up his loss of Atlanta (*See*) by drawing enemy forces out of Georgia to protect their lifeline. After pursuing Hood for a while, his adversary, General William Tecumseh Sherman, decided to leave the Confederate army to the efforts of other Federal detachments in Tennessee, and to pursue a new campaign. This decision would make Sherman one of the great generals of the war and the most hated man in the long memory of the South. He planned to cut away from his vulnerable supply line and march his 62,000 men across Georgia to Savannah and the sea. His troops would forage for food and supplies from the population and destroy everything in their path. 'I will make Georgia howl,' Sherman wrote. In the process he would show the

South and the world that the Confederacy was powerless to stop him.

Atlanta experienced a foretaste of what was coming. Sherman turned the city into a Federal military camp, commandeered its food, and burned all buildings of possible military importance, along with a good many private homes. Half the inhabitants were evicted, and streams of refugees poured out of the city. To protests from Atlanta officials Sherman declared, 'War is cruelty, and you cannot refine it; and those who brought war into our country deserve all the curses and maledictions a people can pour out. . . . You might as well appeal against the thunder-

storm as against these terrible hardships of war. . . . the only way the people of Atlanta can hope once more to live in peace . . . is to stop the war.' (The most famous quote attributed to Sherman, 'War is hell,' he never quite said, but it is an accurate portrayal of the attitude of a general who refused to romanticize his profession.)

Sherman and his army set out east across Georgia on November 16, 1864, making about a dozen miles a day and cutting a 50-mile-wide swath of devastation through the state. Later Sherman described the process of foraging this way: 'Each brigade commander had authority to detail a company of foragers, usually about fifty men. . . . This party would be dispatched before daylight and . . . would proceed on foot five or six miles from the route traveled by their brigade, and then visit every plantation and farm within range. They would usually procure a wagon or family carriage, load it with bacon, corn meal, turkeys, chickens, ducks, and everything that could be used as food or forage.'

There was a good deal more to the march than that – inevitable when hardened soldiers are turned loose on civilians in enemy territory. The foragers were derisively dubbed 'bummers'; soon they took to calling themselves that, with a certain fierce pride. One Northern officer recalled the aspects of the march Sherman did not mention: 'To enter a house and find the feather bed ripped open, the wardrobes ransacked, chests stripped of all contents . . . and all the corn

Federal wagon trains move out of Atlanta in November 1864 in the beginning of General Sherman's celebrated March to the Sea.

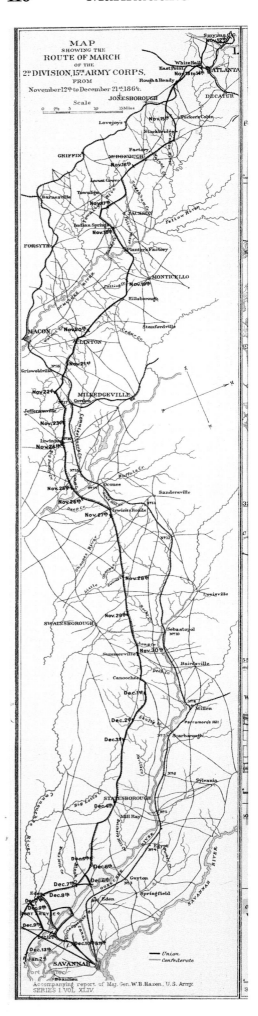

meal and bacon missing, bed quilts stripped from the beds, the last jar of pickles gone, was no uncommon sight, and one to make a soldier blush with indignation.' On the periphery of the march swarmed a rabble of deserters from both sides as well as a number of liberated slaves, all burning and robbing for their private benefit or revenge.

Only a few scattered enemy units and state militia appeared to try and stay the invaders. There was constant skirmishing along the route, but no substantial engagements. By the time Sherman reached Savannah on December 10, 1864, he had proved that the Confederacy was militarily a hollow shell. The last Confederate forces evacuated Savannah on the 21st, and Sherman wired to Lincoln, 'I beg to present you, as a Christmas gift, the city of Savannah.' Lincoln replied that Sherman's march would bring 'those who sat in darkness, to see a great light.' Meanwhile, Hood had lost what was left of his Confederate army in the Franklin and Nashville Campaign (See). Now Sherman would turn his forces north in the Carolinas Campaign (See), a still more destructive march toward union with Ulysses Grant at Petersburg. In the event, the war would be over before he got there.

For all its apparently haphazard destruction, the March to the Sea had served clear military purposes: to destroy the supplies of the Rebel armies, to demoralize the population, and to demonstrate the weakness of the Confederacy. Furthermore, there had actually been few outrages against persons – none of the mass murder visited on civilians by both sides as a matter of normal strategy in World War II. In short, Sherman had done a valuable military service and had done it brilliantly and with some restraint. But by waging war on civilians, he had created an ominous precedent. Future generations would carry the process to ever greater heights of violence in the name of Total War.

Left: A US Army map traces Sherman's route from Atlanta to Savannah and the sea.
Below: Union General George B. McClellan (fourth from right) and staff in 1862.

Marmaduke, John Sappington (1833-1887) Confederate general.

Marmaduke, the son of a governor of Missouri, was graduated from West Point. He left frontier duty to join the Confederates and fought mainly in Arkansas and Missouri, most notably at Shiloh and in Price's 1864 Missouri Raid; he was captured and imprisoned after Marais des Cygnes (See) in October 1864.

Marshall, Humphrey (1812-1872) Confederate general.

This Kentuckian, a West Point graduate and Mexican War veteran, was a lawyer and US Representative. He fought along Big Sandy River in 1861-62 and participated in Braxton Bragg's invasion of Kentucky. Resigning in June 1863, Marshall sat in the Confederate Congress in 1864-65.

Martinsburg, *Virginia*

Confederate troops attacked this town on June 14, 1863, at the beginning of the Gettysburg Campaign. When one regiment, the 106th New York, broke under a shelling, Union forces began a confused retreat toward the Potomac. The Federals reported about 200 missing; the attackers lost three killed and wounded.

Marye's Heights

This is the name given to the range of hills behind Fredericksburg, Virginia. It formed the anchor of the Confederate position at the Battle of Fredericksburg.

Mason, James Murray (1798-1871) Confederate statesman.

This Virginia lawyer and Senator was a states' rights Democrat and prominent secessionist. As a Confederate diplomatic commissioner en route to Great Britain in 1861, he was captured by the Federals in the *Trent* Affair (See); despite years of diplomacy, he

failed in the end to win British recognition of the Confederacy.

Maury, Dabney Herndon
(1822-1900) **Confederate general.**

A Virginian, Maury was a West Point graduate and professor. He fought in the Confederate cavalry at Pea Ridge, Iuka, Corinth, and Hatchie Bridge, and after July 1863 he commanded the District of the Gulf, losing Mobile to Admrial David Farragut and General Edward Canby. Matthew Fontaine Maury (*See*) was his uncle.

Maury, Matthew Fontaine
(1806-1873) **Hydrographer and Confederate naval commander.**

His sea-going career was ended by a crippling accident in 1839, and this Virginian became director of the US Naval Observatory, publishing internationally acclaimed works on navigation and oceanography. As a Confederate navy commander he represented the Confederacy abroad, purchased foreign warships, and invented a system of laying electric mines. After the war he taught physics at Virginia Military Institute. All the sophisticated and valuable pilot charts published by today's Defense Mapping Agency explicitly credit Maury's inspiration.

Maximilian Affair

Taking advantage of wartime confusion, Napoleon III placed the Austrian Archduke Maximilian (1832-1867) on the Mexican throne and ignored American demands to remove the French troops supporting him. Union diplomatic and military pressure failed to dislodge the French, who finally withdrew their forces in May 1866; unprotected, Maximilian was deposed and executed by the forces of Benito Juarez.

Maynard Carbine

The Union government bought more than 20,000 of these breechloading small arms, designed by a Washington, DC, dental surgeon named Edward Maynard. It weighed six pounds, was slightly more than three feet in length, and used a brass cartridge fired by a percussion cap.

Maynard Tape

This primer, patented in 1845, consisted of a roll of glued pellets of fulminate of mercury sandwiched between two strips of varnished paper. This tape was rolled in a coil inside a magazine located in the stock of the weapon. The cocking of the hammer drew one pellet at a time into position. When the hammer struck, the pellet exploded. The inventor of the primer, Edward Maynard, later developed the Maynard Carbine (*See*).

McCausland, John *(1836-1927)* **Confederate general.**

Born in Missouri, he was graduated from the Virginia Military Institute, joined its faculty, then left for the war. McCausland fought at Fort Donelson and defended the Virginia and Tennessee Railroad. He burned Chambersburg, Pennsylvania, in retaliation for Union General David Hunter's destruction in the Shenandoah Valley.

McCoull House, *Virginia*

A landmark at the Battle of Spotsylvania, McCoull House stood at the center of the Confederate line. Confederate General Richard Ewell's troops were entrenched in a horseshoe-shaped line in front of the house, defining the area known as the 'Mule Shoe' or 'Bloody Salient,' which saw the bloodiest fighting of the 1864 battle.

From fortified positions such as these on Marye's Heights the Confederates devastated the Union army at Fredericksburg in 1862.

McClellan, George Brinton
(1826-1885) **Union general.**

It would be McClellan's achievement to build the greatest army the country had ever seen; it would be his tragedy that he was unable to lead it to a decisive victory. Pennsylvania-born and an outstanding West Point student, McClellan saw distinguished service in the Mexican War. A railroad executive when the Civil War began, he re-inlisted as a major general (at age 35) and took over the Department of Ohio. His success in keeping Kentucky and western Virginia in the Union (*See* WESTERN VIRGINIA CAMPAIGN OF MCCLELLAN) brought him to Washington in July 1861, to become commander of the Division of the Potomac and, that winter, general-in-chief of all Union armies. In Washington, McClellan created the Army of the Potomac virtually from the ground up.

But at that point his success had reached its zenith. In leading his army in the field, McClellan would prove consistently slow and indecisive, to the growing consternation of President Lincoln. Prodded into the Peninsular Campaign of summer 1862 – and meanwhile relieved as general-in-chief – McClellan took immensely superior forces to the gates of Richmond, yet somehow ended up retreating without having lost a battle. His generalship at the Battle of Antietam in September 1862 was similarly ineffective, though he was nominally the victor. Lincoln relieved McClellan in November. The general's last hurrah in national politics was his unsuccessful challenge to Lincoln for the presidency in the election of 1864.

McClellan's reputation in history is that of a brilliant administrator, a considerable strategist, and a poor fighter. He carried self-confidence and self-importance to the brink of insubordination, yet he ended the war still a wronged hero to many, and he never lost the affection of his troops.

McClernand, John Alexander
(1812-1900) **Union general.**

An Illinois editor and Democratic politician, he proved a politically ambitious, sometimes insubordinate, and only occasionally effective officer. McClernand commanded troops at Forts Henry and Donelson and at Shiloh, and he led the controversial Arkansas Post expedition *(See)*, later leading XIII Corps in the Vicksburg and Red River Campaigns. He resigned in ill health in November 1864.

McCook Family of Ohio
('The Fighting McCooks.')

The brothers Daniel (1798-1863) and John (1806-1865) McCook and their 13 sons ('the tribe of Dan' and 'the tribe of John') all served the Union with distinction. The elder McCooks served respectively as an army paymaster and surgeon; of their sons, six became generals and three died in the war. The best known of the sons were General Alexander M. McCook, who fought at Shiloh, Perryville, Stone's River, and Chickamauga, and General Edward M. McCook, who commanded cavalry under W. T. Sherman in his Atlanta Campaign.

McDowell *(Virginia)*, Battle of

Two Federal brigades under Robert Schenck attacked Stonewall Jackson here on May 8, 1862, during the Shenandoah Valley Campaign of Jackson. Though Jackson repulsed the attack, his forces suffered nearly twice as many casualties (about 500) as Schenck's. The Federals withdrew, but Jackson was unable to mount a vigorous pursuit.

The second of Wilmer McLean's famed wartime houses was this one, at Appomattox, scene of Lee's surrender to Grant in 1865.

Union General George Meade.

McDowell, Irvin *(1818-1885)*
Union general.

Ohio-born McDowell was graduated from West Point in 1838. He returned to teach tactics there and in addition saw Mexican War, frontier, and Washington staff service. In May 1861 he received the Union's most critical command, leading the Army of the Potomac, but after his defeat at First Bull Run he was immediately demoted to division commander. His performance in leading the short-lived Army of the Rappahannock at Cedar Mountain and Rappahannock Station, and III Corps at Second Bull Run, drew strong criticism, and he was removed from command. Although an inquiry exonerated his performance, McDowell received no further field commands, serving on army boards until receiving his last wartime assignment commanding the Department of the Pacific (July 1864-June 1865). Though an ineffectual field commander, McDowell was an excellent administrator.

McKay, Charlotte Elizabeth
Union Army nurse.

McKay left Massachusetts to enlist as an army nurse in March 1862. She nursed men wounded in the Potomac Army campaigns from Winchester through Spotsylvania, serving in City Point hospital during the sieges of Petersburg and Richmond and earning the Kearny cross. After the war she worked with freed blacks in Virginia.

McLean Houses

Houses owned by Wilmer McLean were the settings for two climactic episodes of the war, one early and one late. After his house on Bull Run was damaged in the first battle there in July 1861, he moved his family to Appomattox. Robert E. Lee surrendered to Ulysses S. Grant in the parlor of McLean's Appomattox house on April 9, 1865.

Meade, George Gordon
(1815-1872) **Union general.**

Born in Spain of American parents, he was graduated from West Point in 1835 and resigned for a brief stint of civil engineering before rejoining the army in 1842 as a military engineer. A brigade leader in the Peninsular and Second Bull Run Campaigns, Meade demonstrated consistent soundness as a field commander, leading a division at Antietam and Fredericksburg and V Corps at Chancellorsville. Assuming command when Joseph Hooker resigned five days before the Battle of Gettysburg, he is deservedly credited with being the main architect of that great Northern victory. Whether he was remiss in not pursuing Robert E. Lee's retreating Rebel army more vigorously in the aftermath of Gettysburg is a much-debated point: Lee's Army of Northern Virginia was then certainly vulnerable to calamatous injury, but

Union General Irvin McDowell's reputation never recovered after his defeat in the Civil War's first major battle.

Meade insisted that the Army of the Potomac was too exhausted to seize the opportunity, and he may well have been right. He led the Army of the Potomac through the rest of the war, fighting from the Wilderness through Appomattox accompanied in the field by his superior, Ulysses S. Grant, an awkward position which by all accounts Meade, who could be temperamental, handled with admirable loyalty and skill. After the war he commanded various military departments.

Meagher, Thomas Francis (1823-1867) Union general.

A nationalist expelled from Ireland, Meagher became the leader of New York's Irish community. He commanded a Zouave company at First Bull Run and the Irish Brigade through the Peninsular Campaign, Second Bull Run, Antietam, Fredericksburg, and Chancellorsville, later commanding the District of Etowah and participating in the 1864 Atlanta Campaign.

Mechanicsville (Virginia), Battle of

Second of the 1862 Seven Days' Battles. On June 26 Robert E. Lee sent John Magruder with 25,000 men to make a feint at the 60,000 Federals on the south bank of the Chickahominy River. With his main body, Lee hoped to overwhelm Fitz-John Porter's 30,000 Federals isolated on the north bank. But Lee's complex plan of attack foundered, due mainly to the slowness of the exhausted Stonewall Jackson and his men. Porter repulsed the attack easily near Mechanicsville.

Memminger, Christopher Gustavus (1803-1888)
Confederate secretary of the treasury.

This German immigrant was a South Carolina lawyer and legislator. As Confederate secretary of the treasury (1861-64), Memminger faced difficult choices: without cotton exports, taxes, or bonds to finance the war, he issued treasury notes which became nearly worthless (*See* Confederate Currency) as the Confederacy's credit collapsed.

Memorial Day

Mississippi declared a state holiday to decorate Civil War veterans' graves on April 26, 1865; the first national observance of Decoration Day, inaugurated by John A. Logan (*See*), was May 30, 1868. State by state, beginning with New York in 1874, the holiday was renamed Memorial Day and was broadened to commemorate all who had fallen in American wars throughout the nation's history.

Meridian Campaign

In preparation for the 1864 Red River Campaign, Federal General W. T. Sherman decided to operate against enemy railroads and resources in central Mississippi. Starting from Vicksburg on February 3, 1864, Sherman got as far as Meridian on the 14th, after a series of skirmishes. After destroying enemy facilities there, he withdrew to Canton to await a supporting force under Sooy Smith. Finding that Smith had been routed by Nathan B. Forrest at West Point, Mississippi, on the 21st, Sherman returned to Vicksburg.

Merritt, Wesley (1834-1910)
Union general.

A young West Point graduate when war broke out, this New Yorker was aide-de-camp to Philip St. George Cooke and George Stoneman. Leading a cavalry brigade and then the Cavalry Corps of the Shenandoah Army, he saw nearly continuous action for the last two years of the war, winning numerous brevets.

Chapultepec, Mexico, is stormed by US troops on September 13, 1847. Many veterans of the Mexican War held high commands in the Civil War, including Lee, Grant, Jackson, Sherman, both Johnstons, Thomas, Meade, and McClellan.

Messes

Early in the war cooking duty rotated among everyone in the military, the men preparing food and eating individually or in squads. Tradition claims that the rotation passed to whoever complained first about the food. In March 1863 Congress ordered food preparation to be shifted to company level, but foraging and cooking by individuals and squads continued throughout the war.

Mexican War

The United States fought a war with Mexico (1846-1848) that had considerable bearing on the Civil War. To begin with, many of the Americans who were most intent on pursuing the war with Mexico tended to be those interested in acquiring more land that could be used by slave-holders, so disagreements over the war tended to reinforce the split already existing between free- and slave-state advocates. When the war ended and the United States found itself with so much new territory, the debate many people hoped had been resolved by the Compromise of 1820 broke out anew: should new slave states be allowed into the Union? The result was the Compromise of 1850, with its recognition of 'popular sovereignty' – effectively saying that each new state could decide for itself whether to be free or slave. From that point on the nation seemed headed down a road to civil war. In another way, too, the Mexican War affected the Civil War: many of the leading Federal and Confederate officers had gained their combat experience fighting side-by-side in the Mexican War – among them, Ulysses S. Grant and Robert E. Lee.

Middleburg, *Virginia*

One of Union General Alfred Pleasanton's cavalry brigades chased Jeb Stuart's forces out of this place after a hot charge by the 4th Pennsylvania Cavalry on June 19, 1863. This early clash in the Gettysburg Campaign cost 99 Federal casualties; Stuart reported 40 of his troopers missing.

Miles Court of Inquiry

On August 10, 1861, this court ruled that insufficient evidence existed to convict Union Col. D. S. Miles of drunkenness during the Battle of First Bull Run. I. B. Richardson brought the charge after Miles ordered changes in the dispositions of two of Richardson's regiments during the battle.

Miles, Nelson Appleton
(1839-1925) **Union general.**

This Boston store clerk received a commission in a Massachusetts regiment in September 1861 and earned rapid promotion. Wounded at Fair Oaks during the Peninsular Campaign, he recovered in time to command the 61st New York at Antietam. He was

The Battle of Missionary Ridge, which broke the Confederate siege of Chattanooga, was freakish in that it was won by an assault that the Union command had not ordered.

wounded at Fredericksburg; he also fought at Chancellorsville, the Wilderness, and Spotsylvania. From July 1864 until the war's end Miles led a division in the II Corps. He commanded the guard over Jefferson Davis, imprisoned after the war in Fortress Monroe. In later years he won fame as an Indian fighter. He became commander-in-chief of the army in 1895 and played a prominent role in the Spanish-American War of 1898.

Mill Springs, Battle of

See LOGAN'S CROSS ROADS

Mine Run, *Virginia*

This was the culminating engagement – or, rather, non-engagement – of the Bristoe Campaign (*See*), in which Robert E. Lee feebly tried to regain some measure of initiative against the Army of the Potomac after Gettysburg. By the end of November 1863 it was clear that Lee's offensive maneuverings had come to nothing, his Army of Northern Virginia had gone back to the defensive, and Union General George Meade was considering a counter-stroke. On November 30 the two armies faced each other across a small brook called Mine Run, and what might be a major, possibly decisive, battle seemed in the offing. But at the last minute the Union field commander, Gouverneur Warren, declined to attack, judging the Rebel positions too

strong. Soon thereafter, both armies went into winter quarters, and Mine Run became one more of history's countless, fascinating 'might-have-beens.'

Minie Ball or Bullet

A French army officer named Minié designed this bullet-shaped projectile to be fired from a muzzle-loading rifle. It had a shallow depression in its after end, which trapped expanding powder gasses and forced the soft-sided bullet hard into the rifling grooves of the barrel, thus eliminating windage and giving the bullet improved accuracy. From its appearance in 1849 the Minie (American soldiers pronounced it 'minnie') substantially increased the deadliness of rifle fire.

Minnesota Sioux Uprising

A six-week uprising of reservation Sioux began on August 17, 1862. Rebellious tribesmen killed nearly 300 white settlers before Union General H. H. Sibley managed to put down the outbreak. On December 6, Lincoln ordered the execution of 39 Sioux; 38 tribesmen were hanged on December 26.

Missionary Ridge *(Tennessee)*, Battle of

Ulysses Grant's Union forces assaulted Braxton Bragg's main defenses here on November

25, 1863, in the decisive battle of the Chattanooga Campaign. W. T. Sherman's attack on the Confederate left, planned as the main effort, made little progress, and late in the day Grant ordered an assault on the center. Two divisions each of the IV and XIV Corps moved forward and easily captured the first defensive line. Though they had been ordered to halt there, the attackers pressed forward on their own initiative and drove Bragg's forces off the summit. The defeat sealed the Confederate loss of Chattanooga, a vital east-west communications link, and opened the way for William Tecumseh Sherman's Atlanta Campaign.

Mississippi Rifle

This US Army rifle, introduced in 1841, fired a round ball from a .54-caliber barrel. The weapon was so named because it armed Jefferson Davis's Mississippi Volunteers during the Mexican War.

Missouri Compromise

See COMPROMISES OF 1820 AND 1850.

Mobile Bay, Naval Battle of

By the autumn of 1864 Union naval operations had shut down most Confederate ports, the major one remaining being that of Mobile Bay, Alabama. On August 5 a Union fleet under Admiral David Farragut steamed in to claim the bay. The admiral led on his flagship *Hartford*, followed by 14 wooden steamships and four *Monitor*-class ironclads. The defending Southern fleet consisted of three wooden gunboats and a powerful new ironclad of the *Merrimac* type, the *Tennessee*. The Confederates placed their main hopes on two forts guarding the bay, Forts Gaines and Morgan, and in a number of mines (then called torpedoes) in the water.

The forts' batteries opened up as Farragut approached; then one of the Union ironclads, USS *Tecumseh*, hit a torpedo and sank immediately. Seeing his seamen shaken by that, Farragut roared his famous words of defiance: 'Damn the torpedoes! Full speed ahead!' The Union ships continued into the bay. For a half hour Union ships circled the *Tennessee* at close range, pounding the ship's armor with gunfire and ramming; finally the ironclad, her steering damaged, gave up. With the loss of their main warship, the Confederates were forced to capitulate. Casualties were high for a naval engagement in the war – the Union lost 319 sailors (93 drowned in the *Tecumseh*) and the South 312. With the closing of the port the South lost one of its last sources of food and supplies.

Mobile Campaign

During March 17-April 12, 1865, Federal General E. R. S. Canby closed in on Mobile, Alabama, with a divided force of 45,000 men. After taking enemy garrisons in the area with

The historic duel between the ironclads, USS *Monitor* vs CSS *Virginia* (ex-*Merrimac*), may have ended the age of fighting sail, but it has somehow drifted into the background in this busy Kurz & Allison print.

considerable losses, his men occupied Mobile on April 12. Ulysses Grant later noted in his memoirs that the capture of the town was costly and too late to be of military importance, since Robert E. Lee had already surrendered at Appomattox.

Monacacy, *Maryland*

As part of Jubal Early's Washington Raid (*See*), Confederate raider Early arrived at the Monacacy River near Frederick on July 9, 1864, to find Lew Wallace's 6000 Federals in his path. A series of largely unplanned Confederate attacks routed the mostly green Union troops; the bulk of the 2000 Federal casualties were listed as 'missing.' Rather than wasting time in pursuit, Early pressed on toward Washington.

Monitor

This generic term described a type of shallow-draft, low-freeboard ironclad Union warship that carried its guns in one or two revolving turrets. The name was taken from USS *Monitor* (*See*), which fought its famous duel with the big Confederate ironclad ram *Merrimac* in March 1862.

A *Harper's Weekly* version of the sinking of USS *Monitor* in a storm. The craft depicted is, however, another type of monitor.

Monitor and *Merrimac*, Battle of

At the beginning of the war both sides knew that the newly developed armored warship would radically change naval warfare, for ironclad ships would be nearly impervious to the fire of existing naval weapons. The initial step toward an ironclad fleet was taken by Confederate Secretary of the Navy Stephen R. Mallory, who had been forced, by the South's lack of materials and industry, to be resourceful. In April 1861 the Union had to abandon its Norfolk, Virginia, Navy Yard, leaving behind the partly-burned steam frigate USS *Merrimac*. The Confederates salvaged the ship with hull and engines intact and rebuilt it into a completely ironclad vessel, 263 feet long, with a sloping citadel made of 24-inch-thick oak and pine covered by two inches of railroad iron. She carried four rifled guns (two 6.4-inchers and two 7-inchers) and six 9-inch smoothbores, and a 1500-pound iron ramming prow projected from her bow. Sailing with her armored decks awash, the ship rather resembled a floating barn roof with smoking stovepipe. She was rechristened the CSS *Virginia*, but history has persisted in calling her the *Merrimac*.

Washington heard of the Southern ironclad project soon after it began, and Union Navy Secretary Gideon Welles made haste to build comparable armored ships. Swedish-born inventor John Ericsson had been working on the idea for some time already and had developed a sophisticated design featuring a hull that was flat on top and covered with iron plates and that floated only a few feet above the waterline. Rising from this iron raft were a stubby pilothouse in front, a short smokestack to the rear, and in the middle a heavily armored rotating iron turret some 9 feet high and 140 tons in weight. The ship was armed with only two 11-inch Dahlgren smoothbore cannons, but the turret enabled them to fire in any direction. The odd-looking result, called the *Monitor*, was finished in January 1862.

It was ready none too soon. On March 8, 1862, the *Merrimac* made a devastating first appearance off the coast of Virginia, at Hampton Roads, where she attacked a Union blockading fleet of wooden ships, sank the 30-gun sloop-of-war *Cumberland* and crippled the 50-gun frigate *Congress*. Union commanders could see their cannonballs bouncing off the *Merrimac* like marbles off a brick wall. In late afternoon the cumbersome ironclad lumbered off with little damage, though the ramming prow had broken off and her captain, Franklin Buchanan, had been injured. Lieutenant Catesby ap Roger Jones took over command.

When the Confederate ironclad steamed out on March 9 to finish off the Federal fleet, however, her sailors saw a bizarre object slip around a grounded Union ship and head for them. They took it for a boiler going for repairs on a raft, until the oncoming *Monitor* fired her first shot.

The two ships closed in, at times touching and firing point-blank, both trying without success to find a weak spot. Several times the *Merrimac* tried to ram the smaller *Monitor*, but Federal Captain Lorimer Worden was easily able to outmaneuver his slow-moving opponent. In the first two hours of fighting the *Monitor* took 21 hits without serious damage; sailors in the sweltering turret were threatened mainly by large screwheads that came loose and richocheted around the chamber with every hit. Federal cannonfire was able to crack but not penetrate the armor of the formidable *Merrimac*.

Just after noon the historic battle trailed off indecisively. Over the next few days the *Monitor* challenged the *Merrimac* several times, but it had been decided not to risk another engagement with the Union ship. She had already done her primary job of preserving the Union fleet in the area.

Neither ship survived the war. The unseaworthy *Merrimac* had to be destroyed by the Confederates when they abandoned Norfolk in May 1862. The *Monitor* was swamped and went down in a gale off Cape Hatteras in December 1862. As the North and South began building more ironclads on the model of these prototypes, governments around the world realized that their wooden fleets had become obsolete in a single afternoon.

Montgomery Convention

A provisional Confederate Congress met in the Alabama capital in February 1861. On February 8 the convention adopted a provisional constitution patterned on the US Consitution. Among other changes, however, it guaranteed the right to own slaves. The following day it elected Jefferson Davis provisional president of the Confederacy.

Morgan, George Washington (1820-1893) Union general.

A Pennsylvanian who attended West Point but was not graduated, he served in the Mexican War and then entered the diplomatic service. Upon the outbreak of the Civil War he was made a brigadier general, served under Don Carlos Buell in Tennessee, led a division in the Yazoo Expedition, and led XIII Corps in the capture of Arkansas Post. Ill health forced his resignation in June 1863.

Morgan, John Hunt (1825-1864) and Morgan's Raids
Confederate general.

A Mexican War veteran, he commanded a squadron of Kentucky cavalry at the start of the war. Promoted to brigade command in April 1862, he embarked the first of three famous raids in July, working in conjunction with Nathan B. Forrest's raids on Union General Don Carlos Buell's supply lines in Kentucky after the battle of Shiloh. Morgan and 800 men captured four Union cavalry

Confederate cavalry leader John Hunt Morgan, famed for his raids behind Union lines.

companies in Tomkinsville and depots at Glasgow and Lebanon, and skirmished with local militia in Cynthiana, returning to Tennessee with some 1200 prisoners. In his second raid, in October 1862, Morgan took Lexington and a number of smaller Federal outposts in Kentucky. The third raid stretched through the end of that year and into January 1863, as Morgan raided William Rosecrans's supply lines in Tennessee and destroyed some $2 million-worth of Federal supplies while taking 1887 prisoners; his own losses totalled two dead and 24 wounded. After these successes, however, Morgan came to grief in the Ohio Raid of July 1863, in which he took some 2500 men on a destructive but fairly random raid around that state. Meanwhile, Federal forces gradually gathered around him, finally running Morgan and his 300 remaining men to ground at New Lisbon, where he was captured on July 26. He escaped from Federal prison, got back go Confederate lines, and resumed his raiding. While making a raid on Greenville, Tennessee, he was surrounded and killed by Union troops in September 1864.

Mortars

These stubby-barreled artillery weapons that fire their munitions in high, arcing trajectories were used to throw heavy shells into enemy fortifications. Field armies carried 8- to 10-inch mortars; heavier ones were used as seacoast artillery and in static siege operations. A 13-inch mortar weighed 20,000 pounds and fired a 220-pound bomb.

Mosby, John Singleton (1833-1916)
Confederate raider.

A lawyer before the war, Mosby rode for a time with Jeb Stuart's Confederate cavalry before creating a band that would have the

The guerrilla cavalry leader John Singleton Mosby (standing, fifth from left), posing with some of his Confederate irregulars.

most success of the war's various guerrilla groups. In January 1863 Mosby and his Partisan Rangers commenced operations in Virginia. They would become known as Mosby's Irregulars, their area of operations in Virginia was called Mosby's Confederacy and their leader 'The Gray Ghost.'

They retained a loose association with Stuart's cavalry, doing advance scouting for him and stealing Union horses. Most of the time they managed to steal all the supplies they needed for themselves from the enemy. Their main business was to impede Federal operations. Mosby and his men first hit the headlines in March 1863 with a raid on a Union camp at Fairfax Court House that netted them the commanding blue general and some 30 other prisoners, plus 58 horses. Eventually Mosby had some 1000 mounted men in his command, but in most of his raids used fewer than 300. He continued operations to the end of the war. Later Mosby became a friend and an ardent political supporter of Ulysses S. Grant, who had once ordered him hanged.

Mud March

Union General Ambrose Burnside's second attempt to cross the Rappahannock after his terrible defeat at Fredericksburg ended in farce. The army started out for Banks's Ford on January 20, 1863, aiming to cross there and turn Robert E. Lee's flank, but two days of heavy rain left the men bogged down in a quagmire. Burnside called off the march on January 23. Lincoln relieved him of command of the Army of the Potomac shortly thereafter, replacing him with the almost as luckless General Joseph Hooker.

Mudd, Dr. Samuel (1833-1883)
Physician.

A Maryland physician who set John Wilkes Booth's broken leg after the Lincoln assassination, he was alleged to have been part of the murder conspiracy. Tried, convicted and sentenced to life imprisonment in the Dry

Tortugas off the Florida Keys, he cared for the garrison and prisoners during a severe yellow fever outbreak. Mudd was at last pardoned in 1869.

'Mule Charge'

Confederate General Braxton Bragg ordered a night raid on Joseph Hooker's Union forces carrying out Cracker Line operations (See) near Chattanooga on October 28-29, 1863. The Federals turned back the attackers in a confused battle, one of the rare night actions of the war. The legend of the 'mule charge' evidently grew out of the stampede toward the Confederate lines of some animals in the Federal supply train.

Munfordville, *Kentucky*

Confederate General Braxton Bragg surrounded the 4100-strong Federal garrison here during Bragg's Kentucky invasion (See) of September 1862. Asked to surrender, the inexperienced Federal commander, an Indiana manufacturer named J. T. Wilder, met under a flag of truce with Bragg's lieutenant, General Simon B. Buckner, to seek advice on what to do. Buckner made no suggestions, but he did permit Wilder to count the Confederate cannon. Wilder surrendered the garrison shortly thereafter.

Murfreesboro, Battle of

See STONE'S RIVER.

Murfreesboro, *Tennessee*

Near this Tennessee town on December 7, 1864, Federals under Robert L. Milroy struck the forces of Nathan Bedford Forrest, who had been ordered by General John B. Hood to raid the area in support of the Franklin and Nashville Campaign. Milroy forced Forrest from the field, in the process capturing over 200 men and 14 guns.

Music in the Civil War

It is safe to say that the entire Civil War was carried on accompanied by music. It was heard on the march, in camp, even in battle: armies marched to the attack to the heroic rhythms of drums and often of brass bands. The fear and tedium of sieges was eased by nightly band concerts, which often featured requests shouted from both sides of the lines. Around camp there was usually a fiddler or guitarist or banjo player at work, and voices to sing the favorite songs of the era.

Songs of the war covered every aspect of the conflict and every feeling about it. There were the patriotic songs for each side: the North's 'John Brown's Body' that Julia Ward Howe made into 'The Battle Hymn of the Republic'; the South's 'Dixie' (originally a prewar minstrel-show song). The slaves had their tradition of songs of hope: 'Follow the Drinking Gourd,' the words said guardedly – meaning follow the Big Dipper north to the Underground Railroad and freedom.

Soldiers sang sentimental tunes about distant love – the popular 'Lorena' and 'Aura Lee' (which in this century became 'Love Me Tender') and 'The Yellow Rose of Texas' –

A group portrait of the band of the 8th New York State Militia taken in 1861. Military bands played an important role in the Civil War, both in camp and in battle.

and songs of loss such as 'The Vacant Chair.' Other tunes commemorated victory – 'Marching Through Georgia' was a vibrant evocation of Sherman's March to the Sea. Soldiers marched to the rollicking 'Eatin' Goober Peas'; they vented their war-weariness with 'Hard Times'; they sang about their life in 'Tenting Tonight on the Old Camp Ground'; they were buried to the soulful keening of 'Taps,' written for the dead of both sides in the Seven Days' Battles. When the guns stopped, the survivors returned to

Part of the cover of a song composed in honor of Union General mcClellan.

the haunting strains of 'When Johnny Comes Marching Home.'

After Robert E. Lee surrendered, Lincoln, on one of the last days of his life, asked a Northern band to play 'Dixie,' saying it had always been one of his favorite tunes. No one could miss the meaning of this gesture of reconciliation, expressed by music.

Mutinies

These were comparatively rare, given the large numbers of volunteer soldiers raised by both sides. On August 14, 1861, troops of the 79th New York mutinied after they were denied furlough; several men were arrested. George McClellan dealt severely with minor outbreaks in the Army of the Potomac in the autumn of 1861. Confederate troops at Fort Jackson, Louisiana, part of the New Orleans defenses, mutinied on April 27, 1862, and many fled into the swamps before their officers surrendered the fort next day.

Muzzle-Loaders

At the beginning of the war most cannon, muskets, and rifles were loaded from the muzzle, which not only meant that the loading process was slow but that the weapons were necessarily single-shot. Gradually large numbers of more efficient breech-loading cannon and small arms, both single- and multiple-shot, came into service.

Myer, Albert James (1829-1880)
Union officer.

This New York-born army surgeon helped develop the 'wigwag' flag-signal system. The army's first signal officer, he served on the staffs of Benjamin Butler, Irvin McDowell, and George McClellan and directed the Signal Corps (See SIGNAL COMMUNICATIONS) before being assigned as signal officer along the Mississippi. Fort Myer, Virginia, is named after him.

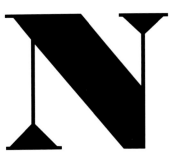

Namozine Church and Willicomack Creek, *Virginia*

After the Five Forks Battle, Federal cavalry from George A. Custer's division caught retreating Confederates at Willicomack Creek on April 3, 1862. Charging dismounted, the Federal troopers took the position, capturing most of a Confederate brigade, and continued the pursuit to Namozine Church. There they paused for the night to wait for the infantry to come up.

Napoleon Gun Howitzer

This 12-pounder muzzle-loader, the most widely-used field gun in both armies, fired a 4.62-caliber shell from a smoothbore barrel at a maximum effective range of over 1000 yards. Its rate of fire was about two rounds per minute. It also fired short-range canister and grape shot. The US Army adopted the Napoleon in 1857; the Confederates captured large numbers on the battlefield, and also manufactured their own copies. The gun's name derived from the fact that its design was credited to Louis-Napoleon of France.

Nashville, Battle of

See FRANKLIN AND NASHVILLE CAMPAIGN

Nashville Convention

In June 1850 leaders from nine Southern states met to discuss the slavery issue, and some spoke openly of secession. The delegates approved a resolution calling for the extension of slavery to the Pacific Ocean south of 36°, 30' – the Missouri Compromise line.

National Union Party

Pro-Lincoln Republicans contested the 1864 national election under this banner to attract the votes of 'loyal' Democrats, the term 'Republican' having acquired an extremist connotation which had cost the party in the midterm elections. The name was resurrected in 1866 by Andrew Johnson supporters who were seeking to mobilize opposition to the Radical Republicans.

A beautifully preserved example of a 12-pounder Napoleon gun, the most widely used artillery weapon in the Civil War,

Naval War

The Civil War was mostly a ground conflict, but the naval arm still played a vital role. The Union began the war with a substandard navy consisting of around 9000 officers and men (some of whom defected to the Confederacy) and 90 vessels, many in poor repair; the loss of the Norfolk Navy Yard in April 1861 further reduced the Union fleet. Under Navy Secretary Gideon Welles, however, the North built back up to 641 vessels, including several ironclads. The Confederate Navy, meanwhile, started from nothing under Secretary Stephen R. Mallory, and also had no shipbuilding capacity. Mallory's main procedure was having ships built in supposedly neutral England and Europe. For more specifics of the war afloat, refer to individual entries, including Blockade, *Monitor-Merrimac*, Burnside's Expedition to North Carolina, New Orleans, Mobile Bay, *Kearsarge*, and *Alabama*. In many land battles, gunboats accompanied infantry operations onshore, contributing substantially, for example, to the Union comeback at Shiloh.

New Bern, *North Carolina*

Federal forces captured this port city on March 14, 1862, during Ambrose Burnside's North Carolina Expedition. The Confederates were never able to recapture the place.

New Madrid (*Missouri*) and Island No. 10

These contained two Confederate garrisons on the Mississippi River, whose batteries forestalled Union operations on the river. On March 13, 1862, the defenders evacuated New Madrid after ten days of siege by Federal

General John Pope. The Federals then turned to Island No. 10, capturing its 3500 men on April 7. This opened a long stretch of the Mississippi to the Union and gave Pope a high reputation for the moment, a reputation he would soon lose in his humiliating defeat at the Second Bull Run Battle.

New Market (*Virginia*), Battle of

Confederate forces under John C. Breckinridge attacked 5100 Union troops under Franz Sigel here late in the morning of May 15, 1864, during the fighting that took place in the aftermath of the Battle of Spotsylvania. The assault gradually forced the Federals back, and at 4:00 pm Sigel ordered a general retreat. Federal casualties were 831; the attackers lost 577 out of 5000 engaged. In the aftermath Sigel was relieved of his command.

New Market Heights (*Virginia*),

(also called Chafin's Farm, Laurel Hill, Forts Harrison and Gilmer)

As part of his 1864 Petersburg Campaign, Ulysses Grant sent troops on a surprise attack on Forts Harrison and Gilmer, part of the city's defenses. In heavy fighting on September 29, Federals captured Harrison but not Gilmer; Robert E. Lee's Confederates failed in an attempt to retake Harrison the following day. Losses in two days of fighting were over 2500 for the North (mostly missing) and 2800 for the South (300 taken prisoner).

New Mexico and Arizona Operations

Action in these territories during the Civil War, though something of a sideshow, arose

A US Army map showing Rebel and Union forces around New Madrid and Island No. 10.

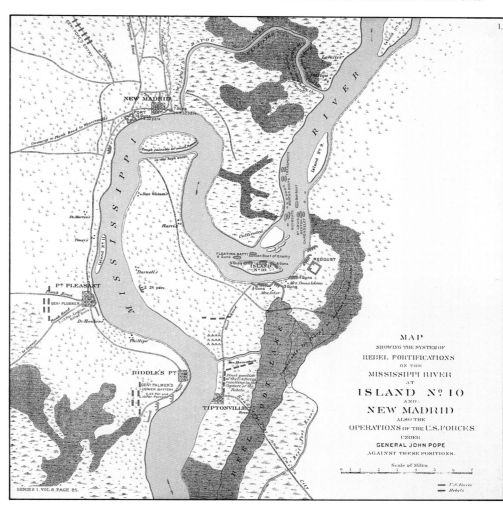

Farragut's daring run past the New Orleans forts in April 1862. Farragut's flagship, USS *Hartford* (upper center), is shown being assailed by a Confederate fireship.

because of an attempt to claim them for the Confederacy. In 1861 John Baylor organized the Confederate Department of Texas. In July of that year he occupied Fort Bliss in El Paso with 300 men; then, at the end of the month, he and 200 men captured a Federal garrison of 700 at Fort Fillmore, after which Baylor proclaimed himself governor of the new Confederate Territory of Arizona.

At the end of 1861 CSA General H. H. Sibley got together a force he called the Army of New Mexico and combined them with Baylor's men for operations against E. R. S. Canby's Federal Department of New Mexico. Sibley's operations began auspiciously when he won the Battle of Valverde (*See*) on February 21, 1862. Sibley then marched his forces, some 2600 men, toward Sante Fe to capture the Union supply depot there. He occupied the town on May 23, only to find the supplies had been withdrawn, and continued on toward Fort Union under increasing harassment from Federal forces organized by Canby. Finally, at the end of March, after losing two skirmishes with the outnumbering bluecoats and failing to secure the supplies he needed, Sibley decided it was time to retreat. He reached Fort Bliss in early May without pursuit from Canby. There he learned that another Federal column was approaching and so continued on to San Antonio, reaching it with less than a thousand men. This effectively put an end to major Confederate efforts to secure the New Mexico and Arizona territories.

New Orleans Campaign

In 1862 New Orleans, Louisiana, was both the South's greatest commercial port and the key to Confederate power in the lower Mississippi Valley. In April of that year Union Admiral David G. Farragut led a combined operation against the city. His forces consisted of a naval squadron – made up of four steam sloops-of-war, an elderly steam frigate, three smaller sailing vessels, and numerous gunboats and towed mortar schooners – and 15,000 army troops led by Benjamin Butler. The city's floating defenses were centered on the formidable ironclad CSS *Louisiana*, the ram *Manassas*, and a large number of gunboats and floating batteries, but far more important were two fixed defenses, Forts Jackson and St. Philip, which stood on opposite sides of the main channel downriver from New Orleans. Farragut tried for a week to reduce these delta forts by naval bombardment, but he got nowhere and in the end was driven to the risky expedient of trying to run his squadron past the forts in darkness. The attempt was made on the night of April 23-24 and nearly came to grief. Fire from the forts was intense and most of the Rebel naval vessels sortied to do battle. Farragut's flagship, *Hartford*, temporarily ran aground and was badly shot up, the sloop-of-war *Brooklyn* was all but sunk by gunfire from *Louisiana* and ramming by *Manassas*, and most of the other Union warships suffered varying degrees of damage. But somehow the squadron got through, the Rebel vessels were one by one silenced, and New Orleans, defended by only a small garrison, was now open for the taking. Butler formally occupied the city on May 1, Forts Jackson and St. Philip

having surrendered two days earlier. (Butler would soon earn international notoriety for his behavior as the city's heavy-handed military governor – *See* 'WOMAN ORDER').

The strategic consequences of this campaign were out of all proportion to the relatively light casualties suffered on both sides. Not only had the South lost its greatest port, the way was now open for the Union conquest of the entire Mississippi. When this would finally be accomplished, over a year later at Vicksburg, the Old South would be completely surrounded and vulnerable to invasion from the west.

New York Draft Riots

Of the nationwide eruptions following the March 1863 draft act, the New York City riots of July 13-16, 1863, were the most violent. As the draftees' names were drawn, a 50,000-strong mob, mostly Irish working men, burned offices and threatened military men, eventually attacking blacks at random in a full-blown race riot. A dozen people died before the Army of the Potomac restored order – at the cost of 1000 casualties.

Norfolk, *Virginia*

The Federals burned the important Gosport Navy Yard here on April 20, 1861, to keep it from falling into Confederate hands, although, in fact, when they occupied the area, the Confederates were able to salvage much useful war matériel that had escaped destruction. Thereafter, Norfolk was closely blockaded by Union ships. In November 1864 the port came under Union control, and Lincoln ordered the blockade to be lifted.

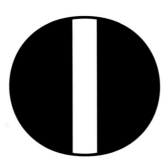

One of the casualties of the inconclusive May 1864 Battle of North Anna River was this demolished railroad bridge.

North Anna River (Virginia), Battle of

After the Battle of Spotsylvania in May 1864 Ulysses Grant hoped to turn R. E. Lee's flank along the North Anna River line. Lee, however, anticipated the move and entrenched his troops at Hanover Junction across Grant's line of advance. Federal forces under Gouverneur Warren crossed the river and attacked the Confederate positions on May 23 without effect. On the following day more Federal forces under Winfield Hancock and Horatio Wright crossed the river, but Lee managed to slip between them and prevent them from joining, thus stalemating them as well. The battle, also known as Jericho Mills, ended in a draw. Grant concluded that Lee's positions were too strong, and he began another turning movement that culminated in the Battle of Cold Harbor.

North Carolina, Department of

The Federal high command created this military district on January 7, 1862, at the start of Burnside's North Carolina Expedition. In mid-July 1863 it was consolidated with the Department of Virginia; it became an independent district again in January 1865.

Northern Virginia, Confederate Department of

Jefferson Davis's government created this military district on October 22, 1861. General J.E. Johnston was its first commander. The district comprised the chief operating area of the Army of Northern Virginia, commanded by Robert E. Lee from June 1, 1862, until his surrender at Appomattox.

Northwest Conspiracy

This abortive operation was to have freed and armed 10,000 Confederate prisoners at Camp Douglas, Illinois, for an attack on Chicago in July 1864. Benjamin J. Sweet, the Union commander of Camp Douglas, discovered the conspiracy and had its leaders arrested.

Nullification Doctrine

South Carolina politician John C. Calhoun argued that the states had a constitutional right to declare null and void any federal law deemed to violate the agreement of Union. He advanced the theory initially as an argument in the debate in 1832 over the Nullification Crisis, in which Andrew Jackson's federal government was threatening military action against South Carolina for having declared the tariff's of 1828 and 1832 void within the state; the dispute was finally settled in a compromise engineered by Henry Clay. The Calhoun doctrine was an early suggestion that states dissatisfied with the federal arrangement might secede.

Oak Grove (Virginia), Battle of
(also called Henrico, King's School House, The Orchards)

This was the opening engagement of the 1862 Seven Days' Battles. Preparing his assault on Richmond, Federal General George McClellan ordered a reconnaissance on June 25. In heavy skirmishing, Union General Joseph Hooker's division drove back Southern outposts near Oak Grove. There were some 500 casualties on each side. The Mechanicsville Battle followed.

Old Capitol Prison

This Washington, DC, prison, formerly the temporary replacement for the US Capitol burned in the War of 1812, held prisoners of war, deserters, and suspected spies.

'Old Fuss and Feathers'

This nickname for General Winfield Scott, commander-in-chief of the US Army at the start of the war, referred to Scott's fondness for military pageantry.

Olustee, Florida

On February 20 Confederate forces attacked and routed a Union division under Truman Seymour at this place, about 20 miles inland from Jacksonville. The Union commander lost more than 1800 of his 5115-man division; Confederate casualties were 934 out of about 5200 engaged.

Ord, Edward Otho Cresap (1818-1883) **Union general.**

This Maryland native, a West Point graduate and 20-year veteran, defended Washington and fought at Dranesville, Iuka, and Hatchie. Ord was a corps commander at Vicksburg, Jackson, and Fort Harrison, and at the Petersburg Siege and in the Appomattox campaign. Several times wounded, he was repeatedly cited for bravery.

Often-breveted Union General Edward Ord was eventually rewarded with the command of the Army of the James in 1865.

Above: A 3-inch Ordnance gun belonging to the Union's 2nd Artillery.
Left: Recovered from President Lincoln's box in Ford's Theatre after his assassination was this playbill for the evening's feature presentation, *Our American Cousin*.

Ordnance Gun

Developed by the US Ordnance Department in 1863, this 3-inch rifled gun was widely used by the horse artillery. Also called the Rodman rifle, it had a maximum range of about 4000 yards.

Organization of Armies

On both sides, Civil War land forces were assigned either to territorial organizations, of which departments were the largest category, or to operational organizations, of which armies were the largest subdivision. Armies were composed of two or more corps; corps of two or more divisions; divisions of two or more brigades; and brigades of two or more regiments. Federals generally named their armies after rivers in their areas of operation (the Army of the Potomac); Confederates named theirs after states or regions (the Army of Northern Virginia).

Osterhaus, Peter *(1823-1917)* Union general.

Prussian-born, he emmigrated to the United States in 1848. He served in Missouri regiments early in the war, and commanded a brigade at Pea Ridge in March 1862. He led a division during the Vicksburg Campaign and the Chattanooga Campaign. From September 1864 to January 1865, he commanded the XV Corps of the Army of the Tennessee.

Our American Cousin

Lincoln was watching a performance of this light comedy at Ford's Theatre the night he was assassinated. The play, written by the English dramatist Tom Taylor, was originally produced in London in 1858; Laura Keene starred in the Washington production.

Page, Charles Anderson
1838-1873 War correspondent.

A young Treasury official released for war reporting, Page became famous for fast, accurate, and vivid dispatches to the New York *Tribune*. He covered the Peninsula, Second Bull Run, the Wilderness, Spotsylvania, and the Petersburg siege and was one of the first reporters into Richmond in April 1865.

Paine, Charles Jackson
(1833-1916) Union general.

A Harvard-trained Massachusetts lawyer, Paine recruited a company in September 1861 and served on the staff of Benjamin F. Butler. He commanded troops at Port Hudson and, as a brigadier general, at New Market and Fort Fisher.

Palmer, John McAuley
(1817-1900) Union general.

Palmer was a Kentucky lawyer, legislator, and 1861 Peace Convention delegate. Joining the 14th Illinois, he commanded troops in the Mississippi, Ohio, and Cumberland Armies, fighting at New Madrid, Point Pleasant, and Island No. 10 and distinguishing himself at Stone's River and Chickamauga.

Palmetto Arms

Ten years before secession South Carolina officials created a small arms industry in the state, awarding rifle, musket, pistol, and saber contracts to the Palmetto Iron Works in Columbia. The factory, renamed the Palmetto Armory, made copies of US arms during the 1850s. During the war, bombs, cannonballs, and Minie balls were manufactured there.

Palmitto Ranch, *Texas*

On May 12, 1865, in the last significant land action of the war, Federals under T.H. Barrett captured a Southern camp at Palmitto Ranch on the Rio Grande, but then withdrew in fear of a counterattack. On the next day the Federals fought their way into the camp again but were repulsed by J.S. Ford's Rebel forces.

A portrait of Grant's staff includes (third from left) Seneca chief Ely S. Parker.

Panada

This hot gruel, invented by Sanitation Commission worker Eliza Harris, was a concoction of army crackers mashed in boiling water, ginger, and wine. An alternate name was bully soup.

Parker, Ely Samuel (1828-1895)
Union officer.

A Seneca chief, Parker trained as a lawyer and then, when refused admission to the bar, as an engineer. He was commissioned captain of engineers in May 1863, serving as J.E. Smith's division engineer and as military secretary to Ulysses S. Grant, a personal friend; Parker transcribed the official copies of Robert E. Lee's surrender.

Parole

Prisoners of war were often released on their pledge of honor not to take up arms again until they had been exchanged. This pledge was commonly called a parole.

Parrott Guns

R. P. Parrott designed a series of rifled guns ranging in size from those firing a 3-inch, 10-pound shell to those firing a 10-inch, 250-pound shell. These muzzle-loaders were more accurate and could fire at greater ranges than smoothbore types.

Partisan Rangers

John S. Mosby first raised this Virginia guerrilla force in January 1863. The rangers specialized in swift raids against Federal rearward supply trains and depots; after an attack, they would disappear into the countryside. Despite intensive effort, the Federals never managed to break up Mosby's band of riders.

Patrick, Marsena Rudolph (1811-1888) **Union general.**

A New Yorker, this West Point graduate and war veteran resigned a college presidency to enlist. After serving on George McClellan's staff and in Washington's defenses, he fought at Second Bull Run, Chantilly, South Mountain, and Antietam; he served as the provost marshal general of the Union army after October 1862.

Pay

Union privates received $13 per month until June 1864, when they were granted a $3 permonth raise. Confederates got $11 per month, raised to $18 in June 1864. A Federal second lieutenant got $105.50 per month; a major general, $457. Confederate officers' monthly pay was slightly less. In both armies, pay was slow and irregular, and this was especially true for private soldiers.

Payne, William Henry Fitzhugh (1830-1904) **Confederate general.**

This Virginia lawyer and public servant commanded cavalrymen at Williamsburg and Chancellorsville, on Stuart's Pennsylvania raid, in Early's Raid on Washington, and at Richmond; he was repeatedly wounded and was captured three times, the last time at the Battle of Five Forks.

Pea Ridge (Arkansas), Battle of (also called Elkhorn Tavern)

In this two-day battle, March 7-8, 1862, Federals under Samuel R. Curtis at Pea Ridge (or Elkhorn Tavern) were assaulted by scraped-together Rebel forces (including Indians) under Earl Van Dorn. Curtis, alerted by scout 'Wild Bill' Hickok of the enemy approach, formed a line of battle on high ground. In the first day of fighting Van Dorn's men got behind Curtis, but the bluecoats faced about and held on; on the other end of the line there was also fierce fighting at Elkhorn Tavern. On the 8th the fighting centered around Elkhorn Tavern and ended in a Northern charge that routed the graycoats. The North suffered about 1384 casualties of 11,250 engaged, the South some 800 of 14,000. Van Dorn had hoped ultimately to be able to march on St. Louis, but this defeat frustrated his plans.

Peace Convention

On February 4, 1861, peace-seeking delegates from 21 Union states (but none of the seceded states) convened in Washington at Virginia's instigation. Led in debate by former President John Tyler, they sincerely but ineffectually tried to save the Union, submitting the Crittenden Compromise (See) and six proposed constitutional amendments to Congress on February 27. None of these was – or could have been – accepted.

Peace Democrats

This influential antiwar group within the Democratic Party succeeded in incorporating a peace plank in the platform for the 1864 presidential election. Although Democratic nominee George McClellan and the majority of the party disavowed it, the peace plank damaged the Democrats on election day.

This photograph of a 10-pounder Parrott gun shows both the rifling and the reinforced breech typical of Parrott's weapons.

Peach Orchard

This lightly wooded area west of Cemetery Ridge was the scene of heavy fighting on the second day (July 2, 1863) of the Battle of Gettysburg when General Daniel Sickles made it the apex of his ill-judged salient in the Union line.

Peach Tree Creek (Georgia), Battle of

Confederate General John B. Hood, taking over from Joseph Johnston the responsibility for Confederate resistance to William T. Sherman's 1864 Atlanta Campaign, made his debut on July 20 with a surprise attack on George Thomas's Federal army at Peachtree Creek. After desperate fighting, often hand-to-hand, Thomas moved up artillery which turned back two hours of desperate Southern assaults. By the end, Hood's forces had sustained nearly 5000 casualties, while Thomas's forces suffered but 1779.

'Peculiar Institution'

This was Southerners' delicate term for slavery. It was coined by John C. Calhoun, who referred to slavery as the 'peculiar domestic institution' in 1830. He intended it to mean 'distinctive' or 'unique,' but many people since then have misinterpreted it to mean 'unusual' or 'strange.'

Southerners often used the euphemism 'our peculiar institution' when speaking of slavery.

Pegram, John *(1832-1865)*
Confederal general.

The Virginian Pegram, a West Point graduate and career soldier, fought a varied war: after surrendering to George McClellan at Rich Mountain during the latter's western Virginia Campaign of 1861, he was an engineer under P.G.T. Beauregard and Braxton Bragg and fought under Kirby Smith, Richard Ewell, and Jubal Early. He was killed in February 1865 at Hatcher's Run.

Pemberton, John Clifford *(1814-1881)* **Confederate general.**

Born into a Pennsylvania Quaker family and married to a Virginian, he was a West Point graduate who fought for the Confederacy. Rapidly promoted, he commanded Southern departments; after he surrendered Vicksburg in July 1863, however, he never received another major command.

Pender, William Dorsey *(1834-1863)* **Confederate general.**

A North Carolinian and West Point graduate (1854), he served on the Northwest frontier until the war began. He earned distinction as a division commander at Antietam and Chancellorsville and, but for his youth, would probably have been given a corps at Gettysburg, where he was mortally wounded on the second day of the fighting. So highly regarded was Pender that some of his admirers compared him to Jackson.

Peninsular Campaign

The progress of the Civil War in the Eastern Theater would largely be in the hands of two armies, the Federal Army of the Potomac and the Confederate Army of Northern Virginia. In the summer of 1862 these armies (the Southern one at that point called the Confederate Army of the Potomac) began their long series of engagements.

Commanding the Southern army at the beginning of 1862 was General Joseph E. Johnston, leader of the victorious forces at the First Bull Run Battle. At the head of the Federal Army of the Potomac was the man who built it, General George B. McClellan. In December 1861, in addition to commanding his forces in the field, McClellan had been named to succeed aged Winfield Scott as general-in-chief of all Union armies. McClellan, a small, ambitious, and energetic man, had created an impressive fighting force, but in the end he would not prove able to lead it to victory. His thoroughness and attention to detail, as well as his fatherly attitude toward his men, proved his greatest liabilities on the battlefield: his elaborate caution and protective attitude toward his army made him ponderous and indecisive whenever he went into action.

In the first months of 1862 General Johnston's Confederate Army of the Potomac lay at Centreville, Virginia, only 30 miles from Washington. On February 22 President Lincoln issued the General War Order No. 1, mandating a movement against the enemy. General McClellan stalled, worrying over his arrangements and alarmed by the erroneous reports of his chief of intelligence, Alan Pinkerton, that enemy forces in Virginia vastly outnumbered Federal strength. (Pinkerton's exaggerated estimates of enemy strength would impede the Union war effort during most of 1862.) Lincoln wanted the Federal Army of the Potomac to advance from the North by land and push Johnston away, staying between the enemy and Washington. Instead, McClellan produced an ingenious plan to move against the Confederate capital at Richmond from the south, by water; he reasoned that Washington's defenses were adequate to any eventuality and that Johnston would be obliged to follow and contest any Federal movement. When Johnston withdrew to Culpeper, Virginia, Lincoln, though still concerned about Washington's vulnerability, consented to McClellan's plan. However, to allow McClellan to concentrate on the campaign, and also because of growing worries about his general, Lincoln relieved McClellan as overall Union commander and took on those duties himself. (Until he found a winning general – Ulysses S. Grant, in March 1864 – Lincoln would involve himself overmuch in army matters.)

McClellan's Peninsular Campaign, aimed at both Johnston and Richmond, began in March 1862, with some 100,000 men, 25,000 animals, 300 cannons, and mountains of supplies beginning the journey on 400 ships to land on the toe of the peninsula between the James and York rivers, about 70 miles southeast of Richmond. McClellan was expecting to be reinforced by the corps of Generals Irvin McDowell and Nathaniel Banks, moving over from their positions in Virginia's

Shenandoah Valley; but during the landing word came from Lincoln that due to the disruptions caused by the Shenandoah Valley Campaign of Stonewall Jackson, McDowell and Banks must stay where they were. This was precisely what Jackson's campaign had meant to accomplish.

Furious at losing the two corps, still convinced by exaggerated estimates of enemy strength, and seeing clearly that Jackson's campaign was intended to tie up Union forces, McClellan fired off a steady stream of letters to Washington demanding reinforcements. In early April, reluctantly, he began

inching his army up the peninsula toward Richmond, but then he stopped in front of Confederate defenses that stretched from Yorktown across the peninsula. These lines

A Union army map shows the main theater in which the Peninsular Campaign was fought.

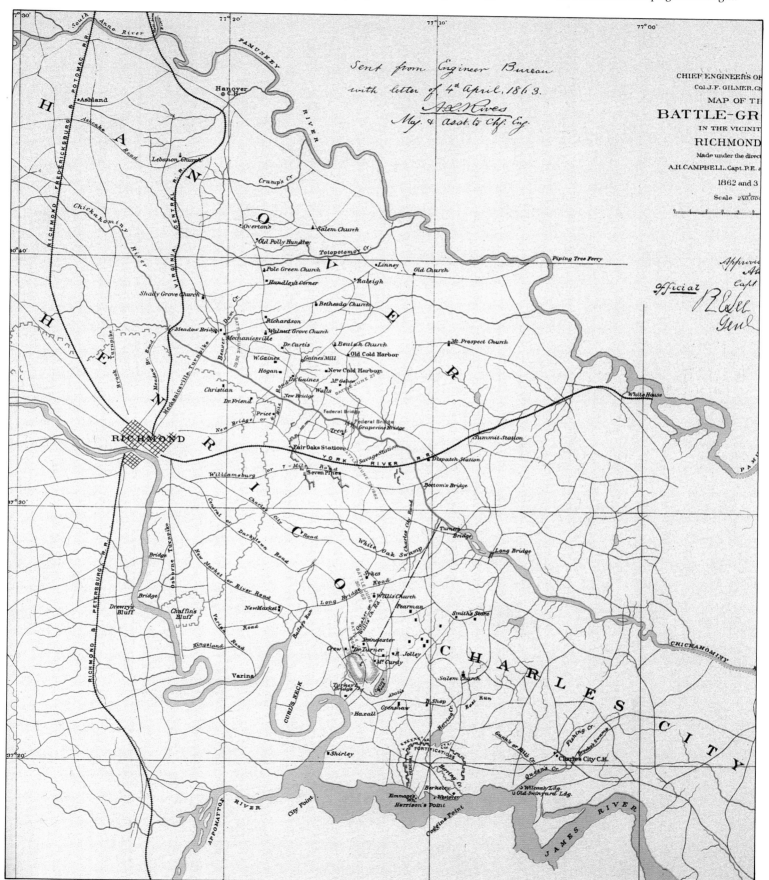

Union troops land on the Virginia Peninsula in 1862. Brilliantly planned, the campaign was wretchedly executed.

were actually manned by less than 13,000 Southerners, but McClellan called this thin defense 'one of the most extensive known to modern times' and spent a month arranging a siege. General John B. Magruder, commanding the Confederate defenses at Yorktown, was an amateur actor, and he produced a splendid show for the enemy, marching the same regiments in and out of various positions to deceive McClellan about the actual numbers. The Union commander was quite ready to swallow these deceptions.

Meanwhile, Federal slowness gave the Confederates plenty of time to make preparations. The plans were formulated by General Robert E. Lee, then serving as military advisor to Confederate President Jefferson Davis. During April, Johnston was given 60,000 men to oppose the Union advance; meanwhile, strong defenses were erected to protect Richmond proper. These defenses completed, Johnston pulled back from Yorktown to Richmond on May 3. On the next day McClellan finally unleashed his attack on the defenses at Yorktown, only to find them nearly deserted. On the 5th, at Williamsburg, advancing Federal forces suffered 2200 casualties in being turned back by the Southern rear guard; this allowed the Confederates to pull away with all their supplies. McClellan then began inching cautiously up the peninsula, beset by an unusually rainy spring and muddy roads.

For a while, Federal prospects of getting to Richmond looked better by way of the James River. As Union gunboats advanced, Confederates were forced to destroy their naval yard at Norfolk, including blowing up the ironclad *Merrimac (See MONITOR AND MERRIMAC BATTLE)*. Before the Union fleet could reach Richmond, however, it was stopped on May 15 by Southern batteries at Drewry's Bluff. That left it solely up to McClellan to try and take Richmond.

In late May 1862 the Federal Army of the Potomac had reached the outskirts of Rich-

mond, some eight miles away, but it was dangerously straddling the rain-swollen Chickahominy River. Confederate General Johnston, finding the Union left wing isolated south of the river, decided to attack there on March 31. The two-day Battle of Fair Oaks and Seven Pines was mishandled by the Confederate commanders but nonetheless had two important benefits for the South: it made McClellan still more cautious, even at the gates of Richmond; and General Johnston was wounded, to be replaced in command by General Robert E. Lee. Lee renamed his forces the Army of Northern Virginia and began the series of operations that would make him the scourge of the North and a celebrated name in history.

McClellan's Peninsular Campaign had now passed its zenith. In June, Lee's chief of cavalry J.E.B. ('Jeb') Stuart took his troopers on a scouting and raiding ride completely around the Army of the Potomac, in the process finding that Fitz-John Porter's Federal V Corps was isolated on the north bank of the

Chickahominy. Lee decided to strike this contingent. The operations related to that offensive began at Oak Grove on June 25, the first of the Seven Days' Battles (*See*).

Though in these subsequent operations Lee would fail to destroy McClellan's forces, they did serve to convince the Federal commander to withdraw down the peninsula to Harrison's Landing. In fact, the Army of the Potomac had fought well throughout the Seven Days and were still in good fighting shape, perhaps better than Lee's forces. But McClellan was already defeated in his mind, and bitterly blaming Washington for everything. The Peninsular Campaign drifted to its conclusion in early August, when the Army of the Potomac began to move northward in support of John Pope's ill-fated forces, then preparing to advance to disaster at the Second Battle of Bull Run.

Pensacola Bay, *Florida*

This bay offered the best natural anchorage in the Gulf of Mexico. Its aged commanding officer surrendered the US Navy Yard there to secessionists in April 1861, but Federal forces continued to occupy outlying positions. When Confederate forces withdrew in May 1862, Pensacola Bay became the headquarters for the Union Navy's West Gulf Squadron during the blockade.

Percussion Caps

These were small, powder-filled wafer-shaped metal objects that were placed on the nipple of a rifle or revolver. When the hammer struck the cap, the powder exploded and set off the charge, propelling the bullet out of the gun. Percussion caps operated more rapidly and reliably than the flintlock firing mechanisms they replaced, and they added considerably to the general rise in firepower that made the Civil War so much more lethal than any earlier wars.

One junior Union officer who did well on the peninsula was Lt. George Custer, shown here in a Waud sketch fording a stream.

Perryville (*Kentucky*), Battle of
(also called Chaplin Hills)

Ordered to halt Braxton Bragg's 1862 invasion of Kentucky (*See*), Federal General Don Carlos Buell marched from Louisville with 60,000 men. Early on October 8, Federals under Philip Sheridan drove back enemy positions near Perryville as blue forces moved into line. In the afternoon, Confederates under Leonidas Polk routed the Union left, but at the same time, Sheridan attacked from the right and drove the enemy back through the town. Buell, nearby with half his Federal army, did not hear the fighting because of an 'acoustic shadow,' and darkness prevented him from following up Sheridan's success. By the next morning Bragg had withdrawn in the face of superior forces; he would soon thereafter abandon his Kentucky Campaign entirely.

Personal Liberty Laws

These laws were adopted in 10 Northern states in reaction to US government's Fugitive Slave Law. They prohibited state officers from aiding in the capture of runaway slaves, denied the use of state jails to hold escaped slaves, and required jury trials before runaways could be returned.

Petard

Military engineers had for centuries used this kind of explosive charge to blow open gates and to knock down walls. It often consisted of an iron receptacle filled with powder and ball, and generally was attached by hooks to a gate or wall before being detonated.

Petersburg, Campaign and Siege

By the summer of 1864 the Confederacy was sinking toward defeat. It had lost most of its important cities and ports, a substantial number of its fighting men, and much of its grip on the slave-labor system that had supported its economy. Already there was talk of enlisting freed slaves in the Confederate army, a manifestly desperate course for the South.

Robert E. Lee and the Confederate Army of Northern Virginia, however, had survived everything Ulysses S. Grant could throw at them and remained a serious impediment to Union hopes of quick victory. After the devastating repulse of Federal forces at Cold Harbor, Virginia, Lee expected his opponent to repeat his previous tactics, slipping around the Confederate flank and again marching on Richmond. Instead, in one of his most brilliant tactical moves, Grant for once surprised his enemy: on the evening of June 12, 1864, the Federal Army of the Potomac quietly pulled out of position at Cold Harbor and headed south for Petersburg. This town protected the southern route to the capital and its vital rail lines. If Petersburg were taken, Richmond would inevitably fall.

Commanding at Petersburg was General P. G. T. Beauregard. For the past month he had been keeping at bay the Union army of General Benjamin Butler, who had been ordered to support Grant by marching toward Richmond from the south. Instead, the inept Union general was thoroughly

Union troops win a surprise victory over the Rebels at Petersburg on June 15, 1864, but will blunder badly by not following it up.

bottled up by the enemy on the peninsula between the York and James rivers, scene of McClellan's earlier ill-fated Peninsular Campaign. Beauregard, realizing that Grant was heading for his 5400 defenders in the city with the full Army of the Potomac, began sending Lee urgent requests for reinforcements. For some days, however, Lee refused to believe that Grant had given him the slip.

On June 15, 1864, 16,000 men of the Union army arrived at Petersburg under General William F. Smith, who had been ordered to attack immediately. At that point Beauregard had not been reinforced and the city was at the Federals' mercy. But the attack was bungled. Smith was slow on the march, and Federal reinforcements got lost on the way, finally arriving at the city in the evening. An assault was nonetheless mounted and made good headway as darkness came on. Then, in a decision that may have prolonged the war for nearly a year, Smith ordered his men to break off for the night. By next morning Beauregard had pulled nearly 10,000 reinforcements off the peninsula into Petersburg, and Lee had finally recognized the threat posed by Grant's maneuver.

As more of the Army of the Potomac arrived during the following days, Grant ordered new assaults on the Petersburg defenses. These costly attacks achieved little; troops and officers alike, drained by weeks of incessant fighting, fell into discouragement and disorganization. On June 18 Lee arrived with the Army of Northern Virginia. Meanwhile, in his futile assaults on the defenses, Grant had suffered over 11,000 casualties. Petersburg was now virtually immune to direct assault. It would have to be reduced by the slow, gruelling process of a siege. Grant now spread his lines east of the city, and in subsequent weeks and months he would extend his stranglehold to the west. Lee's men would contest every Federal move. Meanwhile, at the end of June, Lee sent Jubal Early on his Washington Raid in an attempt, only briefly successful, to force Grant to send some of his troops to the capital.

In July came a glimmer of hope for a quick resolution, but it turned into another disaster. Under the direction of hapless General Ambrose E. Burnside, engineers dug a gigantic mine under the defenses of Petersburg and filled it with powder. When it was touched off on July 30th the largest explosion in American history sent a geyser of earth, guns, and men into the sky, leaving a crater leading straight into the city and a unique chance to storm in while the defenders were still in shock. However, the Federal black troops who had been specifically trained to lead the assault had been withdrawn at the last minute by General George Meade (still nominally in command of the Army of the Potomac), who feared criticism for using the still-controversial black units on such an experimental operation. Discouraged by that change of plans, Burnside was desultory about his orders for the attack. The result was that thousands of unprepared troops were shoveled into the crater and ended up literally at the feet of an aroused enemy. The Union suffered 3748 casualties of 20,708 engaged before the survivors fled. In a bitter irony, the worst struck were the black units originally slated to lead the attack, for they had been thrown in at the end, only to meet devastating fire from the enemy. Legend says that a dismayed President Lincoln responded to reports of Petersburg Mine Assault thus: 'Only Burnside could have managed such a coup, wringing one last spectacular defeat from the jaws of victory.'

So the siege went on, men dying one by one in the trenches and earthworks from the continual depredations of sharpshooters, mortars, and cannons. Finally, in August 1864, Grant sent a detachment under Gouverneur Warren to seize the Weldon Railroad south of Petersburg. The Federals occupied the line on the 18th, and two attacks by A.P. Hill's Confederates could not dislodge them, though the North suffered 4455 casualties to the South's 1600. Now only one Confederate lifeline was left – the South Side Railroad on the west. The next spring, on March 29, 1865,

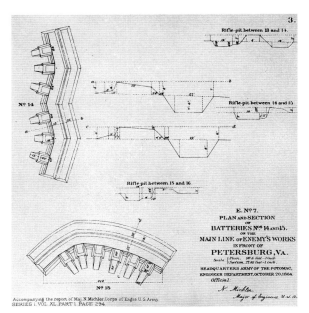

Above: A Union engineers' plan of two of the many batteries (plus intervening rifle pits) that made up the Confederate defensive line during the siege of Petersburg.

Above right: Union troops take shelter in a trench before Petersburg.

Right: A Union map showing a major segment of the opposing lines at Petersburg.

Union General Philip Sheridan led a force of infantry and cavalry to occupy Dinwiddie Court House, near that railroad, and prepared to cut the lifeline of the Army of the Northern Virginia. By then the Army of the Potomac had closed around most of the city, and Lee had failed in a March 25 attempt to break through Union lines at Fort Stedman.

Lee sent out George Pickett with 19,000 men to drive Sheridan away and hold the railroad 'at all costs.' After two days of heavy fighting, March 31 to June 1, around Dinwiddie Court House and Five Forks, the Federals had captured nearly half of Pickett's men and had driven the rest back into Petersburg. On the next day Lee informed President Jefferson Davis that his last rail line had been cut and that the army would have to evacuate Petersburg immediately – which doomed Richmond as well. On April 2, as Grant unleashed attacks that broke through Lee's defenses in several places, the Confederate government evacuated Richmond and fled to Danville, Virginia. Meanwhile, Southern troops blew up factories and munitions works in the capital, touching off fires that consumed much of the city. In the day's fighting at Petersburg, A.P. Hill, one of Lee's ablest commanders, was killed; Lee was visibly shaken by the news.

On the night of April 2 Lee and the starved and exhausted remaining 35,000 soldiers of the Army of Northern Virginia slipped out of the city and marched west toward Amelia Court House, where Lee hoped to put his men on the Danville Railroad for South Carolina to join forces with J.E. Johnston. On the following day Abraham Lincoln walked in the streets of Richmond, to the accompaniment of cheering slaves just freed. In the Appomattox Campaign of the next week, Ulysses S. Grant would finally run his old enemy to ground.

Petersburg Mine Assault

(or Petersburg Crater)
See PETERSBURG, CAMPAIGN AND SIEGE

Pettigrew, James Johnston
1828-1863 **Confederate general.**

This North Carolinian, who had been graduated with the highest marks of anyone who had ever attended the University of North Carolina, led a brigade on the Peninsula, where he was wounded and captured. He was exchanged and at Gettysburg led one of the three divisions (George Pickett and Isaac Trimble led the other two) that made 'Pickett's Charge' on the third day of the battle. He was killed during the retreat from Gettysburg.

Philippi Races

In the opening engagement of the Western Virginia Campaign of McClellan (*See*), at Philippi, West Virginia, on June 3, 1861, Federal troops surprised a force of 1500 Confederates in their sleep and routed them. The derisive term, coined by Northern newspapers, describes their hasty withdrawal.

Pickets

Small detachments of soldiers who guarded the outskirts of a military camp or defensive position. At various times during the war Union and Confederate pickets, away from their officers, would arrange informal truces; they often carried on a brisk trade in coveted goods, Confederates exchanging tobacco for coffee, for example.

Pickett, George Edward
(1825-1875) **Confederate general.**

Virginia-born Pickett resigned his Union captaincy in June 1861, led the Confederate 'Game Cock Brigade' at Williamsburg and

CSA General George Pickett did not in fact order the Gettysburg charge named for him.

Secret Service head Allan Pinkerton (seated right) hindered the Union's 1862 Peninsular Campaign with flawed intelligence reports.

Seven Pines, and participated in Gaines's Mill, Fredericksburg, Gettysburg, Drewry's Bluff, and the Petersburg and Appomattox Campaigns. Defeated at Five Forks and Sayler's Creek, he surrendered with Longstreet at Appomattox. The misnamed 'Pickett's Charge' came on the third day of the Battle of Gettysburg, July 3, 1863: James Longstreet, on Lee's command, ordered the disastrous charge, Pickett merely directing the attacking brigades' placement and then taking part in the charge.

Piedmont (*Virginia*), Battle of

After the Federal defeat at New Market (*See*) in May 1864, Union General David Hunter replaced Franz Sigel and advanced down the Shenandoah toward Staunton, Virginia. He met Confederate forces under W.E. Jones at Piedmont on the morning of June 5 and, after a sharp fight, routed them. Confederate casualties were about 1600, including 1000 prisoners; Union forces lost 780 men. The Federals entered Staunton the next day.

Pierpont, Francis Harrison
(1814-1899) **Governor of Virginia.**

A Virginia lawyer and businessman, Pierpont was a Unionist who supported Lincoln in 1860. After Virginia's secession he organized the pro-Union forces that declared West Virginia a separate state in 1862 (it was admitted to the Union as such in 1863) and served as wartime governor of the Virginia counties under Federal control.

Pike, Albert *(1809-1891)*
Confederate general.

A wealthy newspaperman, he entered Confederate service in August 1861, commanding the Department of Indian Territory. He led Indian troops at the Battle of Pea Ridge (*See*) in March 1862. He resigned his command later in 1862 after being publicly reprimanded by President Jefferson Davis for airing complaints about his political treatment. Out of favor in both North and South, he fled to Canada in 1865 but was pardoned by President Andrew Johnson in 1867.

Pillow, Gideon Johnson
(1806-1878) **Confederate general.**

This Mexican War veteran was a Tennessee criminal lawyer and moderate Democratic politician. Second in command at Fort Donelson, he and his superior, John B. Floyd, relinquished their commands and fled, leaving Simon B. Buckner to surrender to Ulysses Grant. Pillow was reprimanded and received no further significant commands.

Pinkerton, Allan *(1819-1884)*
Detective and secret service chief.

A Scottish emigrant to Illinois, Pinkerton opened America's first private detective agency in 1850. Recruited in 1861 to set up the Federal army's secret service, he worked under George McClellan in the Ohio Department and then in Washington, where he directed counter-espionage activities. The poor quality of the intelligence information and analyses he gave McClellan during the Peninsular Campaign doubtless contributed to the Union general's lackluster performance in that dismal operation. Pinkerton left government service when McClellan was relieved in November 1862. He expanded his agency after the war, winning a controversial reputation as a 'labor union buster'.

Plank Road

Roads on campaign routes were made passable by laying down planks over boggy or otherwise muddy surfaces. The method produced a hasty and impermanent wartime version of the corduroy road. (*See*).

Pleasant Hill (*Louisiana*), Battle of

After their victory at the Battle of Sabine Crossroads during the Red River Campaign, Confederate forces under General Richard Taylor attacked the retreating Union troops of Nathaniel Banks here on April 9, 1864. Taylor's late-afternoon assault made good pro-

As Union engineers became adept at building ponton (or pontoon) bridges, the speed of Federal troop movements greatly improved.

gress at first, but a Union counterassault drove the Confederates back. Nevertheless, Federal forces withdrew during the night. Federal casualties were 1369 out of 12,200 engaged; the Confederates lost about 1500 of their own 14,300 engaged.

Pleasonton, Alfred (1824-1897)
Union general.

Born in Washington, DC, Pleasonton was graduated from West Point and enjoyed a long military career. He led cavalry throughout the Potomac Army's campaigns from the Peninsula through Gettysburg, earning promotion to brigadier general for his role at the Battle of Chancellorsville, distinguishing himself at Brandy Station, and commanding the Union cavalry at the Battle of Gettysburg. In 1864 he routed Sterling Price in Missouri (See PRICE'S RAID IN MISSOURI) at the Battles of Westport and Marais de Cygnes.

Plymouth, North Carolina

Three Confederate brigades, supported by the ironclad ram Albemarle (See), attacked the Federal garrison here on April 17, 1864. The Albemarle sank one Federal warship, disabled a second, and scattered the rest; the garrison, unreinforced, surrendered on April 20. Federal losses exceeded 2800, many of this total being prisoners.

Point Lookout Prison, Maryland

This Federal prison opened in August 1863 on the Potomac where the river empties into Chesapeake Bay. There were no barracks, and all the prisoners – Point Lookout held as many as 20,000 Confederate enlisted men – lived in tents.

Polignac, Prince Camille Armand Jules Marie de (1832-1913)
Confederate general.

This French Crimean War veteran was the only alien to hold high rank (major general) in the Confederate army. Polignac was P. G.

T. Beauregard's chief of staff and fought at Corinth and in the 1864 Red River Campaign. After unsuccessfully seeking French aid for the Confederacy, he retired in 1865.

Polk, Leonidas Lafayette (1806-1864) **Confederate general.**

Born to a prominent North Carolina family related to President James Polk, he was graduated from West Point in 1827. He soon entered the Episcopal ministry, however, and was ordained Bishop of Louisiana in 1841. Hoping to bolster Southern morale, Jefferson Davis persuaded him to accept a commission in June 1861, and Major General Polk took a western departmental command. Belying the largely symbolic nature of this assignment, Polk directed the Mississippi River defenses, occupied Columbus, Kentucky, defeated Ulysses Grant at Belmont, and led four charges at Shiloh. He was second in command at Perryville and, promoted to lieutenant general, fought at Stone's River and Chickamauga. Polk was killed while on a reconnaissance mission during the Atlanta Campaign.

Ponton or Pontoon

Though most Civil War literature and popular usage favor 'pontoon,' 'ponton' (pronounced PON-ton) is the correct modern military spelling for a boat or other floating structure supporting a temporary bridge over a river. The army engineers' ability to construct these rapidly was vital to troop movements and supply lines.

Pope, John (1822-1892)
Union general.

One of several Union generals who started out with some success and proclamations of future victory and then ran afoul of Robert E. Lee, Pope was a West Point man who by early 1862 was commanding the Army of the Mississippi. After leading several successful operations along the Mississippi River, he was named by Lincoln in June 1862 to head the new Army of Virginia.

Taking command, Pope immediately aroused enmity and ridicule on both sides by a blustering address that included, 'Let us

understand each other. I have come to you from the West, where we have always seen the backs of our enemies.' At the Second Battle of Bull Run in August, Pope was thoroughly outwitted and defeated by Lee and Stonewall Jackson. He responded by blaming the loss on subordinates. Relieved of his command shortly after the battle, he spent the rest of the war commanding the Department of the Northwest.

Poplar Springs Church, Virginia

During the Petersburg siege, Ulysses Grant ordered a reconnaissance in force in late September 1864 in an effort to force Robert E. Lee to extend his lines westward from Petersburg. After three days of intermittent fighting, the Federal V Corps under Gouverneur Warren consolidated its positions and linked up with the Federal line to the east, thus achieving Grant's objective of further stretching the enemy's Petersburg defenses. Federal losses in the operation, from September 30 to October 2, 1864, were more than 2800. Confederate casualties are not known.

Popular Sovereignty

In American usage during the pre-Civil War period this term referred primarily to the doctrine that slavery was a matter for the people of individual territories to decide – in other words, was a local rather than a moral or national issue. Senator Lewis Cass articulated the doctrine in 1847. Stephen A. Douglas promoted it in the Compromise of 1850, in the Kansas-Nebraska Act (1854), and in his 1858 debates with Lincoln. Popular sovereignty, understood in this sense, thus became the crux of the explosive North-South split over what the legal status of slavery should be in states newly admitted to the Union.

Arrogant Union General John Pope was taught a lesson in humility at Second Bull Run.

Port Hudson, *Louisiana*

Union forces had unsuccessfully attacked this Confederate Mississippi River strongpoint several times in 1863 before Nathaniel Banks's XIX Corps besieged the place, beginning on May 27, 1863. The garrison finally surrendered on July 9, five days after the upriver fortress of Vicksburg had fallen to Ulysses Grant. The Confederates lost 7200 men, two steamers, 60 guns, and substantial amounts of small arms and ammunition, but the real significance of Port Hudson's fall lay in the fact that it was the last Rebel stronghold on the entire Mississippi River, the last possible impediment to a Union invasion of the Deep South from the west.

Port Royal Expedition

In a large combined operation, a Union fleet of 77 vessels under the command of Flag Officer Samuel DuPont transported 12,000 troops under Thomas W. Sherman to attack the Confederate coastal stronghold of Port Royal, North Carolina, in 1861. The expedition left Hampton Roads, Virginia, on October 29, was nearly undone by violent storms en route, but finally entered Port Royal Sound on November 7. Naval bombardment soon reduced Port Royal's primary defenses, Forts Beauregard and Wagner, which were then occupied by Sherman's troops. This success gave the Union both a strategically important toehold on the Southern coast between Charleston and Savannah and a useful new refueling depot for its naval blockade ships.

Porter, David Dixon *(1813-1891)*
Union admiral.

As a youth he went to sea with his father, Commodore David Porter, a hero of the War of 1812. He joined the Mexican navy at 13 and the US Navy at 16, receiving his first command in the Mexican War. In the Civil War, after aborting his April 1861 expedition to relieve Fort Pickens, he joined the blockade of southern ports. The following spring Porter's mortar flotilla supported David Farragut's operations in the New Orleans Campaign. Given command of the Mississippi Squadron in October 1862, Porter took Arkansas Post with W.T. Sherman and supported Ulysses Grant's assault on Vicksburg. As a rear admiral commanding the lower Mississippi, he led the naval force accompanying Nathaniel Banks's Red River Campaign of 1864 before joining the North Atlantic Squadron and taking Fort Fisher in January 1865. Porter received the Thanks of Congress three times.

Porter, Fitz-John *(1822-1901)*
Union general.

A New Hampshire-born West Point graduate, Porter commanded the siege of Yorktown, fought in the Shenandoah Campaign of Jackson, and led V Corps in the Peninsula (where he distinguished himself at Malvern Hill), Second Bull Run, and Antietam. Cashiered in January 1863 on a charge of having disobeyed orders at Second Bull Run, he tried for 23 years to clear his record, finally winning reappointment in 1886.

Flag Officer David Porter commanded the US Navy's Mississippi Squadron at Vicksburg.

Potomac, Confederate Army of the

Originally referring to P. G. T. Beauregard's troops in the Department of the Potomac after July 20, 1861, this designation included J. E. Johnston's Army of the Shenandoah. After Beauregard went west early in 1862, the term referred only to Johnston's troops in the Peninsula (those in the Valley being called the Army of the North); Robert E. Lee named these combined forces the Army of Northern Virginia on assuming command June 1, 1862.

Potomac, Union Army of the

Named for the Department of the Potomac, created August 15, 1861, this army was the major Union fighting force in the Eastern Theater. The primary succession of commanders included George McClellan, August 15, 1861 – November 9, 1862 (Peninsular and Antietam Campaigns); Ambrose Burnside, until January 26, 1863 (Fredericks-burg Campaign); Joseph Hooker, until June 28, 1863 (Chancellorsville Campaign); and George Meade, until June 27, 1865 (Gettysburg to Appomattox).

Powell, Lewis *(d. 1865)*
Confederate Conspirator.

One of John Wilkes Booth's conspirators in the Lincoln assassination (he was calling himself Lewis Paine at the time), he gravely wounded Secretary of State Seward. He was hanged on July 7, 1865.

Prairie Grove, *Arkansas*

Confederate General Thomas C. Hindman had scraped together a force to defend Little Rock and northern Arkansas. At Prairie Grove on December 7, 1862, Hindman planned to attack Federals under James G. Blunt but instead got himself and his unreliable troops caught between three converging enemy divisions and was forced to withdraw without a fight.

Price, Sterling *(1809-1867)*
Confederate general.

A Missouri lawyer, farmer, and Congressman, he commanded the Missouri State Guard at the Battle of Wilson's Creek in 1861 and later fought at Iuka, Cornith, Helen, and in the Red River Campaign. In 1864 he mounted an unsuccessful raid into Missouri (*See* PRICE'S RAID IN MISSOURI), after which he retreated into Mexico and oblivion.

Price's Raid in Missouri

In September 1864 Confederate General Sterling Price and a somewhat ragtag band of 12,000 cavalry began a guerrilla campaign against Union forces in Missouri. The state had long seen violence between slaveholding

At a review of the cavalry of the Army of the Potomac, Federal General John Buford watches his troopers ride past.

and abolitionist factions, and some of Price's men followed the bloody pattern of that conflict – as when a group including Frank and Jesse James slaughtered two dozen unarmed Federal soldiers from a captured train. That same day, September 27, Price was repulsed with heavy losses in an attempt to take Fort Davidson. Price rode on west, laying waste as he went, as resistance from Union forces under Samuel Curtis, Alfred Pleasanton, and Alfred Smith, as well as local militia, gathered momentum. Finally Price was defeated by Pleasanton at the Battle of Westport on October 23, and again at Marais de Cygnes on the 25th, after which Price was chased into Arkansas with half the forces he started with. Though Price tried to paint the operation as a success, it was clearly a disaster and proved to be the last significant Confederate operation in Missouri.

Prisoners of War

The US Record Office records a total of 462,634 Confederates and 211,411 Federals captured by their enemies during the war. Many were freed by parole or exchange, but hundreds of thousands were held in prison camps where appalling sanitation, diet, disease, and crowding contributed to a death rate among prisoners on both sides of roughly 15 percent. By suspending prisoner exchanges in April 1864, Ulysses Grant increased the Northern death toll.

Privateer

A privateer is a merchant ship given official permission to prey upon enemy shipping for its own profit – in other words, a form of legal

A swarm of Confederate soldiers captured at Spotsylvania in 1864 awaits transport back to Union prisoner-of-war camps.

piracy. Outlawed internationally, privateering was revived by the Confederate government during the war. When the Union captured two privateers – the *Enchantress* and *Savannah* – and condemned the officers as pirates, the Confederacy threatened to hang an equal number of prisoners. The North relented and imprisoned the officers.

Proclamation of Amnesty

President Andrew Johnson issued a proclamation on May 29, 1865, offering a general amnesty to any Confederates who pledged allegiance to the Constitution. This amnesty excluded, among others, high-ranking Confederate military and government officers and wealthy property-owners, who had to apply for individual presidential pardons.

Promotion

Fewer than 150 of the 1080 regular officers serving in 1861 achieved general's rank in the Union army, which followed policy of freezing officers in regular units rather than assigning them in ones and twos to volunteer formations. West Point graduates who had left the army before the war broke out fared better; an even half of the 102 academy graduates who returned to serve in the volunteer forces became generals.

Pryor, Roger Atkinson
(1828-1919) **Confederate general.**

Pryor was a newspaper editor, US Representative, and influential Virginia secessionist. As a brigadier general he fought at Williamsburg, Seven Pines, and Antietam. He resigned after losing his brigade and fought as a private in Fitzhugh Lee's cavalry. Pryor was captured near Petersburg in November 1864.

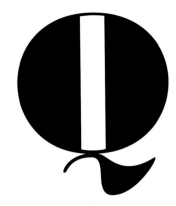

Quaker Road, *Virginia*

The van of the Federal V Corps, moving to envelop the Petersburg defenses at the opening of the Appomattox Campaign on March 29, 1865, met stiff Confederate resistance here. Charles Griffin's 1st Division troops held off Confederate counterattacks at a sawmill beyond the stream, then advanced to the Boydton Plank Road and dug in for the night. Federal casualties were about 370 dead and wounded. The Confederates lost 130 dead and about 200 prisoners.

Quakers

Members of this pacifist religious sect were early abolitionists, opposing slavery and the slave trade from the 18th century on. Many Quakers manned stations on the Underground Railroad.

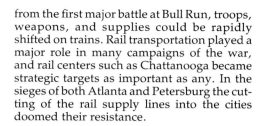

Perhaps the most barbarous guerrilla leader of the war was Rebel William Quantrill.

Quantrill, William Clarke
(1837-1865) **Confederate irregular.**

Quantrill, a onetime schoolteacher, was a frontier thief and gambler. Alias 'Charley Hart,' he drifted into the Kansas and Missouri border skirmishing. He parlayed his involvement in murders, robberies, and raids into a Confederate captaincy after taking Independence, Missouri, in August 1862. While his troops continued raiding in Kansas and Missouri, Quantrill's own operations included the August 1863 pillaging of the free-state stronghold of Lawrence, Kansas, where he killed at least 150 people, and, a few months later, the murder of 17 noncombatants after defeating Federal cavalry at Baxter Springs. He was killed by Union troops in May 1865 en route to Washington to assassinate President Lincoln.

One effect of railroads on the war was to confer mobility on heavy artillery.

Radical Republicans

These extremist Republicans called for emancipation of the slaves early in the war and for a peace settlement that would punish the rebellious states. The Radicals, led by Charles Sumner, Benjamin Wade, and Thaddeus Stevens, advocated the destruction of Southern economic and political power. They led the move to impeach President Johnson, primarily because they considered his Reconstruction policies too lenient.

Railroads

The Civil War was the first conflict in history in which railroads played an indispensable role in moving men and supplies. At the beginning of the war the North had a marked advantage in railroad mileage – some 21,000 miles compared to the South's 9000 – and though this ratio remained roughly the same throughout the war, the North gained a further advantage from the steady improvements it made in operating efficiencies. All this had an important effect on the war's outcome. Whereas throughout previous history troops had moved on foot or horseback, now,

from the first major battle at Bull Run, troops, weapons, and supplies could be rapidly shifted on trains. Rail transportation played a major role in many campaigns of the war, and rail centers such as Chattanooga became strategic targets as important as any. In the sieges of both Atlanta and Petersburg the cutting of the rail supply lines into the cities doomed their resistance.

Rains, Gabriel James *(1803-1881)*
Confederate general.

A North Carolinian, this West Point graduate and career soldier directed the first-ever use of land mines and booby traps in the Peninsula Campaign and further developed other innovative weapons as head of the torpedo bureau. His brother, George Washington Rains, was also one of the leading Confederate munitions specialists.

Rams

These warships, usually ironclad, were fitted with a heavy iron prow that could be driven into the hull of an enemy. The South authorized construction of 14 ironclad rams, the most famous of which was CSS *Virginia* (also known as *Merrimac*).

Ransom, Robert Jr. *(1828-1892)*
Confederate general.

Born in North Carolina, Ransom was a West Point-trained cavalryman. He organized the western cavalry; led troops at the Seven Days' Battles, Harper's Ferry, Antietam, Fredericksburg, Bermuda Hundred, and Drewry's Bluff; and participated in the Weldon Railroad defense and Early's Washington Raid. His brother, Matt Whitaker Ransom, was also a Confederate general.

Ransom, Thomas Edward Greenfield *(1834-1864)*
Union general.

He left an Illinois business career for the war. Wounded at Charleston, Fort Donelson, and Shiloh, he participated in the Battle of Corinth and in the Vicksburg, Red River, and Atlanta Campaigns. He died of illness. Ulysses Grant later called him 'the best man I have ever had to send on expeditions.'

Rappahannock Bridge and Kelly's Ford *(Virginia)*, Battles of

During the 1863 Bristoe Campaign *(See)*, Union General George Meade sent troops under John Sedgwick to attack a Rappahannock River bridge over which Robert E. Lee was retreating. On November 7, in one of the rare night actions of the war (and including a still rarer bayonet charge), the Federals overran the defenders of the bridge. Meanwhile at Kelly's Ford, two Southern regiments were captured. The losses of some 2023 shocked the Southern army.

Rations

The Union ration – one soldier's food for one day – was a 16-ounce biscuit or 22 ounces of bread or flour and 1¼ pounds of meat or ¾

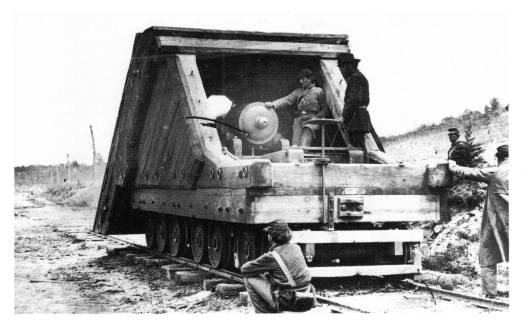

pound of bacon, with additional allocations of beans, rice or hominy, coffee, sugar, vinegar, and salt. Initially adopting the Union ration, the Confederates reduced it in 1862. In reality, soldiers often went without rations, relying on food from home and from sutlers.

Rawlins, John Aaron (1831-1869)
Union general.

A Democratic Illinois politician, he joined the army in August 1861 and became Ulysses Grant's 'most nearly indispensable' advisor. Trusted for his intelligence, honesty, and sound judgment, Rawlins was promoted in tandem with Grant, becoming chief of staff of the US Army in March 1865.

Reagan, John Henninger (1818-1905) Confederate politician.

A Texas legislator, he became postmaster general of the Confederacy in March 1861. In the Confederacy's final months he was treasury secretary. Captured with President Jefferson Davis, Reagan was held in Fort Warren until October 1865. He later served in the US Senate (1887-91).

Reams's Station (Virginia), Battle of

During the Petersburg siege, when Federal forces under Winfield Hancock moved up to cut the Weldon Railroad in late August 1864, Confederates moved to the attack. On August 25 strong forces under A. P. Hill routed John Gibbon's inexperienced division; fresh troops sent into the battle 'could neither be made to go forward nor fire.' The Federals lost more than 2700 men, including 2000 captured, in the action.

Rebel Yell

Confederates on the offensive used this piercing shriek to great psychological effect. Said to derive from a Southern fox hunter's shout, it was first sounded at the First Battle of Bull Run in July 1861.

Reconnaissance in Force

This is an attack by a large force with the mission of finding and testing an enemy's strength. The cavalry clash at Brandy Station, Virginia, on June 9, 1863, during the Gettysburg Campaign is an example.

Reconstruction

The term refers broadly to the North's postwar policies toward the conquered Southern states and to the roughly 10-year period during which those policies were most markedly in effect. The question of under what conditions the Southern states should eventually be re-admitted to the Union had of course been much debated in Washington during the war. The Radical Republicans tended to favor policies of enforcement rather than conciliation, and on the key issue of how fast and in what manner the newly-emancipated black population should be integrated into the mainstream of Southern society, the radicals were dogmatic: integra-

tion must be immediate and complete, regardless of the social disruptions such a course might foster. Lincoln's position was more moderate: in his view the North's general approach should be more conciliatory than punitive, and, with respect to integration, all legal impediments to it should at once be removed, but the North should be wary of trying to force the pace of social change too rapidly, lest the result be counterproductive. Because Lincoln was assassinated almost at the moment of the Union's victory, it was left to his vice president and successor, Andrew Johnson, to try to realize Lincoln's policy.

Johnson moved swiftly but incautiously. Following his Amnesty Proclamation of May 29, 1865, and while Congress was still in adjournment, he rushed ahead with a program in which Southern state governors, appointed by Johnson, would hold conventions that would void their states' ordinances

Reconstruction-era black members of Congress. On the left is H. R. Revels of Mississippi, the first black US Senator.

of secession, abolish slavery, and repudiate Confederate debts. They would then elect new legislatures whose first order of business would be to ratify the 13th Amendment. The Southern states responded well to this plan, and by the year's end all save Texas had new civil governments in operation.

But Johnson's program had been more lenient than well-thought-out. It had made good the emancipation of Southern blacks, but it had done almost nothing to protect their civil rights, and especially their right to vote. Most of the Southern states were quick to take advantage of this, putting into effect a

Ex-Confederate soldiers are administered the Oath of Allegiance to the United States in the Senate Chamber at Richmond, Virginia.

variety of so-called Black Codes which denied Southern blacks access to the polls, to equal economic opportunity, or to anything approaching social justice.

Predictably, this ill-judged show of Southern recalcitrance infuriated the US Congress, which became rapidly more radicalized and activist, and set it on a path towards wresting from Johnson's hands the initiative in the framing of Reconstruction policy. Johnson's efforts to slow this process with vetoes were soon undone by the introduction of the 14th Amendment (proposed in June 1866; ratified in July 1868), which left no room for cavil in its definition of civil rights or in its grant of power to Congress to enforce them.

The culmination of Congress's victory in taking control of Reconstruction policy came with the passage of the Reconstruction Act of March 2, 1867. In this, and ancillary legislation, the South was carved up into five military districts in which army authority would be supreme until new state constitutions satisfactory to Congress were written, and the re-admission of the states would then be contingent on their ratifying the 14th Amendment. The effects of this bulldozer policy on the South were considerable. While ex-Confederates remained largely disenfranchised, new black voters were not yet sufficiently organized or sophisticated to take effective control of local governments. Into the political vacuum poured a host of exploiters – 'carpetbaggers,' 'scalawags,' and the like – who added much to the South's already grave political, economic, and social woes.

By 1870 all the Southern states had been re-admitted, though some Federal troops still remained stationed in the region. But Congress's radical Reconstruction policy had, as Lincoln had feared, created a potent backlash. The Republican Party was all but banished from Southern politics, resentment against the North ran high, and the South's inter-race relations had become almost hopelessly envenomed.

Thanks to the revival of the Democratic Party's national power, Reconstruction effectively ended after the presidential election of 1876, but the after-effects of its failures would persist. Black civil rights would be steadily eroded and would not again make any significant advances until the 1960s. Indeed, whether what the radical Reconstructionists hoped to accomplish, and so mishandled, has yet been fully achieved is moot.

Red River Campaign

As part of Ulysses Grant's overall plan of March 1864 to finish the war, (*See* WILDERNESS CAMPAIGN), the Red River Campaign was assigned to Nathaniel Banks, a politically-appointed general with little battlefield success to his credit. Banks had been gearing up for an operation against Mobile, Alabama, with his Army of the Gulf, but he was diverted from that for this campaign, being directed to move up Louisiana's Red River to expand Union control in the state and seize stores of cotton; only after doing that was he to turn again toward Mobile. In fact, Grant had inherited the plan when he took overall command, and neither he nor W.T. Sherman – or Banks, for that matter – approved of it; all of them felt the

A view of the Union fleet on the Red River, stranded in shallow water above the rapids near Alexandria, Louisiana, in 1864.

move on Mobile should have priority. President Lincoln, however, pushed the campaign through. Thus it began with little military support or justification and was to be led by a weak general.

The plan called for Banks to take 17,000 troops to link up in Louisiana with 10,000 of Sherman's troops from Tennessee under A.J. Smith, plus 15,000 coming from Arkansas under Frederick Steele (the latter would never make it to Louisiana – *See* ARKANSAS CAMPAIGN.) Accompanying the ground forces marching along the Red River would be a formidable flotilla that included 13 ironclads and seven gunboats under Admiral David Dixon Porter. Obstacles the expedition faced included low water, inhospitable country, and Confederate forces under General Richard Taylor.

Smith's troops left Vicksburg on March 10, taken onto the Red River by the Union flotilla. On the 18th Smith and the fleet arrived at Alexandria, Louisiana, without obstruction from Taylor, and Banks's forces arrived a week later. Despite low water on the river and orders to return Smith to Sherman by April 15, Banks continued on to his next objective, the taking of Shreveport. His land forces ended up marching in a thin line on a narrow road, encumbered by a wagon train stretching 12 miles through enemy-held wilderness; meanwhile the ships were making poor headway through the shallow waters of the Red River.

Taylor, having massed his Confederate forces, finally made an appearance in force on April 8, moving his troops out of Mansfield to obstruct the Federal advance at the communications hub of Sabine Crossroads. There a battle broke out in late afternoon, and it ended in a rout of the Union forces. Banks withdrew to a defensive line at Pleasant Hill, where his troops decisively repulsed a full-scale assault by Taylor on the 9th. With the Southern troops now in disarray, Banks had the upper hand, but in light of Steele's failure in Arkansas, the unnerved Federal general decided to pull back. The Red River Campaign was now in retreat, but that would also prove to be a difficult proposition.

As the Union forces withdrew, they were steadily harassed by the enemy on both land and water. One of the ironclads, struck by a mine, had to be destroyed. The Federals began to arrive in Alexandria on April 25, relatively intact but in serious danger. The Red River was now so low that a number of ships were marooned above the rapids near town. On the 26th Southern artillery hit the gunboat *Cricket* with 19 shells; the ship lost 31 of her 50-man crew before the others escaped. Two Federal pumpboats were also destroyed; one, the *Champion*, exploded from a hit in the boiler and some 200 black crewmen – runaway slaves – died in the scalding steam. It seemed that Porter's massive fleet had become a collection of sitting ducks. Then Union Lieutenant Colonel Joseph Bailey stepped in with an extraordinarily imaginative scheme to free the fleet.

Bailey used an old lumberjack trick to raise the Red River: a series of wooden dams with gates that could be swung open in the middle to spill water and boats down the river. At the end of April, under fire, the troops began to build these wing dams and then wait for the water to rise behind them. From the first to the eighth of May Confederate depredations came down heavily on the Federals, destroying five Union boats. Finally, on May 9, the first Union ship spilled through a gate; the rest of the surviving fleet would follow over the next few days. Banks continued his retreat with constant skirmishing. Bailey produced one more engineering feat in the middle of May, using steamers to create a 600-yard bridge across the Atchafalaya River, over which the Federal wagon train and troops crossed. By May 26th the expedition had at last reached comparative safety in Donaldsonville, Louisiana.

The Red River Campaign turned out an unmitigated disaster. The Mobile Campaign had to be aborted, Smith's command never made it back to rejoin Sherman, and Southern troops were thereafter available to reinforce Sherman's opponent, Joseph Johnston, in Georgia during Sherman's Atlanta

Campaign. It would be Banks's last field command; he also had to undergo a Congressional investigation and official censure. To be sure, the current of the war was now running inexorably against the South, but this ill-advised campaign had made no contribution to the Union's success.

Reed Projectile

Similar to the projectile fired from the Parrott Gun, it was named after the Alabama doctor who developed it in the late 1850s. It was widely used in the Confederate service.

Regular Army

The United States Army in 1861 consisted of 1080 officers on active service and approximately 15,000 enlisted men, most of them in scattered garrisons on the frontier. Only a handful of private soldiers deserted on the outbreak of war, but nearly a third of the the regular army officers resigned to join the Confederate service.

Remington Carbine

Developed in 1863 and in service late in the war, this single-shot weapon fired a .50-caliber Spencer (*See*) cartridge.

Reno, Marcus Albert *(1835-1889)* Union officer.

An 1857 West Point graduate from Illinois, he served as a cavalry officer and was wounded at Kelly's Ford, Virginia, in March 1863. A court of inquiry would later investigate his conduct during George Armstrong Custer's defeat by the Sioux in 1876.

Republican Party

The Kansas-Nebraska Act of 1854 was a catalyst for the formation of this party, which drew Free-Soil and antislavery adherents into its membership. Republicans steadily gained strength through the 1856 and 1858 elections, finally electing Lincoln president in 1860 and 1864. Anti-Southern Radicals dominated the party after Lincoln's death. By the time the Republicans lost the White House in the election of 1876, a new, solidly Democratic South had emerged.

Resaca *(Georgia)*, Battle of
(also called Sugar Valley, Oostenaula)

Early in his 1864 Atlanta Campaign, W.T. Sherman struck Joseph Johnston's defenses at Resaca. There was skirmishing on May 13th, then heavy fighting on the following day as Sherman tried unsuccessfully to crack the enemy lines. On the 15th the action was renewed, inconclusively until Johnston discovered that Federals had crossed the Oostenaula River and were moving on his rear, forcing him to withdraw.

Opposite top: The first battle in Sherman's relentless advance on Atlanta began on May 13,1864, at Resaca, Georgia.
Opposite bottom: Revetments of earth, logs, sandbags and gabions protect this battery of big Union Parrott guns.

Revetments

These are walls that support the sides of trenches, gun emplacements, or other fortifications. During the Civil War, they were often made of wire and wooden posts, woven brushwork, or sandbags.

Revolvers

Many varieties of handgun saw service on both sides. The several models of Colt cap-and-ball pistols were probably the most widely used; Federal ordnance officers bought 146,000 of Colt's 1861 .44 caliber Army revolver and his .36 caliber Navy model, which appeared in 1862.

Reynolds, Alexander *(1817-1876)* Confederate general.

A pre-war regular officer (West Point, 1838), he was dismissed in 1855 for discrepancies in his accounts. He was reinstated, then dismissed again in 1861 after he left his post to join the Confederate service. He commanded a brigade at Vicksburg and Chattanooga and during the Atlanta Campaign.

Reynolds, John Fulton *(1820-1863)* Union general.

A Pennsylvanian, he was graduated from West Point in 1841 and fought with distinction in the Mexican War. In July 1862 he was captured at Gaines's Mill during the Seven Days' Battles but was exchanged in time to lead a division at Second Bull Run. As commander of the Army of the Potomac's I Corps he fought at Fredericksburg and Chancellorsville. He was killed on the first day of the Battle of Gettysburg while directing the Union defense to the west of the town. Reynolds enjoyed a very high reputation in the Union army, and many believed that he, rather than George Meade, should have been appointed to replace Joseph Hooker as commander of the Army of the Potomac.

When John Reynolds was killed at Gettysburg the North lost one of its best generals.

the Death of Reynolds

Reynolds, Joseph Jones *(1822-1899)* Union general.

An Indiana businessman when the war broke out, this West Point alumnus secured West Virginia for the Union at Cheat Mountain. He led divisions at Hoover's Gap and Chickamauga, was chief of staff of the Cumberland Army at Chattanooga, and, among other commands, led VII and XIX Corps and the Department of Arkansas.

Rhett, Robert Barnwell *(1800-1876)* Confederate politician.

A South Carolina planter and legislator, this 'Father of Secession' was an influential secessionist from the 1850s onward, agitating in South Carolina and helping draft the Confederate constitution. He spent the war years promoting extremist, anti-Davis views in the *Charleston Mercury*.

Rhodes, Elisha Hunt *(1842-1917)*

The son of a sea captain, he left his job as a harness-maker's clerk to enlist in the 2nd Rhode Island Volunteers in June 1861. He was 19. Rhodes kept a detailed and eloquent diary of his war service, in which he saw action at Bull Run, on the Virginia Peninsula, and at Antietam, Fredericksburg, Gettysburg, Petersburg, and Appomattox.

Rice Station, *Virginia*

During the Appomattox Campaign, Confederate General James Longstreet's command reached this place on April 6, 1865, while the balance of the Army of Northern Virginia fought at Sayler's Creek (*See*). Though Longstreet's forces made contact with the enemy, there was little fighting before he withdrew toward Farmville (*See*).

Richardson, Albert Deane *(1833-1869)* War correspondent.

The Massachusetts-born Richardson reported the troubles in Kansas in 1857, accompanied an expedition to Pike's Peak, traveled clandestinely in the South during the secession crisis, and covered the war in Virginia and the West. Captured near Vicksburg, he spent 18 months in a Southern prison before he escaped and walked 400 miles to his freedom. His adventures came to an abrupt and violent end in the office of the New York *Tribune* when he was shot and mortally wounded by a jealous husband.

Richmond *(Kentucky)*, Battle of

Two hastily-assembled Federal brigades under William Nelson were sent to defend this town from General Kirby Smith's invading Confederates (*See* SMITH'S INVASION OF KENTUCKY) in August 1862. In a powerful attack on August 30 Smith's forces routed one of the brigades and sent the second retreating in confusion. The Federals lost 5300 of 6500 engaged, including 4300 missing. Confederate casualties were about 450. Smith would have a few more successes, but his final objective, the capture of Kentucky, would never be realized.

Richmond, *Virginia*

Capital of both Virginia and of the Confederacy, Richmond was the ultimate target of every major Union offensive in the Eastern theater throughout the Civil War. The city finally fell to the Union on April 3, 1865, as a result of the collapse of the Confederate defense of Petersburg.

Richmond Armory and Arsenal

This Virginia facility produced roughly half of all the ordnance supplied to Confederate land forces. In four years of war the arsenal issued more than 300 big guns, 1300 field pieces, 323,000 infantry arms, more than 900,000 rounds of artillery ammunition, and 72,500,000 rounds of small arms ammunition. The totals include work done by contractors, including the Tredegar Iron Works (*See*), also in Richmond.

Rifle

Rifles are single-shot firearms distinguished by grooves cut into the bore, spinning the projectile and giving it a more accurate flight. At the beginning of the war military inventories included both old flintlock and the newer percussion rifles. The war stimulated the emergence of breech-loading rifles like those designed by Sharps, Smith, Maynard, and Burnside and of repeating rifles: the Spencer and Henry (later called the Winchester) were developed during these years. (*See* also US REGULATION SHOULDER ARMS).

Rifle Pits

Soldiers dug these shallow holes on the battlefield to give themselves minimal protection from enemy fire. In later American wars they were called fox holes.

This line of Union rifle pits is so closely spaced that it forms a semi-trench.

Robertson, Jerome Bonaparte
(1815-1891) **Confederate general.**

A Texas doctor, public official, and Indian fighter, Robertson led Texans in the Seven Days' Battles, Second Bull Run, Boonsboro Gap, Fredericksburg, Gettysburg, and Chickamauga, suffering three wounds in 40 battles. A mediocre general, he was twice relieved of his brigade command; he eventually led the Texas reserves.

Robinson, John Cleveland
(1817-1897) **Union general.**

A New Yorker, this career officer led troops continuously and gallantly in the Potomac Army's operations from the Peninsula through Spotsylvania, where he lost a leg and left field service. His valiant stand at Gettysburg is commemorated by a statue on that battlefield.

Rock Island Prison

This Federal prison, on an island on the Mississippi between Rock Island, Illinois, and Davenport, Iowa, opened in December 1863. It held as many as 8000 Confederate soldiers who lived in 84 poorly heated barracks.

'Rock of Chickamauga'

Union General George H. Thomas earned this nickname for his XIV Corps' stubborn stand on the left wing at Chickamauga in September 1863 while the rest of William Rosecrans' Federal army was giving way before the Confederate advance. Thomas's soldiers had another nickname for him: Pap.

Rocky Face Ridge, *Georgia*

Opening his 1864 Atlanta Campaign, Federal General William T. Sherman ordered a series of actions to dislodge his opponent, Joseph Johnston, from strong positions at Rocky

Legend wrongly credits author Edmund Ruffin with firing the Civil War's first shot.

Face Ridge. Individual engagements were called Tunnel Hill, Mill Creek Gap, Buzzard Roost, Snake Creek Gap, and Varnell's Station, as well as an unnamed action near Dalton. These efforts failed in their attempt to cut Johnston's line of retreat, but they did force him to withdraw from Dalton.

Rodman Guns

Guns of this type were manufactured by casting iron cast around a water- or air-chilled core. This left the metal stronger and more capable of standing the pressure of repeated firing. The method, named after T.J. Rodman, who developed it, was used mainly for large-caliber smoothbores such as the Columbiad (*See*).

Romney Campaign

Stonewall Jackson's forces left Winchester, Virginia, in early January 1862 to attack the Baltimore & Ohio Railroad and locks on the Chesapeake & Ohio Canal. Federal forces moved down from Maryland to protect these communications lines; they met in a series of skirmishes in what is sometimes called the Romney Campaign.

Rosecrans, William Starke
(1819-1898) **Union general.**

This Ohio-born West Point alumnus (1842) and professor resigned from the army in 1854 to pursue various business interests. He joined George McClellan's staff in April 1861 and soon assumed a Western Virginia command, winning an early victory at Rich Mountain and helping bring West Virginia to statehood. Succeeding John Pope in June

1862, 'Old Rosy' led the Mississippi Army at Iuka and Corinth and then led the Cumberland Army through Stone's River (for which he received the Thanks of Congress) and the Tullahoma Campaign. A mistake in an order to the front at Chickamauga cost the Federals the battle and Rosecrans his command; he saw no further significant action. Rosecrans was nevertheless a gifted strategist.

Rosser, Thomas *(1836-1910)*
Confederate general.

He quit West Point after Fort Sumter and fought at First Bull Run. After the Peninsular Campaign, in which he was wounded, he was named to command the 5th Virginia Cavalry, which he led at Second Bull Run, Chancellorsville, and Gettysburg. As a brigade commander, Rosser clashed in the Shenandoah and during the Appomattox Campaign with Union forces led by his friend George A. Custer. Rosser was adept at raiding, and a series of three raids he led into West Virginia – January 1864, November 1864, and January 1865 – is remembered as 'Rosser's Raids.'

Round Top

The hill at the extreme southern end of the Union position at the Battle of Gettysburg.

Rousseau, Lovell Harrison *(1818-1869)* Union general.

A lawyer and legislator in Indiana and then Kentucky, this Unionist held commands in the Armies of the Ohio and the Cumberland, figuring prominently at Shiloh, Perryville, and Chickamauga. From November 1863 to July 1865 Rousseau commanded the District of Nashville.

But for his defeat at Chickamauga, Federal General William Rosecrans would probably be remembered as an outstanding commander.

Ruffin, Edmund *(1794-1865)*
Secessionist.

This Virginian, an agriculturist, author, and early secessionist, joined the Palmetto Guard before the attack on Fort Sumter, where some sources erroneously state he fired the first shot. Too old for field service, Ruffin shuttled between his plantations and Charleston until June 1865, when, distraught after the surrender, he committed suicide.

Ruggles, Daniel *(1810-1897)*
Confederate general.

A Massachusetts-born career officer trained at West Point, Ruggles joined the Confederate army in 1861 and served along the Potomac and at New Orleans; he fought at Shiloh and commanded the Department of the Mississippi. In 1865 he was commissary general of prisoners.

Russell, David Allen *(1820-1864)*
Union general.

A West Point-trained frontier veteran, this New Yorker led the 7th Massachusetts in the Peninsula, at South Mountain, and at Antietam. As a brigadier general he subsequently commanded troops at Fredericksburg, Gettysburg, Rappahannock Bridge, the Wilderness and Petersburg. After joining Philip Sheridan in the latter's Shenandoah Valley Campaign he was killed at the Battle of Winchester in September 1864.

Russell, Sir William Howard *(1820-1907)* **War correspondent.**

An English war correspondent famous for his Crimean War dispatches, he covered the Civil War for the pro-Confederate London *Times* in 1861-62. Russell's account of the Federal rout at First Bull Run made him unpopular in the North, but in fact Russell soon became a Union sympathizer.

Sabine Crossroads *(Louisiana)*, Battle of (or Mansfield)

As part of his 1864 Red River Campaign, Nathaniel Banks's Federal ground forces had reached Sabine Crossroads, near Mansfield, Louisiana, on April 8; there they ran into Richard Taylor's defensive lines, involving nearly 9000 troops. In the late afternoon Taylor moved forward, crumpling both Federal flanks. Fighting ended with the Union line retreating under pursuit to Pleasant Hill, where Taylor was repulsed the next day. The crossroads would be Banks's farthest point of advance in the ill-fated campaign.

Sabine Pass, *Texas*

A combined land-sea Federal assault failed here on September 8, 1863. When Confederate fire from land batteries disabled two of the Union gunboats (they eventually surrendered), William B. Franklin, the Federal commander, called off the operation.

St. Albans *(Vermont)* Raid

On October 19, 1864, a band of Confederate raiders, mostly escaped prisoners of war, crossed the border from Canada into St. Albans, Vermont. Intending to burn the town, they succeeded only in robbing three banks. Eleven who escaped back to Canada were arrested but released, the Canadians disavowing jurisdiction. Such raids forced Lincoln to maintain troops along the border and contributed to tensions among the US, Canada, and Britain.

Salem Church *(Virginia)*, Battle of

During the Battle of Chancellorsville in May 1863 beleagured Union General Joseph Hooker ordered John Sedgwick to take his VI Corps from its defensive position at Fredericksburg and move on Robert E. Lee's rear at Chancellorsville. Sedgwick started out, making fairly good headway at first, but Lee, taking the risk of dividing his army, sent a powerful 20,000-man force to intercept Sedgwick, which it did on the afternoon of May 3 at Salem Church. By the following morning

Sedgwick was nearly surrounded and was Obliged to retreat northward to Banks's Ford, where he withdrew across the Rappahannock on the night of May 4. Hooker followed him in retreat the next day.

'Salient, The'
See 'BLOODY ANGLE.'

Salisbury Prison, *North Carolina*

The Confederates converted a former cotton factory here into a prison in November 1861. By March 1862 about 1500 Federal soldiers were being held in reasonably good conditions. By late in the war, however, conditions had seriously deteriorated; in the prison it is estimated that more than 3400 Union prisoners died in Salisbury between October 1864 and February 1865.

Salm-Salm, Prince and Princess

Felix Constantin Alexander Johann Nepomuk, Prince Salm-Salm (1828-70), a Prussian veteran, sailed to America in 1861 to fight for the North, serving as aide-de-camp to Louis Blenker, commander of a 'German' division, and fighting with various New York regiments. His wife Agnes (1840-1912), a one-time circus performer, accompanied him in the field, eventually earning a captaincy for her hospital service.

Salomon Brothers

They were Prussian refugees from the 1848 revolution. Carl Eberhard and Frederick Sigel Salomon became Union officers, Frederick rising to the rank of brigadier general. A third brother, Edward S., wartime governor of Wisconsin, was a conspicuously successful military recruiter.

US Sanitary Commission field quarters. The humanitarian work done by the Commission was on a scale unprecedented in US history.

Salt Beef

Standard soldiers' ration, the meat was preserved in such a strong brine solution that it had to be thoroughly soaked in water before it could be eaten. Soldiers also called it salt horse (a term long used by sailors).

Sanitary Commission

Founded in 1861 by Henry Whitney Bellows and William H. Van Buren, the Sanitary Commission was one of the great triumphs of private humanitarian enterprise during the Civil War. It was created to make up for the grievous shortcomings of the Union army's small and inefficient Medical Bureau, and the Commission, along with its impressive women's auxiliary, soon became the largest and most advanced national agency devoted to the care of casualties of war, supplying ambulances and medicines, staffing hospitals with doctors and nurses, inspecting camps, and much else. Among its distinguished commissioners were Cornelius R. Agnew, Alexander D. Burke, Wolcott Gibbs, Elisha Harris, and Frederick Law Olmstead. Its energetic treasurer, George Templeton Strong, raised nearly $5 million for the Commission during the war.

Santa Rosa Island, *Florida*

Confederate General R. H. Anderson led a raid on Union positions on Pensacola Bay on the night of October 8-9, 1861. About 1000 raiders landed undetected and surprised the 6th New York Zouaves in camp, but returned to their boats and withdrew when Federal forces marched out of Fort Pickens (*See*) to counterattack.

Sap Roller

Engineers building a trench toward an enemy's lines would roll this cylindrical device, often made of woven branches and

saplings, ahead of them to provide cover from hostile fire.

Savage's Station and Allen's Farm *(Virginia)*, Battle of
(Also called Peach Orchard)

On the fifth day of the 1862 Seven Days' Battles, June 29, the Army of the Potomac was withdrawing in good order to the southeast. That day at Savage's Station, three miles south of the Chickahominy, Rebel General John Magruder made a weak attack on George McClellan's rear guard, with Stonewall Jackson straggling some distance behind and no use to Magruder.

Sawyer Projectile and Gun

This specialized weapon fired a projectile fitted with six rectangular ribs that matched corresponding grooves in the bore of the gun, thus guaranteeing the projectile's spin.

Sayler's Creek *(Virginia)*, Battle of

Strong Federal forces attacked Richard Ewell's and John Gordon's corps of Robert E. Lee's weakened army here on April 6, 1865, in one of the concluding battles of the Appomattox Campaign. The outnumbered Confederates lost more than 7000 men, perhaps a third of Lee's remaining effective strength. The Federals, under Philip Sheridan and Horatio Wright, reported losses of fewer than 1200 killed or wounded.

Scammon, Eliakim Parker *(1816-1894)* Union general.

Born in Maine, this West Point-trained war veteran and educator was promoted to brigadier general in October 1862 for gallantry at South Mountain. He held commands in West Virginia, Missouri, and the Carolinas, his field service being interrupted by capture in 1864 and imprisonment at Libby Prison.

Schofield, John McAllister *(1831-1906)* Union general.

An 1853 West Point graduate, this successful Federal soldier served in Missouri early in the war and fought at Wilson's Creek (*See*). He commanded the XXIII Corps, Army of the Ohio, during the Atlanta Campaign in 1864, during the Franklin and Nashville Campaign late in 1864, and during Sherman's Carolinas Campaign in early 1865. He was Andrew Johnson's secretary of war in 1868-69 and by 1888 had risen to the command of the US Army. He retired a lieutenant general in 1895.

Schurz, Carl *(1829-1906)*
Union general.

He settled in Wisconsin after fleeing his native Germany when the Revolution of 1848 failed. He commanded a division at Second Bull Run, fought at Chancellorsville, Gettysburg, and Chattanooga, ultimately commanding XI Corps in the Army of the Cumberland. He campaigned extensively for Lincoln during the election of 1864. In later

Union General Winfield Scott.

life he became a US Senator and served as secretary of the interior in the administration of Rutherford B. Hayes. As a writer and political and social reformer he continued to hold a position of great influence and respect into the early years of the twentieth century.

Scott, Winfield (1786-1866)
Union general.

Scott, a national hero after the War of 1812 and the Mexican War, had by 1861 served as general-in-chief of the army for 20 years and had become the first American lieutenant general since George Washington. Experienced in diplomacy and public affairs, Scott early foresaw the enormity of the coming war; he unsuccessfully urged President James Buchanan to reinforce Southern forts in 1860, himself raised and trained an army to defend Washington, and devised the strategically-crucial Anaconda Plan (*See*). Of the officers not trained at West Point, this Virginian was the only Southerner who stayed in the Union army. He was too aged and ill to direct the war, however, and retired in November 1861.

Secession, Sequence of

South Carolina became the first state to secede, on December 20, 1860. Following were: Mississippi, January 9, 1861; Alabama, January 11, 1861; Georgia, January 19, 1861; Louisiana, January 26, 1861; Texas, February 1, 1861; Virginia, April 17, 1861; Arkansas, May 6, 1861; North Carolina, May 20, 1861; and Tennessee, June 8, 1861. The Confederate States formed a provisional government in early February 1861.

Secessionville, *South Carolina*

A subordinate Federal commander, H. W. Benham, ignored orders not to undertake offensive operations and sent two divisions against Confederate positions here on James Island in Charleston Harbor on June 16, 1862. The assaults failed, with a loss of nearly 700 men; Benham was relieved of his command in consequence.

Sedgwick, John (1813-1864)
Union general.

This career officer was born in Connecticut and educated at West Point. His men affectionately called him 'Uncle John.' Competent and hard-fighting, he early won recognition in the Peninsular Campaign, where he was wounded. He was wounded again (twice) at Antietam but recovered in time to serve with distinction at Fredericksburg. As a major general commanding VI Corps, he tried unsuccessfully to reinforce Joseph Hooker at Chancellorsville (*See* SALEM CHURCH), and he commanded the Union left wing on the third day of the Battle of Gettysburg. He soldiered on until May 1864, when he was killed by a Rebel sharpshooter at the Battle of Spotsylvania.

Selma Raid

Union General James H. Wilson led three cavalry divisions from Tennessee against Selma, Alabama, one of the last important Confederate military centers, in late March 1865. There Wilson attacked Nathan B. Forrest, who had 2500 cavalry and 2500 militia in strong positions, on April 2. The militia fled, and Forrest's troopers escaped during the night. Wilson went on to capture Montgomery on April 12, then crossed into Georgia. It was in Macon, on April 20, that he learned that the war had ended.

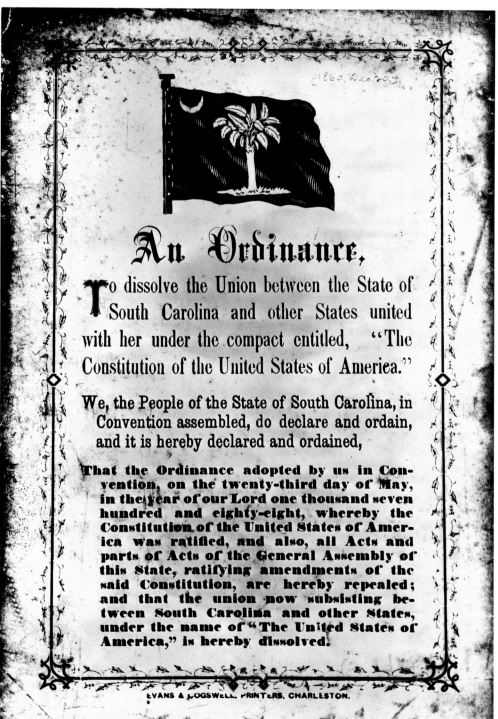

South Carolina's Ordinance of Secession. The first state to secede and the first to fire a shot, South Carolina would be marked out by Sherman for reprisal in 1865.

Raphael Semmes, captain of the Confederate commerce raider *Alabama*, in 1864.

Semmes, Raphael *(1809-1877)*
Confederate naval officer.

An Alabama resident, this US naval officer resigned after secession. He became a Confederate hero as a commerce raider in the Atlantic and Indian oceans. As commander of the raiders *Sumter* and *Alabama*, Semmes captured or destroyed a total of 82 Northern merchantmen valued at more than $6 million before being defeated off Cherbourg by the USS *Kearsarge* in June 1864. He later commanded the James River squadron.

Seven Days' Battles

When, in the midst of the Peninsular Campaign, Robert E. Lee took command of the most important of the Confederate armies after the Battle of Fair Oaks on May 31, 1862, he renamed his forces the Army of Northern Virginia. Under that name, Lee and his army

During the first big encounter of the Seven Days' Battles in 1862 Rebel troops evacuate Mechanicsville, Va., under Union fire.

would engineer a remarkable series of victories, usually against superior Union forces, over the next two years. However, Lee's first major engagements during the so-called Seven Days' Battles, did not show the dash and coordination of his later ones, though they did produce the desired effect of driving the enemy from the gates of Richmond.

After the Battle of Fair Oaks, General George B. McClellan and his Federal Army of the Potomac remained along the Chickahominy River near Richmond, most of the men on the south bank, but Fitz-John Porter's V Corps to the north of the river. Thus, as he had done before Fair Oaks, McClellan had left a detachment of his army dangerously unsupported on the opposite bank of the river. On June 12 Lee asked his flamboyant cavalry leader, Jeb Stuart, to scout the enemy's exposed wing. Stuart responded to the order by riding completely around the Army of the Potomac, raiding as he went. He returned to inform Lee of Porter's position and strength. Lee decided to hold the 75,000 Federals on the south bank with a screening force of only 27,000 under John Magruder, and use most of his strength, 60,000 men, in an attempt to annihilate Porter's 30,000. Lee now had the services of Stonewall Jackson, just arrived from his brilliant but exhausting Shenandoah Valley Campaign.

As Lee prepared to attack, the always-cautious McClellan, convinced enemy strength was 200,000, ordered a reconnaissance toward Richmond, in the process touching off the Seven Days' Battles. At Oak Grove, on June 25, McClellan's men ran into some Confederate outposts and a spirited skirmish broke out, producing some 500 casualties on both sides. In the next day's Battle of Mechanicsville, Lee took the initiative, first sending Magruder to make a feint against the much larger Union contingent on the south bank. Jackson was then supposed to strike Porter's flank in force. But throughout this week of fighting Jackson would prove to be uncharacteristically ineffectual, probably due to profound fatigue from his recent campaign in the Shenandoah; several times he would be found asleep in the midst of battle. On the 26th Jackson failed to engage Porter at all. In late afternoon A. P. Hill

ordered his men to attack Porter's well-entrenched forces near Mechanicsville and suffered 1500 casualties to the Union's 360. Despite this easy repulse, that night McClellan decided to retreat, pulling his forces back to a base on the James River and abandoning his plan to besiege Richmond. Though his attacks in the next days would falter, Lee had already gained the initiative.

On the following day, June 27, Lee tried an assault on Porter's new defensive position in the Battle of Gaines's Mill. In heavy fighting, with Jackson again lethargic, Porter was driven back before his line firmed up and the fighting ended inconclusively. That night Porter got most of his men across the river to rejoin the main body, which had been kept in place by Magruder's bluffing with his skimpy forces – marching in circles, making feints, shouting orders to nonexistent troops. So effective was Magruder that McClellan and his generals were convinced they were under attack by superior numbers on both sides of the river. The North had lost some 4000 killed and wounded and 2800 captured that day at Gaines's Mill, but Lee had lost 9000, in what would be one of his most costly days in the entire course of the war.

June 28 saw minor skirmishes at Garnett's and Golding's Farms, west of Richmond. By the next day the Army of the Potomac was withdrawing in good order to the southeast. Over the next three days Lee tried to turn that retreat into a rout, ordering a concentric series of attacks that failed to produce much effect, due to a combination of poor coordination, Jackson's maddening slowness, and strong Federal resistance. At Savage's Station on June 29, three miles south of the Chickahominy, Magruder made a weak attack on McClellan's rear guard, while Jackson straggled behind. The following day, at White Oak Swamp, Union forces pulled together to repulse another uncoordinated attack by James Longstreet and A. P. Hill; in fierce fighting, the Southerners took 1000 prisoners but suffered 3500 casualties. Once again, a seemingly sleepwalking Jackson failed to move his forces into action.

The Seven Days' Battles ended on July 1 with a battlefield disaster for the South. Lee, sensing McClellan's demoralization but failing to sense the ample fighting spirit left in the Army of the Potomac, threw his forces into a withering Union artillery barrage from the heights of Malvern Hill. Few Confederate units even made it within rifle range of the enemy; rarely in the war would artillery play such a commanding role. That day the South suffered 5500 casualties to less that half that for the North.

Lee and his generals had bungled most of the fighting in the Seven Days and had lost 20,000 men, a quarter of the army, to 16,000 for the Army of the Potomac, which was still not seriously damaged. Yet the South won the campaign for the simple reason that General McClellan considered himself defeated and on the brink of disaster; he wired Washington that he had been 'overpowered' by superior enemy numbers and was settling into a defensive position at Harrison's Landing on the James River. Lee had successfully driven the enemy from Richmond; McClellan had come within sight of the capital with immensely superior forces

The June 27, 1862, Battle of Gaines's Mill. Lee won none of the Seven Days' Battles yet, thanks to McClellan, won the campaign.

but then had let himself be maneuvered into retreat while winning nearly every engagement. Assessing the weakness of his command structure during the fighting, Lee banished some ineffective generals and reorganized the Army of Northern Virginia into two large infantry corps under Longstreet and Jackson (correctly seeing Jackson's real potential despite his failures in the Seven Days), plus Stuart's cavalry. In short, Lee emerged from the tactical defeats of the Seven Days with a strategic victory and a command structure that would take him to triumph on the battlefield again and again, until finally, in 1863, the Army of the Potomac would find the generals it needed.

Seven Pines

See FAIR OAKS AND SEVEN PINES

Seward, William Henry (1801-1872) Union statesman.

A strong opponent of slavery in the US Senate, he joined the newly formed Republican Party in 1856. He twice tried and failed to win the party's presidential nomination.

Seward was an able secretary of state for Lincoln during the war years, particularly on issues involving Britain, which built warships and provided other aid to the Confederacy. He was seriously wounded in the Lincoln assassination plot, but he continued to serve in his cabinet post throughout the administration of Andrew Johnson. His bargain-price purchase of Alaska from Russia in 1867 was dubbed 'Seward's Folly.'

Seward-Meigs-Porter Affair

Bureaucratic confusion in Washington led to embarrassment on the eve of the war when, in April 1861, the Union was still debating whether to reinforce specific Federal outposts in the South. Secretary of State William Seward, on his own authority, sent the USS *Powhatan*, with naval forces under Lieutenant David Dixon Porter and troops under Captain Montgomery Meigs, to support Fort Pickins on the Gulf coast of Florida. This precipitate action, made at a time when government policy had not yet been decided, resulted in the *Powhatan*'s being unavailable for the relief of Fort Sumter.

Seymour, Truman (1824-1891)
Union general.

A Vermonter, Seymour was a professional officer trained at West Point. In a varied war career from Fort Sumter through Sayler's Creek he was seriously wounded at Fort Wagner, suffered defeat at Olustee, and was captured in the Wilderness.

Union cannon pour withering fire on Rebels attacking Malvern Hill on July 1, 1862.

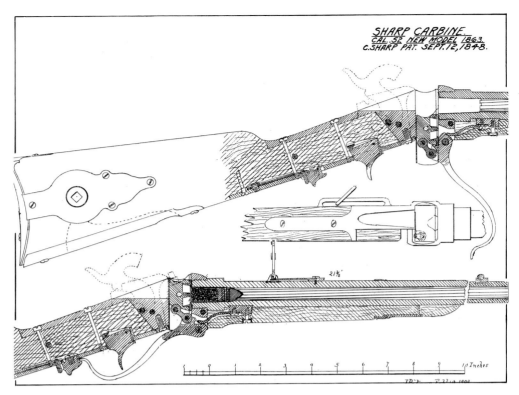

SHARP CARBINE.
CAL. 52 NEW MODEL 1863.
C. SHARP PAT. SEPT. 12, 1848.

A patent drawing of the action of the Sharps carbine, activated by the trigger guard.

Sharps Carbine and Rifle

The Sharps weapons were the most advanced breechloaders in America when the war began. The Union bought 9100 Sharps rifles and more than 80,000 Sharps carbines during the war. Confederate forces bought small numbers of these weapons. The rifles were used by the US Sharpshooters, while the carbine was mainly a cavalry weapon. Both were single-shot, were accurate up to 600 yards, and could fire at a rate of about 10 rounds per minute.

Sharpsburg, Battle of

See ANTIETAM

Sharpshooters, Regiments of

Union Colonel Hiram Berdan proposed forming units of outstanding riflemen, largely equipped with Sharps rifles, in 1861, and as a result the 1st and 2nd regiments of US Sharpshooters were organized. The 1st Sharpshooters fought on the Peninsula and at Chancellorsville and Gettysburg. The 2nd Sharpshooters' first significant action was at Antietam. Both regiments fought at the Wilderness and Spotsylvania. For the entire war, both units had casualty rates approaching 40 percent.

Shaw, Robert Gould (1837-1863)
Union officer.

This Boston abolitionist's son organized and led the Union's first black regiment, the 54th Massachusetts Colored Infantry, which left Boston on May 28, 1863. Shaw was killed amid the heavy Federal losses at Fort Wagner on July 18. As a mark of contempt for this white officer's championing blacks, Confed-erates threw his body into a common burial pit with the bodies of his black troops.

Shelby, Joseph Orville
(1830-1897) **Confederate general.**

'Jo' Shelby, a wealthy Kentuckian, joined the Confederate army as a cavalry captain and fought at Wilson's Creek, Lexington, and Pea Ridge. He later participated in many raids and skirmishes in Arkansas and Missouri. Rather than surrender at the war's end, he led his brigade into Mexico to join Emperor Maximilian's forces.

Shell

The term, casually used to describe any type of artillery projectile, refers specifically to one that contains a bursting powder charge. In the Civil War shells were sometimes ineffec-tive, either because of poor fuses or because the charges were insufficiently powerful to break up and scatter the cast iron casing.

Shenandoah, CSS

The Confederacy purchased this commerce-raiding cruiser in England in September 1864. Fitted out in Madeira under Captain James Waddell, the *Shenandoah* set out for the Pacific, where she captured or destroyed 36 vessels, together valued at $1.4 million, much of this damage being inflicted after the war was over (a fact of which Waddell was un-aware). *Shenandoah*'s depredations figured prominently in the *Alabama* Claims (*See*).

Shenandoah Valley Campaign of Jackson

In March 1862 General George B. McClellan began his Peninsular Campaign with the Federal Army of the Potomac, the goal being to capture the Confederate capital at Rich-mond. Confederate President Jefferson Davis knew that McClellan had the strength to do that unless extraordinary measures were taken (few yet suspected the timidity that would hobble all McClellan's cam-paigns). Besides organizing forces to protect the capital itself, Robert E. Lee, then an advi-sor to Davis, ordered a diversionary cam-paign in Virginia's Shenandoah Valley. This campaign was assigned to General Thomas J. ('Stonewall') Jackson, who was already in the valley with his Stonewall Brigade. The result was one of the legendary operations of mili-tary history.

The Shenandoah was critically important to the Confederacy. Its fertile farmland made it the South's breadbasket, and it was also the ideal route for Confederate armies marching north. Because of its strategic importance, the Union had sent forces there under Natha-niel Banks, a politically-appointed general with little battlefield skill. In March 1862 Banks had chased Jackson's men from Win-chester and occupied the town, along with nearby Strasburg. From there Banks planned to march east to join McClellan's campaign to take Richmond. Jackson's assignment was to tie up the Federal forces of Banks and General Irvin McDowell and keep them in the Shenandoah, away from McClellan.

Just before being ordered on his diversion, Jackson had suffered a major defeat in the valley. On March 22 he had sent cavalry to attack a detachment of Banks's army at Kern-stown; on the next day he sent in his infantry. Initially the attack made progress, but then Banks counterattacked with superior num-bers and sent the graycoats running. Jackson lost 700 of 4200 men engaged at Kernston, the Union 590 of 9000. Nonetheless, this defeat turned out to be as good as a victory from the Confederate point of view.

A sketch of T. J. 'Stonewall' Jackson made six months after his Shenandoah Campaign.

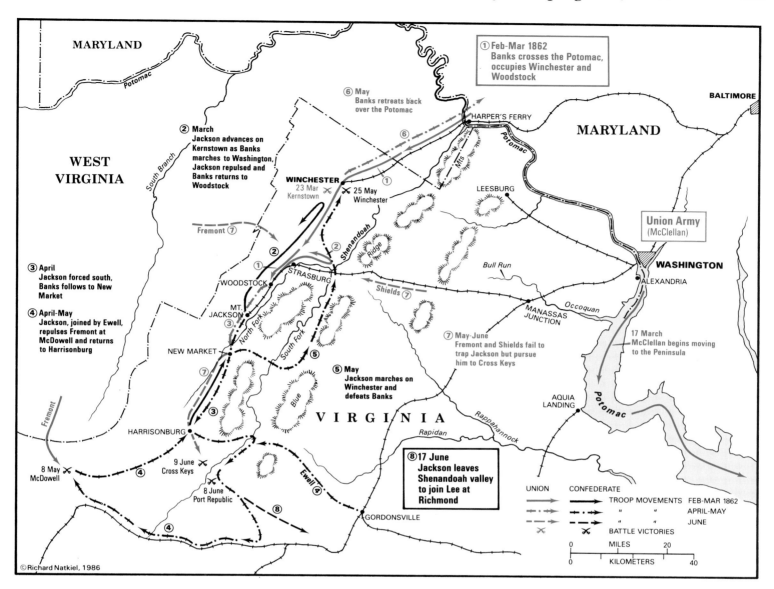

① Feb-Mar 1862
Banks crosses the Potomac, occupies Winchester and Woodstock

⑥ May
Banks retreats back over the Potomac

② March
Jackson advances on Kernstown as Banks marches to Washington, Jackson repulsed and Banks returns to Woodstock

③ April
Jackson forced south, Banks follows to New Market

④ April-May
Jackson, joined by Ewell, repulses Fremont at McDowell and returns to Harrisonburg

⑤ May
Jackson marches on Winchester and defeats Banks

⑦ May-June
Fremont and Shields fail to trap Jackson but pursue him to Cross Keys

⑧ 17 June
Jackson leaves Shenandoah valley to join Lee at Richmond

17 March
McClellan begins moving to the Peninsula

Union Army (McClellan)

MARYLAND
WEST VIRGINIA
VIRGINIA
BALTIMORE
HARPER'S FERRY
WINCHESTER — 23 Mar Kernstown — 25 May Winchester
LEESBURG
WASHINGTON
ALEXANDRIA
WOODSTOCK
STRASBURG
MT. JACKSON
NEW MARKET
HARRISONBURG
MANASSAS JUNCTION
AQUIA LANDING
GORDONSVILLE
8 May McDowell
9 June Cross Keys
8 June Port Republic
Bull Run
Fremont ⑦
Shields ⑦
Potomac
South Branch
North Fork
South Fork
Shenandoah
Blue Ridge
Rappahannock
Rapidan
Occoquan
Ewell

UNION   CONFEDERATE
→ TROOP MOVEMENTS   FEB-MAR 1862
→ " "   APRIL-MAY
→ " "   JUNE
✕ BATTLE VICTORIES

0   MILES   20
0   KILOMETERS   40

© Richard Natkiel, 1986

That was because in Washington, President Lincoln and his cabinet were shaken by this enemy show of strength in the Shenandoah and immediate reversed the orders for Banks and McDowell to reinforce McClellan. In turn, McClellan became even more cautious and tentative than usual, with fatal consequences for his campaign. Thus, in the end, Jackson's defeat at Kernstown may well have preserved Richmond and prolonged the war by three years. His ensuing diversionary campaign would be marked by an unbroken string of victories.

Washington ordered the separate commands of Banks, McDowell, and, to the west, General John C. Frémont to deal with Jackson. Unfortunately for the Union, none of the three would prove equal to his opponent. With Banks beginning a cautious pursuit and the other Federal contingents advancing, Jackson withdrew south (which was considered *up* the valley) with his 6000 men, developing his strategy as he went. Jackson was a strange, secretive man, shabby in his dress, devoutly religious (he tried not to fight on Sunday), suspected of insanity by his own officers, and a wildcat on the battlefield. Robert E. Lee wrote approvingly of him, 'A man he is of contrasts so complete that he appears on one day a Presbyterian deacon . . . and, the next, a reincarnated Joshua. He

lives by the New Testament and fights by the Old.' The heart of his concept of strategy, Jackson said, was, 'Always mystify, mislead, and surprise the enemy.' His Valley Campaign would be the perfect demonstration of that maxim.

As Banks marched in pursuit, Jackson

Above: A map showing the movements of the armies during Jackson's masterly Shenandoah Valley Campaign of 1862.
Below: A portrait of Jackson superimposed on a scene of his boyhood home. It was the Shenandoah Valley Campaign that first gave rise to the larger-than-life Jackson legend, a legend seemingly confirmed at Chancellorsville.

made a forced march to Swift Run Gap, in the eastern mountains, which placed him on Banks's flank and forced the Northern general to stop and protect his supply line. Meanwhile, Jackson was reinforced by Richard Ewell, bringing his total command to 17,000 men, which would be its maximum strength. His operation went into high gear when Jackson learned that Frémont's force was about to join Banks. That had to be prevented. Ordering some cavalry feints to hold Banks, Jackson took the rest of his men to Staunton, putting out the word that he was retreating (his own men believed so until they reached Staunton). In fact, Jackson was taking a roundabout route to the town of McDowell, to which he went from Staunton by forced march. So fast did his troops march – up to 30 miles a day – that they took to calling themselves 'foot cavalry.'

At McDowell, on May 8, Jackson confronted some 6000 Federals who were on their way to join Frémont. The bluecoats attacked Jackson's force of 10,000, but the Confederates struck back and chased the enemy into West Virginia. Jackson then headed his men for Harrisonburg. At that point, as far as the Northerners were concerned, Jackson disappeared into thin air. On May 23, with his full contingent, he reappeared to strike Union troops at Front Royal; his men captured or killed 904 of the 1063-man garrison.

Learning of the disaster at Front Royal, Banks pulled his men back from Strasburg to high ground at Winchester. Before they could dig in, however, Jackson was on them – after an all-night forced march. Jackson

So fast did Jackson's infantry march in the Valley, they called themselves 'foot cavalry'.

A skirmish between Jackson's men and Union troops on June 7, 1862. In the next 48 hours Jackson would beat two Union armies in turn.

attacked the Federals on both flanks and dealt the final blow in the center. Banks then withdrew across the Potomac and out of the Shenandoah for good; he had lost 3000 of the 8000 in his command; Jackson's casualties were about 400 of 16,000. After resting a couple of days, Jackson marched to the northern end of the valley near Harpers Ferry, a feint to convince the enemy he was going to cross the Potomac. There he was threatened by converging forces under Frémont and James Shields (the latter dispatched by McDowell).

Jackson ordered the Stonewall Brigade to prevent Banks from recrossing the Potomac and pulled the rest of his men south on May 30. When his forces were widely scattered, he learned that the two enemy generals were approaching fast. He responded by sending detachments to hold them up, concentrating his forces, and continuing south with 15,000 men and a double wagon train of captured supplies seven miles long. His pursuers could make only weak strikes on Jackson's rear; he had burned all the bridges. Finally, by June 7, Frémont and Shields had caught Jackson squarely between them and began to fire on both Southern flanks. The most remarkable achievement of the campaign followed. On June 8 Frémont advanced from Cross Keys in the west, but Ewell's 6500 graycoats stopped these 10,500 in their tracks. With Frémont kept at bay by a burned bridge and a token force, Jackson on the next day struck Shields, who was somewhat to the east at Port Republic, with nearly his full forces. After putting up stiff resistance, the heavily outnumbered Federals were soundly defeated and driven back.

With some 17,000 men Jackson had bested 33,000 Union troops, outmaneuvering and usually outnumbering his opponents in every engagement; in military terms he had 'defeated the enemy in detail.' Moreover, in one month his men had marched 300 miles, had fought four pitched battles and constant skirmishes, and had captured more than 400 prisoners and enormous quantities of arms and supplies. It had been an historic demonstration of mobile striking power – one that

the Germans would study with profit before World War II. As Jackson marched his men east to rejoin Robert E. Lee in Virginia, the war in the Eastern Theater was firmly under Confederate control. And though Jackson and his men would stumble unaccountably in the coming Seven Days' Battles, this commander had proved his irreplaceable value to the Southern cause.

Shenandoah Valley Campaign of Sheridan

As Ulysses S. Grant began the siege of Petersburg, Virginia, in summer of 1864, General Philip Sheridan and the cavalry of the Army of the Potomac spent weeks making minor raids on Southern rail lines. Meanwhile, Grant became increasingly concerned about the presence in Virginia's Shenandoah Valley of Confederate General Jubal Early, who, both before and again after his Raid on Washington (*See*), had cleared the valley of Union troops. The fertile farms of the Shenandoah thus continued to feed all the Southern armies.

So in August, Grant created the Army of the Shenandoah, 48,000 infantrymen, cavalrymen, and artillerymen, and sent them into the valley under the ambitious and energetic Sheridan. Their immediate objective was to take care of Early and, if possible, raider John Singleton Mosby as well. The larger task, however, would be to wreck farms, burn crops, and confiscate livestock. Grant ordered Sheridan to turn the Shenandoah 'into a barren waste . . . so that crows flying over it for the balance of this season will have to carry their provender with them.' If that could be done, the South and her armies would begin to starve in earnest.

On September 19, pushing into the Shenandoah, Sheridan located Early at Winchester and moved to the attack. Unused to leading a combination of mounted troops and infantry, Sheridan nearly let his slippery opponent get away, but finally the Confederates were in battered retreat south, with Union cavalry in pursuit. Three days later Sheridan attacked Early again at Fisher's Hill, where the graycoats had dug in strongly. Sheridan hit the enemy flank first and then personally led a frontal attack with his full force. The Confederates were routed again. With Early apparently subdued for the moment, the Federals resumed their progress through the valley, beginning their intended work of destruction. By October 7 Sheridan could report to Grant that his men had 'destroyed over 2000 barns filled with wheat, hay, and farming implements; over seventy mills filled with flour and wheat; have driven in front of the army 4000 head of stock, and have killed and issued to the troops not less than 3000 sheep.'

But his opponent had not given up. Collecting men and supplies for a new offensive, Early set his men to nipping at the heels of the enemy, much to Sheridan's irritation. After dismissing one of his generals for lack of aggressiveness, Sheridan ordered his cavalry commander, Alfred Torbert, to 'Whip the enemy or be whipped yourself!' Taking Sheridan at his word, Torbert and his men proceeded to thrash Early's cavalry at Tom's Brook on October 9.

Again assuming that he had ended the threat from Early, Sheridan went to Washington on October 16 to confer with his superiors. On the way back two days later, he stopped off for the night in Winchester, some 20 miles from where his army was encamped at Cedar Creek, near Middletown. On the following morning Sheridan awoke to the sound of firing in the distance. An orderly told him it was probably skirmishing, so the general did not hurry his preparations. But the shooting continued, and Sheridan mounted his charger Rienzi and took to the road in growing concern, stopping occasionally to put his ear to the ground and listen (the earth could carry the sounds of battle better than air). As he approached Cedar Creek he realized that the firing was approaching him faster than he was approaching it: that could only mean that his army was retreating under pursuit. Now he spurred Rienzi to a gallop.

Riding over the last ridge, Sheridan saw his army coming toward him in full flight, the fields and roads covered by a tangle of men, horses, and wagons. Early had mounted a surprise attack on the left flank of the sleeping Federals at Cedar Hill, and four divisions had bolted out of camp and run for their lives. Sheridan saw numerous officers and men marching in their underwear, but to his satisfaction he noticed that nearly everyone had a rifle in hand. He charged down the road waving his hat, the soldiers beaking into cheers as he rode by. In response, he rose up in his saddle and shouted in his usual profane style, 'God damn you, don't cheer me! If you love your country, come up to the front. There's lots of fight in you men yet!'

Word of his return spread out through the scattered army, electrifying the troops. A participant later wrote, 'Such a scene as his presence and such emotion as it awoke cannot be realized but once in a century.' Many of the veterans had stopped to brew coffee along the road while they waited for orders,

A half-finished sketch of Federal General Philip Sheridan on his famous ride.

and the cavalry and VI Corps had not scattered. As Sheridan rode by, men began to kick over their coffeepots, pick up their rifles, and head back to the front.

Sheridan's ride to Cedar Creek would be one of the legendary moments of the war,

Sheridan's Union troops move relentlessly up the Shenandoah Valley in the winter of 1864. They would conquer it all by March 1865.

Union General Philip Sheridan leads his men to victory over Jubal Early's Confederates at Cedar Creek, Va., on October 19, 1864.

material for poetry and song, but it was not a matter of riding down the road and creating an immediate charge. It took some two hours of painstaking work before the army was rounded up and formed into line of battle. Many of Early's men, meanwhile, had stopped at the captured Yankee camps to sample the abundant food and liquor. When his troops were ready to attack, Sheridan rode down the battle line waving a banner and shouting, 'We've got the goddamndest twist on them you ever saw!' The Federals swept out to the attack; in short order the surprised and disorganized Confederates were running for their lives, losing a thousand men who were taken prisoner and most of their artillery and their supplies.

The Battle of Cedar Creek finally ended Jubal Early's power in the Shenandoah. In early March of 1865 George A. Custer's cavalry wiped out the remains of the Confederate forces in the valley at Waynesboro; Early and two officers escaped with only 20 men. By that time Sheridan had completed the sacking of the valley, destroying or confiscating its farms, crops, animals, mills, powder works, barns, tanneries, and railroads. He had failed only in rounding up Mosby. Then Sheridan and his men headed back to join Grant in the final acts of the war, at Petersburg and Appomattox.

Sheridan, Philip Henry
(1831-1888) **Union general.**

After an undistinguished education at West Point and undistinguished service in Texas and the Northwest, New York State-born Sheridan began the Civil War in desk jobs. However, when the short and feisty Sheridan was given combat duty his career sky-

rocketed, one of his early commanders describing him as 'worth his weight in gold.' His immense energy and fierce fighting spirit would take him to the command of the Army of the Potomac's cavalry, a post in which he

An heroic version of Sheridan, astride his horse Rienzi, rallying his retreating men before the Battle of Cedar Creek.

Sheridan (left) and staff. Wesley Merritt is in the center, George Custer on the right.

would soon become General Ulysses Grant's strong right arm.

His combat career in the Civil War began in May 1862 when he was appointed colonel of the 2nd Michigan cavalry and took part in the Union advance on Corinth, Mississippi, winning the Battle of Booneville over Rebel cavalry in July. He was subsequently made a brigadier general and given a division in the Army of the Ohio. He distinguished himself at the Battle of Perryville in October 1862 and at the Battle of Stone's River in December. In the Chattanooga Campaign of 1863 he played important roles in both the Battle of Chickamauga and the Battle of Missionary Ridge. In April 1864 Grant gave him command of all the cavalry of the Army of the Potomac, and within a month, during the Wilderness Campaign, Sheridan was making a raid on Richmond (May 9-24) that, among other things, produced the Battle of Yellow Tavern, in which the South lost its own premier cavalry leader, J. E. B. Stuart. From August 1864 to early 1865 Sheridan was engaged in his most famous wartime operation, his Shenandoah Valley Campaign. Soon after he had rejoined Grant before Petersburg, his victory at the Battle of Five Forks precipitated the end of the lengthy Petersburg siege. In the aftermath of the fall of Richmond he closely pursued the retreating Army of Northern Virginia, finally forcing Robert E. Lee's surrender at Appomattox Court House.

He held various military commands after the war, mainly in the South and West, and in 1884 he succeeded W. T. Sherman as commander-in-chief of the US Army. Though not quite on a par with such master strategists as Grant and Sherman, he is remembered as a brilliant tactician, a formidable warrior, and by far the greatest cavalry commander produced by the Union during the war.

Sheridan's Ride

See SHENANDOAH VALLEY CAMPAIGN OF SHERIDAN

Sherman, William Tecumseh
(1820-1891) **Union general.**

Sherman ended the war with two distinct reputations: in the North, as one of the most admired generals, in the South, as the most hated enemy of all. He was born on February 8, 1820, in Lancaster, Ohio, and, orphaned, was largely reared by a family friend, a prominent state politician. He was graduated from West Point and first saw action in the Mexican War. After the Civil War began he fought as a colonel of infantry in the First Bull Run Battle of July 1861; that August he was promoted to brigadier general and briefly assigned to Kentucky.

Soon thereafter Sherman took over the Department of the Cumberland, but he soon quarreled both with his superiors and with the press, mainly due to his obstinate insistence (entirely correct, as it turned out) that it was going to be a long war that required far more commitments of men and matériel than the North had yet made. In response, the army declared Sherman unstable and removed him from command, at which point he did indeed have some sort of nervous breakdown and considered suicide. By March 1862 he was judged recovered and given command of a division of the Army of the Tennessee under Ulysses S. Grant. There he became the prime partner of the Union's greatest general; their combined leadership would profoundly affect the war.

In the Battle of Shiloh in April 1862 Sherman and his division were instrumental in preventing a total rout after the initial surprise Rebel attack; Grant issued Sherman a commendation. Given command of the District of Memphis, Sherman fought alongside Grant in the long and ultimately triumphant Vicksburg Campaign. When Grant was given command of the Department of the Mississippi, Sherman stepped into his partner's shoes as head of the Department of the Tennessee; together, they directed the breakout of Federal forces in the Chattanooga Campaign. Grant then being elevated to general-in-chief of Union armies, Sherman took over his vacated post once again.

As a vital part of Grant's overall strategy to win the war, articulated in March 1864, Sherman was ordered to begin his Atlanta Campaign. Moving out of Chattanooga in May, he proceeded in a brilliant series of maneuvers against the Confederate forces of Joseph E. Johnston, steadily driving his opponent south. By early September, Southern forces (now under John B. Hood) had been forced out of Atlanta. Sherman moved in and ordered the destruction of all buildings and matériel of potential military importance, turning a good deal of Atlanta into a ruin, streams of refugees pouring from the city. Then, proclaiming 'I will make Georgia howl,' Sherman set out on the campaign that would take him into history – the famous March to the Sea.

In this campaign Sherman followed Grant's lead in the later stages of the Vicksburg Campaign, cutting his army away from supply lines and having his men forage off the enemy countryside, seizing all the food that could be found in his path. This had two primary objectives: it avoided the problem of having to strip his forces to protect a steadily lengthening supply line, and it struck a blow at the spirit of the enemy people, showing that the Confederacy was unable to protect its populace. Though Sherman ordered that there be no looting, destruction of private property, or violation of persons, all those things occurred in the course of what amounted to systematic stealing on a grand scale (there were, however, relatively few atrocities by the standards of later wars). The South, naturally indifferent to the valid mili-

William Tecumseh Sherman, by George Healy. National Portrait Gallery, Washington, DC.

Carolinas, marching his army north with the intention of joining Grant in striking Robert E. Lee at Petersburg. In terms of difficulty this campaign was a far greater challenge than the March to the Sea, it was even harsher in its conduct, and, by putting pressure on Lee, it probably had a greater impact on the outcome of the war; yet for some reason history has chosen to dwell almost exclusively on the Georgia episode. Together, the two campaigns probably did more to break the South's will to fight than anything that had happened previously, and it is at least arguable that in so doing they may have saved a good many thousands of lives.

Lee surrendered in April 1865, while Sherman was still in North Carolina; Johnston surrendered the last major Confederate army to Sherman later in April. The generous surrender terms Sherman offered to Johnston were bitterly criticized and rejected by Washington; Johnston surrendered anyway, under terms similar to Lee's, but Sherman was outraged by the criticism and never forgot it. The affair was one of the main reasons he stayed away from politics after the war (his brother John was a prominent Senator). To admirers who wanted to draft him for the presidency in 1884, Sherman replied succinctly: 'If nominated I will not accept. If elected I will not serve.'

After the war Sherman once again suc-

Above: Union General W. T. Sherman reads the terms of surrender to his old adversary, Joseph E. Johnston, in April 1865.
Below: A Union Wisconsin regiment attacks a New Orleans battery on the second day of the Battle of Shiloh, April 7, 1862.

tary purposes of the campaign, would remember Sherman with a hatred it would feel for no other Northern figure.

After reaching the end of his march at Savannah in December 1864 Sherman, in February 1865, launched a campaign into the

ceeded Grant, in 1869 becoming commander-in-chief of the US Army. He died in New York City on February 14, 1891. One of the many mourners at his funeral was Joseph E. Johnston. Despite the warnings of friends, the old Confederate general insisted on standing bareheaded in a cold rain as Sherman's casket passed. As a result, he contracted penumonia and died soon thereafter. But as Johnston had no doubt rightly said, Sherman would never have remained covered at *his*, Johnston's, funeral.

Throughout his career Sherman rejected any glorification of war; thus his most famous statements: 'War is barbarism; you cannot refine it,' and 'War . . . is all hell.' Whether these were examples of anti-romantic wisdom or means of justifying his own ferociously effective strategy is a question for historians. He has been called the prophet of what came to be called Total War, the practice of waging war on enemy populations as a whole, but whether he would in fact have endorsed such methods as the terror bombing of civilians carried on by most great powers in the twentieth century is by no means certain.

Shiloh, Campaign and Battle

By the middle of 1862 Robert E. Lee and his Army of Northern Virginia were dominating the Eastern theater of the war. In the Western theater, which included most of the Deep South, there were no comparable Southern commanders of major armies. And in the first full year of fighting the linked disciplines of strategy, tactics, and intelligence-gathering had not reached the level they would later attain on both sides. An example of the situation early in the war is the Battle of Shiloh,

which set the pattern of Union dominance in the Western theater.

Many in the North, hoping for a quick victory, had not yet realized that, in order to win, the Federal armies had to invade and occupy the South. Washington's first major task toward that end would be to split the Confederacy from north to south by gaining control of the Mississippi River. To this end, and fresh from his celebrated victories at Forts Henry and Donelson, Union General Ulysses S. Grant was preparing for new operations in the South during March 1862. The bulk of his Army of the Mississippi was encamped on the western bank of the Tennessee River near Pittsburg Landing, Tennessee, awaiting reinforcements from Don Carlos Buell's Army of the Ohio.

Meanwhile, in nearby Corinth, Mississippi, Confederate General Albert Sidney Johnston had assembled an army of 40,000 men for the purpose of destroying Grant. Second in command there was General P. G. T. Beauregard. Johnston's plan was to spring a surprise attack, to envelop the Union left flank by the river (cutting off Buell's reinforcements), and then to drive the Federals back against Owl Creek for the kill.

Before dawn on April 6, 1862, Grant left Pittsburg Landing and his 33,000 troops (most of them green) to confer with General Buell in Savannah, Tennessee. Grant and his close subordinate W.T. Sherman knew about the enemy concentration in Corinth and were planning an eventual offensive against it, but Grant was confident that the enemy would not strike him first. He had recently written to Henry Halleck, the new Union general-in-chief, 'I scarcely have the faintest idea of an attack . . . being made on us.'

He was wrong. Soon after Grant left, on April 6, Johnston's attack smashed into the camps of the sleeping Federals, driving many of them toward the river in panic. It appeared that a rout was imminent. But over on the left flank, where Johnston had planned his envelopment, Sherman organized his men to stand their ground and fight back. The surprised Confederates pulled up, thus slowing the whole advance.

Thousands of raw Northern recruits saw their first action and ran that day, yet by midmorning scattered bands were, on their own, beginning to contest the Confederate onslaught. Johnston allowed his attack to become disorganized – units intermingled, commands became confused, and the intended envelopment became a disorderly piecemeal advance. Meanwhile, Grant had arrived back at Pittsburg Landing and begun to organize his resistance: Lewis Wallace was ordered to rush his 5000 troops down from their position five miles north at Crump's Landing. Buell was urged to hurry, and Union stragglers were rounded up at gunpoint. On the left center a group of 4500 bluecoats under Benjamin Prentiss fought back so fiercely that the Confederates dubbed the area the 'Hornet's Nest.' Grant ordered Prentiss to hold out as long as possible. The initial Southern impetus was finally lost in midafternoon, when A.S. Johnston, whom the Confederacy considered one of its finest generals, bled to death after a stray bullet cut an artery in his leg. His replacement, General Beauregard, was ailing.

As the afternoon ended Grant's army re-

The 'Hornet's Nest,' the key to the Union's defense on the first day at Shiloh.

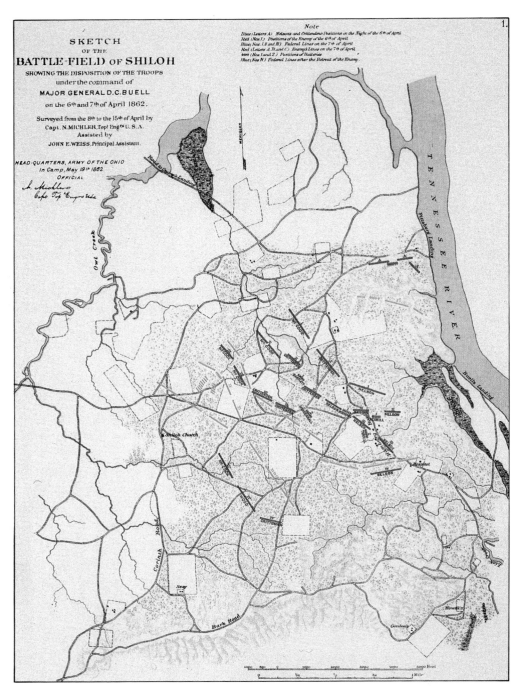

A Union map of the Battle of Shiloh.

on the first day. On the whole, Shiloh was a 'soldier's battle,' a matter of the courage and resourcefulness of individual leaders and units. And the Union victory proved incomplete, since the Southern forces had escaped (it was more Grant's style in those days to swallow enemy armies whole).

Yet as a result of the Battle of Shiloh the Confederacy would never be as strong in Tennessee as it had been before, and the North was one step closer to conquering the Mississippi River. Though Grant's reputation suffered as a result of his initial surprise, President Lincoln would be quick to perceive this general's value. To demands for Grant's head, Lincoln replied 'I can't spare this man. He fights.' As for Grant and many other Union leaders, Shiloh led them to realize that this was not going to be a quick war; later, Grant wrote that after the Battle of Shiloh he 'gave up all idea of saving the Union except by complete conquest.'

Shoddy

This name for the material used in making Union uniforms at the start of the war soon became a synonym for cheapness. 'Soldiers, on their first day's march or in the earliest storm, found their clothes, overcoats and blankets scattering to the wind in rags, or dissolving into their primitive elements of dust under the pelting rain,' the magazine *Harper's Monthly* reported.

Shot

Unlike the term 'shell,' this refers to a solid artillery projectile that contains no explosive. Shot can be spherical, for use in smoothbore cannon, or oblong, for use in rifled cannon. In the days before delayed-action fuses had been perfected it was often the preferred munition to be used against fortifications and armor plate.

Shrapnel

This hollow projectile was filled with lead bullets. A fuse-detonated explosive charge burst the cast-iron shell and scattered the balls, to deadly effect. It was also, more loosely, called case shot (*See*).

Sibley, Henry Hastings (1811-1891) Union general.

A Michigan-born lawyer and fur trader, he worked for the organization of a Minnesota Territory. He represented it in Washington, and when it became a state (1858), he was elected the first governor of Minnesota. He was commissioned a brigadier general of volunteers in September 1862. He led a brigade against the Sioux in the Indian rebellion of 1862 (*See*). Taking 2000 prisoners, Sibley tried 400 Sioux by court martial and executed 38 of them on December 26, 1862.

Sibley Henry Hopkins (1816-1886) Confederate general.

This Louisiana-born Indian fighter was made commander of the Army of New Mexico early in the war and conducted the South's generally unsuccessful New Mexico and

mained in desperate shape. The left had been driven back almost to Pittsburg Landing, where Buell's reinforcements had yet to come in from across the river. The Hornet's Nest had been overrun after 11 enemy charges; Prentiss finally surrendered in late afternoon. But the effort it took to round up Prentiss's 2200 surviving troops wasted valuable time for the South. By the time the Confederates made their last push of the day Union batteries and two gunboats were in position to slow the advance. At the same time, Buell's reinforcements arrived on the opposite bank and began crossing on boats; not knowing of that, Beauregard called off the fighting at about 6:00 in the evening. The decision probably cost him the battle. That night the Confederates slept in the captured enemy camps, convinced that the next day would cement their victory. All through a rainy and miserable night, however, Grant

was busy organizing his forces, including 25,000 reinforcements from Buell, for a counterattack.

Early on the morning of April 7 Grant unleashed his attack, and by early afternoon his men had recaptured their camps. For a time the Southerners mounted fierce resistance near Beauregard's headquarters at Shiloh Church, which would give the battle its name. But the Confederate commander had only 20,000 troops left fighting, and reinforcements from the west had been halted by high water on the Mississippi. At 2:30 in the afternoon Beauregard gave the order to retreat to Corinth.

The Battle of Shiloh was the bloodiest in the war to that time: 1754 Federals were killed and 8408 wounded of 62,682 engaged; the South lost 1723 killed and 8012 wounded of 40,335 engaged. None of the top commanders had managed his troops particularly well, although Grant had mounted a brilliant counterattack after being surprised

Although Shiloh was a Union victory, that the Rebel attack had taken Grant by surprise was a fact much criticized by his superiors.

Arizona operations (*See*) in 1862. He subsequently led various commands in Louisiana, south of the Red River. He is perhaps best remembered as the inventor of the Sibley tent.

Sibley Tent

This lightweight conical tent could shelter 12 soldiers and their equipment. It was designed before the war by then-Major Henry Hopkins Sibley (*See*).

Sickles, Daniel Edgar *(1825-1914)*
Union general.

A New York lawyer, diplomat, and US Senator, Sickles raised the Excelsior Brigade of New York City and led it in the Peninsular Campaign, at Antietam, and at Fredericksburg; he led III Corps with distinction at Chancellorsville and at Gettysburg, where he advanced his unit ahead of the Union line without authorization, helping to stop the Confederate advance but seeing his troops decimated and losing his leg. He was instrumental in later making Gettysburg battlefield a national park.

Sigel, Franz *(1824-1902)*
Union general.

The German-born Sigel emigrated to the US after the Revolution of 1848. Director of schools in St. Louis at the start of the war, he received a commission as brigadier general of volunteers in May 1861 and fought at Wilson's Creek and, with some distinction, at Pea Ridge. Sigel held a series of senior commands in the Shenandoah, where he suffered a serious defeat at New Market, and in West Virginia before he resigned in May 1865. Though considered a mediocre general, he recruited thousands of German immigrants for the Union forces.

Signal Communications

The Civil War saw many signal 'firsts': the first signal corps, the first air-to-ground telegraph, the first field-telegraph system, and the earliest extensive use of electrical telegraphy. The Union Signal Corps, established on June 21, 1860, was eventually restricted to visual signals, losing a struggle for primacy with the elaborate Military Telegraph System (*See* TELEGRAPHY). The Confederate Signal Corps, which was not established until 1862, developed a comparatively primitive set of communications systems.

Slavery

The causes of the American Civil War were many and complex, but most of them surged around the issue of human slavery, visited on black people in America for two centuries before the war. In 1860 the Southern states of the US were among the last places in the Western world to maintain the institution of slavery. The Dutch had first brought African slaves to America in the early seventeenth century; by the time of the American Revolution, there were half a million slaves in the country, most of them shipped under brutal conditions by the British slave trade. In the South, where three-quarters of the country's slaves lived, they made up 40 per cent of the total population.

The contradiction between American ideals and slavery was too manifest to be ignored forever, though it caused little overt political friction until the second decade of the nineteenth century. In the Declaration of Independence, the second sentence had proclaimed 'all Men are created equal.' America had been the first country in history to erect that principal as the foundation of a state, yet by protecting slavery the US Constitution denied that very principal. The resulting moral (and ultimately political) dilemma troubled the founding fathers; Thomas Jefferson said, 'I tremble for my country' at the thought of what slavery was leading to. Yet Jefferson owned slaves; like most Southern planters, he could not imagine how else to work his land.

Unwittingly, Jefferson provided the ideological basis that extended the life of slavery – his idea of States' Rights. He saw the primacy of state governments as the bastion of democracy. During the nineteenth century, that idea would be taken up by political theorists such as South Carolinian John C. Calhoun and made into the means of protecting slavery: it was a matter for each state to decide, and the federal government had no right to interfere. If the national government passed laws objectionable to a state, that state had the right to nullify them – or to secede from the Union if Federal interference went too far.

The legal tensions aroused by slavery and the nullification doctrine grew steadily during the nineteenth century. Beginning with the Quakers around the time of the Revolution, an abolitionist movement grew up. Congress began to chip away at the institution, starting by abolishing the overseas slave trade in 1808. A series of Congressional compromises – that fully satisfied no one – protected slavery in the South but placed barriers to its spread into new territories. Begin-

Military communications improved steadily during the war. This log platform near the battlefield at Antietam was part of a chain of Union semaphore signal stations.

A sense of what Hannah Arendt called 'the banality of evil' pervades this chilling Brady photograph of a slave pen in Alexandria, Va.

ning with Rhode Island in 1774, states north of the Mason-Dixon line had abolished slavery by 1846, and territories north of the Ohio River entered the Union as 'free' states. Meanwhile, the population of slaves in the South increased to over four million by 1860, a third of the population (though less than a third of Southern whites owned slaves). Slaves were considered the indispensable foundation of the region's agrarian economy, which had become firmly based on cotton after the invention of the cotton gin in the early part of the nineteenth century.

Well aware of the economic facts, the South became steadily more defiant in its defense of both its slavery and its culture. Southerners took to calling themselves 'Southrens'; they imagined their society as superior to that of the North, a chivalrous land full of bold cavaliers and elegantly re-fined ladies. As the uncompromising section-alism of the South grew, so did the fury of antislavery sentiment in the North; the fulmi-nations of abolitionists such as Boston minis-ter William Lloyd Garrison became increas-ingly violent. Educated blacks such as Frederick Douglass, who had escaped from slavery, wrote eloquent and heartfelt attacks on the institution. The Underground Rail-road was organized to give slaves a means of escaping north to freedom – a humanitarian effort entirely illegal by existing laws. In 1852 Harriet Beecher Stowe's novel *Uncle Tom's Cabin* electrified the North and outraged the South with its indictment of slavery.

Stowe and others exposed the old South-ern myth that blacks were happy and well-treated under slavery and did not yearn for freedom. In reality, treatment of slaves ranged from mild and paternalistic to cruel and sadistic; but in all cases slaves had no legal means of protesting any treatment whatever. Nor did they have any recourse

when families were broken apart, when owners attempted to breed slaves as if they were livestock, or when whites took slaves as mistresses or simply raped them – as occurred regularly. The latter practices created a large mixed-race population in the country, all of whom, no matter how minute the black ancestry, were considered Negro. Abolitionist literature was replete with stories of women and men being sold into slavery for having one-sixteenth or less of black blood, and these stories were more often than not true.

Uncle Tom's Cabin, or rather, the climate of rising indignation it represented, was part of the web of events that led inexorably toward war. Its publication followed by two years the Fugitive Slave Act, which alarmed abolition-ist forces by mandating stringent penalties, even in the North, for aiding fugitive slaves in the Underground Railroad or otherwise. In 1857 came the Dred Scott Decision by the con-servative Supreme Court; it defined slaves as subhuman property, with no rights of citizenship. In the mid-1850s a virtual war raged in the territory of Kansas between pro- and antislavery factions. And finally and most ominously of all, came the spectre of the South's greatest fear, that of a slave revolt: in October 1859 fanatical abolitionist John Brown led an armed group of blacks and whites to seize the Federal arsenal at Harpers Ferry, Virginia, to realize his dream of ignit-ing a general uprising of slaves. Brown was quickly captured and hanged, but the story of his exploit broke over the entire country like a thunderclap.

By then a new political party had formed, the first one explicitly to oppose slavery. The emerging leader of this Republican Party was an Illinois lawyer named Abraham Lincoln. His election as president in November 1861, precipitated the secession from the United States of most of the slave states in the country, who would thenceforth call them-selves the Confederate States of America. The years of political maneuver and com-promise were now over, and violence would decide the future of slavery.

Slidell, John *(1793-1871)*
Confederate diplomat.

A New Yorker by birth, this New Orleans lawyer was an influential Democratic polit-ician. In 1861 he was captured on a diplomatic mission to seek French recognition for the Confederacy (*See* TRENT AFFAIR), a goal he never achieved. His nephew, Ranald Slidell MacKenzie, was a Union general.

Five generations of slaves on a plantation in Beaufort, South Carolina, pose – or, more probably, are compelled to pose – for a gloomy family portrait.

Slocum, Henry Warner
(1827-1894) **Union general.**

A West Point alumnus, he was a New York lawyer and legislator. He commanded a division at First Bull Run, where he was wounded, fought through the Peninsular Campaign, and commanded V, XI, and XII Corps at Fredericksburg, XII Corps at Chancellorsville, and XII Corps at Gettysburg, where he held the Union right wing. In 1864, toward the end of the Atlanta Campaign, he took over XX Corps from Joseph Hooker and then continued to serve under W.T. Sherman during the March to the Sea and the Carolinas Campaign. After the war he resigned his commission and returned once again to the practice of law.

Sloop-of-War

Not a sloop in the modern sense, this was a type of wooden-hulled full-rigged naval ship (*i.e.*, one with three square-rigged masts and a bowsprit) that carried its main battery uncovered on its uppermost deck. Many Civil War sloops-of-war had auxiliary steam power and were sometimes called 'steam sloops' or 'screw sloops.' They were less powerful than frigates (*See*). Although not a term then used in the US Navy, the designation 'corvette' referred to essentially the same type of ship.

Smith, Andrew Jackson
(1815-1897) **Union general.**

A Pennsylvania-born West Pointer (1838), he served on the frontier and in the Mexican War. He led a division during the Vicksburg Campaign and the right wing of XVI Corps during the Red River Campaign of 1864. Smith also led large formations at the Battle of Nashville in December 1864 and in operations around Mobile in 1865.

Confederate General Edmund Kirby Smith.

Smith, Edmund Kirby
(1824-1893) **Confederate general.**

A Floridian, Smith was graduated from West Point (1845), participating in the Mexican War and Indian fighting and teaching at the Military Academy before the war. He helped organize the Shenandoah Army before leading a brigade at First Bull Run, where he was wounded. Promoted to major general and commanding the Department of East Tennessee, he led Smith's Invasion of Kentucky (*See*) and fought at Perryville, earning the Thanks of the Confederate Congress. He commanded the Trans-Mississippi Department after February 1863. There he repulsed Nathaniel Banks's Red River Campaign of 1864, led the Arkansas Campaign, and, cut off from the east, effectively governed what became known as 'Kirby Smithdom.' Smith's surrender on June 2, 1865, was the last of the war.

Smith, Gustavus W. *(1822-1896)*
Confederate statesman and general.

A Mexican War veteran, he was street commissioner in New York City when the war began. He joined the Confederate service in 1861 and was secretary of war briefly in November 1862. Smith resigned from the army in 1863 when several generals were promoted over his head. Commanding Georgia militia in 1864, he retreated before W.T. Sherman's March to the Sea. Smith surrendered at Macon, Georgia, in April 1865.

Smith, William ('Extra Billy') *(1796-1887)*
Confederate general and politician.

A Congressman and governor (1846-49) of Virginia, his nickname referred to the extra government payments he received to subsidize his mail-coach service from Washington to Milledgeville, Georgia. He led the 49th Virginia at First Bull Run, in the Peninsular Campaign, and at Antietam. He led a brigade at Gettysburg. He took office a second time as governor of Virginia in January 1864.

Smith, William Farrar *(1824-1903)*
Union general.

Trained at West Point as an engineer, he fought at First Bull Run and led a brigade and then a division during the Peninsular Campaign. He commanded the VI Corps at Fredericksburg in 1862. When the Senate refused to approve his major general's commission, he reverted to divisional command. Sent to the West in 1863, Smith organized Grant's defenses at Chattanooga and helped open the 'Cracker Line' (*See*). Returning east, he led the XVIII Corps in the initial assault on Petersburg in June 1864, but he performed poorly and was relieved in consequence. It was Smith's last command of the war.

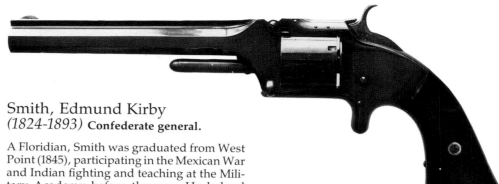

The Smith & Wesson .32 caliber Army Model 2, one of the first true cartridge revolvers.

Smith & Wesson Revolvers

These cartridge revolvers were introduced in 1857, but were of too small a caliber to be of much use in combat. The Smith & Wesson 'Number One,' for example, was only .22 caliber, and a direct short-range hit was needed to disable an enemy. The company developed a .32 caliber revolver later in the war, but it, too, saw little service.

Smith's Invasion of Kentucky

In August-September 1862 Confederate forces under Kirby Smith were ordered to march from Knoxville, Tennessee, and drive George Washington Morgan's 8000 Federals from Cumberland Gap. Arriving at Cumberland Gap on August 18, Smith decided that Morgan's main body was too strong to attack; instead, marching to Richmond, Kentucky (*See*), he routed enemy troops on August 30, then occupied Lexington. Smith then planned to join forces with Braxton Bragg during the latter's invasion of Kentucky (*See*).

South Anna River, *Virginia*

Federal forces conducted diversions here during the Gettysburg Campaign in late June 1863 in an effort to force Robert E. Lee to divert forces southward. There was some fighting around bridges over the South Anna, but local forces were adequate to contain the Federals, and Lee did not detach troops from the main army.

Spanish Fort, *Alabama*

Federal forces under Edward Canby besieged this strongpoint near Mobile beginning on March 27, 1865. On April 8, a brigade led by the 8th Iowa pierced a section of the Confederate works, taking 500 prisoners; the rest of the defenders then withdrew into Mobile.

Spencer Repeating Carbine

A Connecticut gunsmith, Christopher M. Spencer, patented this breech-loading repeater, by far the most advanced weapon of its kind, in 1860. By 1864 it had become the standard Federal cavalry weapon. The Spencer weighed 8¼ pounds, was 39 inches long, and carried a seven-cartridge magazine in its stock. After each shot a new cartridge could be fed from the magazine into the

Above: A Union cavalryman poses with his saber and his Spencer repeating carbine.
Below: Confederate and Union troops clash at Laurel Hill during the inconclusive but bloody Battle of Spotsylvania in May 1864.

breech simply by flipping an operating lever that doubled as a trigger guard. By the end of 1865 the government had bought more than 77,000 Spencer carbines.

Spiking Cannon

A gun could be disabled by driving a spike or a large nail into the vent (and/or by wedging a shot into the bottom of the bore). Sometimes a cannon could be unspiked by blowing the obstruction out with a charge of powder.

Spotsylvania, Battle of

Following the Battle of the Wilderness of May 5-6, 1864, General Ulysses S. Grant slipped his Army of the Potomac around the right flank of Robert E. Lee's Army of Northern Virginia and headed toward the Confederate capital of Richmond. Lee, anticipating the move, put his forces on the march to confront the Northerners at a little Virginia road crossing called Spotsylvania Court House. Shooting broke out briefly when the Federals reached Spotsylvania on May 8, but the blue-coats were too tired to mount a serious attack. That night and the next day both armies built strong breastworks. The following two days saw mainly light skirmishing, though on the 10th Lee's troops drove back a somewhat more coordinated enemy move directed against the Southern left.

Lee's lines followed the shape they had fallen into during the fighting on the 8th – a large, irregular crescent. In the middle was a bulging salient the soldiers dubbed the 'mule shoe'; history would remember it as 'Bloody Angle.' On the evening of the 10th young Colonel Emory Upton convinced Grant to let him try a charge on the salient. Grant agreed, and Upton led out a brigade at the run. His spearhead drove through a hail of bullets right over the breastworks, the very center of the Confederate line. Finally, when Southern artillery turned back blue reinforcements, Upton was forced to withdraw. Impressed, Grant decided to send a corps against the salient. The next day Grant sent his famous telegram to Washington: 'I propose to fight it out on this line if it takes all summer.' In the end it would take a good deal more time and blood than anyone could have imagined, given the desperate state of the Confederacy by that summer.

The attack came on the rainy dawn of May 12, when 20,000 bluecoats of Winfield Hancock's II Corps rolled out of the fog and, despite hundreds of casualties, flowed over the breastworks of the salient. Lee, listening at the base of the salient, realized that the center of his line was about to be broken. He found Virginia reserves moving out under James B. Gordon and rode to the head of the column, intending to lead them into battle himself. Immediately he was surrounded by troops shouting, 'General Lee to the rear!' They virtually carried their commander to the rear, horse and all, then moved forward. Their counterattack fell heavily onto the disorganized Federals in the salient, driving them back over the breastworks. Instead of

A Union Parrott battery struggles through rain and mud toward Spotsylvania in this engraving by war artist Edwin Forbes.

fleeing, however, the bluecoats turned and fought on the other side of the works. The result, mainly at the Bloody Angle, was a day of fighting as nightmarish as anything ever seen in warfare: a savage hand-to-hand fight in driving rain across the log barricades.

Rank after rank was riddled by shot and shell and by bayonet-thrusts through the works, the dead and wounded trampled into the mud as fresh troops moved up. Cannons were run up close to the parapet, and double charges of cannister were discharged point-blank. The fence-rails and logs in the breastworks were shattered into splinters, and in some places trees over a foot and a half in diameter were cut in two solely by rifle fire. It went on for 18 hours. A Union survivor later wrote, 'I never expect to be fully believed when I tell what I saw of the horrors of Spotsylvania, because I should be loath to believe it myself were the case reversed.'

At 3:00 in the morning the Confederates pulled back to a new line across the base of the salient, and the Union claimed the breastworks and their chest-high heaps of dead and wounded. The Union had suffered 6800 casualties to the South's 5000; once again, the Army of Northern Virginia had survived the full power of the outnumbering Army of the Potomac. Skirmishing and maneuvering continued at Spotsylvania for another seven days. Then, on May 19, Grant once again slipped around Lee's right flank toward Richmond, and once again Lee raced to block the way. They would soon meet again at the Battles of North Anna and Cold Harbor.

Springfield Arsenal, *Massachusetts*

This was the North's main small arms factory. By the end of June 1864 it was producing 300,000 'Springfield' rifles a year. The arsenal manufactured nearly 800,000 rifles from 1861 to 1865.

Stanton, Edwin McMasters *(1814-1869)* **Union secretary of war.**

Ohio-born Stanton was a US government special counsel and President James Buchanan's attorney general. An outstanding executive, he was Lincoln's secretary of war from January 1862 onward; he efficiently manned, equipped, and reorganized the military, rooted out fraud and corruption, and instituted harsh security measures such as press censorship and arbitrary arrests. Initially opposed to Lincoln, Stanton became one of his most loyal supporters. When, in 1868, President Andrew Johnson dismissed Stanton from his cabinet post in defiance of the Tenure of Office Act, Stanton's Radical Republican colleagues in Congress used the action as an excuse to vote the impeachment of the president, with whom they had long been at odds over Reconstruction policy.

Wary of Lincoln at first, Secretary of War Edwin Stanton came to admire him greatly.

Star of the West

South Carolina troops fired on this unarmed steamer on January 9, 1861, as she attempted to resupply the besieged garrison at Fort Sumter – among the first shots of what would soon become the Civil War. Confederate forces captured the vessel later in 1861 and eventually sank her in the Tallahatchie River in 1863 in an effort to bar the Federals' passage during the Vicksburg Campaign.

Starr Army Percussion Revolver

The US government bought nearly 48,000 examples of this .44 caliber, six-shot revolver during the war. Nearly a foot long and weighing about three pounds, the Starr fired a cartridge but also could be loaded with loose powder and ball.

States' Rights

The debate over the balance between federal and state powers began with the framers of the Constitution. John C. Calhoun used this term to refer to the doctrine of state sovereignty, particularly with regard to regulating slavery, and it became the rallying cry of the Southern states to justify secession.

Steedman, James Blair *(1817-1873)* **Union general.**

Steedman, an Ohio newspaper editor and legislator, fought at Perryville, Stone's River, and in the Tullahoma Campaign, and later with great gallantry at Chickamauga, where his division provided crucial aid to George Thomas in his defense of the Union left wing. He later commanded the post of Chattanooga, and during the Battle of Nashville he led the District of Etowah.

Steele, Frederick *(1819-1868)* **Union general.**

A New York-born veteran of the Mexican War, he was a major at the outbreak of the Civil War. He was made a major general in 1862 and served with some distinction in Missouri and, in the following year, under Ulysses Grant at Vicksburg. He led the generally disastrous Arkansas Campaign of 1864 (*See*) and finished the war assisting in the final operations around Mobile.

Stephens, Alexander Hamilton *(1812-1883)* **Confederate vice president.**

This Georgia lawyer and Congressman, a prominent Unionist, remained a voice of moderation as Jefferson Davis's vice president, working for prisoner exchanges and opposing Davis's centralization of power and the suspension of civil rights. He published a constitutional study of the war (1868-70).

Stevens, Thaddeus *(1792-1868)* **Union politician.**

A strongly abolitionist Pennsylvania lawyer and Congressman, Stevens was a founder of the Radical Republicans (*See*). As wartime chairman of the House Ways and Means Committee, he controlled military appropria-

The year 1863, the most decisive of the war, began with the indecisive Battle of Stone's River, near Murfreesborno, Tennessee.

tions, providing the government critical support. He was later instrumental in passing the radical Reconstruction Acts and in the impeachment of President Johnson.

Stevenson, Carter Littlepage (1817-1888) **Confederate general.**

A Virginian, Stevenson was trained at West Point and was a Mexican War and frontier veteran. After fighting with Braxton Bragg in Tennessee and Kentucky, he commanded Confederate troops in the Vicksburg Campaign, at Chickamauga and Missionary Ridge, and in the Atlanta, Nashville, and Carolinas Campaigns.

Stone Fleets

In a bid to close Southern ports to blockade runners, the US Navy filled small vessels with stones and sank them in harbor entrances. The project failed, however, for the ships' timbers soon rotted and the stones sank in the harbor mud.

Stoneman, George (1822-1894)
Union general.

An 1846 West Point graduate, he had served in the Mexican War and on the frontier. He commanded the Army of the Potomac's cavalry division during the Peninsular Campaign, III Corps at Fredericksburg, and the newly established Cavalry Corps during the Chancellorsville Campaign. Stoneman led W. T. Sherman's cavalry during the Atlanta campaign until he and 700 of his troopers were taken prisoner in what is known as Stoneman's and (Edward) McCook's Raid to Macon. Freed a few months later, he led cavalry strikes in support of the Franklin and Nashville Campaign and throughout the Carolinas Campaign.

Stone's River (Murfreesboro), Battle of

The year 1863, the critical one of the war, began with the costly but inconclusive battle of Stone's River, near Murfreesboro in western Tennessee. The forces involved were the Federal Army of the Cumberland under William S. Rosecrans and the Confederate Army of Tennessee under Braxton Bragg. The latter had just been thwarted in an attempted invasion of Kentucky, but he still controlled Tennessee.

On December 31, 1862, the battle began at dawn when Southerners struck Rosecrans's right wing. Heavy fighting surged back and forth for hours before the Union line was pushed back on the pivot of the left flank. From that point the Federals fought desperately to hold their line against successive Confederate attacks.

The next day saw minor skirmishing. On January 2 graycoats drove Federals from the top of a hill to the north, but in attempting to pursue they were mowed down by blue artillery and forced to withdraw. That ended the battle in a bloody draw: Rosecrans had suffered 12,906 casualties of 41,400 Federals engaged, Bragg, 11,379 of 34,739. The two armies would rest and maneuver for months before meeting again in the autumn at the Battle of Chickamauga.

Stonewall Brigade

Thomas Jonathan Jackson trained and was the first commander of this famous Confederate fighting formation. Both it and its great commander won the sobriquet 'Stonewall' at First Bull Run. It fought in the Shenandoah Valley Campaign of Jackson, at Antietam, at Fredericksburg, at Chancellorsville, at Gettysburg, in the Wilderness, and at Spotsylvania. The original brigade, 4500 strong, consisted of the 2nd, 4th, 5th, 27th, and 33rd Virginia infantry.

Stowe, Harriet Beecher
(1811-1896) Abolitionist author.

Her antislavery novel *Uncle Tom's Cabin* (1851-52 – *See*) sold over a million copies in ten years and became a potent abolitionist weapon. Reviled by Southerners, the novel made Stowe an international celebrity, a position she used to raise large sums for the antislavery movement.

Stuart, James Ewell Brown
(1833-1864) Confederate general.

Probably only Robert E. Lee and Stonewall Jackson stand higher in the South's pantheon of Civil War heroes than does this lengendary cavalry commander. A Virginian and West Point graduate (1854), 'Jeb' Stuart served in 'Bloody Kansas' and as Lee's aide-de-camp at Harpers Ferry. As colonel of the 1st Virginia Cavalry he fought at First Bull Run and was made a brigadier general soon thereafter. During the Peninsular Campaign he per-formed the first of his famous 'Rides Around McClellan,' in three days (June 12-15, 1862) leading 1200 troopers in a complete circuit of the Union army, the while raiding and gathering valuable intelligence. In the following month he was given command of all the cavalry of the Army of Northern Virginia. He fought in the Battles of Second Bull Run (before which he made his celebrated Catlett's Station Raid – *See*) and Antietam, and he made his 'Second Ride Around McClellan' in October (*See* CHAMBERSBURG RAID OF STUART). Following the Battle of Fredericksburg in December 1862 he made yet another daring raid on the Army of the Potomac's supply lines (*See* DUMFRIES RAID OF STUART). After Jackson's death at Chancellorsville, Stuart briefly took over II Corps, but he soon returned to cavalry operations in the Gettysburg Campaign, receiving his first major setback at the Battle of Brandy Station and, due to unclear orders, embarking on a long reconnaissance that, though spectacular in itself, kept him from taking part in the crucial Battle of Gettysburg. In 1864 he played an active role in the Battle of the Wilderness, but soon afterward, on May 11, he was fatally wounded in a battle with Philip Sheridan's Union troopers at Yellow Tavern.

Stuart's reputation as the embodiment of the South's romantic ideal of dash and chivalry was already high at the time of his death, and it has grown ever since. He has been called a 'gay knight-errant of the elder time' and the 'flower of cavaliers.' Fortunately, such excesses of adulation have not been sufficient to obscure his very real accomplishments.

The dashing James Ewell Brown (Jeb) Stuart, the South's most famous cavalry leader.

Sturgis, Samuel Davis *(1822-1889)*
Union general.

This Pennsylvania-born veteran, a West Point alumnus, saved Fort Smith, Arkansas, for the Union in April 1861. He held commands in the Armies of the Potomac and the Ohio, drawing criticism for his actions at Wilson's Creek and an investigation for his disastrous loss to Nathan B. Forrest at Brice's Cross Roads.

T. J. Jackson leads the Stonewall Brigade in prayer. Seated lower left is A. P. Hill. Second from Jackson's left is R. S. Ewell.

Confederate *David*-type torpedo boats were semi-submersible, making them very difficult targets. They carried an explosive charge or 'torpedo' on a spar mounted on the bow.

Submarines/Submersibles

Experimental submersible vessels in the US dated back to the Revolution, but Confederate attempts to make the idea workable had scant success. At Charleston Harbor in October 1863 the steam-powered semi-submersible *David* damaged a Union warship with a torpedo on a spar – but sank itself in the process. The little hand-cranked experimental sub *Hunley* dove with its crew in several trials before it sank the USS *Housatonic*, as well as itself, in February 1864. In the end, Southern subs proved more dangerous to their crews than to Union shipping.

Suffolk, *Virginia*

With two divisions, Confederate General James Longstreet invested this town, occupied by as many as 25,000 Federals, for a few weeks in April and May 1863. The place proved too strong to take, but Longstreet foraged the surrounding farm districts for much-needed supplies.

Sumner, Charles *(1811-1874)*
Union politician.

Massachusetts Senator Sumner was an uncompromising abolitionist whose uninhibited oratory made him profoundly influential. Narrowly surviving a retaliatory beating on the Senate floor in 1856 after denouncing a South Carolina member, Sumner maintained his staunch advocacy of emancipation and equal rights for blacks throughout the war.

Surratt, John and Mary

A Confederate spy and an alleged conspirator in Lincoln's assassination, John Surrat avoided arrest by fleeing to Canada. He returned to the United States in 1867; his trial ended in a hung jury. His mother, Mary, ran the Washington boardinghouse in which John Wilkes Booth and his conspirators plotted the president's murder. She was tried, convicted, and hanged for her role in the conspiracy in 1865.

Surrender Dates

Robert E. Lee asked for an armistice and surrendered to Ulysses S. Grant at Appomattox on April 9, 1865. J. E. Johnston signed an armistice on April 18, surrendering to W. T. Sherman on April 26. Confederate General Richard Taylor sealed Union victory east of the Mississippi by surrendering to E. R. S. Canby on May 2 (officially, May 4), while the Trans-Mississippi Department was surrendered to Canby by E. Kirby Smith on May 26. In the last significant Confederate surrender, Brigadier General Stand Watie surrendered a Cherokee battalion in the Oklahoma Territory on June 23, 1865.

Swamp Angel

This was the nickname for an 8-inch Parrott gun with which the Federals shelled Charleston, South Carolina, on August 22-23, 1863. The gun, fired from Morris Island at a range of 7900 yards, blew up after the 36th round.

Swinton, William *(1833-1892)*
War correspondent.

The New York *Times* sent Swinton to the front as a special war correspondent. His constant verbal attacks on generals and his underhanded methods of newsgathering – including eavesdropping on a Meade-Grant conference during the 1864 Virginia campaign – finally led the war department to ban him from the field.

Sykes, George *(1822-1880)*
Union general.

A Delaware-born veteran of the Seminole and Mexican Wars, he led a division in the Army of the Potomac's V Corps and, intermittantly, the corps itself, notably at the Battle of Gettysburg. In the autumn of 1864 he commanded the District of South Kansas.

Taliaferro, William Booth *(1822-1898)* **Confederate general.**

This Virginia veteran and legislator served with distinction under Stonewall Jackson in the Shenandoah Valley and led the Stonewall Brigade at Cedar Mountain, Second Bull Run, and Fredericksburg. He later commanded at Fort Wagner and James Island. He surrendered with J.E. Johnston in North Carolina in April 1865.

Taney, Roger Brooke *(1777-1864)* **Chief Justice of the Supreme Court.**

Presiding over the Supreme Court from 1836 until his death, Taney ruled on cases that highlighted the growing North-South rift. The most explosive of these was *Dred Scott v. Sandford* (1857 – See), generally regarded as a major cause of the Civil War.

Controversial Chief Justice of the Supreme Court Roger Brook Taney.

Tattnall, Josiah *(1795-1871)*
Confederate commodore.

This Georgian, a career naval officer, directed the Confederate naval defenses of Georgia and South Carolina and then of Virginia, where he commanded CSS *Virginia* (formerly *Merrimac*) after her fight with USS *Monitor*, later ordering her destruction during the evacuation of Norfolk. Tattnall later challenged the Federal blockade and defended the Savannah River until W. T. Sherman took the city in December 1864.

Taxation

Both sides levied taxes to pay for the war. On August 2, 1861, seeking to raise $500 million, Congress authorized tariffs and the first-ever income tax, which was not levied until a revised bill of July 1, 1862, specified a graduated rate of 3 percent to 5 percent. The Southern tax bill of April 24, 1863, called for a graduated income tax and taxes on agricultural products, licenses, food, clothing, and iron.

Taylor, Richard *(1826-1879)*
Confederate general.

Zachary Taylor's son, he was a Louisiana planter and secessionist. He fought in Jackson's Shenandoah Valley Campaign and the Peninsular Campaign, later commanding armies in the Gulf, where he stopped Nathaniel Banks's Red River Campaign of 1864. Taylor surrendered the last Confederate army east of the Mississippi to Edward Canby in May 1865.

Telegraphy

Field and long-distance telegraphy were vital to the Union army. American Telegraph Co. and Western Union constructed the extensive Military Telegraph System for the war department. Run by civilians reporting to the secretary of war, this system employed 12,000 civilian telegraphers, laid 15,000 miles of wire, and, by 1862, was handling 3300 messages a day. The semi-independent Confederate telegraph system was much smaller, employing only 1500 workers. (*See also* SIGNAL COMMUNICATIONS.)

Tennessee, CSS

Union forces captured this ironclad ram during the Battle of Mobile Bay on August 5, 1864. The 209-foot vessel, commissioned in Mobile in February 1864, carried six heavy Brooke rifled cannon and was sheathed in armor six inches thick.

Terry, Alfred Howe *(1827-1890)*
Union general.

This Connecticut lawyer served at First Bull Run, led the 7th Connecticut in the Port Royal Expedition, and led a division in the attack on Fort Wagner. He later held James Army corps commands in Virginia and the Carolinas. He received the Thanks of Congress for taking Fort Fisher in January 1865. After the war he won fame as an Indian fighter; George Custer commanded cavalry under Terry in the 1876 campaign against the Sioux in which Custer was killed.

Thanks of Congress

Fifteen Union officers were voted the Thanks of Congress during the war. The first was Nathaniel Lyon, for the victory at Wilson's Creek, Missouri, in December 1861. Others thanked included William Rosecrans, Ulysses Grant, Nathaniel P. Banks, Ambrose Burnside, Joseph Hooker, George Meade, O. O. Howard, W. T. Sherman (twice), Joseph Bailey, A. H. Terry, Philip Sheridan, George H. Thomas, Winfield Scott Hancock, and Newton M. Curtis.

Union General George H. Thomas won fame as 'The Rock of Chickamauga'.

Thayer, Sylvanus *(1785-1872)*
Military engineer and 'Father of the Military Academy.'

A West Point alumnus (1808), Thayer superintended the Academy (1817-33) and engineered east-coast harbor improvements (1833-66). His insistence on excellence and enduring reform of procedures and curriculum at West Point influenced the US Army through generations of graduates.

Thomas, George Henry *(1816-1870)* **Union general.**

A Virginia-born career soldier who elected to serve the Union rather than the Confederacy, Thomas proved to be one of the Civil War's most effective commanders. A West Point graduate (1840), he was a veteran of the Seminole War and the Mexican War. Appointed a brigadier general in 1861, he won his first notable victory at the Battle of Logan's Cross Roads in January 1862. He served under Don Carlos Buell at Shiloh, Corinth, and Perryville and commanded XIV Corps at Stone's River. He won national fame as 'The Rock of Chickamauga' for his gallant defense of the Union left wing in that disastrous battle. He played a prominent role in the Battles of Lookout Mountain and Missionary Ridge and led the Army of the Cumberland in W. T. Sherman's Atlanta Campaign. At the end of the Franklin and Nashville Campaigns he all but destroyed John Bell Hood's Army of Tennessee at the Battle of Nashville. He remained in the army after the war, dying while still in command of the Military Division of the Pacific.

Thompson's Station *(Tennessee)*, Battle of

Confederate cavalry under Earl Van Dorn surrounded two Union brigades here on March 4-5, 1863. The Union cavalry escaped the trap, but an infantry brigade and a battery of artillery were forced to surrender. The Federals reported total casualties of about 1700, including 1300 missing.

A Union field telegraph station. Telegraphy revolutionized military communication.

Todd's Tavern, *Virginia*

Cavalry clashed at this place, which lay about a mile from the southern edge of the Wilderness, during the Wilderness and Spotsylvania Campaigns of May 1864. Union cavalry under James Wilson and David Gregg encountered Thomas Rosser's Confederate cavalry here on May 5. In a skirmish on May 8 Gregg's 2nd Cavalry Division reported 250 casualties and estimated enemy losses at about the same.

Tom's Brook, *Virginia*

Philip Sheridan ordered his cavalry to turn and fight the Confederates here during his Shenandoah Valley Campaign of 1864. On October 9 Union troopers under Alfred Torbert routed the Confederate divisions of Thomas Rosser and L. L. Lomax while Sheridan watched from a nearby hilltop. Federals called the action the 'Woodstock Races.'

Toombs, Robert Augustus
(1810-1885)
Confederate statesman and general.

A Georgia planter, lawyer, and politician, Toombs was briefly and unhappily Confederate secretary of state in 1861 before joining the army. Opposed to the South's defensive strategy and denied promotion after Malvern Hill and Antietam, he resigned in March 1863, later serving in the Georgia militia.

Torpedo

These were what are now called land and sea mines. Sea mines could be detonated either by striking the hull of a ship or by an electric current from shore.

US officers remove two CSA commissioners from the British ship *Trent* in 1861.

Townsend, George Alfred
(1841-1914) **War correspondent.**

He reported the Seven Days' Battles and Cedar Mountain for the *New York Herald* and became famous for his fine New York *World* coverage of the last battles of the war and Lincoln's assassination. Townsend later erected a monument at South Mountain to 157 Civil War correspondents.

Tragic Era

This was Southerners' term for Reconstruction (*See*), in which federal authority oversaw the restoration of civil government in the Confederacy and the readmission of the defeated states to the Union.

Tredegar Iron Works

This Richmond, Virginia, foundry and machine shop manufactured revolvers and gun carriages before the war, and made cannon, machinery, and ship's armor for the Confederacy after hostilities broke out. The works were just west of the Richmond Armory and Arsenal (*See*).

Trent Affair

On November 8, 1861, the British mail steamer *Trent* was stopped by a Union warship off Havana. Two Confederate commissioners, James Mason and John Slidell, traveling to Europe to seek British and French support for the Confederacy were taken off and held in Boston. While popular with the Northern public, this illegal seizure precipitated an international crisis that threatened war. Secretary of State William Seward, acting on the instructions of an alarmed cabinet, eventually ruled the detention improper, and the commissioners were released into British custody on December 30.

Black abolitionist Harriet Tubman.

Trevilian Raid

Ulysses S. Grant ordered Philip Sheridan to lead a Union cavalry diversion as a cover for Grant's move from Cold Harbor across the James River toward Petersburg in June 1864. Robert E. Lee sent two Confederate cavalry divisions under Wade Hampton and Fitzhugh Lee to shadow Sheridan's command, also two divisions, as it moved north and west of Richmond. The two forces clashed at Trevilian Station on June 11 in a confused and inconclusive battle. On the 12th, Sheridan attacked the now entrenched Confederates and was checked. With Hampton astride his line of advance, Sheridan called off the westward raid and rejoined Grant.

Trimble, Isaac Ridgeway
(1802-1888) **Confederate general.**

Raised in Kentucky and educated at West Point, Trimble disrupted Union supplies in 1861 by destroying railroad bridges north of Baltimore. He later constructed batteries along the Potomac and fought in the Peninsular, Second Bull Run, and Gettysburg Campaigns. At Gettysburg he led one of the three divisions in 'Pickett's Charge.'

Tubman, Harriet *(c. 1821-1913)*
Abolitionist.

Born a slave named 'Araminta' in Maryland, she escaped to the North in 1849 and, working in the Underground Railroad (*See*), helped more than 300 slaves to freedom. Tubman nursed Federal soldiers in South Carolina during the war and occasionally spied behind enemy lines.

Tucker, John Randolph
(1812-1883)
Confederate naval commander.

The Virginian Tucker, a professional naval officer, directed the James River defenses, commanding the *Patrick Henry* at Hampton Roads. He later attacked the Federal blockade and commanded the squadron at Charleston

and the fleet off Drewry's Bluff. Tucker fought on shore as well, in Robert E. Lee's army at Sayler's Creek.

Tullahoma Campaign

Following the Stone's River Battle at the beginning of 1863 (*See*), Federal General William Rosecrans was ordered to operate against Braxton Bragg's Confederate army, to keep them occupied in Tennessee and unable to send reinforcements elsewhere. With an effective series of maneuvers on June 23-30, Rosecrans feinted at Bragg's left; deceived, Bragg responded, only to find two blue corps behind his right. The Southern commander was forced to pull back to Tullahoma, and soon after to Chattanooga; Chickamauga and the Chattanooga Campaign followed.

Tupelo, *Mississippi*

William Tecumseh Sherman, making an attempt to stop Nathan Bedford Forrest's raids on his supply line during the 1864 Atlanta Campaign, sent some 14,000 men under A.J. Smith to deal with Forrest. The forces met in light skirmishing on July 13 at Tupelo; over the next two days Forrest mounted a series of costly and unsuccessful assaults on the blue line. Despite inflicting over 1300 casualties to his own 700, Smith pulled back on the 15th, leaving Forrest slightly wounded but still at large.

Turchin, John Basil *(1822-1901)*
Union general.

This Russian immigrant, a Crimean War veteran, fought in Missouri, Kentucky, and Alabama, notably at Stone's River, Chickamauga, and Missionary Ridge, before resigning in October 1864. Turchin's wife accompanied him as a nurse throughout his campaigns, once even leading a Northern regiment into battle.

Turkey Ridge, *Virginia*

Late in the Peninsular Campaign, Confederates attempting to envelop the Federal south flank during the Battle of White Oak Swamp (*See*) attacked here on June 30, 1862. George Sykes's division, supported by Federal gunboats, checked the attempt. There were minor engagements here before and after the Malvern Hill Battle (*See*) of July 1.

Turner, Nat *(1800-1831)*

This slave preacher led a slave uprising in Southampton County, Virginia, in August 1831. Around 55 whites were killed before troops crushed the rebellion. Turner and 16 of his followers were subsequently condemned and put to death.

Twenty Negro Law

Passed on October 11, 1862, this law reflected the Confederates' concern with internal security by exempting owners of twenty slaves – 12 percent of the Southern population – from military service. Conscription, introduced on April 9, 1862, provoked spirited opposition throughout the South; the slaveholders' exemption was especially unpopular with non-slaveholding whites, who viewed it as proof that the conflict was a 'rich man's war and a poor man's fight.'

Twiggs, David *(1790-1862)*
Confederate general.

A War of 1812 veteran, he also fought in the Seminole and Mexican Wars. In February 1861 he surrendered all Union forces in Texas to the Confederates, then resigned and joined the Confederate service. In poor health, he died in July 1862.

Uncle Tom's Cabin

Harriet Beecher Stowe's antislavery novel, published in 1851-2 and popularly dramatized, was enormously influential. Captivated by characters who were to become American icons – Simon Legree, Little Eva, Uncle Tom, and Eliza – millions rallied to the antislavery cause: Lincoln called Stowe the 'little lady' who caused the Civil War.

Underground Railroad

Neither underground nor a railroad, this was a network of individuals who helped slaves to escape from the South to the North and then – since legally they could be returned from the North – often into Canada. Although individual slaves had been escaping over many decades, the term 'under-

Little Eva and Topsy, two of the characters in Harriet Beecher Stowe's influential 1852 antislavery novel *Uncle Tom's Cabin*.

The capture of Nat Turner, who, in 1831, led one of the most serious of the slave revolts in the antebellum South.

Above: *A Ride for Liberty*: *Fugitive Slaves*, by
Eastman Johnson.
Above right: Confederate privates' uniforms. Note
the differences in the tone of the colors.
Right: Union officers' uniforms.

ground railway' and the system itself did not
really come into use until about 1830. Special
well-traveled routes soon developed, much
like railroad lines. Enhancing the image of a
railroad, designated hiding places for escaping slaves were known as 'stations,' and
those who actively guided the runaway
slaves north were known as 'conductors' –
the best known of these being Harriet Tubman (*See*). Thousands of slaves escaped this
way between 1830 and 1861, usually traveling
at night and fed and supported by abolitionists and others determined to undermine the
institution of slavery.

Uniforms

In the early years of the war soldiers' dress on
both sides was characterized by a random
assortment of styles and colors that were inappropriate for field service and confusing on
the battlefield. The Confederates soon prescribed gray uniforms, but because various
dyes were used, the hue sometimes tended
toward brown. In any case, as the war pro-
gressed privation caused CSA uniforms to
become increasingly non-standard. The blue
Union uniform, prescribed early in 1862, was
finally standard issue by winter 1863.

Upperville, *Virginia*

Union pressure drove J. E. B. Stuart's four
Confederate cavalry brigades back toward
Robert E. Lee's army as it was advancing
north toward Gettysburg in June 1863. On
June 21 Union infantry and cavalry attacked
Stuart here. Though one regiment broke
under the pressure, countercharges held off
the Union attackers, and Stuart managed to
withdraw into a strong defensive position in
the vicinity of Ashby's Gap.

Union General Emory Upton.

Upton, Emory (1839-1881)
Union general.

Commissioned second lieutenant upon his 1861 West Point graduation, this New Yorker earned steady promotions in action with the Army of the Potomac from First Bull Run through Spotsylvania, Cold Harbor, and Petersburg, later fighting at Opequon and in Alabama and Georgia. Several times wounded, Upton was repeatedly breveted.

US Regulation Shoulder Arms

Although many types of shoulder arms were used by both sides in the Civil War, the Union authorities attempted to maintain a degree of standardization by designating certain widely-produced infantry shoulder arms as 'US Regulation' weapons. Such weapons were mainly produced by Federal arsenals, such as those at Harpers Ferry, Virginia, and Springfield, Massachusetts, but in some cases their manufacture was also subcontracted to private firms. Among the principal types of regulation infantry shoulder arms used in the war were the US Model 1855 percussion rifle, the US Model 1861 rifle musket, and the US Model 1863 rifle musket. Of these – all single-shot rifled muzzle-loaders – the Model 1861 was numerically the most important, around 700,000 examples having been produced by the war's end; it used a simple percussion cap mechanism and fired a .58 caliber bullet from a 40-inch barrel.

Utoy Creek (Georgia), Battle of

During his 1864 Atlanta Campaign, W.T. Sherman made a second attempt (the first being at Ezra Chapel – See) to envelop the left flank of his Confederate opponent, John B. Hood. On August 5-6, the forces of John Schofield, George Thomas, and Oliver Howard attacked enemy positions around Utoy Creek, but Hood's lines held firm. At the end of the month Sherman would drive Hood out of Atlanta as the result of Union success in the Jonesboro Battle (See).

Vallandigham, Clement Laird (1820-1871) **Politican and lawyer.**

He was an Ohio lawyer, journalist, and politician who strenuously opposed the war and tried, as a US Congressman, to obstruct war-related legislation. He was prominent among the Copperheads (See). Lincoln banished him to the South after his conviction for treason by a military commission in 1863. Vallandigham re-entered the North via Canada and campaigned vigorously against Lincoln's re-election in 1864, but his influence on both political parties and on the public at large was waning and would in fact never revive.

Valverde (New Mexico), Battle of

The Confederate Army of New Mexico moved up the Rio Grande in early 1862 (See NEW MEXICO AND ARIZONA OPERATIONS) and challenged the Federal garrison at Valverde under Edward Canby to a battle. After a two-hour action on February 21 the

Lincoln banished Copperhead leader Clement Vallandigham to the South in 1863.

Confederates routed the Federals and captured a battery. Federal casualties were about 260 out of 3800 engaged; Confederate losses were fewer than 200 out of a force of 2600.

Van Dorn, Earl (1820-1863)
Confederate general.

A veteran of the Mexican War and many Indian battles, he commanded the Confederate Department of Texas at the start of the war and captured the Star of the West (See) at Galveston. He later fought at Pea Ridge and at Corinth. On May 8, 1863, he was shot and killed at Spring Hill by a local man who had accused Van Dorn of being involved in an affair with his wife.

Van Lew, Elizabeth L. (1818-1900)
Union spy.

A Virginian educated in Philadelphia, she early opposed slavery. Openly Unionist, Van Lew was the Federals' link with Richmond throughout the war. Besides relief work at Libby Prison, she gathered intelligence and helped Union prisoners to escape.

Velasquez, Loreta Janeta (1842?-1897)
Confederate officer and spy.

Cuban-born and educated in New Orleans, she followed her American husband into the Confederate army by posing as a man. She fought at First Bull Run and Fort Donelson, continuing to fight after her husband's death and spying behind enemy lines.

Veteran Reserve Corps

This organization grew out of an Invalid Corps, formed in April 1863, of wounded or ill Union soldiers who had recovered sufficiently to take on light duties as guards, nurses, and cooks. By September more than 20,000 men were assigned to the corps. The name change came in March 1864.

Vicksburg, Campaign and Siege

Vicksburg, Mississippi, situated on bluffs overlooking the Mississippi River, was one of the two strategically most vital cities of the Confederacy (the other being the rail center of Chattanooga). From the West through Vicksburg poured a stream of food, cotton, and other supplies necessary to keep the South alive and fighting. If that supply line could be cut the Confederacy would begin to wither on the vine; and if the nation's greatest river were in Federal hands a path would be open to the Union to mount an offensive from the West that could effectively cut the Old South in half.

   The city became the objective of Ulysses S. Grant in late October 1862, when he took command of the Federal Department of the Tennessee. A week later he set his Army of the Tennessee marching down a railroad line toward Vicksburg. The advance soon ran into trouble – Confederate cavalry destroyed Grant's supply depot at Holly Springs, and Nathan Bedford Forrest's men tore up 50 miles of railroad that the Union army needed for resupply. At around the same time forces

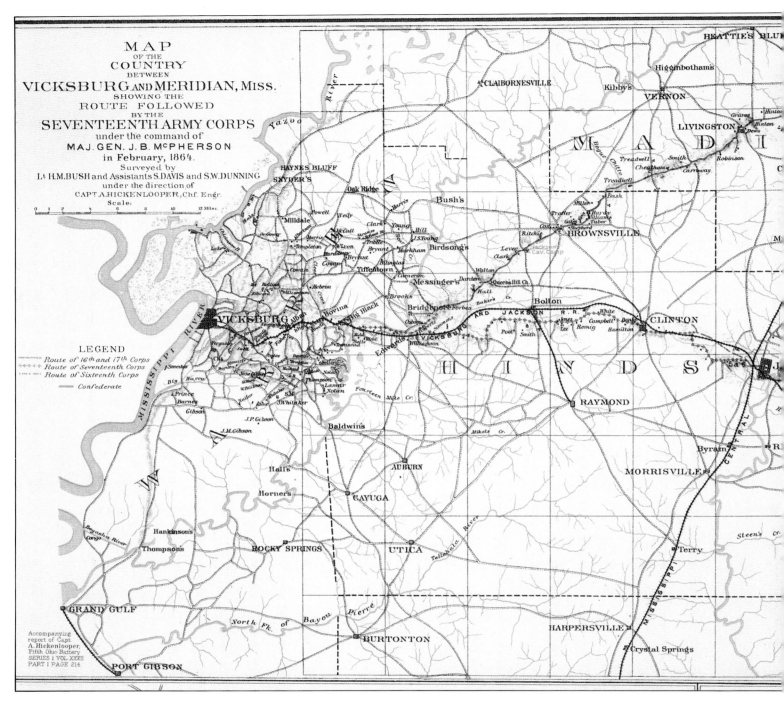

Previous pages: The surrender of Vicksburg.
Above: The Vicksburg-Jackson region, where Grant conducted his 1863 Vicksburg Campaign.

under Grant's subordinate, William Tecumseh Sherman, suffered a costly repulse in attempting to attack the bluffs overlooking Chickasaw Bayou, north of Vicksburg. That ended Grant's hopes of taking the city with relative dispatch.

As winter settled in Grant faced an unpromising situation. He had learned that he could not simply march in and besiege Vicksburg; besides the enemy forces in Mississippi, there was the barrier of swampy land surrounding the area, made worse by a rainy winter. The city could only be attacked from high and dry ground to the east – that is, from enemy territory. Meanwhile, hundreds of Grant's soldiers were dying from swamp-born diseases. Yet Washington was not likely to countenance letting Grant spend the

winter doing nothing, and neither would the Northern press, which was becoming ever more critical of him. Finally Grant shifted his base to a point nearly opposite Vicksburg on the western (Louisiana) bank of the river and commenced a series of experiments.

The Federal navy had already secured most of the other major river towns – Memphis, to the north, and Baton Rouge and New Orleans, to the south. To be useful for Grant's operations, the Union flotilla, then north of Vicksburg, had to get downriver past the extensive batteries trained on the river from city. For that purpose Grant first had the army dig a canal so that the fleet could bypass the batteries; but the canal turned out to be too shallow to float the ships. At the same time, he sent a corps to try to open a passage from Lake Providence that would put Federal vessels on to waters south of Vicksburg. This operation was abandoned in favor of a more promising one in the Yazoo

Delta, 400 river-miles to the north. Cutting through a levee to enter the Tallahatchie River, the Union fleet made some progress, but an inconveniently-located Confederate fort then drove the ships away. In the spring Grant tried the last of his experiments, trying to move the fleet through a tangled mass of streams and backwaters called Steele's Bayou. In that nightmarish operation the ships were slowed by trees felled by the enemy and attacked from shore by Rebel infantry, while the Union sailors had to contend with snakes and wildcats that fell on them from overhanging trees. Finally Sherman's infantry had to come and rescue the fleet, which barely made it out of the waterway, steaming backwards for miles.

Having tried every conceivable roundabout way to bypass Vicksburg, and with summer coming on, Grant now set a bold new plan in motion. The ground had dried out just enough to allow his army to march

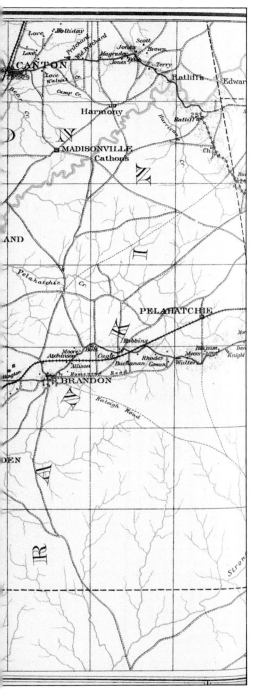

The first and most daunting element, running the batteries, began just before midnight on April 16, 1863. Admiral Porter's fleet floated quietly downstream, boilers damped to prevent telltale sparks. The ships were protected by barges towed alongside and by bales of cotton lashed along the hulls. But when flotilla reached Vicksburg it was spotted from the shore, and the guns opened up. The ships put on steam for the final dash. In the end, the fleet made it through with losses of only one ship and a few barges. Admiral Porter came to rest at Hard Times, Louisiana, where Grant's army was gathering after their march down the western shore. A few days later more Union ships ran the gauntlet of the the batteries.

Sherman then made his feint on Haines's Bluff with equal success: General John C. Pemberton, commanding in Vicksburg, was convinced that Sherman's was the main assault on the city. His job done, Sherman marched south to join Grant. Pemberton was further confused when Colonel Benjamin H. Grierson's 1700-man Federal cavalry brigade set off on their diversion, riding south through Mississippi in mid-April and raiding as they went. For over two weeks, Confederate riders tried in vain to round up the Federal horsemen. By the time Grierson and his men arrived in Baton Rouge, they had accounted for 100 enemy casualties, taken 500 prisoners, destroyed 50 miles of railroad, captured 1000 horses and mules, and

This Union army map of the Siege of Vicksburg shows both the disposition of US forces and the formidable ring of Rebel fortifications.

south on the Louisiana side of the river. Once the infantry troops were south of Vicksburg, the Federal fleet might be able to ferry them across the river. But this would mean that Admiral David Dixon Porter would have to run his ships downriver past the formidable Vicksburg batteries. In addition, the enemy's attention would have to be diverted from what was going on. To mask his troop movement Grant would order two diversionary operations, one by Sherman's corps attacking Haines's Bluff near Vicksburg, the other, a showy cavalry raid south through Mississippi. But after all that, Grant would still face the daunting task of taking the city. In short, Grant's strategy consisted of four separate operations involving thousands of men and horses and dozens of ships, all of whom had to work in perfect concert if the campaign were not to fail. He issued his orders over the objections of Sherman and, indeed, the entire staff.

suffered only 24 casualties of their own, while riding 600 miles through hostile territory. Grierson's raid would count as one of the finest cavalry exploits of the war.

Now three parts of Grant's four-pronged strategy had come to fruition. The hardest part remained – moving over enemy ground to conquer a well-fortified city, and doing it before Southern reinforcements could reach Pemberton. On May 1 Grant finished ferrying his army across the river unopposed. At that point his orders from Washington instructed him not to move on Vicksburg yet; he was supposed to march south and join General Nathaniel Banks in attacking Port Hudson on the Mississippi. After that town fell he and Banks were to return to Vicksburg together. But upon learning that Banks was busy instead with the elaborate (and ill-fated) Red River Campaign (See), Grant made a bold and historic change of plans: he would cut away from his supply and communications lines – something almost never heard of in warfare – and move east across the state to occupy Jackson, the capital of Mississippi, thus discouraging enemy reinforcements from advancing from that direction. Then he would march west and besiege Vicksburg. Throughout the operation his army would move with only the supplies they could carry and would forage whatever else they needed from the surrounding countryside. A year later Grant's subordinate, Sherman, would adopt the same tactics in Georgia.

Sending Sherman to make a feint at Vicksburg, Grant headed west and arrived at Jackson on May 13. Inside the city were General Joseph E. Johnston and 6000 men; they were supposed to be helping Pemberton in Vicksburg, and more Southern reinforcements were on the way. As the bluecoats gathered around the city, Johnston wrote to Pemberton ordering him to cut Grant's supply line and then attack from the rear with his whole

Opposite top: Union Admiral Porter's fleet runs past the Vicksburg batteries.
Opposite bottom: The Siege of Vicksburg.
Below: River-borne supplies reach Grant as he prepares his offensive against Vicksburg.

force. Refusing to leave the city unoccupied, the Vicksburg commander wasted a day marching a detachment back and forth in an effort to find the nonexistent Union supply line. By the time Pemberton gave up and marched the detachment east to attack Grant, Jackson had fallen. Grant then sent his forces out to meet Pemberton.

Some 22,000 Confederates ran into 29,000 of Grant's soldiers at Champion's Hill on May 16, and the biggest battle of the campaign broke out. After hours of heavy but indecisive fighting that claimed well over 2000 casualties on both sides, the Northerners threatened the only Southern road of retreat, and Pemberton pulled his men back toward the city. On the next day Grant tried to cut off Pemberton's retreat at the Big Black River Bridge but captured only 1700 men. Pemberton finally reached Vicksburg with most of his forces.

The city's fortifications were perhaps the strongest in the Confederacy: a line of works

A Vicksburg woman, reduced to living in a cave to escape the dangers presented by the incessant Union bombardment of the besieged city, prays for safe deliverance.

and trenches nine miles long, with nine forts as strongpoints; broken ground in the area also worked to the advantage of the Confederates. Nevertheless, Grant mounted a full-scale assault on May 19; it gained only a few yards. Impatient with the prospect of a siege, he ordered another attempt a few days later; it failed, costing 3200 Union casualties to Pemberton's 500. Grant would later admit that these assaults were bad mistakes.

The Northerners then settled into a siege, gradually extending their lines around the city. Inside Vicksburg the slowly-starving soldiers and civilians dug into the hills to escape incessant shelling from Union batteries and gunboats. The end came on July 3, 1863, when white flags appeared on the ramparts. Pemberton and Grant, who were old army acquaintances, sat on a hillside and came to terms. The defenders would surrender on July 4, and Grant would parole them until they could be exchanged, rather than making them prisoners (such paroling was still fairly common at that stage in the war).

As he had done previously at Fort Donelson, Grant had captured an entire Confederate army. He had also conducted one of the most complex and brilliant strategic campaigns of the war, as well as one that was, on the tactical level, comparable to Robert E. Lee's maneuvering at Chancellorsville and Stonewall Jackson's in his Shenandoah Valley Campaign. As the 30,000 ragged and hungry Southern soldiers filed out of the city on July 4 Grant forbade any victory celebration by his troops. Far to the east, the South had lost another critical battle that week, at Gettysburg, but it was in Vicksburg that the fate of the Confederacy was decided. After Port Hudson – now something of a footnote – fell to Banks on July 8 the Mississippi River belonged entirely to the Union and the South was broken in two. 'The Father of Waters,' wrote Lincoln, 'runs unvexed to the sea.'

From her wagon a vivandiere furnishes Union soldiers at Bailey's Crossroads, Virginia, with food, drink, tobacco and other goods.

Vicksburg, Union Naval Bombardment of

Before Ulysses S. Grant's Vicksburg Campaign began, the Union attempted to reduce that strategic confederate stronghold on the Mississippi by naval bombardment, Union warships under Flag Officer David Farragut attacking Vicksburg from May 18 to July 26, 1862. Cruisers and gunboats began the shelling and were later reinforced by mortar vessels. The defenders refused to give in under the bombardment, however, and casualties were light – only 22 killed or wounded inside the fortress. Eventually heat, illness, and low water forced Farragut to return to New Orleans. It was now clear that there could be no quick, easy, or inexpensive way of capturing well-defended Vicksburg.

Villard, Henry (1835-1900)
Journalist.

A Bavarian-born war correspondent, he reported in 1861 for the Cincinnati *Commercial* that War Secretary Simon Cameron considered W.T. Sherman, then commanding in Kentucky, insane. The report led to quarrels that were, at least in part, responsible for Sherman's dismissal from that command. Villard later joined the staff of Greeley's (*See*) New York *Tribune* and became one of the war's outstanding correspondents. He married William Lloyd Garrison's daughter.

Virginia, CSS

See MONITOR AND *MERRIMAC*

Vivandiere

This was the female attendant who accompanied regiments in many European armies. Frequently a soldier's wife, she served as nurse and/or provider of food and liquids. Far from a camp follower, she was a respectable woman with an acknowledged position in the regiment. A few vivandières served in the Civil War, generally with regiments of foreign-born troops. The word is taken from the French term for such a person; the English equivalent is 'sutler.'

Volunteers

The Union and Confederate armies consisted overwhelmingly of volunteers, organized by the states and mustered into the national service. At first volunteers enlisted for periods as brief as three months; by mid-1861 Lincoln had issued his first call for hundreds of thousands of three-year enlistees.

Von Steinwehr, Adolph (1822-1877) **Union general.**

Prussian-born, he came to America to fight in the Mexican War and eventually settled down to farming in Connecticut. He became colonel of the all-German 29th New York at the start of the war. He led a brigade at Second Bull Run and a division at Chancellorsville and Gettysburg. He briefly commanded the XI Corps in Virginia and, later, during the Chattanooga Campaign.

Wade-Davis Manifesto

In 1864 Radical Republicans Benjamin F. Wade and Henry W. Davis issued this call for a harsh Reconstruction in the defeated Southern states. Both men fought the moderate Reconstruction policies of Lincoln and, after the assasination, Andrew Johnson. It has been suggested that one reason Wade pressed for Johnson's impeachment was that Wade, as president of the Senate, stood next in line for the US presidency.

Walker, Leroy Pope (1817-1884)
Confederate general and secretary of war.

A lawyer and powerful Democrat in Alabama, he was Confederate secretary of war from February to September 1861. Inexperienced and overwhelmed, he resigned and was commissioned a brigadier general, but, denied an active command, he soon resigned. He thereafter sat on a military court until the war's end.

Three Confederate volunteers in the Third Georgia Infantry. Two, half-brothers, would be killed in the Seven Days' Battles.

A double portrait of Dr. Mary Walker, the first woman surgeon in the US Army.

Walker, Mary Edwards
(1831-1919) Union surgeon.

This New Yorker received her medical certification in 1855. Early in the war she was an army nurse and sometime spy; in 1864 she was commissioned as the first woman surgeon in the US Army. After the war she was a physician, inventor, and active suffragist.

Wallace, Lewis (1827-1905)
Union general.

Wallace had a varied career before the war; in 1861 he was adjutant-general of Indiana. He fought at Romney and Harpers Ferry and, rapidly promoted, led divisions at Fort Donelson and Shiloh and VIII Corps at Monocacy. His substantial administrative service included the courts martial of Lincoln's assassins and Henry Wirz. A prolific author, he wrote *Ben Hur* (1880) while serving as governor of New Mexico.

War Democrats

This faction of the Northern Democratic Party, led by Stephen A. Douglas and Andrew Johnson, supported Union war policy. The opposing faction, the 'Peace Democrats,' called for a negotiated settlement with the rebellious states.

Warren, Gouverneur Kemble
(1830-1882) Union general.

An 1850 West Point graduate, he served in the pre-war army as an engineer. He led the 5th New York at the start of the Peninsular Campaign, then commanded a brigade in the 2nd Division, V Corps, from Second Bull Run to Fredericksburg. As the Army of the Potomac's chief engineer Warren played a decisive role at Gettysburg by directing reinforcements to the threatened Union left at Little Round Top on the second day of the battle. He commanded the V Corps at the Wilderness, Spotsylvania, Petersburg, and in the start of the Appomattox Campaign. In a celebrated incident, Philip Sheridan sacked him for lack of aggressiveness after the battle of Five Forks only a few days before Robert E. Lee's surrender. Fourteen years later a court of inquiry cleared Warren of Sheridan's charges. Warren died less than a year later.

Washington Artillery

Wealthy, socially prominent men of New Orleans filled the ranks of this famous Confederate unit. Formed in 1838, the battalion saw service in the Mexican War; it was mustered into the Confederate Army in May 1861. Four batteries fought with the Army of Northern Virginia, while a fifth served in the West in the Army of Tennessee.

Waud, Alfred R. (1828-1891)
War correspondent.

As the principal war artist for *Harper's Weekly*, Waud produced hundreds of frontline sketches of some of the war's most important events (as, more modestly, did his less talented and prolific brother, William). Because of the state of mid-nineteenth-century printing technology, however, few of Waud's contemporaries ever saw the sketches themselves, but only hasty and often coarse wood-block prints made from them by the periodical's engravers. Fortunately, many of the original sketches have survived, together forming an invaluable graphic record of the Civil War.

Wauhatchie Night Attack

During the Chattanooga Campaign on the night of October 28, 1863, Confederate General Braxton Bragg sent forces under James Longstreet to attack an isolated division of Joseph Hooker's army at Wauhatchie. The action, one of the rare night attacks of the war, was extremely confused, officers of both sides hardly knowing the enemy from their own. After intensive fighting, each side suffering over 400 casualties, the Confederates were driven back. This victory secured protection for the 'cracker line' that would supply the besieged Union forces in Chattanooga. A legend of the battle was that some terrified Union mules stampeded toward Confederate troops, who fled, thinking that they were being charged by cavalry. This led to the wry suggestion that the mules should be declared honorary horses.

Waynesboro, *Georgia*

On November 26, 1864, early in his March to the Sea, W. T. Sherman sent Hugh Judson Kilpatrick's Federal cavalry to destroy a railroad bridge near Waynesboro. Harrassed from the outset by Joseph Wheeler's Con-

Harper's Weekly's noted war artist Alfred R. Waud is shown sketching at Gettysburg in this photograph by Timothy O'Sullivan.

General Sherman reviews H. J. Kilpatrick's cavalry division before sending it out to burn the Waynesboro railroad bridge in 1864.

federate cavalry, the blue horsemen abandoned the operation; on the 28th one division had to fight their way through Wheeler's entire corps. They were finally able to rejoin Sherman on the following day.

Waynesboro (*Virginia*), Battle of

Union General Philip Sheridan finished off the remnants of Jubal Early's Confederates here on March 2, 1865, during the concluding phase of the Sheridan's Shenandoah Valley Campaign. George A. Custer's 4800-strong Union cavalry division overwhelmed a force of about 1000 Confederates; only Early and about 20 others managed to escape.

Weldon Railroad Expedition

During the Petersburg siege, Union General Gouverneur Warren's V Corps, with an extra infantry divison and a cavalry division attached, broke up the railroad to Hicksford 40 miles south of Petersburg in a neat operation conducted between December 7 and 11, 1864. Confederate General A. P. Hill led out a force to protect the vital rail line, but Warren had completed the work of destruction before Hill could arrive.

Welles, Gideon (*1802-1878*)
Union secretary of the navy.

A Hartford newspaper proprietor, he became secretary of the navy in 1861 and, despite his inexperience, served ably throughout the war. Welles quickly assembled a navy, defined strategy, and promoted new technology, the success of his naval operations making him an important member of Lincoln's cabinet.

West Point, *Mississippi*

In February 1864, as part of the Meridian Campaign, some 7000 Federal cavalry under William Sooy Smith set out from Memphis,

Tennessee, to break up the Mobile & Ohio Railroad from Okolona, Mississippi, southward and then to join W. T. Sherman in Meridian. The Federals made contact with Nathan B. Forrest's Confederate cavalry at West Point on February 20, and after a minor skirmish on the 21st Smith ordered a withdrawal. Another skirmish at Okolona on the 22nd ended in a Federal rout, though portions of two brigades turned to face Forrest at a place called Ivey Hills – a stand that ended what had been an aggressive Confederate pursuit. Sherman later censured Sooy Smith for his handling of the operation.

West Virginia

As frontier farming country, the western part of Virginia was economically and culturally divergent from the aristocratic plantation society in the east, and as early as 1776 western Virginians had petitioned for their own

Though inexperienced, Gideon Welles proved an excellent Union secretary of the navy.

government. Western loyalists refused to recognize Virginia's secession in April 1861. At three conventions at Wheeling from May to August they elected their own US Senators and loyalist Governor Francis Pierpont, and called for the formation of a separate state. Their new constitution, drafted in November, provided for the abolition of slavery. The 50 counties of West Virginia were admitted to the Union as the 35th state in June 1863.

Western Virginia Campaign of McClellan

When, soon after the fall of Fort Sumter in April 1861, the Virginia State Convention passed an ordinance of secession, it began to appear that the large and generally pro-Union western part of the state might not be willing to follow Richmond's lead. To exploit this situation, and to protect the vital B&O railroad lines in western Virginia, young General George McClellan, then commander of the Department of the Ohio, mounted an expedition into the region. On June 3 one of his lieutenants, General T. A. Morris, routed a Confederate force at Philippi – a small fight but a big propaganda victory (Northern newspapers dubbed the Rebel flight 'the Philippi races') that so encouraged western Virginia Unionists that they declared Richmond's ordinance of secession void. By now alarmed, the Confederate government rushed a new commander, Robert S. Garnett, into the area but failed to give him adequate men and supplies for the task at hand. Garnett attempted to set up a defensive line based on Rich and Laurel Mountains, but on July 11 another of McClellan's lieutenants, General William S. Rosecrans, overran the Rich Mountain position, and Garnett's right flank at Laurel Mountain inevitably collapsed soon thereafter. McClellan caught up with the retreating Garnett on the 13th at Carrick's Ford; in the ensuing action Garnett's small force was badly mauled and Garnett himself was killed. McClellan then occupied Beverly and was all for pushing on, but at that point Washington intervened, calling a halt to the campaign on the grounds that its objectives had already been accomplished.

The historical consequences of this militarily minor campaign were considerable. Not only was West Virginia permanently lost to Virginia and the Confederacy (it would be admitted to the Union as a new state in 1863), the campaign had so enhanced George McClellan's reputation that it would seem only logical to Washington, in the aftermath of Irvin McDowell's disaster at First Bull Run, to name McClellan the general-in-chief of all the Union armies. It thus would be McClellan who, in 1862, would preside over the even more disastrous Peninsular Campaign.

Westport (*Missouri*), Battle of

Federal forces defeated the Confederates of Price's Raid (*See*) here on October 23, 1864. Sterling Price with 9000 men initiated the battle, attacking Samuel G. Curtis's Army of the Border in positions along Brush Creek. Curtis counterattacked, forcing Price to withdraw. At this point Alfred Pleasanton's Federal cavalry fell on the Rebels, turning their withdrawal into a rout.

Wheat, Chatham (1826-1862)
Confederate officer.

The adventuring son of an Episcopal minister, he fought in the Mexican War, then served as a mercenary officer in the Mexican Army and with Garibaldi's insurgents in Italy. Wheat led the Louisiana Tigers at First Bull Run. He was mortally wounded at the Battle of Gaines's Mill during the Peninsular Campaign.

Wheat Field

This patch of cultivated ground halfway between Little Round Top and the Peach Orchard was the scene of heavy fighting on the second day of the Battle of Gettysburg.

Wheeler, Joseph (1836-1906)
Confederate general.

A Georgian West Point graduate, Wheeler left frontier fighting when war broke out. He fought at Shiloh, Perryville, and Stone's River, commanded the Army of the Mississippi's cavalry and led raids against Federal communications; one such raid on Federal supply lines, conducted between October 1 and 9, 1863, during the Chattanooga Campaign, was so successful that it came close to forcing the besieged Union troops in Chattanooga to evacuate the city. He subsequently participated in the Knoxville and Atlanta campaigns and fought W.T. Sherman during his March to the Sea. 'Fightin' Joe' was said to have fought in 1000 engagements and skirmishes before his capture in May 1865. He later played a prominent role in the Spanish-American War.

'Whistling Dick'

This famous gun defended the Confederate fortress of Vicksburg on the Mississippi. Built as a smoothbore, the subsequent rifling of the barrel put a spin on its projectiles that produced a weird sound in flight. 'Whistling Dick' sent the Federal gunboat *Cincinnati* to the bottom on May 27, 1863.

The 18-pounder 'Whistling Dick', most famous of the Rebel guns defending Vicksburg.

Pugnacious Rebel General Joseph Wheeler well deserved his nickname, 'Fighting Joe'.

White Oak Swamp (Virginia), Battle of

In this sixth engagement of the Seven Days' Battles on June 30, 1862, Robert E. Lee made an elaborate plan to strike the retreating Army of the Potomac, but once again his generals were ineffective, and only two of the seven divisions got into action. James Longstreet's and A. P. Hill's divisions did fight fierce engagements, but by nightfall they had gained little ground. Federal casualties were 2853 for the day, Southern 3615. That night McClellan withdrew to Malvern Hill (*See*).

Whiting, William Henry (1824-1865) **Confederate general.**

An 1845 West Point graduate, he served as an engineer officer in the prewar army. He joined the Confederate service in the spring of 1861 and fought at First Bull Run. Whiting

commanded a division under T.J. Jackson in the latter's Shenandoah Valley Campaign. He subsequently served as commander of the military district of Wilmington on the North Carolina coast; he was mortally wounded at Fort Fisher on January 15, 1865.

Whitman, Walt (1819-1892) **Poet.**

Already mildly notorious for his poetry, Whitman went to Washington, DC, in December 1862 to assist his wounded brother; he stayed for the duration, serving as a volunteer nurse in military hospitals. His war poems were published as *Drum-Taps* (1865) and *Sequel to Drum-Taps* (1865-6). His most celebrated masterpiece, *Leaves of Grass*, was published in 1871.

Whitworth Gun and Rifle

Confederates used small numbers of the English-made Whitworth rifled gun, including 6-, 12-, and 70-pounder types. One authority called the accurate and powerful Whitworth the best gun in either army, but it was somewhat prone to jamming. Small numbers of the muzzle-loading Whitworth rifle were used by Rebel marksmen.

Wickham, Williams Carter (1820-1888) **Confederate general.**

A Virginia planter, lawyer, and anti-secessionist legislator, he fought steadily in the Eastern Theater from First Bull Run to Cold Harbor, joining Jubal Early for the fighting in the Shenandoah Valley in 1864 before resigning from the army in November 1864 to sit in the Confederate Congress.

Wigwag

Union signal officer A. J. Myer and E. P. Alexander, who would serve as a senior Confederate artillery officer, developed this semaphore signal communication system when they served together in the 1850s.

American poet Walt Whitman.

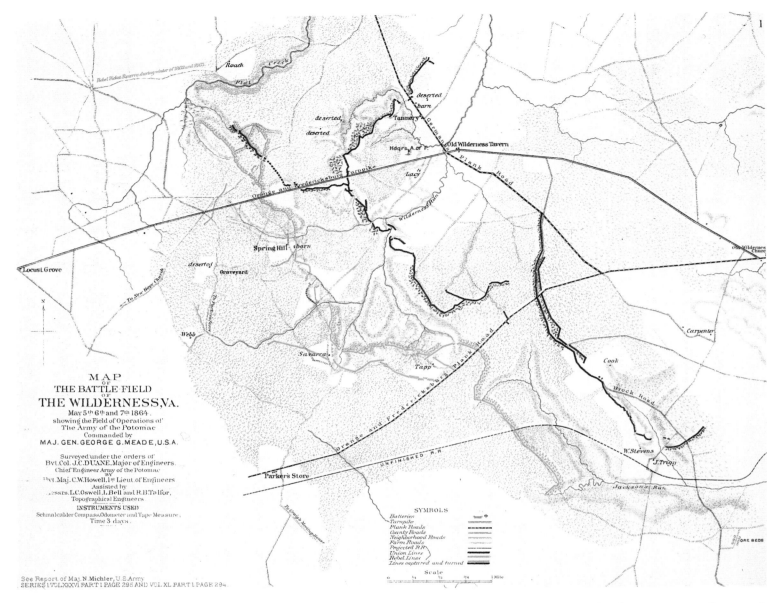

MAP
OF
THE BATTLE-FIELD
OF
THE WILDERNESS,VA.
May 5th 6th and 7th 1864.
showing the Field of Operations of
The Army of the Potomac
Commanded by
MAJ. GEN. GEORGE G.MEADE,U.S.A.

Surveyed under the orders of
Bvt.Col. J.C.DUANE, Major of Engineers.
Chief Engineer Army of the Potomac
BY
Bvt.Maj.C.W.Howell,1st Lieut.of Engineers
Assisted by
Messrs.L.C.Oswell,L.Bell and R.B.Talfor,
Topographical Engineers
INSTRUMENTS USED
Schmalcalder Compass,Odometer and Tape Measure.
Time 3 days.

See Report of Maj. N.Michler, U.S.Army
SERIES 1 VOL.XXXVI PART 1 PAGE 295 AND VOL. XL PART 1 PAGE 294.

SYMBOLS
Batteries
Turnpike
Plank Roads
County Roads
Neighborhood Roads
Farm Roads
Projected R.R.
Union Lines
Rebel Lines
Lines captured and turned

Scale

The positions of Lee's and Grant's armies at the beginning of the confused, bloody Battle of the Wilderness in May 1864.

Wilderness, Campaign and Battle

On May 4, 1864, General Ulysses S. Grant and the Federal Army of the Potomac reached the edge of the Virginia Wilderness, scene of the previous year's humiliation of the army in the Battle of Chancellorsville. Grant had just been named commander of the entire Federal war effort, but he decided that his headquarters would be in the field with the primary Union army. His goal was to capture the Confederate capital of Richmond; but before that he would have to subdue Robert E. Lee and the Army of Northern Virginia. He planned to meet Lee on open ground south of the Wilderness. In that assumption Grant fell prey to his main weakness as a commander: planning his own strategy without adequately considering what his enemy was doing in the meantime.

Meanwhile, as part of Grant's overall strategy for winning the war, General Benjamin Butler had been ordered to move on Richmond from the south, Franz Sigel was to march through Virginia's Shenandoah Valley, and W.T. Sherman was to head for Atlanta. Of those three operations, only Sherman's would be successful, but it would be a very great success (*See* ATLANTA CAMPAIGN).

At that point in early May the Army of the Potomac had 115,000 well-fed and well-equipped soldiers to Lee's 66,000 ragged and hungry ones. Nonetheless, Lee was prepared to ambush Grant in the Wilderness, knowing that the impediments of thick trees and brush and uneven ground would compensate for much of his enemy's numerical superiorty. On May 5, marching into the woods, General Gouverneur Warren notified Grant that an enemy force was on the Orange Turnpike. Thinking it was an isolated detachment, Grant ordered Warren to attack, but he then found himself fighting with an enemy in force. As the battle developed through a day of severe fighting, units on both sides grappled nearly blind in the thick brush. Opposing lines mingled in the confusion, both sides often firing on their own men. One participant recalled that the fighting was 'simply bushwacking on a grand scale . . . I knew a Wisconsin infantryman named Holmes who walked right into the Rebel skirmish line. He surrendered, and a Rebel was sent to the rear with him. In two minutes Holmes and his guard walked right into our own lines, and that in broad daylight.'

Late in the afternoon Southern General A. P. Hill's advance along the Plank Road was met by Union General Winfield Scott Hancock; a separate and equally desperate contest ensued. As evening fell neither side had made significant progress. During the night troops of both sides frequently wandered into enemy lines. Grant had ordered a general attack for 5:00 in the morning, but before that could get underway Confederates struck the Union right flank. This was actually a diversion – Lee was waiting for James Longstreet to move up and spearhead the main effort on the Union left flank. Soon the fighting had spread along the line, and the superior Union forces drove the Confederates steadily back.

As the Union men pressed forward, however, they became disorganized due to the tangled thickets and swamps. For a time, Federal General Hancock enveloped the weakened forces of A. P. Hill along the Orange Plank Road. Finally the Federals arrived at the clearing containing Lee's headquarters. But as Hancock paused to regroup, Longstreet's men, having just arrived in the area, made a dramatic appearance, moving up the Plank Road at a trot and pitching into the enemy. Lee had to be dissuaded from personally leading Longstreet's advance units. In short order Hancock was being pushed back. Learning of an unfinished railroad cut that led to the Union left flank, Longstreet sent a detachment along it to the attack; they devastated the enemy forces they encountered and soon were in position to roll up and destroy the Northern line.

The tide of battle quickly swung again when Longstreet was seriously wounded by his own men firing blindly into the woods, some three miles from where the same thing had happened to Stonewall Jackson the year before. As Longstreet was carried from the field the Southern attack faltered. Grant ordered a new attack on the middle and right of the enemy line for 6:00 am. But again Lee got the jump; the Confederates pushed forward and claimed part of the breastworks erected by the Federals – partly because the log barricades had caught fire, forcing the bluecoats to fight the enemy and the fire at the same time. Meanwhile, repeated Union attacks on the north flank had failed to breach Southern positions. In the process, John Sedgwick's Union corps had drifted off, leaving itself 'in the air.' Late in the afternoon

Right: Frustrated by Lee in the Wilderness and at Spotsylvania, Grant (left, leaning over Meade's shoulder) unwisely elected to 'fight it out' at Cold Harbor in June 1864.
Below: The Battle of the Wilderness.

An Edwin Forbes sketch of Union troops in the Wilderness. The area's dense woods made organized maneuver nearly impossible.

John Gordon's division of Confederates fell onto Sedgwick's flank, again endangering the whole Union line. This time the Union was saved by the coming of night, which ended Gordon's assault and the battle.

In two days of inconclusive fighting in the Wilderness casualties had been staggering for both sides. The North had lost 2246 killed and 12,073 wounded of 101,895 involved; Confederate casualties were estimated at 7750 of 61,025 engaged. As had happened at the Battle of Chancellorsville, hundreds of wounded men died during the night in forest fires that had started during the battle.

After their previous battle at Gettysburg, both armies had spent months in recovery and tentative maneuvering. This time Grant was determined not to let up the pressure. He issued orders to slip around Lee's right flank and resume the advance toward Richmond. Lee, guessing what Grant would do, put his forces on the march to stop the enemy at Spotsylvania. The Wilderness Battle, as it turned out, was only the beginning of a long summer of incessant and devastating struggle between the two armies.

Wilkes, Charles *(1798-1877)*
Union naval officer.

He entered the Navy as a midshipman in 1818. In 1838, he led a six-ship squadron carrying a scientific expedition to Antarctica. As captain of the USS *San Jacinto*, Wilkes stopped the British steamer *Trent* route to England on November 8, 1861, and arrested Confederate commissioners Mason and Slidell, precipitating a diplomatic crisis with Britain (*See* TRENT AFFAIR). Wilkes later won considerable acclaim as commander of the 'flying squadron,' a naval flotilla which captured a number of Rebel blockade-runners in West Indian waters.

Williams Rapid-Fire Gun

This was the first true machine gun to be fired successfully in battle – by Confederate gunners at Seven Pines on May 31, 1862. Designed by a Confederate army captain, it was a 1-pounder breech-loader that fired 18-20 rounds per minute at a range of 2000 yards. Several batteries of the Williams saw service.

Williamsburg *(Virginia)*, Battle of

Federal cavalry, with two infantry divisions trailing, followed John B. Magruder's Confederates to this colonial town after they withdrew from Yorktown during the Peninsular Campaign of 1862. Union forces attacked on May 5. After a hard fight the Confederates continued their withdrawal up the Peninsula that night. The Federals reported 2239 casualties out of more than 40,000 engaged; the Confederates lost 1603 out of about 31,900 committed to the battle.

Union naval Captain Charles Wilkes.

Wilmot Proviso

Introduced in Congress in 1846 by Representative David Wilmot of Pennsylvania, this clause in a Mexican War appropriation bill outlawed slavery in any territory acquired from Mexico. Passed by the House in 1846 and 1847, it failed in the Senate. John C. Calhoun implicitly rejected the Compromise of 1820 in the Senate debate on the Wilmot Proviso, enraging Free Soil partisans and deepening the North-South rift.

Wilson, James Harrison
(1837-1925) **Union general.**

Graduated from West Point in 1860, this Illinois native was a major general by 1865, having served under W. T. Sherman, David Hunter, and George McClellan, directed the Cavalry Bureau, and, in 1864-65, led a cavalry corps. His troops captured Jefferson Davis in May 1865 after his (Wilson's) Selma Raid (*See*). In a notable earlier raid during the Petersburg siege, Wilson and August V. Kautz had taken 5000 troopers to attack the Southside Railroad, one of the city's main supply lines; between June 22 and July 1, 1864, they destroyed many miles of vital railroad track, but they were eventually beaten off by the Confederate defenders, having suffered some 1500 casualties.

Wilson's Creek, Campaign and Battle

In an effort to stymie Confederate operations designed to take control of Missouri, Federal General Nathaniel Lyon attacked Benjamin McCulloch's Rebel forces at Wilson's Creek, near Springfield, Missouri, on August 10, 1861. The early morning attack made progress at first, but then a gray counterattack checked the Federals. Fighting raged all morning, the now-outnumbered bluecoats on Oak Hill repulsing three Confederate charges; during the first two Lyon was wounded twice, then killed. Despite his line's holding, Major Samuel D. Sturgis, who had succeeded Lyon, ordered a retreat, for which he would be much criticized. It was one of the hardest-fought battles of the war: the 5400 Federals suffered 1235 casualties; the Confederates 1184 of 11,600 engaged.

Winchester, Battles of

On May 25, 1862, the first Battle of Winchester, Virginia, took place as part of the Shenandoah Valley Campaign of Stonewall Jackson. Union General Nathaniel Banks, assigned by Washington to deal with Jackson, was at Strasburg when he learned of the Confederate attack at Front Royal. Though he did not at first realize the threat posed to his forces, Banks withdrew to high ground south and west of Winchester, thereby probably preserving his army from a worse disaster than occurred; after taking the garrison at Front Royal, Jackson was on the Federal flank with twice Banks's numbers.

Jackson drove his forces all night to reach Winchester, slowed both by the weariness of his men and by Turner Ashby's undisciplined Rebel cavalry, which stopped to loot a captured wagon train. Jackson's attack on the

Federal left came at dawn, before the enemy had been able to fortify their positions on the hills. The attack made little progress at first, but about 7:30 Southern units under Richard Taylor and Richard Ewell gained both Federal flanks; Taylor drove into the left flank, and then Jackson moved forward with his center and right. Soon the Federals broke into full flight toward the Potomac. Jackson was unable to pursue due to the slowness of some of his officers. Of over 8000 effectives, Banks had lost some 3000 in the battle, while Jackson lost only 400. The Federal general and his men crossed the Potomac to safety, out of the campaign for good. Jackson rested his men for a couple of days before marching north toward Harpers Ferry to continue his astonishing Valley campaign.

The Second Battle of Winchester took place on June 13-15, 1863. In support of Lee's invasion of Pennsylvania (*See* GETTYSBURG CAMPAIGN), Southern General Richard Ewell was dispatched to subdue an enemy garrison at Winchester under General Robert H. Milroy. The Federals had two primary sets of fortifications on the hills west of town, called the Main and Star Forts. Ewell began by driving in some enemy outposts, then, on the 14th, made some demonstrations in front of the forts to divert the enemy while he sent a detachment around to attack from the rear. In the early evening that detachment opened up its cannons from the west and captured Milroy's artillery post. The Union general pulled his men into the Main Fort and

decided to retreat in the morning, which was just what Ewell had prepared for. On the next day the retreating Federals ran into heavy fire and were overwhelmed. Over the three days Ewell had captured 3500 bluecoats and killed or wounded over a thousand

Above: Federal troops try to drive Rebels from behind a stone wall in the disastrous (for the Union) First Battle of Winchester, which was fought on May 25, 1862.
Below: An impressionistic A. R. Waud sketch of the Third (here called Second) Battle of Winchester, fought on September 19, 1864.

more, while losing some 269 of his own troops. Milroy later had to defend himself at a court of inquiry but was acquitted. Nevertheless, he had overseen what amounted to a serious setback for the Union.

The Third Battle of Winchester took place on September 19, 1864. The most severe of the struggles around Winchester, it was the opening battle of the Shenandoah Valley Campaign of Sheridan. For some weeks Philip Sheridan, the pugnacious Federal general, had submitted to Ulysses Grant's orders to move carefully with his Army of the Shenandoah and follow a defensive strategy against his opponent, Jubal Early. Then Sheridan learned from one of his spies, a Quaker schoolteacher named Rebecca West, that Early had sent one of his divisions to Robert E. Lee, who was then besieged at Petersburg. With Grant's two-word approval – 'Go in' – Sheridan marched to strike the weakened Early at Winchester.

Early, for his part, had deduced from Sheridan's previous caution that his opponent was the timid sort. He would learn otherwise. With his 33,600 infantry and 6400 cavalry, Sheridan ordered a concentric attack on Early's 8500 infantry and 2900 cavalry, who were scattered in various units north to southeast of the town. The bluecoats moved

Previous pages: Third Battle of Winchester.
Below: The execution of Confederate prison commandant Henry Wirz in November 1865.

to the attack on the wings as planned, but then the main attack in the center faltered when the troops of one unit got tangled in the wagon train of another. The confusion created a gap in Federal lines, toward which Early's men struck just before noon; after some fierce and confused fighting, the gap was filled, and the Confederates were driven back. But so far, cavalryman Sheridan, unused to commanding a mixture of infantry, cavalry, and artillery, had not been able to move his considerably superior forces effectively against the Confederate position.

Yet as dusk approached Early's units had been forced back to a tight line northeast of town, and Sheridan had reorganized his forces. Then a broad Federal attack along the line inevitably sent the smaller number of Southerners running. The Northern cavalry made good use of their repeating carbines, but also captured hundreds of graycoats with an old-fashioned saber charge. The Union men suffered a heavy 5018 casualties of 37,711 engaged, but Early was deprived of a quarter of his army – of some 16,377 engaged, he lost about 4000, nearly half of them captured, including three important officers killed and two others wounded.

Sheridan would follow up this victory with an easier and equally decisive one at Fisher's Hill on September 22. Both victories considerably raised the spirits of the North and Lincoln's sagging electoral campaign against General George B. McClellan. A Northern

commentator wrote that week, 'Sheridan has knocked down gold and G.B. McClellan together. The former is below 200 and the later is nowhere.' (In fact Lincoln's election was only finally secured by the fall of Atlanta in September.)

Winder, John Henry *(1800-1865)*
Confederate provost marshal general.

Born in Maryland, Winder was a West Point graduate and professional officer who commanded Libby, Belle Isle, and Andersonville Prisons and eventually became commissary general of all prisoners of war in the east. The degree of Winder's responsibility for the appalling conditions in prisons under his perview remains a controversial issue.

Wire Entanglements

Used for the first time in any war – by the Union forces at Fort Sanders November 29, 1863 – this was smooth telegraph wire stretched among trees and stumps; it caught the Confederates off guard, as it did again at Drewry's Bluff. It would eventually be replaced by barbed wire.

Wirz, Henry *(1822-1865)*
Confederate officer.

Swiss-born Wirz was a Louisiana physician. First a clerk in Libby Prison, he was wounded

Y

A Union cavalry charge at the Third Battle of Winchester (Opequon) in 1864.

at Seven Pines and became Confederate messenger and purchasing agent in Europe in summer 1863, returning in January 1864 to become commandant of Andersonville Prison, where he stayed until the war's end. In the only postwar execution for war crimes, he was hanged in November 1865 for atrocious cruelty to prisoners.

Wise, Henry Alexander
(1806-1876) Confederate general.

A lawyer, he served as a Congressman from Virginia and was governor of the state in 1858 when John Brown carried out his famous raid (he signed Brown's death warrant). Commissioned a brigadier general in the Confederate Army in June 1861, he served in the South Carolina coastal defenses and, later, in Richmond, at Petersburg, and during the 1865 Appomattox Campaign.

'Woman Order'

The nickname given to the notorious General Order No. 28, issued on May 12, 1862, by

Commander of the *Monitor* John Worden.

Union General Benjamin Butler when he was commanding the occupied city of New Orleans. He warned that any women in New Orleans who 'by word, gesture, or movement insult or show contempt' for any Federal soldier would be treated as prostitutes.

Wood, Thomas John *(1823-1906)*
Union general.

A Kentucky West Point alumnus and frontier fighter, he commanded an Ohio Army division at Shiloh, Corinth, and Perryville, then fought in the Army of the Cumberland at Stone's River, the Tullahoma Campaign, Chickamauga, Missionary Ridge, Knoxville, and the Atlanta Campaign. He commanded IV Corps at Nashville.

Wool, John Ellis *(1784-1869)*
Union general.

A veteran of the War of 1812 and a Mexican War hero, Wool lived to become the fourth-ranking Union general in the Civil War. He occupied Norfolk and Portsmouth after the Confederate evacuation and commanded the Department of the East, the Middle Department, and VIII Corps, retiring from active duty in August 1863.

Worden, John Lorimer
(1818-1897) Union naval officer.

This New Yorker, a career naval officer, earned national celebrity after commanding the *Monitor* against the *Merrimac*. Worden also commanded the USS *Montauk* in the South Atlantic Blockading Squadron early in 1863 and spent the remainder of the war supervising the construction of ironclad warships in New York.

Wright, Horatio Gouverneur
(1820-1899) Union general.

A Connecticut-born army engineer, he was Chief Engineer for the expedition to destroy Norfolk Navy Yard and served at First Bull Run and on the Port Royal expedition. Wright fought in South Carolina and Florida, at Rappahannock Bridge, and on the Bristoe Campaign; he led VI Corps from the Wilderness through Appomattox.

Yancey, William Lowndes
(1814-1863) Confederate politician.

This Alabama planter resigned his Congressional seat in 1848 to agitate for states' rights. A leader of the 'Fire-Eaters' (*See*), Yancey was a pivotal figure in the secessionist movement. He was a Confederate commissioner to Europe in 1861. He died in office in the Confederate Senate in 1863.

Yazoo Expedition

As part of Ulysses S. Grant's Vicksburg Campaign, what is called Sherman's Yazoo Expedition was an operation involving 32,000 men (W. T. Sherman's and John McClernand's corps) who were shipped up the Yazoo River north of Vicksburg and ended by failing to take the heights in the battle of Chickasaw Bluffs (*See*).

William L. Yancey, an ardent secessionist, served the Confederacy in Europe.

Federal ordnance destined for Union General George McClellan's Peninsular Campaign is stockpiled in Yorktown, Va., in 1862.

Yellow Tavern (*Virginia*), Battle of

During Philip Sheridan's 1864 Richmond Raid, Federal cavalry ran into J. E. B. Stuart's troopers at Yellow Tavern on May 11. The fighting had surged back and forth for several hours when Union Private J. A. Huff took a potshot at an enemy officer sitting on a horse. The officer turned out to be Stuart, who was

A Confederate gun that burst while in action during the somewhat pointless Union siege of Yorktown in the spring of 1862.

taken off the battlefield mortally wounded and died next day. The fighting ended with a Southern retreat.

Yorktown, *Virginia*

In the Peninsular Campaign to take Richmond, Union General George McClellan's strategy called for first taking Yorktown, located on the coast near the southeastern tip of the peninsula. Union troops arrived outside Yorktown by April 4, 1862; although greatly outnumbering the Confederate forces, the Federals settled in for a formal siege, which dragged on until the Confederates evacuated Yorktown on May 3 – another of McClellan's time-consuming and ultimately hollow victories.

Zollicoffer, Felix Kirk (*1812-1862*)
Confederate general.

Born in Tennessee, he fought in the Seminole War, held several offices in Tennessee, was a US Congressman, and attended the 1861 Peace Conference in Washington (*See*). Appointed a brigadier general, he was killed in his first major battle, Logan's Cross Roads.

Zouaves

Originally Zouaves were French colonial Algerian troops noted for their exotic uniforms and flashy drill routines. Both before and during the War certain Northern and Southern regiments adopted the look of these Zouaves – baggy trousers, turban or fez, even in some instances shaved heads – as well as the elaborate drill. Early in the War, however, it was realized that the Zouaves' attention-getting uniforms were a real liability on the battlefield; the wearing of the uniforms was soon relegated to parade functions, and in time this colorful form of dress passed out of US military use entirely.

Below: The death of Rebel General Felix K. Zollicoffer at Logan's Cross Roads in 1862.
Opposite top: Zouaves of the Union's 114th Pennsylvania Infantry Regiment.
Opposite bottom: The Philadelphia Zouave Corps parades in their colorful uniforms.

PHILADELPHIA ZOUAVE CORPS.
PENNSYLVANIA VOLUNTEERS.